ASTONISHING BATHROOM READER

YOUR **N° 2** SOURCE TO ALL THE FLUSHING **FACTS** JAMMING **TRIVIA** & GASSY **MYSTERIES** OF THE **UNIVERSE!**

Diego Jourdan Pereira

RACEHORSE PUBLISHING

Copyright © 2020 by Diego Jourdan Pereira

All rights reserved. No part of this book may be reproduced in any manner without the express written consent of the publisher, except in the case of brief excerpts in critical reviews or articles. All inquiries should be addressed to Racehorse Publishing, 307 West 36th Street, 11th Floor, New York, NY 10018.

Racehorse Publishing books may be purchased in bulk at special discounts for sales promotion, corporate gifts, fund-raising, or educational purposes. Special editions can also be created to specifications. For details, contact the Special Sales Department, Skyhorse Publishing, 307 West 36th Street, 11th Floor, New York, NY 10018 or info@skyhorsepublishing.com.

Racehorse Publishing™ is a pending trademark of Skyhorse Publishing, Inc.®, a Delaware corporation.

Visit our website at www.skyhorsepublishing.com.

10 9 8 7 6 5 4 3 2

Library of Congress Cataloging-in-Publication Data is available on file.

Cover and interior art and design by Diego Jourdan Pereira

Mechanical design by Kai Texel

Muara Rough font designed by Surotype at Fontbundles.net. Used under license.

Print ISBN: 978-1-63158-589-0

eISBN: 978-1-63158-590-6

Printed in the United States of America

CONTENTS

Introduction.

V

I. Gassy Universe

1

II. Loaded Science

101

III. Jamming History

195

IV. Clogged Culture

295

V. Bursting Sports

410

VI. Flushing Phenomena

490

Acknowledgments

590

About the Author

590

Dedicated to my grandmother, **Hedy Glocker**, the fiercest, most independent woman I've ever known.

INTRODUCTION

"If you don't make mistakes, you don't make anything."

—Joseph Conrad

Always thought writing was reserved for novelists, poets, or pundits, but not me. I was well set to work as a comics artist or an illustrator for life.

Twenty years of hard labor later (there are shorter prison sentences), I found myself sent out to pasture by that fine meat grinder some clueless folks call the "comics industry." Quoting Lennon (who in turn quoted comics writer Saunders), "life is what happens to you while you're busy making other plans," so no hard feelings.

In truth, I saw it coming, and had a contingency plan in place—I would return to the university (dropped out in 2000) to complete my studies and find a teaching position somewhere. All I can say is the Almighty is still laughing aloud at that one!

Fortunately, other than burning through my savings to get a completely useless degree, the university gave me another gift. Turns out my thesis paper was written in solid enough Spanish prose to be published locally in Chile, where I live, and then in neighboring Argentina. I was on my way to becoming an author!

Unfortunately, professional writing in Latin America is indeed reserved for novelists, poets, or pundits. Gatekeepers who attend all the cocktail parties, hound every grant, give every lecture. Not being the brown-nosing type I figured if I found a way to become a comic artist for companies in the US, the UK, and India, maybe I could give the English language book publishing world a spin as well. Sure, I'm no Joseph Conrad (king among exophonic writers!), but have a skill he never had at his disposal: marketing!

Well, marketing teaches us that while it's more important to be the first at something than being the best at it, there's nothing wrong with being second banana (Pepsi to Coca-Cola, Burger King to McDonald's, and the list goes on and on). That's what this book is all about, being the best number two it can be; solid, but squishy enough to find its way out painlessly, with no hard chunks or corn kernels doing any damage while seeking the light at the end of the tunnel.

Profound (ahem!) metaphors aside, the objective is to write and package (graphic design being part of my skill set too) a heavy-duty volume anyone may bring into the ol' W.C., to liven up the experience without any clogging headaches—"releasing the kraken" is hard enough!

Think of me as your friendly restroom attendant. Soon I may be replaced by robots (*domo arigato*, Japan!), but in the meantime will strive to provide the best constipation-free facts, printed in enough cellulose to make a difference should you find yourself in a toilet paper roll emergency, or in need of a doorstop.

Don't forget to leave a tip on the way out!

Diego Jourdan Pereira

I
GASSY
UNIVERSE

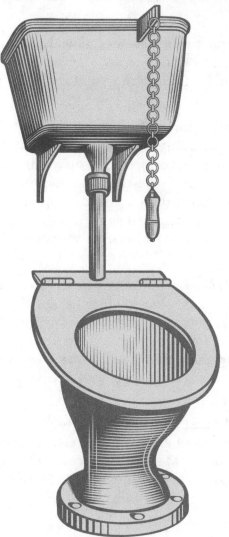

WE DON'T KNOW SH*T

As much as mankind has discovered over the centuries, the Universe at large is still clogged with unsolved questions.

Time: As far as physics is concerned, time is pretty much an illusion: everyone experiences it differently. The fact humans remember the past but not the future also seems to be entirely arbitrary!

Space: Forget what you think you know. Up, down, left, right, are all meaningless. According to theoretical physicist Dr. Michio Kaku (b.1947) the universe is comprised of eleven dimensions, of which humans can grasp three at best. This is given away by particles, such as electrons, tending to disappear and reappear in different places, leading scientists to suspect they get through higher dimensional planes in order to move from one point to another.

Gravity: Really? Didn't Newton figure it out ages ago? Of the four basic forces holding the Universe together, gravity has no associated particle, and the way it functions still makes no sense. Both amazingly weak (less than simple magnetism) and incredibly strong (holding entire planetary systems together), once we get down to the molecular level it, well, disappears!

Planets: The vast majority of our very own Solar System remains uncharted. Even our best telescope can't see squat between the Sun and Mercury on account of that area being too bright, nor much else kneeling behind Pluto on account of it's darkness.

MORE THAN MEETS THE EYE

There may be eleven dimensions, but just how big is the universe in the three we can see? So vast in fact, new units had to be devised to accommodate its distances to our teeny-tiny brains, but I won't bother you with AUs, light-years, or parsecs. Let's try to keep it down to simple Earth miles instead.

Observable universe (region comprising all matter that can be seen from Earth or its space-based telescopes at the present time):
544,887,000,000,000,000,000,000 miles wide.

Milky Way (our home galaxy):
621,371,000,000,000,000,000 miles wide.

GN-z11 (currently the most distant known galaxy):
13,400,000,000 miles away from us.

Solar System (our galactic suburb):
7,440,000,000 from the Sun to Pluto (**14,880,000,000** miles wide).

Sun (needs no introduction):
864,938 miles in diameter, located **92,955,807** miles away from our home, sweet home: Earth!

Of course, what do we really see? Until William Herschel (1738-1822) discovered *infrared* light in 1800, and Johann W. Ritter (1776-1810) detected *ultraviolet* light in 1801, we thought we saw every color in the spectrum!

BING BANG BOOM

The "Big Bang" is the prevailing model for the observable universe, and it states that every galaxy is moving away from every other galaxy, which means the whole universe is expanding from a single, smaller, hotter, and denser state of the cosmos.

1. It was first theoretically proposed by Soviet mathematician Alexander Friedmann (1888-1925) in 1922, then confirmed by Jesuit priest Georges Lemaître (1894-1966) in 1927, and finally observed by Edwin Hubble (1889-1953) and Milton Humason (1891-1972) in 1929!

2. CMB (Cosmic Microwave Background) is a radiation leftover from the Big Bang first detected during the sixties as a radio "noise" that seemed to come from everywhere in space. Recent precise measurements of CMB temperature lock it at -455°F.

3. Based on measurements of supernovae and temperature fluctuations in the CMB, we know the event itself, or "singularity," happened 13.8 billion years ago.

4. The Big Bang is not an explosion of matter moving outward to fill a dark, empty universe, but rather, space (and time) itself ever-expanding everywhere at an ever-accelerating rate—no "Big Crunch" in sight!

5. After the singularity took place, most of the helium, hydrogen, and lithium of the universe was already formed. Later on, all of the elements heavier than the latter were generated inside newly formed "ovens" we now call *stars*!

SEQUENTIAL QUARK

We now know the Big Bang wasn't a violent explosion, but rather a super-fast expansion, currently theorized to have happened in the following stages:

1. Gravity separated from three other forces (electromagnetic, strong nuclear, and weak nuclear) in little over ten seconds.

2. Electromagnetic, strong nuclear, and weak nuclear forces then took another ten seconds to split among themselves.

3. Cosmic inflation began.

4. Ten microseconds later, quarks* combined to make particles.

5. Light atoms nuclei were born after three minutes.

6. Took another 500,000 years for complex atoms to form.

7. Gassy clouds of Hydrogen and Helium began to condense, forming stars and galaxies.

*A quark is an elementary particle which combines with other quarks to form composite particles called hadrons, the most stable of which are protons and neutrons, which comprise the nuclei of atoms, and therefore matter itself!

POWER OF THE ATOM

So quarks make atoms, but what's an atom exactly?

1. All solids, liquids, gases, and plasma are composed of atoms and no body, living or non-living, would exist without them.

2. By volume, the nucleus and electrons are so small that an atom is theoretically 99.999% empty space.

3. Atoms are like a mini-solar system with the nucleus at the center, with electrons moving around it like planets.

4. Electrons lack a well defined outer boundary. Rather than going through clear orbital motions, they seem to disappear and reappear at different points at random!

5. The actual mass of an atom at rest is often expressed using the unified atomic mass unit (u), also called Dalton (Da).

6. There are 92 naturally occurring atoms, of which a dozen or so are quite common.

7. Twenty-four manmade atoms were created between 1944 (Curium) and 2010 (Tennessine).

8. The most uncommon and highly elusive element, Technetium, was first predicted by Russian chemist Dmitri Mendeleev (1834-1907). It has been found to be naturally present in red giant stars!

9. The human body contains 7,000,000,000,000,000,000,000,000,000 atoms, 99% of which are hydrogen, oxygen, carbon, and nitrogen.

10. "Atom" is a name shared by several fictional American super-heroes, as well as the original name of "Astro-Boy," the Japanese manga and cartoon character created by Osamu Tezuka (1928-1989). He was first known as "Mighty Atom."

BONUS FACTS!

- A transcript of one of Abraham Lincoln's speeches written in 1862 contains the first-ever "wink" emoticon!

- By diluting your blood's sodium level, too much water will make you feel "drunk."

- Torrington, a village in Alberta, Canada, holds the world's one and only "Gopher Hole Museum," which exhibits stuffed gopher dioramas of every kind.

- Connecticut seal hunter John Davis (1784-1864) was the first man to set foot in Antarctica in 1820!

- The woodpecker's tongue wraps around its skull to protect its brain from the shock of drilling trees with its beak.

ANTIMATTER BANANAS

Simply put, antimatter is matter with its electrical charge reversed. Theoretical physicist Paul Dirac (1902-1984) first conceptualized it in 1928, but it remains mysterious for a number of reasons.

1. Matter and antimatter cancel each other out. While the Big Bang produced matter and antimatter in equal proportions, instead of creating an even bigger bang, antimatter was seemingly phased out of existence by regular matter.

2. Small amounts of antimatter constantly rain down on the Earth in the form of cosmic rays, which are energy particles from space. Some is even formed above thunderstorms!

3. Bananas produce antimatter, when their decaying potassium releases one positron (the antimatter equivalent of an electron) every seventy-five minutes!

4. Scientists have managed to create teeny tiny amounts of antimatter in lab settings (in places such as CERN), and trap some of it so it won't collide with matter particles and disappear.

5. Making a single gram of antimatter would require approximately twenty-five quadrillion kilowatt-hours of energy and cost over a quadrillion dollars, and still probably wouldn't be enough to even boil water for a cup of coffee.

6. Antimatter rocket propulsion is hypothetically possible and currently under study!

INTERGALACTIC

There are hundreds of billions of galaxies in the universe, each one containing billions of stars, which gives an estimated total of ten billion trillion stars in the universe... more stars than the number of grains of sand here on Earth!

Dwarf galaxy: Most galaxies in the Universe are small, containing only a few billion stars, and many orbit a single larger galaxy (the Milky Way has at least a dozen of these!)

Spiral galaxy: These cosmic pinwheels are made by a rotating disk of stars around a central bulge of generally older stars, extending out of which are bright arms.

Elliptical galaxy: Ranging from nearly spherical to highly elongated, they are populated by older, more evolved stars orbiting the common center of gravity in random directions.

Shell galaxy: These occur naturally when a larger galaxy absorbs a smaller companion galaxy, resulting in a galaxy where the stars in the galaxy's halo are arranged in concentric shells.

Ring galaxy: With a ring of stars, gasses, and dust surrounding a bare core, these originate when a smaller galaxy passes through the core of a spiral galaxy... boom!

Dominican friar and Hermetic occultist Giordano Bruno (1548-1600) proposed that the stars were distant suns surrounded by their own planets, which could have life of their own.

GALAGA

Not all galaxies can be neatly typified. Some are, in fact, plain weird!

Antennae Galaxy: Actually two galaxies violently merging in the Corvus constellation, and discovered in 1785.

Evil Eye Galaxy: Discovered in 1779, in the Coma Berenices constellation, "M64" is made of two systems rotating in opposite directions, with a red core surrounded by a dark band of dust, which gives it a garish look!

Centaurus "A" Galaxy: In the Centaurus constellation lies this massive galaxy harboring a supermassive black hole in its midst, which projects "ghost" spiral tentacles, only seen in X-Ray frequencies … and H. P. Lovecraft's lore.

NG 660 Galaxy: Considered a rare occurrence, this Pisces constellation galaxy has an outer ring which rotates over the poles of its core (hence called a polar-ring galaxy), most likely siphoned from a galaxy that passed nearby aeons ago.

Sombrero Galaxy: Like the popular Mexican hat, this Virgo constellation galaxy has a nucleus made of several separate clusters of stars, with an intricate (and yet, unexplainable) dust brim surrounding it.

All the stars, galaxies, and black holes comprise about 5% of the Universe's mass, while the other 95% is unaccounted for, and has been labeled "dark matter" by scientists.

SPILT MILK

Gazing at the Milky Way has kept mankind busy for ages, and continues to enthrall and mesmerize the best of us, but there are milky facts unknown to most of us.

1. Mankind used to think it was the whole universe until astronomer Edwin Hubble (1889-1953) disabused us of that notion in 1924.

2. As far as galaxies go, it holds between 100 and 400 billion stars (of which we can see about 2,500), so it's considered pretty mid-level (gassy too), but that's only 10% of its mass. The other 90% is made of unknown "dark matter," which gives it a mysterious invisible halo.

3. It's shaped like a warped vinyl record, a side effect of the gravitational pull of neighboring galaxies known as the Large and Small Magellanic clouds.

4. It spins at 1,400,000 mph and is on a collision course against the Andromeda galaxy!

5. Living 26,000 light years away from the galactic center (most likely a super-massive black hole tentatively named "Sagittarius A"), humans obviously cannot take a picture of it from above, so its spiral nature still remains uncertain. If you have seen nice, shiny pictures of the whole shebang, they're likely illustrations done by artists!

6. American astronomer Carl Sagan (1934-1996) estimated there may be a million advanced alien civilizations living on planets orbiting the Milky Way alone, but the 100-400 billion stars in our galaxy make their search downright daunting.

BORN TO DIE

Stars are classified according to their life-span, which is huge but not infinite.

Protostar: A collection of gas which collapsed down from a giant molecular cloud, a protostar is what you have before a star forms. This "childhood" phase lasts about 100,000 years, before actual nuclear fusion begins.

T Tauri star: With the gravitation holding the star together as the source of its energy, a protostar becomes a T Tauri Star, giving off powerful X-ray flares in a phase that lasts about 100 million years, almost as long as a person's teenage phase these days!

Main sequence star: While they may differ in size, mass, and brightness, most stars in our galaxy, including our Sun, are main sequence, adult stars which convert hydrogen into helium in their cores.

Red giant star: The senior adult of the universe, when a main sequence star has consumed its load of core hydrogen, fusion stops and the hydrogen around the core ignites, causing it to increase in size dramatically before this fuel runs out completely and it becomes a ...

White dwarf star: When the fusion reaction stops and the star collapses inwardly, the senior star still smolders and shines, but there's no fusion reaction happening anymore.

TV star: Quoting Carl Sagan (him again?), "The nitrogen in our DNA, the calcium in our teeth, the iron in our blood, the carbon in our apple pies were made in the interior of collapsing stars."

SPACE ODDITIES

Of course, nothing is simple or normal upon close examination, and the universe's stars prove no different!

Red dwarf star: These are main sequence stars, like our Sun, but with much lower mass, and running far cooler, keeping the hydrogen in their core much longer than other stars, which allows them to burn for up to ten trillion years!

Neutron star: Resulting from the supernova explosion of a giant star, combined with gravitational collapsing that compresses the core past white dwarf star density. In fact, they are the smallest and densest stars, not counting black holes.

Theoretically, if the stability of the star core is broken further, the neutrons forming most of it would merge into quark matter, turning it into a **quark star** instead.

When a neutron star emits a powerfully focused beam or electromagnetic radiation, we call it a **pulsar**.

Giant, supergiant, and hypergiant stars: The largest stars in the Universe are monsters many, many times bigger that our Sun, but their size also means they're destined to explode as supernovae, at a relatively young age, or collapse onto themselves, becoming black holes!

Diamond star: Orbiting pulsar PSR J2222-0137 in the Aquarius constellation, in 2004 scientists discovered a collapsed white dwarf star turned into a gigantic diamond that is ten billion trillion trillion carats!

HARD, ROUND POOP

In case you are wondering, other than crystals or broken minerals, most space objects are round or started out as such, which proves the early universe wasn't getting nearly enough fiber or water in its diet.

1. Sphere-shaped objects are predominant in the universe.

2. Big cosmic objects become spherical due to gravity and energy. Stars, in fact, are almost perfectly spherical, as is our Sun.

3. Whenever you see a spherical solid object, it probably formed while molten.

4. Mountains only get as big as gravity allows them, but on a cosmic scale, if we were a gigantic god-like being of science fiction floating around, planets and stars would feel as smooth as marbles to the touch.

5. According to NASA, Earth is definitely round (an oblate spheroid, to be precise), but the Milky Way and the universe itself are now FLAT as pancakes (and apparently equally consistent). Truth is, the faster they spun, the flatter they got!

Spinning, however, doesn't justify the pseudoscientific theories originally espoused by whacky Englishmen Samuel Rowbotham (1816-1884) and Samuel Shenton (1903-1971), which are currently championed by those candid internet loonies known as "flat-earthers."

LET THERE BE LIGHT

Stars are the source of light in the universe, but what exactly is light and what does science know about it?

1. Essentially, it is electromagnetic radiation of any wavelength that can be perceived, either directly by our eyes (or by other species' eyes), or by indirect means such as experimentation and technology.

2. Its properties include: intensity, propagation direction, frequency (wavelength spectrum), and polarization.

3. Its speed in a vacuum, 186,282 miles per second, is considered a constant in the universe.

4. Light waves travel in a completely straight line until they hit an object. When they do, they are reduced to the minimum particle of light, or *photon*, at the point of collision.

5. A person could travel thousands of light years in a single human life-span without exceeding the speed of light.

6. The sunlight we see actually left the sun ten minutes before we perceive it, and is so powerful it reaches 262 feet into the ocean!

7. Astronauts see random flashes of light while in space. They're caused by cosmic rays hitting their optic nerves, which we don't see on Earth because the magnetosphere filters them out.

COSMIC A-HOLES

Black holes were first proposed to exist in the eighteenth century, but remained only a curiosity until the first one, Cygnus X-1, was found in 1964. Many questions about black holes are yet to be answered, but the ones that have been are presented here.

What are they?

The remains of dead, unstable stars so huge they collapse in on themselves, becoming so dense their gravitation distorts light, space, and time around them. They come in different sizes, from the common stellar-mass (meaning the size of a regular star) to the supermassive (either the product of a gigantic star or a combination of several holes).

Do they suck everything in?

They're not the giant vacuums of science-fiction, but may trap anything (mainly gas and dust) that passes their "event horizon" (the point at which escape becomes impossible).

Do they get bigger and bigger?

Black holes may indeed grow while absorbing a lot of surrounding gas and dust but they can't grow indefinitely. Black holes spin so fast, the surrounding cloud of ignited gas and dust and eventually the black hole's own mass end up evaporating into space, as Stephen Hawking (1942-2018) correctly predicted in 1974. The speed of this "Hawking radiation" emission is nearly the same as the speed of the light!

Could Earth fall prey to one?

Even if the Sun turned into a black hole (and it just won't), Earth would go about its business around it undisturbed.

How can we see them?

In 2019, a global network of radio telescopes called EHTs (Event Horizon Telescopes) produced the first accurate image of supermassive black hole Messier 87 (M87 for short), including its glowing event horizon, accurately measuring its mass, axis, and spin direction (clockwise).

The biggest black hole known, S5 0014+81, is so bright that if it were 100 light years away from Earth, it would appear just as bright as our sun!

BONUS FACTS!

- An old, red postbox was altered for the underwater collection of cards and installed in Japan's Susami Bay. Since then, 32,000 items of mail have been posted there by divers.

- During World War II, the crew of the British submarine *HMS Trident* kept a gift from the Russians aboard: a fully grown reindeer called Pollyanna!

- An entire family from isolated Appalachia, the Fugates of Troublesome Creek, have had blue skin for many generations—a rare genetic condition known as Methemoglobinemia!

- A "jiffy" is the time it takes for light to travel 0.39 inches in a vacuum, which is about 33.3564 picoseconds.

HERE COMES THE SUN

There is no "doo doo doo doo" when it comes to our nearest and most visible hydrogen bomb ... er, star.

1. A perfect hot plasma sphere, and classified as a G2V yellow dwarf, it orbits the center of the Milky Way within the Orion Spur.

2. It's made of hydrogen (73%), helium (25%), and smaller quantities of heavier elements, including oxygen, carbon, neon, and iron.

3. If a pinhead could be brought to the same temperature here on Earth, it would set fire to everything in a 60 mile radius!

4. Other than light and heat, it also generates radio waves, first discovered by British Army research officer, physicist James Stanley Hay (1909-2000) during World War II. Hey would also track a radio signal coming our way from Cygnus, which is odd considering that's exactly where the Sun and its planetary system are headed to!

5. Has its own storms in the form of cyclical gigantic magnetic disturbances that emanate outward, creating areas called "sunspots," which appear darker due to being more than 1,800°F lower than standard solar surface temperature. Sun storms mess with our transmissions, but could do a lot worse, if it weren't for Earth's own magnetosphere, instead giving birth to colorful lights in both the northern (aurora borealis) and southern (aurora australis) hemispheres.

6. It hasn't changed dramatically for more than four billion years, and

will remain fairly stable for another five billion. Then it'll begin to expand, reaching maximum size in 7.6 billion years, engulfing and completely disintegrating Mercury, Venus, Earth, and possibly Mars too! Life as we know it, of course, will be completely toast well before that. The Sun itself will end its days as a gargantuan ball of red glowing gas with a tiny core.

7. Contrary to popular belief, staring at a solar eclipse won't cause instant blindness, but exposure should be limited to less than a minute. Typical impairments may be as minor as visual field discoloration, but recovering normal vision shouldn't take more than a few weeks.

BONUS FACTS!

- A new aerobic, rod-shaped species of bacteria that lives in hairspray was discovered in 2008.

- Ten percent of all the world's salt is used by the US just to salt roads!

- China makes 70% of the world's air-conditioners, 58% of the world's shoes, and prints 90% of all the world's Bibles!

- Static can bend flowing water!

- American cow-bison hybrids are called "beefalos."

INTO THE SUN

Layered like the best murder mystery plots, our sun is made of complex strata worth taking a closer look at.

Core: At 27,000,000°F, this is where the nuclear fusion of hydrogen into helium occurs, releasing massive amounts of energy, with helium gradually accumulating to form an inner core within the core itself.

Radiation Zone: Where energy transfer occurs by means of radiation, at 12,500,000°F.

Tachocline: The transition region between the radiation and convection zones.

Convection Zone: Things get interesting here, where almost 2,000,000°F heat transfers outward due to the bulk movement of molecules!

Photosphere: The Sun's visible surface at a "cozy" 10,000°F.

Chromospere: Sitting above the photosphere at 45,000°F, it is actually rosy red hued.

Transition Region: A thin and irregular layer of the Sun's atmosphere (only seen with UV sensitive telescopes), where temperature flowing down from the corona to the chromosphere changes rapidly from 1,800,000°F to about 45,000°F.

Corona: The "crown" or aura of plasma that surrounds the Sun extends millions of miles into outer space. At 1,800,000°F on average, it runs much hotter than the Sun's surface!

Heliosphere: The thin, outermost atmosphere of the Sun, it is filled with solar wind plasma, which flows through the Solar System for billions of miles, far beyond even the region of Pluto. Ironically, it protects this system and us from baking in cosmic radiation!

BONUS FACTS!

- John Wayne's real name was Marion Morrison (1907-1979). His first named deemed "girly," he originally assumed "Duke Morrison" as his stage name.

- An average person can survive for up to a month without food, eleven days without sleep, and three to eight days without water.

- Walt Whitman not only wrote his seminal *Leaves of Grass*, but also handled its first and subsequent editions typesetting and design.

- A million bacteria, 10,000,000 viruses, and 100 worm eggs are generally contained in 0.035 ounces of human feces.

NEIGHBORHOOD WATCH (PART 1)

Sometimes grass seems so green on the other side of the fence, we forget everything over there is made to kill us on the spot. Same goes for the Solar System's lovely collection of planets beyond our own.

Mercury: With a solid iron core allowing it to withstand the impact of large asteroids, no life to complain about surface temperature extreme fluctuations (-280 to 800°F), a thin atmosphere, and rugged pox-ridden cratered terrain not unlike our Moon, it's one of the least hospitable planets in our system.

Venus: Rotating in the opposite direction to the rest of the planets, and enveloped by an atmosphere made of carbon dioxide and sulfur dioxide that keeps the planet at a scorching 932°F, the unlucky astronaut ever to crash land there would suffocate and roast at the same time. Not to mention be squeezed to a pulp at the same time, by atmospheric pressure amounting to 1,500 pounds per square inch.

Mars: Enjoying seasons not unlike our own and the presence of water, it may seem more hospitable than other planets, but its dust storms cover the whole planet for months on end, and it has no magnetic field—meaning if you lived there, your cancer would get cancer! Unlike Earth, it has two moons, quaintly named Phobos (god of fear) and Deimos (god of dread), the former expected to crumble into a ring of rocks in the next 20-40 million years.

Ceres: Beyond Mars lies a belt of asteroids (some of which have been nudged our way by Jupiter), housing little known, dwarf-planet Ceres. It may even have a remnant ocean of liquid water underneath its icy surface, sprinkled by reflective sodium-carbonate crystals!

DEATH FROM ABOVE

While comets are basically made of ice, asteroids are made of bad-ass metal. When they bump into each other, the small chunks that break off are called meteoroids. When a meteoroid enters our atmosphere, leaving a streak of light (which romantics call a "shooting star"), it becomes a meteor, and when it hits the ground we call it a meteorite. The Torino Scale color-codes the scale of possible impact danger:

1. White—No Hazard: Zero collision likelihood, not counting smaller bodies such as meteoroids.

2. Green—Normal: Applies to routine near-Earth (and "near" here applies to far off space distances) passes, usually blown out of proportion by news media.

3. Yellow—Meriting Attention: A discovery or close encounter deemed of astronomical interest, this category is divided in three sub-categories which go from near zero to 1% collision chances on a local or regional level, and could be worthy of public attention if the probability of such an encounter is less than a decade away.

4. Orange—Threatening: A close encounter also subdivided into three sub-categories according to the threat it may or may not pose in a ten to 30 year period, and requiring critical attention from astronomers, as well as government contingency plans.

5. Red—Certain Collision: When impact is imminent and divided in three sub-categories depending on the damage scale (local, regional, global).

GREATEST HITS!

If you're thinking space is too far away to do any real damage to planet Earth, think again. Some of the largest impact craters found on Earth today include:

Chicxulub: Found in Mexico's Yucatan peninsula, its diameter (186 mi) makes scientists believe it was caused by the original dino-buster: an asteroid about 6.2 miles wide which possibly helped wipe out the dinosaurs 60 million years ago!

Vredefort: This South African behemoth is the world's largest-known (190 mi diameter) and second-oldest (2 billion years ago) impact crater, and was declared a UNESCO World Heritage Site in 2005.

Sudbury Basin: The 81 miles wide result of a nasty bolide (super bright, exploding meteor) of an estimated size of 6.2–9.3 miles wide impacting Ontario, Canada, 1.8 million years ago. Fragments blown away by the impact can be found as far as Minnesota!

Woodleigh: As peculiar as Australian fauna, this crater was discovered hiding underground in 2000, and a 2010 study suggests its crater could be between 37 and 99 miles in diameter, and was produced by a comet or asteroid 3.7 to 7.5 miles wide.

Chesapeake: Thirty-five million years ago, 125 miles from Washington, DC, a pesky bolide crashed at 37 miles per second, leaving a hole of about 53 miles wide (twice the size of Rhode Island!) and 0.81 miles deep (nearly as deep as the Grand Canyon!). It would one day be called the Chesapeake Bay.

Yarrabubba: Discovered in 1979, the world's oldest asteroid crater is located in Western Australia. It was recently dated at 2.2 billion years old and some even think it may have put an end to the Ice Age!

Tunguska: A large explosion attributed to the air burst of a large meteor over Eastern Siberian in 1908, which flattened 770 square miles of forest (no human casualties were reported).

It left no crater behind!

BONUS FACTS!

- Mouth kissing actually transmits less bacteria than shaking hands, but saliva does transmit rabies and Hepatitis B among other viral diseases.

- The leotard body suit got its name after French acrobat and trapeze artist Jules Léotard (1838-1870).

- László József Bíró (1899-1985) was a Hungarian-Argentine inventor who patented the first commercially successful ballpoint pen. His technology was adapted to create the first rollover deodorant in the fifties.

- The English language has more words than any other. An average dictionary contains 600,000 words, but English-speaking people use only about 60,000 in their lifetime.

GATHERING MOSS

While "younger" meteors are blown to bits either by the atmosphere or upon impact, some large ones have encrusted themselves on Earth's surface, where they remain to this day. Smaller ones, on the other hand, are constantly being dissected like frogs.

Hoba: This virtually immovable (132277.4 lb) Namibian iron juggernaut was discovered by chance in 1920, when the owner of the land, Jacobus Hermanus Brits, ploughed the field with an ox. It is the world's largest single-piece meteorite.

Agnighito: Known to Greeland's Inuit as Saviksoah ("great iron") it was used by them as a source of molten metal for tools and harpoons. What's left of it currently sits at the American Museum of Natural History in the Arthur Ross Hall, weighting 68343.3 pounds.

Gancedo: The largest known chunk of a meteor shower that struck Campo del Cielo, in Argentina, 4,500 years ago, it weights 67902.38 pounds and was discovered underground in 2016.

Willamette: Held sacred by indigenous peoples of the Willamette Valley, who call it Tomanowos ("spiritual power"), the 34,000-pound nickel nugget was acquired by the American Museum of Natural History in 1906.

Mbozi: Once the sacred stone of the people of Tanzania, who call it Kimondo, this iron beast weights 35273.96 pounds.

Tita'a hanga 'o te henua: This large, ovoid-shaped stone 31.5 inches in diameter was, according to legend, brought by the founding king of

the Rapa Nui people to its current resting place in Easter Island. It is said that this magnetic iron rock concentrates a supernatural energy called "mana," and many nutty visitors rub their hands on the meteorite to capture it. So many in fact, it may account for the stone's unnatural smoothness!

Murchison: Well observed while it fell near Murchison, Victoria, in Australia, in 1969, it is one of the most studied meteorites due to its mass (220 lb) and the fact it contained 70 types of life-enabling amino acids. In 2019, American and Swiss scientists discovered the oldest material on Earth, 7.5 billion year old dust grains, within it. The oldest of these grains were formed in stars long before our sun was even born!

BONUS FACTS!

- The president of Iceland, Gudni Th. Jóhannesson (b.1962), has stated pineapple should be banned from pizza.

- One percent of women will climax just by simply stimulating their breasts.

- Almost half of the entire world's population has no toilet, and must make use of public toilets and/or other public areas to relieve themselves daily.

- Horatio Magellan Crunch is Cap'n Crunch's full name.

- The Eiffel Tower grows six inches every summer.

SMALL POTATOES

About 500 small (rock to pea sized) meteors fall to earth every year. Some fall in the sea and in unpopulated areas, but most are just vaporized while puncturing our atmosphere before hitting land or sea. Hence, being hit by one is like the lotto: someone could win, but the odds are it won't be you. Registered winners, however, include:

1. Entire families and cattle were reportedly killed during well-documented showers in China, in the years 1321, 1490, 1907, and 1915.

2. Pious men seem to be the preferred victims of meteors in Italy, as a monk in 1511 and a Franciscan friar in 1633 respectively passed from wounds caused by "celestial stones."

3. Between 1647 and 1654, en route to Sicily from Japan, two sailors were killed when a meteorite struck their ship in the middle of the Indian Ocean.

4. In 1897, a meteor exploded over the town of New Martinsville, West Virginia, and knocked a man unconscious, while a loose chunk decapitated a horse!

5. A wedding party in 1929 Yugoslavia was struck by a meteor with one person being killed on the spot.

6. A shower allegedly killed twelve people, injured twenty, and killed many animals near Teheran, Iran, in 1951.

7. The best known meteor injury in America was sustained on the left hip and arm while napping, by Annie Hodges, of Sylacauga, Alabama, in 1954.

8. The Chelyabinsk meteor in Russia detonated in the sky, injuring an estimated 1,500 people and damaging 3,000 buildings in 2013!

9. Most recently, in 2016, a tiny meteor crashed into the gardens of the Bharathidasan Engineering College in Tamil Nadu, India, hurting two gardeners and a student, and possibly killing a 40-year-old bus driver, although this has been disputed.

10. The first documented case of a car being struck by a meteor occurred on September 29, 1938, in Benld, Illinois, when one made a hole in the roof of Edward McCain's garage, embedding itself in the seat of his 1928 Pontiac Coupe!

BONUS FACTS!

- Sixty-five percent of the world's hard drugs are consumed in the United States, which explains why 90% of all dollar bills contain traces of cocaine!

- Theobromine is a highly toxic alkaloid present in chocolate, which can kill dogs, cats, and even bears, yet deemed "safe" for humans.

NEIGHBORHOOD WATCH (PART 2)

Even deadlier planets await us on the wrong side of the tracks, beyond the asteroid belt!

Jupiter: If a manned vehicle would somehow be lured in by the gas giant's gravity, and if it managed not be torn apart by its four rings, nor crash into any of its 79 known moons (some larger than planets), it would have to endure penetrating Jupiter's colossal and stormy hydrogen atmosphere, withstanding its freakishly strong centrifugal force, and it would then need to survive the deadly ammonia and methane clouds (which would be at -220°F, and giving off incredibly powerful lightning), before crashing into its solid core … if it even exists (no one knows!).

Saturn: This madhouse of a planet isn't the only ringed planet in the system, but its rings are certainly the most visible, its 62 moons the fanciest (including planet-sized Titan, which has its own atmosphere and possibly even life!), and visiting would present challenges similar to Jupiter's, only with winds reaching 1,118 miles per hour, colder clouds (-274°F) and an inner temperature of 21,000°F (so it's frying, not freezing for us), which means it strangely radiates 2.5 times more energy into space than it gets from the Sun!

Uranus: Tilted and rolling at 98 degrees, this ice giant's poles are in the middle, while its equator runs from top to bottom, surrounded by 13 known rings and 27 known moons! Nevertheless, Uranus seems hotter at its equator than at its poles, but scientists still haven't figured out the reason for this. "Hotter," of course, means very little at an average −371°F, which makes it the coldest planet in the system (even colder than Neptune, which should be much, much colder!).

Neptune: Denser and physically smaller than Uranus, its atmosphere has visible weather patterns driven by the strongest sustained winds of any planet in the Solar System, with recorded speeds as high as 1,500 miles an hour (take that, Saturn!). Its dark, organic rings and 13 moons were only discovered recently, in the twentieth century. Of the latter, Triton seems more like a dwarf-planet trapped by Neptune's gravitational pull than a moon itself.

Planet X: Since 1906, this ninth planet has been hypothesized and searched for but never actually found. In 2015, astronomers Konstantin Batygin and Mike Brown announced "new evidence" of a giant planet tracing an unusual, elongated orbit in the outer solar system, but failed to produce solid proof.

BONUS FACTS!

- According to the World Health Organization, 1.5 billion people suffer from roundworm infection, while another 800,000,000 are infected by whipworms, and 740,000,000 by hookworms!

- Female kangaroos have three vaginas, while male kangaroos have a bifurcated penis!

- Two-thirds of the world's executions happen in China!

- In 1942, TV star Lucille Ball (1911-1989) claimed her dental fillings had picked up radio transmissions from Japanese spies!

PLUTO AND FRIENDS

Regrettably labeled by their size, gender, and ethnicity, ice dwarf trans-neptunian planets discovered so far include:

Pluto (1930): The first dwarf to be discovered and the only one with an atmosphere (which goes from gassy to snowy depending on its distance from the Sun), it has five moons, the biggest of which, Charon, is almost as big as Pluto itself.

Haumea (2004): This one rotates so fast, it's shape has been compressed into something akin to a football. Not happy with its odd shape, this dwarf planet also has two moons and a ring system!

Eris (2005): Twenty-eight percent more massive than Pluto, it is also the most distant from the Sun. It has a bad-ass moon of its own: Dysnomia (after the Greek goddess of lawlessness who was Eris's daughter).

Makemake (2005): Much like Pluto, it has a reddish, irregular surface, but lacks an atmosphere. A moon, nicknamed MK2, has been found orbiting it as recently as 2016.

Sedna (2015): Its exceptionally long and elongated orbit (taking approximately 11,400 years to complete) has been widely speculated about in scientific circles.

Gonggong (2007): Aptly code-named "Snow White," it is currently the largest unnamed body in the Solar System, but an online poll had it christened as Gonggong, the Chinese water god, which was since been submitted to the International Astronomical Union for approval.

ABOVE AND BEYOND

"Exoplanets" are the astronomical equivalent to "clickbait," and have been widely discussed in the media, where they provide a good filler when no news is available. But what do we really know about them? As of 2019, 4,016 have been discovered, 97% of which were found via bouncing radio signals, which means the astronomers' guesses are as good as yours or mine.

PSR B1620-26 b: One of the oldest known extra-solar planets, believed to be about 12.7 billion years old, and aptly nicknamed "Methuselah, the Genesis planet." It orbits not one but two stars.

55 Cancri e: Roughly twice the size of Earth, it has 8.63 times our planet's mass. One of the running theories is the planet's solid core is made of diamond!

J1407 b: We don't know if it's a gas giant, like Saturn, or a brown-dwarf (imagine Jupiter and the Sun having a baby), with a ring system so big you'd think it'd have trouble hiding, but the truth is astronomers haven't manage to re-locate it since 2007!

Gliese 436 b: With a surface temperature estimated at 822°F, this weirdo is a white-hot version of Neptune, leaving a trail of evaporating atmosphere on a misaligned orbit around its red-dwarf star (which suggests another planet may be skewing it).

Meet the Keplers: In 2015 astronomers concluded that the exoplanets Kepler-62f, Kepler-186f and Kepler-442b are likely the best candidates for being habitable. Of these, Kepler-186f is similar in size to Earth, and is located on the outer habitable edge around a red star.

PLANET HOLLYWOOD

While we're at it, let's have a look at some of the best known fictional planets!

Arrakis: Imagined by author Frank Herbert (1920-1986) for his *Dune* series of novels, it is a desert planet inhabited by giant sand-worms and the Fremen tribes which harvest the most valuable commodity in the universe: the melange or "spice."

Cybertron: The Transformers home world (its name is the Japanese name for "Autobot"), is an artificial planet the size of Saturn, hollow, and traversed by tunnels, with a breathable atmosphere but no water, nor any toilet facilities for carbon-based life forms either.

Gallifrey: An orange planet located in a binary star system, 250 million light years from Earth, it is home to *Doctor Who*'s "Time Lords" civilization, and has been destroyed, lost in time, and brought back as many times as it suited the show's writers.

Krypton: The birthplace of Superman (a.k.a. Kal-El, a.k.a. Clark Kent), Krypton was once the seat of an advanced, if cold, civilization, tragically destroyed when the planet exploded. The cause of the planet's destruction has also been changed to match the times, often due to the expansion of its red sun, but lately being attributed to ecosystem abuse.

Mongo: In the classic comic strip, this rogue planet is a lot like ours, processing an atmosphere compatible with Earth life, and inhabited by a diverse roster of intelligent, human-like species, ruled with an iron fist by tyrant Ming, the Merciless. Its collision course with Earth is fortunately thwarted by Flash Gordon and his friends.

Tatooine: The original home of Luke Skywalker (in the 1977 film *Star Wars*) is a desert planet orbiting a pair of binary stars, and inhabited by human and alien settlers alike.

Klendathu: Home of the "Arachnids" in Robert A. Heinlein's (1907-1988) *Starship Troopers* 1959 militaristic novel, and the 1997 film based on it.

The Planet of the Apes: In the 1963 novel by Pierre Boulle (1912-1994), it's an Earth-like planet orbiting the star Betelgeuse (don't say it three times!) where apes are the dominant species, and humans live in the wild like animals. However, the 1968 film's ending revealed it to be our own Earth in the far future!

Solaris: **When Earth builds an orbiting space-station around a distant sentient planet and tries to prod it into communicating, the planet retaliates, tormenting the scientists onboard with their most painful memories. The original 1961 novel by Polish writer Stanislaw Lem (1921-2006) thus established the notion of humans being completely unable to understand a truly alien intelligence.**

BONUS FACT!

- On October 21, 1988, a poodle named Cachy fell off the thirteenth floor of a building in Buenos Aires, Argentina, killing three people: Marta Espina (75) on impact, Edith Solá (46) who was hit by a bus while hurrying accross the street to help, and an unnamed male witness who suffered a stroke at the gruesome sight!

THE FARTING LEMON

Capturing mankind's attention since the dawn of history, we didn't lay a finger on our Moon for 4.5 billion years, until the Soviet Luna 2 robotic spacecraft crashed there in 1959. What science has found about it since, reveals a much more complex natural satellite than previously dreamed of.

It's getting away:

Distance from us (238,856 mi) gradually increasing 1.5 inches a year, and no manmade object on Earth can be seen from it, not even the Great Wall of China!

It's shy:

Completes a full orbit around the Earth in 27.3 Earth-days, and it takes it exactly the same time to spin around its own axis. Hence, we only see one side from Earth, while its far side has only been seen by artificial craft and astronauts.

It's ugly:

In 2014, scientists came to the conclusion it is actually shaped like a lemon, with an equatorial bulge.

It farts:

Colored lights have sometimes been seen briefly across its surface and are speculated to be gas leaks from deep within!

It smells:

Apollo astronauts have actually described its odor as akin to spent gunpowder!

It's pox-marked:

Cataclysmically hit with meteorites three to four billion years ago (in what scientists call a Late Heavy Bombardment), one of the largest craters (1,600 mi wide) in the Solar System, the South Pole-Aitken, can be found on its far side.

It has competition:

Astronomers have discovered several asteroids that are more or less following the Earth as it moves around the Sun. The two biggest ones are called 3753 Cruithne and 2002 Aa29.

It's soft on the inside:

Holds a probably liquid core of about 20% of its radius.

It's complicated:

The Apollo missions returned with 850 pounds of rocks and dust. When exposed to the latter, Earth bacteria died, but sea algae thrived and grew greener! Corn, as usual, remained unaffected.

BONUS FACTS!

- Realizing that lack of human contact would take its toll during the 2020 Coronavirus pandemic lock-down, the Dutch National Institute for Public Health recommended that people find stable "sex buddies" as a means to cope with stress.

- Ancient Greeks invented spiked dog collars to protect them from wolf attacks.

FLY ME TO THE MOON

With Soviet, American, Japanese, Chinese, European, Israeli, and Indian (whew!) missions either crashing, or softly landing there on purpose, there's an ever-growing amount of manmade stuff left behind on the Moon, which so far includes:

96

BAGS OF URINE, FECES, AND VOMIT

62

UNMANNED SPACE VEHICLES

16

ASCENT/DESCENT STAGES

6

AMERICAN FLAGS

5

MIRRORS

3

MOON BUGGIES (Yay!)

2

GOLF BALLS (Yay?)

1

GOLDEN OLIVE BRANCH

1

FALLEN ASTRONAUT MEMORIAL

1

FAMILY PHOTO (Apollo 16 astronaut Charles Duke's family)

1

FALCON FEATHER AND A HAMMER
(Dropped at the same time to prove a point)

1

THE ASHES OF PLANETARY GEOLOGIST EUGENE SHOEMAKER
(1928-1997)

1

DIGITAL LIBRARY (Sandwiched in-between, highly-resistant tardigrades were also included, and may stay alive on the moon for many years!)

1ST

BUZZ ALDRIN (b.1930) may have been the second man to walk on the moon in 1969, but according to record was the first to urinate and defecate on it!

MOONAGE DAYDREAM

Since the dawn of time, Earth's most brilliant minds still can't figure out why our moon appears larger when closer to the horizon than it does higher up in the sky. This is called the "moon illusion," and remains largely a mystery.

1. All atmospheric refraction, apparent distance, relative size, and angle of regard theories have been largely ruled out as explanations.

2. The moon isn't physically closer to Earth when showing above the horizon. Actually, it's closer when placed directly overhead.

3. The moon doesn't look bigger compared to trees, mountains, and buildings. Airplane pilots experience the same mirage without any of these visual reference points.

4. The moon creates a 0.0059 inch image of itself on our retina no matter its position in the night sky.

5. Since the seventeenth century, it has been purported as a strictly psychological phenomenon, related to our perception of the sky as a flattened dome instead of half a sphere. Said perception is also tainted by unconscious expectations of size and distance. In a nutshell, our brain is playing a nasty trick on us!

Five mirrors were planted on the lunar surface during the Apollo program (US) and the Lunokhod missions (USSR). They bounce back laser lights shot from Earth observatories, helping us determine the moon's true distance from our planet, which turns out to be huge.

PALE BLUE DOT

Fact is, we live on a backwater planet that is spinning on its axis while rotating around a star that is revolving around a galaxy that is plunging through space. If this makes you dizzy, wait till you read the following!

1. It has a waist line problem: It's not actually round but a "geoid," which means it has a delicate bulge toward the equator, caused by rotation.

2. It spins fast: It rotates on its 23.45° tilted axis at 1000 miles per hour!

3. It's unequal: Hudson Bay in Canada, for instance, has less gravity than other regions of the globe due to its lesser land mass.

4. It flips: The planet's magnetic poles flip every several hundred thousand years. The last major pole reversal happened 780,000 years ago, probably messing with the magnetic field a great deal in the process.

5. It has a force-field: A powerful magnetic field protects life on this planet from solar radiation, and is the result of possessing a rotating iron core.

6. It's dense: Made mostly of iron (88%), making it the densest Solar System planet that we know of.

7. It's slowing down, but not that much: At about 17 milliseconds every hundred years. In 140 million years our days will be 25 hours long!

SH*T SANDWICH

Earth's name derives from the Old English word "ertha" and the Anglo-Saxon word "erda" which mean ground or soil, but what do we really know about the planet layers under our feet?

Inner Core: The 1,712 miles thick, dense (90% iron, 9% nickel, 1% sulfur) and extremely hot (8,100°F) center of the Earth, is also speculatively enriched with gold and platinum!

Outer Core: Viscose, fluid, turbulent, and molten, it is 1,500 miles thick, and even hotter, with temperatures ranging from 14,000 to 4,000°F.

Mantle: An 1,800 miles thick, semimolten (392 to 7,230°F) layer of silicate (iron-magnesium) rock between the crust and the outer core, and makes up for about 84% of Earth's total volume.

Oceanic Crust: Overlying the solidified and uppermost layer of the mantle, it is less than 200,000,000 years old, and about five miles thick (though twice as dense as continental crust), its hollows obviously filled with water.

Continental Crust: About 30 miles thick, and four billion years old, this is the layer of rock that forms continents and underwater continental shelves, currently occupying around 40% of Earth's surface.

Trapped in the continental crust we find the best record of Earth's history: fossils! Dinosaurs in Utah, palm trees in Britain, and even relics of marine life atop mountains, for most parts of the world have been undersea in our geological past.

ROCK OF AGES

Carbon dating estimates Earth to be around 4.54 billion years old, and geologists have measured the time of Earth's distant past, and organized it into units, according to the phenomenons that took place, which are in turn marked by major events, such as mass extinctions!

A few clarifying terms:

EON: Largest division of Earth's time, encompassing several eras.

ERA: Several periods of geological time.

PERIOD: Large division of time and geological strata.

EPOCH: Part of a period.

AGE: A stage within an epoch.

CHRON: Part of an age, and the smallest division of geological time.

Major eras of Earth's formation:

1. PRECAMBRIAN ERA (4.6 billion to 542 million years go): Divided into three eons (Hadean, Archean, Proterozoic), from the formation of Earth to the development of bacterial and multi-cellular life, to the first hard-shelled creatures appearing in abundance.

Mass extinction event: The **Oxygen Catastrophe** saw almost all life on Earth to that point go extinct!

2. PALEOZOIC ERA (542 million to 250 million years ago): Divided into six geologic periods (Cambrian, Ordovician, Silurian, Devonian, Carboniferous, and Permian), which saw explosive growth in species diversification from the sea onto dry land.

MEE #1: Caused by what is believed to have been a gamma-ray burst originating from a hypernova within 6,000 light-years of Earth, the **Ordovician–Silurian event** combo killed off 85% of all marine species.

MEE #2: The **Late Devonian extinction** affected marine life due to environmental changes of unknown origins, during a very extended period of time.

3. MESOZOIC ERA (250 million to 65 million years ago): Divided into the Triassic, Jurassic, and Cretaceous periods, it saw the splitting of the Pangea super-continent, the appearance of flowering plants, dinosaurs, and mammals, but was marred by three mass extinctions!

MEE #3: The **Permian–Triassic event** was made possible by an apparent sharp increase of atmospheric CO_2, which decimated 96% of all marine species, 70% of terrestrial vertebrate species, and 83% of all insects!

MEE #4: The **Triassic–Jurassic event** wiped out a number of land and sea creatures, and has been blamed on climate-change or unusual volcanic activity.

MEE #5: Perhaps the most famous of all, the **Cretaceous–Paleogene event** asteroid made sure no four-legged creatures weighing more than 55 pounds survived—say goodbye to dinosaurs!

4. CENOZOIC ERA (65 million years ago to the present): The current era saw continents moving into their current positions, the rise of mammals, and the beginning of a cooling climate period, now reversed by a new, hairless primate species hell-bent on ecocide...

A February 2012 study predicted that in 200 million years time a new continent would be made by Asia and North America colliding over the North Pole: Amasia!

DRY HUMP

There's plenty of action to be found on the planet's surface:

1. Earth's ground is gradually being broken down into smaller pieces by the atmosphere, in a phenomenon called "weathering" (which explains the little evidence of asteroid and meteor impacts).

2. Other than meteor impacts and weathering, two other mechanisms shape the Earth's surface: volcanic activity and orogeny (mountain-making earthquakes)!

3. Our rocky surface gets recycled by volcanoes, which spits it out as magma. When magma cools down, it dries, hardens, and crackles, creating rocks which either get sucked down (by earthquakes) or pushed down (by a new layer of rocks from above), to be molten again around the planet's core.

4. As far as volcanoes go, on a small island in the Tyrrhenian Sea, off the north coast of Sicily, Italy, Mount Stromboli (which gives the island its name) has been continuously erupting since the time of Jesus!

5. The highest land point on Earth is Mount Everest (29,029 ft) in the Himalayas, while the 1960 Valdivia (Chile) earthquake remains the highest in magnitude ever recorded (9.4–9.6 Richter Scale).

6. The largest and oldest living organism on land is an Armillaria mushroom fungus. "Humongous Fungus" covers 2,385 acres of Malheur National Forest in Oregon, and is estimated to be around 8,650 years old!

NEED A FLOWER FOR THAT VASE?

Among Earth's many weathering cracks (which include gorges, valleys, fissures, faults, trenches, and fumaroles) canyons caused by a river cutting deep between cliffs or mountains are by far the most magnificent.

Yarlung Tsangpo Grand Canyon: The world's deepest (19,714 ft) and longest (313.5 mi) canyon is located in Tibet, China.

Capertee Valley: It measures 279 miles and while not cutting very deep (it's a "young" one in geological time), it's 18.6 miles wide, so it is considered the world's second largest canyon.

Cotahuasi Canyon: Carved between two Peruvian mountain ranges, Coropuna and Solimana, this is the second deepest canyon in the world at 11,004 feet.

Colca Canyon: Also located in Peru, this canyon runs deep at 10,730 feet, for over 62 miles.

Grand Canyon: Arguably the most famous canyon in the world, it stretches for 277 miles and its depth is about 5,900 feet.

Kali Gandaki Gorge: At an 8,270 feet floor elevation, this old Nepalese canyon is considered one of the world's deepest.

Blyde River Canyon: With a maximum depth of 4,500 feet, this gorge splits through 16 miles of South African lush wilderness.

Tara River Canyon: The deepest in Europe; the depth of this Montenegro canyon is about 4,265 feet, and it is almost 50 miles long.

Fish River Canyon: This Namibian wonder cuts 1,804 feet deep through almost 100 miles, while stretching 16.7 miles wide in some places.

Charyn Canyon: While the length (95.6 mi) and depth (984.2 ft) of this Kazakh gorge may seem somewhat modest, it is considered the most beautiful on Earth.

Valles Marineris: The widest known canyon (the room between its walls would span the width of the entire continental United States), and running 10 times deeper that the Grand Canyon, this unique rift is located ... on Mars!

BONUS FACTS!

- One pound of peanut butter may contain up to 150 bug fragments and five rat hairs.

- The first silver dollar coin was minted 500 years ago in the Czech town of Jáchymov, which now only accepts Czech koruna as currency.

- The oldest "yo' mama" joke on record dates back to ancient Babylon, over 5,000 years ago!

RISE ABOVE

Earth's own acne, mountains, are looked upon by some as something worth climbing—and littering—mercilessly, while others have seen it fit to classify them from a safe distance.

TYPE:

Dome: Flat, their slope gradually merges with the lowlands (think the South Dakota Black Hills).

Fault-block: Caused by faults in the crust which uplift blocks along linear fracture zones (think Sierra Nevada).

Fold: Formed by tectonic plates collision (think the Appalachians).

Volcanic: Actual volcanoes (think Mount Fuji in Japan) or made by volcanic residue (like Wyoming's Devil's Tower).

STRUCTURE:

Base: The lowest flat point from which they rise.

Foothills: After the base, this is where plants and trees still manage to grow.

Alpine zone: Where the treeline ends and hardly anything grows.

Summit: The mountaintop or peak.

LENGTH:

Andes (South America): World's longest mountain range at 5,500 miles.

Rockies (North America): World's second longest mountain range at 3,000 miles.

Himalayas (Asia): World's third longest mountain range at 2,400 miles.

Eastern Highlands (Australia) and **Transantarctic Mountains** (Antarctica): World's fourth longest mountain ranges at 3,000 miles each.

HEIGHT:

Everest (Himalayas): Highest mountain on Earth (29,000 ft).

Aconcagua (Andes): Second highest mountain at a nifty 22,800 feet.

Mount McKinley (Alaska Range): Third highest peak at 20,300 feet high.

Kilimanjaro (Eastern Rift): Fourth highest volcano mountain at 19,300 feet.

Olympus Mons: Earth tallest elevations pale against this 72,000 feet volcano located on Mars!

BONUS FACTS!

- Though it may be considered a felony if done to a native species, contrary to popular belief, cutting a cactus in Arizona will not land anyone in jail.

- Vatican City ATM machines have Latin as one of their language options.

- As Assistant Secretary of the Navy, Franklin Delano Roosevelt (1882-1945) created and oversaw "Section A," an undercover unit dedicated to investigating and persecuting homosexuals at Newport's Naval Base.

BOOM SHAKALAKA BOOM!

Mankind has a strong love-hate relationship with volcanoes. On one hand, at their best these magma-spitting ruptures on Earth's crust give a great show, inspiring great disaster films. On the other, while we could outwalk certain types of lava flow, others would incinerate us in a split second. At their worst, not even Usain Bolt (b.1986) could outrun the steaming avalanche of hot ash and gas known as pyroclastic flow!

Huaynaputina: In the year 1600, this Peruvian volcano starred the largest historical eruption in South America, which was heard all the way to Lima, and caused disruptive effects all over the Earth, including floods, cold waves, and famines in places as far as Russia.

Mount Tambora: This still active Indonesian volcano had the biggest eruption ever recorded. In 1815, it shot approximately 18,000,000,000 tons of lava, killing 71,000 people instantly, and many more afterwards by causing a global climate and agricultural disaster known as "The Year Without a Summer."

Krakatoa: Another Indonesian *Kaiju* monster, its cataclysmic 1883 eruption followed by a series of smaller ones completely obliterated the island it sat on, and generated a tsunami which killed 34,000 people. The Arabian Peninsula, 7,000 miles away, also registered the increase in wave heights! New eruptions in December 1927 produced the Anak Krakatau ("Child of Krakatoa") volcano, currently active at the center of the caldera produced by the 1883 eruption.

Santa Maria: A very violent 1902 eruption broke the 500 year old slumber of this Guatemalan volcano, its pyroclastic flow claiming the lives of at least 5,000 people.

Novarupta: This "newly formed" (the meaning of its name) Alaskan volcano was built in 1912, during the largest recorded eruption of the twentieth century, which shot 30 times the volume of magma of the 1980 eruption of Mount St. Helens. Fortunately, despite its magnitude, no direct deaths were caused by this eruption.

Mount Pinatubo: The 1991 explosion of Mount Pinatubo in the Philippines was so mean, it sent a twelve mile high ash column into the atmosphere, collapsing the mount's summit in the process, damaging at least 16 commercial aircraft, and killing more than 847 people in its wake, which coincided with the arrival of Typhoon Yunya! It reduced the amount of sunlight reaching the planet by an estimated 10%, and is thought to have played a part in the 1993 "Storm of the Century."

Mount St. Helens: Rather than a single eruption, it started out as a series of earthquakes and phreatic explosions (steam blasts caused by magma heating groundwater), followed by a massive landslide and a supersonic, superheated lateral pyroclastic blast! While smaller in scale (compared to previously mentioned eruptions), this volcanic event was the most disastrous ever recorded in the continental US, its ash column rising 80,000 feet into the atmosphere, subsequently blanketing eleven states and two Canadian provinces, and killing 57 people.

BONUS FACT!

- Gerald Ford (1913-2006) turned down a Green Bay Packers contract to study law instead. He did generally well for himself, becoming America's thirty-eighth president in 1974.

HITTING CLOSE TO HOME

According to the 2018 Update of the U.S. Geological Survey National Volcanic Threat Assessment, *of the 161 active American volcanoes listed, 18 were designated a "very high threat."*

1. Mount Kilauea, Hawaii.
2. Mount St. Helens, Washington.
3. Mount Rainier, Washington.
4. Redoubt Volcano, Alaska.
5. Mount Shasta, California.
6. Mount Hood, Oregon.
7. Three Sisters, Oregon.
8. Akutan Island, Alaska.
9. Makushin Volcano, Alaska.
10. Mount Spurr, Alaska.
11. Lassen volcanic center, California.
12. Augustine Volcano, Alaska.
13. Newberry Volcano, Oregon.
14. Mount Baker, Washington.
15. Glacier Peak, Washington.
16. Mauna Loa, Hawaii.
17. Crater Lake, Oregon.
18. Long Valley Caldera, California.

Yellowstone National Park actually sits in the caldera of a gigantic super-volcano! In 2013 scientists reported a huge magma-filled chamber bubbling underneath it!

DEEPEST DEPRESSIONS

Not all of Earth's surface manages to rise above itself, and no amount of psychotherapy will make the following feel any better!

Dead Sea: Considered to be the Earth's lowest point on land at 997 feet deep, it is also one of the world's saltiest bodies of water.

Trupan: The second lowest depression on the planet (505 feet deep), it is also the hottest and driest area in China.

Qattara: Located in the Western Desert of Egypt, it lies below sea level at 436 feet deep, covered with salt pans, sand dunes, and salt marshes.

Karagiye Trench: At 433 feet below sea level, it is the lowest point in Kazakhstan and all of Central Asia.

Danakil: A 383 feet deep geological depression, resulting from the presence of three tectonic plates in the Horn of Africa.

Death Valley: It's floor is the second lowest depression in the Western world at 282 feet.

Salton Sink: The lowest point within a basin in Colorado's Sonora Desert lies at a 235 feet.

Byrd Glacier: While covered in ice, this 9,120-foot-deep Antarctic glacier valley extends 85 miles long, and 15 miles wide!

CAN I BORROW A FEELING?

People love rocks, be that for collecting, painting, throwing, or studying them, but minerals are dull enough not to care what we do with them. They know we will all eventually be turned to dust.

SIZE & GRAIN:

Colloid: Smallest rock in size and grain at 0.0001 inches.

Clay: Second smallest at 0.0002 inches.

Silt: From coarse to very fine, at 0.0039 inches.

Sand: From coarse to very fine, at 0.062 inches.

Gravel: From 0.75 to 1.5 inches big.

Pebble: 1.5 to 2.5 inches big.

Cobblestone: 2.5 to 10 inches big.

Boulder: Ten inches and bigger.

TYPE:

Magma: Molten rock.

Igneous: Formed from molten magma, may be considered extrusive (volcano-ejected magma) or intrusive (cooled down magma).

Sedimentary: Formed on earth's surface by accumulation and cementation.

Metamorphic: The result of subjecting igneous or sedimentary rocks to enough heat or pressure to change its mineral type or form.

AGE:

Alluvium: Loose and eroded sediment.

Limestone: These are often composed of fragments of marine organisms.

Sandstone: The most resistant to weathering processes, they are composed mainly of silicate particles.

Conglomerate: Coarse-grained rocks made of a substantial fraction of rounded to gravel-size rock fragments, often cemented by calcium carbonate, iron oxide, silica, or hardened clay.

Metamorphic (again?): Rocks which saw their chemical components and crystal structures change without melting (the rock remains a solid), through heat and pressure alone. They are among the oldest on Earth!

In 2019, NASA reported the discovery of the oldest known Earth rock—on the Moon! Nicknamed "Big Bertha," it had been brought back decades ago by the Apollo 14 mission. Containing quartz, feldspar, and zircon, all common on the Earth but highly uncommon on the Moon, it was carbon-dated to be 4 billion years old.

BONUS FACTS!

- The two main charges Joan of Arc was sentenced to be burned at the stake for were having visions, and wearing soldier's clothing.

- An estimated 2,000 serial killers currently roam the United States, looking for their next victim!

- Wild boars actually wash their food clean in water streams before eating it!

FRAGGLE ROCK

Friedrich Mohs (1773-1839) spent his life classifying rocks by their resistance to, well, scratching. It's a list too odd not to share here—wonder what the guy's nails looked like!

1. Scratched by fingernail:

1.1. Talc

1.2. Rocksalt

2. Scratched by red penny:

2.1. Calcite

3. Scratched by knife:

3.1. Apatite

3.2. Fluorite

4. Scratched by steel needle:

4.1. Orthoclase feldspar

5. Scratched by streak plate (hard, unglazed porcelain):

5.1 Quartz

6. Scratch-resistant:

6.1. Topaz

6.2. Corundum

6.3. Diamond

SHAKE YOUR BOOTY

Volcanoes are not the only weapon the planet uses to shake us off its back like fleas. An average 20,000 noticeable earthquakes strike without warning, all year round, at any time, day or night, anywhere in the world, killing an average of 8,000 people a year.

1. Don't fret! Only 70 to 75 major (7.0 and up on the Richter magnitude scale) earthquakes hit populated areas each year (most occur in uninhabited land, or under the ocean floor).

2. Eighty percent of all the planet's earthquakes take place along the Pacific Ocean's "Ring of Fire" (also home to 75% of the world's volcanoes).

3. All 50 US states are vulnerable to earthquakes, with California and Alaska being hit by the largest and most damaging ones—the largest US earthquake on record was a 9.2 magnitude one that struck in Alaska in 1964.

4. The largest earthquake ever was a 9.5 magnitude event which hit Valdivia, Chile, on May 22, 1960, sending seismic waves around the entire planet for many days, and causing a destructive tsunami that hit Hawaii, Japan, the Philippines, eastern New Zealand, southeast Australia, and the Aleutian Islands!

5. The 2004 undersea Indian Ocean earthquake lasted ten minutes and generated a gigantic tsunami which wiped out 227,898 people in 14 countries. After the Chilean and Alaskan earthquakes, at 9.1 magnitude it is the third largest ever recorded.

6. On February 27, 2010, another huge 8.8 Chilean earthquake (actually several quakes combined in line throughout the territory) shortened Earth's day and slightly changed the planet's axis!

7. The 9.0 magnitude Tōhoku earthquake and ensuing tsunami in 2011 caused the Fukushima Daiichi Nuclear Power Plant nuclear disaster, and is considered the world's fourth strongest.

8. From 1811 to 1821, a series of earthquakes (three of which were above 8.0 in Richter magnitude) hit Missouri for three months, from 1811 to 1812, and were felt all over the Eastern Seaboard.

9. The 6.9 magnitude 1995 Kobe (Japan) earthquake killed 6, 434 people, left 300,000 homeless, and leveled over 100,000 buildings, all in approximately 20 seconds!

10. The 2010 Haiti earthquake (7.0 magnitude), wiped out 160,000 people, and collapsed 280,000 buildings in less than 30 seconds.

11. Parkfield, California, the most closely observed earthquake zone in the world, lies along the San Andreas Fault, and has a bridge over two tectonic plates.

12. Moonquakes were first registered by seismometers placed by the Apollo 12, 14, 15, and 16 missions, which were switched off in 1977.

13. Marsquakes on the other hand are very rare (one every million years or so), with the first, very faint one, being measured by NASA on April 6, 2019.

WATER CLOSET

Paraphrasing Ambrose Bierce (1842 - c.1914), water fills about two-thirds of a world seemingly made for humanity ... a species with no gills. Maybe that's why we have only explored 5% of it all.

1. While initially closeted within the planet, water was brought to the surface by volcanic activity.

2. Of the water currently covering 70% of Earth's surface, only 3% is fresh, while 97% is salted. Of that 3%, over 2% is frozen in ice sheets and glaciers, meaning we may actually get to drink less than 1% of all water on the planet (hence its enormous importance).

3. Seventy percent of all fresh water and 90% of all ice on Earth lie in Antarctica, while the Pacific Ocean basin contains 50% of all free (liquid) water on Earth.

4. The ocean is where life first developed, and currently still contains more living organisms than rainforests, and also its largest living structures—coral reefs.

5. The longest mountain range on Earth is underwater, stretching for 80,000 km around the world and is completely volcanic.

6. The deepest place on Earth is the Challenger Deep in the Mariana Trench, seven miles below the surface of the ocean. Only three people have ever been there!

7. Oceans hold nearly 20 million tons of—very diluted—gold, while enough undissolved gold sits on the sea floor to put 15-20 US dollars in every pocket on Earth if ever extracted (and equally distributed)!

While technically dead as a doornail, iron-manganese rocks do grow by slowly collecting chemical elements from seawater. 200 billion tons of these rocks litter the world's oceans steadily growing at a rate of 0.04 inches every million years so, unlike human beings, they do not pose any immediate danger to life on Earth.

BONUS FACTS!

- Johnny Appleseed (1774-1845) did plant apple trees, but rather than feeding people, they were meant for cider-making!

- *Sphenopalatine ganglioneuralgia* is the scientific term for "brain freeze."

- In 2001, an eight-year-old boy got a three day suspension from school for pointing a breaded chicken finger at his teacher and uttering "Pow-Pow-Pow!"

- Yamaguchi Tsutomu (1916-2010) survived the atomic bombings of both Hiroshima and Nagasaki!

- The world's largest furnace is a solar-powered marvel built in France in 1970, which burns at an amazing 6,000°F.

COOL AS ICE

Pop culture abounds in ice-powered characters, and here's a list of some of the coolest (pun intended) ones!

Iceman: Chief among cold super heroes, this 1963 Marvel Comics "Omega level" mutant has made it off the printed page into film (the *X-Men* film franchise) and TV (*Spider-man and His Amazing Friends*, 1981-1983). He can become ice, change his shape and size, make ice weapons, and even slide in his own ice toboggan!

Killer Frost: This 1978 DC Comics female villain turned anti-hero can make deadly ice-based weapons, and may absorb heat from various sources, including humans, with usually deadly results. She can also be seen on TV's *The Flash* (2014).

The Night King: Sprung from the pages of George R R Martin's *A Song Of Ice And Fire* fantasy series into the *Game of Thrones* TV show (2011-2019), he is the subtly ironic leader of a race of super powerful ice-zombies known as "White Walkers," who are nigh-indestructible, can make ice-based weapons, and turn human and animal victims into mind-controlled zombies. Obsidian daggers and fictional Valyrian steel swords seem to be their only weaknesses.

Mr. Freeze: Another tragic DC Comics villain from 1959, Victor Fries is a cryogenics scientist whose body temperature is accidentally lowered to sub-zero levels while attempting to cure his wife, Nora, from a terminal illness. Forced to wear a special suit to survive, he also makes a "freeze gun" he uses to exact revenge on those he blames for his tragedy. Mr. Freeze has been interpreted on the screen by a roster of well-known stars, including Eli Wallach (1915-2014) and even Arnold Schwarzenegger (b.1947)!

Captain Cold: Created in 1957 on the pages of DC Comics *The Flash*, Leonard Snart is a hardened criminal driven by his desire for money, women, and killing The Flash, of course! To that effect he dons a blue parka, Eskimo snow goggles, and a "cyclotron" gun he uses to freeze objects and people, shoot deadly icicles, and anything the plot requires to slow his nemesis down.

Elsa: Loosely based on Hans Christian Andersen's *The Snow Queen*, the distraught anti-hero of Disney's successful *Frozen* films is a woman capable of commanding ice and snow at will. She can shoot ice from her fingertips, freeze anything she touches, and build complex ice architecture as well as sentient creatures she controls.

Frozone: A supporting character in Disney/Pixar's film franchise *The Incredibles*, Lucius Best can freeze water, but is limited by the amount of available liquid or atmospheric water. He may also use the moisture of his own body if needed be, though at serious dehydration risk.

Richard Kuklinski (1935-2006) was an American hitman and mass-murderer. Originally known in the criminal underworld as "The Polack" or "The Devil himself," he was given the nickname "The Iceman" by law-enforcement after his M-O was discovered: freezing the body of his victims to disguise the time of death—a technique allegedly learnt from another ice-themed killer, who went by the name "Mister Softee!"

BONUS FACT!

- Alfred Hitchcock's *Psycho* (1960) was the first film to show a toilet being flushed.

COLDPLAY

Earth's climate alternates between ice ages and greenhouse periods. Ice ages see a reduction in Earth's surface and atmosphere temperature, with a subsequent expansion of ice sheets and glaciers.

1. Ice ages are long term phenomenons which last for many million years.

2. Glacial (colder) and interglacial (warmer) periods alternate within ice ages.

3. Major ice ages include the Huronian, Surtian/Marinoan, Varangian, Ardea, Saharan, and Karoo epochs.

4. Currently we are living through the Great Ice Age or Pleistocene, which began 1.8 million years ago. The last glaciation ended about 15,000 years ago. The reason we don't experience colder climate is we are currently in an interglacial period, the Holocene, which is still going on.

5. During the Climatic Optimum period, which began 10,500 years ago (sooner in the Southern than the Northern Hemisphere) and lasted roughly 5,000 years, the temperature was even warmer than it is today, with rainfall basically forming otherwise arid Central Asia and green grass sprouting all over Africa's Sahara, which was dotted with lakes teeming with crocodiles, hippos, and other fauna.

6. A "Medieval Warm Period" lasted a few hundred years between 950 and 1250AD, and fostered Norse colonization of Greenland and North America.

7. The "Medieval Warm Period" was followed by a "Little Ice Age," starting around the early fourteenth century, and lasting until the nineteenth century, when some societies collapsed to famine and chaos, while others, like the Dutch, adapted to the new conditions and thrived exponentially.

8. Since the twentieth century, manmade emission of greenhouse gases is bringing about a rise of temperature on a global scale, which contributes to the retreat of glaciers, permafrost, and sea ice.

BONUS FACTS!

- Light doesn't always travel at 186,000 miles per second. The slowest ever recorded light moved at 38 miles per hour!

- *Toxoplasma gondii* is a parasite that only breeds in the guts of cats. To this end, it infects rats and twists their brains to make them less scared of cats.

- "Casu Marzu" is a Sardinian cheese delicacy known as "walking cheese," as it contains live, wriggling maggots!

- Many in showbiz owe their careers to New Jersey machinist Henry Ruschmann (1905-1989), who accidentally invented glitter in 1934, while trying to find better ways to grind plastics.

- Dogs may in fact recognize up to 165 English words!

MR. PURPLE SKY

This wondrous and odd blue marble we live on is enveloped by an atmosphere of strange gases which mostly cushion and protect us from the perils of sun radiation, cosmic rays, and meteor strikes. On top of it all, inhaling and exhaling some of these gases (which we candidly call "air") allow us to stay alive.

1. Early on, plants, algae, and cyanobacteria used carbon dioxide for photosynthesis and farted oxygen as waste, which got most anaerobic primordial life extinct, but in turn gave rise to oxygen-breathing creatures, and eventually us! Currently our atmosphere is composed of 78% nitrogen, 21% oxygen, and trace amounts of other gases including argon (0.9%) and carbon dioxide (0.04%).

2. The atmosphere is made of five main layers of variable density: troposphere, stratosphere, mesosphere, thermosphere, and exosphere, the latter reaching about 430 miles above sea level to around 6,200 miles, where it gets swept by solar wind.

3. Indeed our atmosphere isn't an air-tight glass bubble—most of its gasses leak into space. In the far future, hydrogen depletion in particular might end up drying our oceans out, shutting out this planet to life everywhere but at its poles.

4. Atmospherical temperature depends on humidity, solar radiation, and altitude. Meaning it gets colder at the mesopause, a zone which joins the mesosphere and thermosphere, and then much warmer due to increasing sun radiation.

5. When elevation increases, air pressure drops, as does the boiling point of water. Atop Mount Everest it boils at 162°F.

However, at stratospherical height (60,000 ft), water boils at 98.6°F, which means all our bodily fluids (such as saliva and blood) will boil at our average body temperature, killing us from within in less than a minute. It is called the Armstrong Limit!

6. Atmospherical friction disposes of most meteors and space junk it meets, incinerating them in temperatures reaching up to 3,000°F.

7. The atmosphere doesn't just contain gases but also water: 37.5 quadrillion gallons of it, in vapor form!

8. The sky above us doesn't just house birds but microbes too. According to scientists, 75% are similar to those in oceans and freshwater, but 25% are similar to those found in feces.

9. The sky appears purple because when sunlight gets scattered by the gases present in the atmosphere, violet light gets scattered more than other colors on account of its short wavelength; an effect that even gives the planet a purplish halo when seen from outer space too ... wait, what? As it turns out, we see the planet's sky blue both from within and without Earth due to a physiological limitation: the human eye is more sensitive to blue light than violet!

BONUS FACT!

- A virus (seastar-associated densovirus) discovered in the 1940s makes starfish tear off their own limbs until they die!

AIRHEADS

By now you're probably thinking it's best to stay informed on the many atmospherical levels, if only to avoid freezing, boiling from the inside, choking, losing our sight, or falling to our certain death like a misinformed Icarus.

Troposphere:

Eleven miles high at its upper edge, it is the atmosphere's densest (80% of the whole atmospherical weight) layer, which houses all life (including the birds in the sky), plane flights, and meteorological phenomena!

Stratosphere:

Thirty miles high at its upper edge, it houses the ozonesphere, a belt of maximum ozone concentration, which absorbs a great amount of the UV rays.

Mesosphere:

Fifty miles high at its upper edge, it is the atmosphere's coldest layer where ice clouds form, and falling meteors and other space junk burns.

Thermosphere:

At 250 miles high at its upper edge, this is where UV radiation created what we call the ionosphere within it. It may reach high temperatures (4,530°F) during daytime, and houses the International Space Station (ISS).

Exosphere:

From 250 to 40,000 miles above us, it reaches into space and is made mainly of runaway, sun-swept hydrogen. It has a glowing zone called Geocorona which extends more than 62,000 miles away from Earth.

Magnetosphere:

Formed by the interaction of the solar wind with Earth's magnetic field, it starts at the ionosphere, and reaches well beyond the exosphere, protecting Earth from the solar wind and cosmic rays that would otherwise burn it to a crisp.

Karman Line: The boundary between atmosphere and outer space is closer than you think: 62.1 miles, or 100 kilometers according to the *Federation Aeronautique Internationale*. If you take that into account, the Great Wall of China can be seen from that altitude but, come on, it is hardly "outer space" at all!

BONUS FACTS!

- A single mega-colony of Argentinian ants has colonized Europe, the US, and Japan, the vast extent of their global conquest paralleled only by human society!

- It has been found that farting reduces high blood pressure.

- Women have twice as many pain receptors and an equally higher tolerance to pain than men.

- Dinosaurs weren't scaled at all, but feathered like birds!

AIR QUALITY INDEX

No hint of irony in the title above, as the AQI, which debuted in 1968, is used by the Environmental Protection Agency (EPA) to inform the public how polluted the air currently is or is about to become at any given time.

0-50: Good and damn fresh.

51-100: Moderate but some particles may cause allergies.

101-150: Unhealthy for some sensitive folks.

151-200: Unhealthy for the elderly or ill, who should stay indoors.

201-300: Very unhealthy for the general population who need stay indoors and reduce all physical activity.

301-500: Hazardous. The stuff apocalyptical science fiction is made of!

Twenty percent of the world's population breathes heavily contaminated air, especially with carbon monoxide, sulfur dioxide, and methane.

BONUS FACT!

- **Most toilets produce an E flat note when flushing.**

AIR SUPPLY

Around the world, AQI monitoring tracks levels of dangerous particulates, the most harmful of which, PM2.5, contains tiny particles small enough to enter the bloodstream through the lungs, killing an estimated 7 million people a year! The world's ten most PM2.5-heavy cities include:

1. Kanpur (India): The most polluted in the world, this city is famous for its leather industry, which releases dangerous chromium into the air!

2. Faridabad (India): As with many other cities, its smog levels rise during wintertime, as cold temperatures trap pollutants nearer the ground. Not surprisingly, it is a leading industrial center.

3. Gaya (India): Located 62 miles south of Patna, this city is surrounded by hills, which lock the smog in.

4. Varanasi (India): Considered to be the spiritual capital of India, a construction boom has increased the poor air quality in the city.

5. Patna (India): As with any other Indian cities, heavy industrialization and a rising standard of living are the most common causes of high concentrations of PM2.5.

6. Delhi (India): Once the most polluted city in the whole world, it still struggles with smog stemming from the burning of rice paddies, municipal waste, and fuel.

7. Lucknow (India): The fourteenth-most populous city and the twelfth-most populous urban agglomeration of India, with the main root of its pollution lying in vehicle emissions, it is all out of luck.

8. Bamenda (Cameroon): The most polluted city outside of India, the reason lies not in industry but deforestation and climate change.

9. Agra (India): Home of the famous Taj Mahal, its visible smog is caused mainly by the burning of scrap tires to extract iron!

10. Gurugram (India): Located southwest of New Delhi and ironically a tech business hub, its PM2.5 ranking is 12 times over WHO recommended levels.

While below the pollution levels seen in the top ten most contaminated cities above, many Chinese towns suffer an air-quality crisis unseen in human history, killing hundreds of thousands of denizens and making cancer the country's leading cause of death. Adding insult to injury, China's highly polluted air causes acid rain in South Korea and Japan too!

BONUS FACT!

- Donald Duck is the most popular children's character in Finland. So popular, in fact, that when a Helsinki councilman proposed discontinuing the use of city funds to purchase *Aku Ankka* subscriptions for youth centers, it cost him his 1978 bid for reelection!

IT'S MY AEROPLANE

Over a hundred years since the Wrights' first flight, it seems navigating above the clouds, inside a pressurized aluminum tube, through air that's too thin to breathe, and chilling enough to turn us into icicles, is taken largely for granted.

1. The air is filled with 7,000 flights at any one time. Every month, local flights transport more than a million people between Tokyo and Sapporo in Japan, 680,000 between Hong Kong and Taipei in China, and 350,000 between Los Angeles and San Francisco.

2. The average flight travels at 35,000 feet above Earth's surface, at 550 miles per hour, with outside temperatures of around -65°F.

3. Flying isn't as polluting as some might think, amounting to barely 2% of human CO_2 emissions. For very practical reasons (like not crashing down), planes are highly fuel-efficient machines (70% more so now than when "jettos," as originally called, first trailed the skies).

4. Flying is indeed the safest way to travel, planes being designed to withstand any problems, from single engine failure (all they need to fly is one engine), fire (pilot-activated, built-in cabin extinguishers), engine blades that don't fall off, and oxygen masks when there's a sudden loss of cabin pressure.

5. Aboard passenger planes, air pressure may cause discomfort, be it from ear blockage pain (which becomes unmanageable if affected by a cold or the flu), numbing down your taste buds (making airplane food seem flavorless), or, worst of all, having your genitals ripped out if you flush the toilet while still seated!

6. It is mainly US carriers and international low-cost carriers who charge for meals; 100,000 meals per day are served by airlines.

7. Most airlines depend completely on business and first class passengers to turn a profit. Baggage fees which know no class boundaries, on the other hand, generate them a nifty 3.35 billion dollars a year, with another 3 billion bucks made by change fees.

8. A 2017 report indicated newer passenger planes are coming in with much smaller bathrooms, but before the late 1930s most planes did not have any toilets to speak of, so both crew and passengers had to urinate and defecate inside boxes, bottles, or buckets, which would sometimes tip during turbulence, ruining the whole experience for everybody.

BONUS FACTS!

- Their cloaca being highly vascularized, some species of aquatic turtles can literally breathe through their butts!

- Radical feminist Valerie Solanas (1936-1988) attempted to shoot and kill painter Andy Warhol (1928-1987) in 1968, seriously wounding him for the rest of his life.

- South Africa's boomslang snake's poison will make you hemorrage from every hole in your body faster than Ebola!

- Adam Rainer's (1899-1950) dwarfism was reversed by a pituitary gland tumor which made him grow 7.8 feet tall!

HOLE IN THE SKY

High concentrations of ozone (O_3) which are toxic to people and plants at ground level, save us all from 97-99% of the Sun's UV light when flowing in the lower zone of Earth's stratosphere we call the ozone layer (or shield, or belt). While mankind managed to mess with it too, the following timeline is proof we're well capable of fixing our own messes.

1913: First detected by Charles Fabry (1867-1945) and Henri Buisson (1873-1944), and further studied by Gordon Miller Bourne Dobson (1889-1976).

1930: Thomas Midgley Jr. (1889-1944), Albert Leon Henne (1901-1967), and a team of others developed "Freon," the first chlorofluorocarbon (CFC) to be used as a non-flammable refrigerant by the Frigidaire division of General Motors.

1974: Scientists Frank S. Rowland (1927-2012) and Mario J. Molina (b.1943) revealed that the ozone layer was being depleted by CFCs which, since they tend to amass at low temperatures, were creating an ozone "hole" above Antarctica.

1987: Fifty-seven countries adopted the Montreal Protocol, an agreement to cut CFC production and take further steps toward the worldwide elimination of CFCs from aerosol cans and refrigerators (ACs seem to have gotten a free pass).

2003: A significant slowdown on ozone depletion was announced.

2016: Three decades after the signing of the Montreal Protocol

enactment, and despite a few volcanic eruptions interrupting the process during 2015, the Antarctic ozone hole finally showed signs of disappearing.

In addition to ruining the ozone layer, Thomas Midgley Jr. is also sadly remembered for inventing highly toxic leaded gasoline, which caused catastrophic damages to air, sea, land, and human health for over a century.

Considered the single most destructive man in human history, this walking, breathing, ecocidal maniac accidentally strangled himself to death in 1944, thanks to a system of ropes and pulleys devised to lift himself up after being paralyzed by polio.

BONUS FACTS!

- Norway's Bouvet Island is the most remote in the world, lying 720 miles east of the South Sandwich Islands.

- White, yellow, and orange are the most visible, and therefore safest, of car colors.

- The word "nerd" was first used by Dr. Seuss in his 1950 book *If I Ran the Zoo.*

- A Southeast Asia delicacy, "Balut" is a duck egg which has been incubated for 15-20 days, thus containing the duck's *fetus* as a special treat!

UNDER PRESSURE

Meteorological phenomena may be restricted to troposphere, but its moving force is none other than the Sun, which heats the land differently according to a number of factors, so let's have a look at those places on Earth where things get ... dicey.

Vostok Station (Antarctica): At this Russian base in Antarctica, thermometers went down to the coldest temperature ever recorded: -128.6°F, on July 21, 1983. To gauge how cold that is, just imagine the coldest town on the planet, Oymyakon in Russian Siberia, with average winter temperature of merely -49°F, once registered a freezing -98°F in 2013.

Furnace Creek (USA): The hottest temperature ever was recorded at the aptly named town of Furnace Creek, located in the even more aptly named Death Valley, on July 15, 1972: 201°F. Imagine back in the 1960s the ghost town of Dallol in Ethiopia, Africa, was thought to be the hottest place on the planet at "just" 95°F.

Mawsynram (India): If you think the Amazon rainforest receives the most rain, think again. The record belongs to the Indian town of Mawsynram, which got 1,000 inches of rainfall in 1985, and has an annual average of 467.4 inches, a record disputed by López de Micay, a town in Colombia which reported 507.6 inches of rain between 1960 and 2012.

Loma (USA): This sleepy, 85 person town in Montana registered the most dramatic temperature swing on record, between January 14 and 15, 1972: a rise from -54 to 49°F (103°F change!). Loma beat the nearby town of Browning, which registered a drop from 44 to -56°F back in 1916.

Paradise (USA): According to the National Park Service, Paradise, an area located 5,400 feet up on the slope of Mount Rainier, in the state of Washington, is the snowiest place on the planet, and numbers back their claim, with a max annual snowfall record of 93.5 feet. The ski town of Niseko, Japan, holds the next record at 49.5 feet.

McMurdo Dry Valleys (Antarctica): Everybody knows the driest place on Earth must be the Atacama Desert (Chile), right? Wrong! While the Atacama houses a thriving ecosystem and freshwater sources, surrounded by hostile mountains which won't even allow ice to flow in there from glaciers, McMurdo is by far the world's most extreme desert; so dry, in fact, that no living organisms have been found there, except for bacteria hiding out inside rocks!

BONUS FACTS!

- Safely built into rock overhangs, the Spanish town of *Setenil de las Bodegas* is thought to have been occupied by humans since the stone age!

- Most of Emily Dickinson's (1830-1886) poems were never published during her lifetime.

- The earliest representation of a sailing ship was found on a 5,000 year old painted disc in Kuwait.

- The German Chocolate Cake has nothing to do with Germany, but was invented by English-born baker Samuel German in 1852.

AGAINST THE WIND

The bulk movement of air we casually call "wind" is a crazy weather phenomenon with its own rules, quirks, and plain strange facts.

1. In Greek mythology, the wind was ruled by "anemoi" gods for every compass point: *Boreas* (N), *Notus* (S), *Erus* (E), *Zephyr* (W), *Euroclydon* (NE), *Caurus* (NW), *Euroauster* (SE), and *Afer* (SW).

2. Romantically, meteorologists called the instrument that measures wind speed an "anemometer," while the instrument that measures wind direction got the more pedestrian "weather vane."

3. A gale blows between 32 and 63 miles per hour, a breeze does so from 4 to 31 mph.

4. Wind speed at sea is measured in knots—one knot equals 1.15078 mph.

5. Sea breezes occur because heat from the Sun takes longer to warm the sea than the land, creating a difference in air pressure.

The world's wind speed records include:

- **A 253 miles per hour gust of wind recorded on Barrow Island (Australia) on April 10, 1996.**
- **The fastest tornado spin at 318 mph on May 3, 1999, in Oklahoma.**
- **Typhoon Nancy hitting Japan at 215 mph in 1961.**
- **Antarctica's Commonwealth Bay being regularly slapped by freezing "katabatic wind," which may reach up to 150 mph.**

LET THE WIND BLOW

Over centuries, mankind has learned to harness the wind's energy to power machines and transport for both practical and recreational use.

1. Early forms of windmills were created to crush grain or pump water, but these days futuristic wind turbines create 4% of the whole planet's electricity.

2. Power-generating mills have existed longer than one might think. The very first house to be electrically powered by wind was in Kincardineshire, Scotland in 1887.

3. Both early windmills and wind turbines used to turn counter-clockwise (as viewed from the front), but have shifted toward clockwise rotation in modern times.

4. Wind turbines are highly complex machines, 290 feet tall on average (and getting higher to reach more powerful winds), with approximately 184 feet long turbine blades which spin at 200 mph.

5. By the end of 2018 the United States' wind power capacity reached 96,433 megawatts, providing over 10% of the total power generation in 14 states, and more than 30% in Kansas, Iowa, and Oklahoma.

American singer Christopher Cross admittedly wrote his seminal 1980 Grammy-winning "Ride Like the Wind" song while on an acid trip.

BLOWIN' IN THE WIND

Kiting fed mankind's dream of conquering the skies for thousands of years and its amazing craft continues to capture the imagination of people young and old!

1. Invented most certainly in Asia, the oldest depiction of a kite is a 9,000 year old cave painting found on Muna Island (Indonesia).

2. Fifth century philosophers Mozi (c.470-391BC) and Lu Ban (c.507-444BC) are said to have developed paper kites in China. The Chinese name for kite is *fen zheng*, which means "wind harp." Later on, flying kites were banned in China during Mao's Cultural Revolution (1966 through 1976).

3. Kites were also banned in Japan during the eighteenth century. Apparently they were so popular most people chose to fly them rather than go to work! Fortunately, that didn't take. The Japanese still love kite-making and are famous for making huge ones for their many festivals, including a record-breaking 3,307 pound behemoth built for the Yōkaichi Festival in 1994.

4. The fastest recorded speed of a kite is over 120 mph; another stayed up in the air for 180 hours, and the highest a kite has ever flown is 16,009 feet!

5. There are many safety issues related to kite-flying, mostly related to the use of glass-laced, throat-cutting string in developing countries (such as India and Chile), which kills around 12 people a year.

WIND OF CHANGE

Wind's most common classifications have to do with either range or their relative damage:

Planetary winds: Also known as *prevailing* winds, they blow all year long, from one latitude to the next.

Periodic winds: They are the winds that change with the season, like monsoons and several types of breezes.

Local winds: They have a much more reduced range, and tend to have folksy names, like *Sirocco* (hot wind from the Sahara) or *Pampero* (cold wind sweeping through the Argentinian pampa).

Macroburst: Outward burst of strong winds when a strong downdraft (small-scale column of air) reaches the surface.

Microburst: A small and concentrated downburst that produces an outward burst of strong winds at or near the surface.

Derecho: A cluster of many microbursts and downbursts that comes with a wide band of rapidly moving showers or thunderstorms.

Gust front: The front edge of rain-cooled air that clashes with warmer thunderstorm air flowing in opposite direction.

**Straight-line wind: Obviously, any storm wind that is …
not a tornado.**

GONE WITH THE WIND

For some, this novel and the 238 minute (with overture, intermission, entr'acte, and exit music) run-time film classic based on it didn't go fast enough, but it went on to become a cultural staple nonetheless.

1. Twenty-five-year-old Margaret Mitchell wrote the original novel the film is based on out of sheer boredom, when on leave from her job over an ankle injury.

2. It took Mitchell ten years to finish the book, which she went to great lengths to hide from both friends and relatives.

3. While she never intended to publish it, she took it to an editor after a friend made some derisive comments over her supposed inability to write prose.

4. Mitchell considered calling it "Bugles Sang True" or "Not in Our Star," before settling on the title we all know, which she took from verses by Ernest Dowson:

I have forgot much, Cynara! gone with the wind,
Flung roses, roses riotously with the throng,
Dancing, to put thy pale, lost lilies out of mind ...

5. Oh yeah, Scarlett's original name was Pansy!

6. David O. Selznick (1902-1965) purchased the movie rights for $50,000 in 1936, the highest "option" ever paid at that time.

7. Production of the film was delayed for two years because of Selznick's determination to secure Clark Gable (1901-1960) for the role of Rhett Butler.

8. Butler's last line, "Frankly, my dear, I don't give a damn," became one of the most famous lines in movie history, and Gable would later state continued re-releases of the film never failed to revive his popularity as a major star.

9. Around 1,400 women were auditioned for the part of Scarlett O'Hara, which fell on Vivien Leigh (1913-1967), who won the Best Actress Academy Award for it.

10. Margaret Mitchell was hit by a speeding car on August 11, 1949; she died from her injuries a few days later.

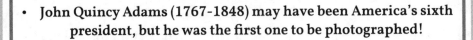

BONUS FACTS!

- John Quincy Adams (1767-1848) may have been America's sixth president, but he was the first one to be photographed!

- An ear of corn has 800 kernels on average, which come lined up in rows of 16.

- A 2014 study revealed one of every nine Americans believes that, rather than a programming language, HTML stands for a type of STD.

THE FAST AND THE FURIOUS

Tornadoes are among the greatest, most destructive forces in nature, and here's a top ten "worst of the worst" list for your twisted enjoyment!

1. 1989 Daultipur and Salturia (Bangladesh) tornado:

Killed 1,300 people, leaving another 80,000 people homeless—every tree and home in a 3.75 square mile area in its path was uprooted or destroyed!

2. 1925 Tri-State (USA) tornado:

Ripped through Missouri, Illinois, and Indiana at 73 mph for 219 miles, killing 695 people.

3. 1973 Manikganj, Singair, and Nawabganj (Bangladesh) tornado:

Leveled entire towns and wiped out 681 people.

4. 1969 East Pakistan tornado:

Caused 660 deaths, hitting the shanty-town of Demra the worst with 90 mph winds.

5. 1551 Valletta (Malta) watersprout:

This Mediterranean Sea water-tornado capsized four galleys stationed at the town's Grand Harbor and killed 600 people.

6. 1964 Magura and Narail (Bangladesh) tornado:

Wiped seven villages off the map and killed an estimated 500 people.

7. 1851 Sicily (Italy) tornado:

Beginning as watersprouts, two tornadoes ravaged through Sicily killing 200 people in the town of Castemare alone, and an estimated 500 people.

8. 1977 Madaripur and Shibchar (Bangladesh) tornado:

Tore through Madaripur, killing 500 people.

9. 2015 Yangtze River (China) tornado:

While relatively small and "harmless," it killed 442 passengers aboard a cruise ship which capsized.

10. 1984 Ivanovo (Russia) tornado:

Hitting north Moscow with both wind and hail, this multiple vortex tornado caused 400 deaths and leveled 1,180 homes.

A 1960s study revealed that, if you live in America, the safest area of your house to hide from a tornado would be the north side, both above and below ground!

BONUS FACTS!

- The first Canadian national superhero is "Nelvana, of the Northern Lights," who debuted in 1941.

- "J" was the last letter added to the English alphabet, and currently is the only one not on the periodic table!

ROCK YOU LIKE A HURRICANE

Don't let their cute names fool you. Tornadoes may be fast and furious, but hurricanes topple them in sheer massive destruction capacity.

1. The Great Hurricane of 1780:

The worst storm in human history, it rampaged through Barbados, Martinique, and St. Lucia, murdering 22,000 people, including American and British soldiers.

2. Mitch:

The worst to hit the Western Hemisphere since 1780, slow-moving Mitch reached Honduras in 1998, causing deadly mudslides which killed 11,000 people there, and another 2,000 in Nicaragua.

3. Galveston Hurricane:

People were more serious about hurricanes at the turn of the century, so no funny names were given to this one. The storms and flash floods it created destroyed 3,600 homes and killed 6,000 to 12,000 people in Texas, before hitting Oklahoma and Kansas too.

4. Maria:

Making landfall on Dominica on September 18, 2017, before moving on to destroy Puerto Rico almost completely on September 20, its death toll amounted to 2,975 people.

5. Katrina:

Inundated 80% of New Orleans, killing 1,833 people (displacing 400,000!) and costing 125-150 billion dollars in damages alone.

On a wider scale, Katrina caused a diaspora of over 1,000,000 people from the central Gulf coast to elsewhere across the United States.

6. Labor Day Hurricane:

Back in 1935, this one hit the Florida Keys at 200 mph, killing approximately 400 people.

7. Gilbert:

In 1988 its 500 nautical miles diameter engulfed the entire island of Jamaica, damaging 80% of its homes and killing 100 people, before moving on to Mexico where it killed another 200.

8. Camille:

This nasty beast hit Virginia at 200 mph, pouring 20 inches of rain that created the ensuing floods which killed 256 people in 1969.

9. Sandy:

Hard-hitting Jamaica, Cuba, and Haiti on its way to New York, it touched ground on October 2012, flooding Manhattan, decimating the Jersey Shore, and killing 117 people in the US alone, as well as 69 others in Canada.

10. Harvey:

This monster hit Texas in 2017 at 130 mph, flooding Houston with 50 inches of water, claiming 82 lives, while displacing 30,000 others in Texas alone, while also affecting Louisiana, Alabama, and Tennessee.

In case you were wondering, powerful 1984 song "Rock You Like a Hurricane," by rock band Scorpions, is one of the most popular rock songs of all time, used in numerous TV shows, films, and sporting events.

IT'S THE END OF THE WORLD AS WE KNOW IT

Let me tell you a little secret: the world is always ending, except it really isn't. Prophets of doom abound in every age and culture, but their inherent pessimism blinds them to mankind's ability to overcome every obstacle—climate change included!

Sandro Botticelli (1445-1510): A gifted yet oversensitive painter, he believed his age was the biblical Tribulation, and that the end of the world would begin in 1503.

Christopher Columbus (1451-1506): Thought that the world would come to an end in 1658. He also believed he had reached Asia by sea in 1492, so he clearly had issues.

Martin Luther (1483-1546): Declared the world would end no later than 1600, but didn't live to see if his prophecy came true.

Nostradamus (1503-1566): Famously predicted the end of the world to happen in 1999.

Nicolas C. Flammarion (1842-1925): Proclaimed Halley's Comet would poison our atmosphere and snuff out all life on the planet in 1910.

Ronald Reagan (1911-2004): In 1971, he ascertained everything was in place for Christ's Second Coming.

Greta Thunberg (b.2003): Currently vaticinates that by 2030 an irreversible chain reaction beyond human control will most likely lead to the end of our civilization.

II
LOADED
SCIENCE

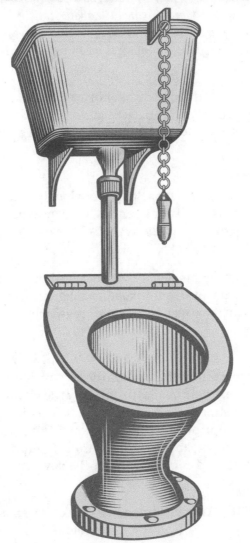

LIVE AND LET DIE

The Life Expectancy statistic measures the average time someone's expected to live based on a number of factors (year of birth, age, gender, and whatnot). Death, however, would appear to care little about statistical science, knocking on the door whenever she pleases, which explains the development of the far more useful science of medicine to keep her at bay.

1. Pre-historic human life was shorter than most pets' today. Twenty-five to thirty years on average everywhere in the world, and that is if we managed not to die in infancy and live up to our teenage years.

2. In classical Greece (sans Sparta, obviously) and Rome, if we managed to survive until our twenties, we'd be expected to die at our current middle age (40-50 years old).

3. Life expectancy in medieval Europe stayed pretty much the same as in the ancient world, but in medieval Islamic countries, where people had learned to wash their hands regularly, a man could die at 84 years of age.

4. Europe had to wait until the scientific advances (including doctors regularly washing their hands) fostered by the eighteenth century's Age of Enlightenment. These went even further in the nineteenth century, when improved health care, sanitation, immunizations, clean running water, and better nutrition all improved the living standards and survival rates of the developed world.

5. Since the 1900s, average human life expectancy has doubled and is now at 75 years old.

6. While equal opportunities, decent public health, and a good diet means the average Japanese citizen can live up to 84.5 years old, Sierra Leone people will kick the bucket at 49.3 years old, according to the World Health Organization.

7. Even within certain countries, life expectancy may show great variations. Living 20 years less than those from well-to-do neighborhoods, the poor of most countries wish they actually lived in Sierra Leone!

8. While life expectancy remains high in the US (78.6), it has recently shown a decline not seen since World War I, attributed mainly to the escalating opioid epidemic and rising suicide rates, specially among males.

9. Some scientists believe by the twenty-second century people will live beyond their centennial birthday. Sadly, if current suicide, Alzheimer's, and IQ decline rates persist, a significant number will kill themselves before they do, while others won't even remember they wanted to kill themselves in the first place, and the rest will be dumb as doorknobs anyway!

BONUS FACTS!

- In 2012, a Disneyland employee playing the White Rabbit refused to hug a black child! That lawsuit was privately settled in 2013.

- The word "freelancer's" original meaning is quite literal, "free lancer," and it was applied to Old World mercenaries.

BODY MOVIN'

Other than the fact it sooner or later calls it quits, what do we know for certain about our human body?

1. Our adult body contains 206 bones, 650 muscles, and 50,000 miles' worth of blood vessels, connected to a heart which pumps 60 million gallons of blood in our lifetime, our kidneys filtering eight quarts of it per hour.

2. Our largest organ is the skin covering us: 20 square feet for men, and 17 square feet for women on average; and we shed 600,000 particles an hour (1.5 pounds a year!).

3. The ear conveniently contains no blood vessels. Otherwise, the sound of our own pulse would be deafening!

4. Our nose will keep growing until we die, which might explain why the air from a single sneeze can reach 100 mph!

5. Our two feet can produce more than a pint of sweat a day, from their 500,000 sweat glands.

6. A lifetime of human saliva may fill up to two swimming pools with spit!

7. Fingernails grow faster than toenails due to exposure to the elements, but don't tell that to Louise Hollis, who has managed to grow six inch long toenails since the 1980s.

8. A grown man's testicles will shoot 1,500 sperm cells per second during ejaculation. If one of these hits its target and the woman does get pregnant, her blood volume will balloon up a whole 25% during pregnancy.

9. The human body is not an island: Four main groups of bacteria live cozily within and without us, 600,000,000 on the skin alone (516,000 of which nest in our armpits).

10. Our body hair is also host to the *Demodex folliculorum* mite (think a tiny spider), while the *Herpex simplex* virus inhabits the nerves of 90% of human adults, causing sores when tickled by intense heat or cold.

BONUS FACTS!

- Gui Khury (b.2009) from Brazil made the first 1080° skateboard turn in 2020, breaking Tony Hawk's (b.1968) previous 900° spin from over two decades earlier!

- BIC's ballpoint pen caps have holes as a safety measure to prevent small children from choking should they swallow one!

- Author Louisa May Alcott (1832-1888) always hated the idea of marriage, and was not particularly keen on having children either.

- You will forget 80% of what you manage to learn from this book today.

NIP/TUCK

Not happy with your body or genetics? No problem! According to the American Society of Plastic Surgeons, cosmetic procedures continue to be on the rise (less glamorous reconstructive procedures don't bring in any extra cash), especially among middle-aged Caucasian women. The most popular invasive surgeries from the 2018 ASPS Statistics Report include:

Breast augmentation: 310,000 procedures (on the rise).

Liposuction: 259,000 procedures (on the rise).

Nose reshaping: 213,000 procedures.

Eyelid surgery: 206,000 procedures.

Tummy tuck: 130,000 procedures.

Gender reassignment: 4,118 procedures.

Less invasive cosmetic procedures, like the lifting of one's "Cupid's Bow," have risen 200% since the 2000s—blame it on current selfie-mania!

BONUS FACT!

- **Congress forgot to officially make Ohio a state until 1953!**

FUNNY BONE

Along with God, duty, and country, our skeleton also does a pretty good job holding us straight.

1. While we are born with 350 bones, some fuse overtime until we are left with only 206.

2. Out of those 206 bones, 54 are in the hand if we count the wrists, with the bottom housing 26 and the face 14.

3. Despite being made of 75% water (spongy marrow!), bones are stronger than granite and concrete.

4. Bones manufacture blood cells and, since they are indeed living tissue, they grow and regenerate.

5. Out of 100 joints, some move a lot (their cartilage ends up creaking with age) while others do not move at all (the ones in the skull).

6. While they lack collagen for flexibility, teeth are part of the skeleton too.

7. The femur in the thigh is the longest bone in our body, while the middle ear houses the three tiniest, known as auditory ossicles: the malleus (hammer), incus (anvil), and stapes (stirrup).

8. In the USSR, "ribs" (*рёбра*) were bootleg copies of forbidden popular Western music albums printed on used X-ray plates!

MONKEYBONE

The congenital anomaly known as Polydactylism gives a person more fingers or toes (though most can barely be moved at all), and while it looks weird, enough notable people have suffered from it to prove it doesn't interfere with genius.

Anne Boleyn (c. 1501-1536): Queen of England from 1533 to 1536, as second wife to King Henry VIII, she had an extra finger on one of her hands and an unconfirmed third breast, though she ended up losing her head instead!

William (1800-1883) and Robert Chambers (1802-1871): Influential Scottish publishers and politicians, both brothers had extra digits.

Hampton Hawes (1928-1977): This noted American jazz pianist was born with six fingers on each hand, which were surgically cut off after birth.

Lucille Clifton (1936-2010): The 1980 Juniper Prize winner poet had her two extra fingers removed as a small child.

Drew Carey (b.1958): In his autobiography, the comedian confessed to have been born with an extra toe.

Antonio Alfonseca (b. 1972): A professional baseball player, this Dominican pitcher became known as *El Pulpo* ("The Octopus") for having an extra finger on each hand.

Gemma Arterton (b.1986): This famous British actress was born with extra fingers too, but got them removed soon after birth.

Akshat Saxena (b.2010): Born in India, he has seven fingers on each hand and ten toes on each foot, a world record!

Diphallia (double penis) is an even rarer anomaly (100 cases reported since 1609) affecting one in 5.5 million American males, some of which, like book author "DDD" (obviously a *nom de plume*), become minor underground celebrities, while others have had the extra penis removed in order to lead a normal life.

BONUS FACTS!

- Christmas wasn't a national holiday in America until 1890.

- Charles Darwin (1809-1882) thought Shakespeare's plays were intolerably dull.

- The spiky *candiru* fish of the Amazon river is attracted to human urine, and will enter a swimmer's body through the anus and dig its way into the penis!

- Once imported from the Arabian peninsula, Australia now exports its camels to Saudi Arabia!

- The rare grizzly-polar bear hybrid is called "Pizzy Bear."

MAN'S GOTTA EAT

We spend so much time thinking about, buying, and cooking food to eat, we might as well have a look at some hard digestive facts:

1. In our lifetime, we eat an average of 35 tons of food, while our stomach can stretch to hold up to four pounds of food per meal.

2. The average American spends 62 minutes a day eating, while the average Frenchman spends 131.5 minutes a day. The amount and quality of the food ingested isn't correlated to the time spent at the table though.

3. Our digestive system is approximately 30 foot long from mouth to anus, digestion and excretion itself taking between 24 and 72 hours on average.

4. Digestion begins when we put food in our mouth. Chewing and saliva reduce whatever delicacy we choose to munch into a formless "bolus" which is swallowed into the stomach, which breaks it down for the small intestine to absorb the nutrients, leftovers then being passed down to the large intestine which absorbs the remaining water and stores the waste in feces, to be expelled from the body by defecation via our rectum and anus ... whoa!

5. Our esophagus waves the bolus down through muscle movements known as peristalsis in around seven seconds. It requires no gravity, so technically we may swallow even when standing upside down!

6. The stomach's rumbling due to the peristaltic movements in the gut has its own fancy name: *borborygmi*!

7. The stomach's hydrochloric acid can dissolve even metal, and if it weren't for mucus lining it, it would devour itself!

8. Despite its corrosiveness, the stomach's acid has no effect on plastic, nor on chewing gum which, unless an inordinately large chunk of it, will usually come out painlessly.

9. The small intestine is 22 foot long (2,700 ft surface area) but only one inch in diameter. The large one is short but thick: five feet long, and up to four inches in diameter—we are indeed full of sh*t!

10. Our digestive system has its own little brain, the ENS (Enteric Nervous System), regulated by neurotransmitters like serotonin, just like our main brain. Maybe it's a form of sibling rivalry, but communication between the two is usually delayed by 20 minutes!

11. Alexis St. Martin (1802-1880) was a Canadian frontiersman with a gunshot wound that never fully healed, leaving a literal window to his stomach which was scientifically studied, and led to a greater understanding of human digestion.

BONUS FACTS!

- A 28-foot squid specimen (caught in 2004) named "Archie" is kept at the London Natural history Museum.

- The *Nisiyama Onsen Keiunkan* hot springs hotel in Japan has been open since 705 AD.

EAT IT!

Eating has been a staple of human life and culture for centuries, and not even popular music can resist its charm. Here are ten of the best songs ever made about ingesting food:

"Eat It"

This "Weird" Al Yankovic (b.1959) classic from 1984 parodies Michael Jackson's 1983 single "Beat It."

"Eat the Rich"

A 1987 heavy metal song composed by Motörhead for Peter Richardson's film of the same name.

"Don't Eat the Yellow Snow"

Frank Zappa's (1940-1993) 1974 tune about a man dreaming to be Nanook, an Eskimo alerted by his mother to "Watch out where the huskies go, and don't you eat that yellow snow."

"Alice's Restaurant"

The best known of Arlo Guthrie's (b.1947) folk repertoire, this one's a satirical talking blues song.

"Thanksgiving Song"

Hard not to love Adam Sandler's (b.1966) jagged, falsetto ode to turkey, gravy, and baby oil from 1992!

"Every Time I Eat Vegetables I Think of You"

A 1983 wholesome punk ballad by The Ramones!

"Eat or Be Eaten"

Iggy Pop (b.1947) knew what it was like to be down on his luck, and this 1982 song shows it.

"Cheeseburger In Paradise"

Jimmy Buffett (b.1946) survived on a canned food and peanut butter diet during a boating accident in the Caribbean, and nothing makes you dream of good ol' diner food like being stranded in the middle of nowhere!

"Don't Eat Stuff Off the Sidewalk"

From the inventors of the *psychobilly* music sub-genre, The Cramps, came this unforgettable "B" side punk tune.

"Savoy Truffle"

Perhaps the least remembered song by The Beatles, "Truffle" is basically a warning from George Harrison (1943-2001) to Eric Clapton (b.1945) not to overindulge with chocolate—and possibly also a coded message about the dalliance between Clapton and Harrison's wife Pattie Boyd (b.1944)!

Nobel Prize for Literature winner Pablo Neruda's (1904-1973) *Elemental Odes* book series contained poems dedicated to tomatoes, onions, and Cusk-eel stock among other foods!

BONUS FACT!

- The Walmart chain hires only 2.6% of its job applicants.

SHAMELESS PLUG

A bezoar is a mass that, once intentionally or accidentally ingested, may get trapped in our digestive system and require surgery to remove it. This ball of fun has many different types, including:

Boli: Not to be confused with the Italian sport known as Bocce, but equally obstructive, it includes fruit pits, bubble gum, seeds, and soil.

Lactobezoar: Mainly thickened formula milk drunk by infants.

Pharmacobezoar: A semi-liquid mass of pills from an overdose.

Phytobezoar: Indigestible plant material which may be effectively washed down with Coca-Cola!

Trichobezoar: A badass hairball, commonly found in people who chow their own hair, a disorder known as the "Rapunzel Syndrome!"

Bezoars may also be classified by their location, so a "choke" is what we call an esophagus bezoar, while a Tracheobezoar is bezoars in the windpipe, and a Fecalith is a rock-solid, immovable poop boulder plug which can develop in the rectum as a result of constipation—ouch!

BONUS FACT!

- Celery was once considered a trendy, upscale veggie.

CODE BROWN

Except for bezoars, everything that comes in, must come out eventually. Since there's no avoiding "potty talk," let's get down and dirty!

1. We spend 1.5 years of our lives in the bathroom, approximately 92 days of which are spent on "the throne."

2. A newborn baby's first bowel movement is a dark, odorless, tar-green substance known as meconium.

3. Squatting, as opposed to toilet sitting, is by far the most efficient and painless method to defecate.

4. Human feces are made of 75% water, and a 25% combo of living and dead bacteria (80%), mucus, and fiber.

5. The average adult stool weighs four ounces.

6. The bile secreted from the liver is what gives feces their distinctive brown color after three days. If it comes out before that time, it will be greenish.

7. Black feces, however, may reveal either too much iron in your diet, or serious health conditions resulting in internal bleeding—not to be confused with red poop as a result of eating beets!

8. Floating feces are due to a greater amount of gas and/or animal fat contents; so if you're pretending to go vegan to please a partner

or a spouse, but still indulge the occasional cheeseburger, "unflushables" might give you away!

9. Among his many accomplishments, Bill Gates (b.1955) also funded the Omniprocessor, a machine that turns feces into drinking water. If online videos are to be trusted, Gates actually drank a glass full of it!

10. The "Mariko Aoki Phenomenon" is a condition in which the smell of books and magazines in a bookstore triggers an irresistible urge to defecate.

BONUS FACTS!

- Actor Sean Connery (b.1930) wore a perfectly trimmed and combed hairpiece in every James Bond movie he starred in!

- A standard No. 2 pencil lead wears out after about 35 miles' worth of writing.

- Penguins run as fast as most men. Sadly, that isn't enough to outrun sea lions, which sexually abuse them on a regular basis.

- "Spaghetto" is spaghetti's singular form.

- Apple co-founder, and universal remote control inventor, Steve "Woz" Wozniak (b.1950) survived a plane crash in 1981.

PENNIES FROM HEAVEN

Ever been pooped on by a pigeon? How about a sperm whale? It goes downhill from there ...

1. If you're looking for a sign your cat is angry at you, see if it poops in places other than its litter box.

2. Termite nests are made of their own wood-based dung.

3. House flies never stop vomiting and pooping everywhere they land, so watch out!

4. Scared and startled rats and mice will defecate on the spot.

5. Civet coffee is made of half-digested coffee cherries which have been defecated by the Asian "toddycat," and then harvested by Indonesians to sell at exorbitant prices.

6. Bat guano is used both as a fertilizer, and as a key component of facial creams and lipstick.

7. Flesh-eating vultures actually poop on their own feet and claws to clean them!

8. Capybaras have two types of feces: black or dark brown, which is hard and inedible, and soft green which other capybaras will indulge in from time to time.

9. Parrot fish eat coral and poop sand, which actually makes most of the white Hawaiian beaches!

10. Divers in different parts of the world have been known to be engulfed in whale diarrhea. It isn't a pretty sight, but it's even worse for the diver.

11. Adorable Australian wombats' almost cubic, pellet-shaped feces acquire their distinctive shape after the marsupial's digestive system has extricated every drop of valuable water from them. Adult members of the species may poop up to 100 hard, dry pellets every single night!

BONUS FACTS!

- After beheading, a person may stay alive for another 15 seconds.

- Cows drink more than 50 gallons of water per day.

- Vice-Admiral Horatio Nelson (1758-1805) lost his right eye in battle in 1794. The left one saw his right arm amputated in 1797.

- The famed Witches Market of La Paz, Bolivia, sells many types of folk cures and remedies, including desiccated llama fetuses, commonly placed under the foundation stones of buildings throughout the country.

CAPTAIN'S LOG

Forget the fifty shades of gray! What about the seven consistencies of poop instead? The Bristol Stool Scale is a medical tool which classifies the form of poop.

Type 1: Separate nut-hard lumps which are hard to pass.

Type 2: Sausage-shaped, but lumpy (ouch!).

If you fall in the previous two categories, consider adding magnesium to your diet, which draws water into the bowel, making poop softer and less painful on its way out.

Type 3: Like a sausage but with cracks on its surface

Type 4: Like a sausage or snake, smooth and soft

Type 5: Soft blobs with clear cut edges (easy to pass)

Types 3, 4 and 5 are the best, but #4 in particular is the nicest!

Type 6: Fluffy pieces with ragged edges, a mushy stool

Type 7: Watery, no solid pieces, entirely liquid

Types 6 and 7 fall in the dreaded diarrhea category!

WELCOME TO THUNDER DOME!

While some deem it a disgusting habit, others find it as normal as sneezing, and science certainly proves it a natural occurrence. Human beings fart 402,000 times in their lifetime (14 times per day on average), so what's all the fuss about?

1. The hard-to-digest sugars found in fruit, beans, cabbage, and Brussels sprouts pass the stomach unaffected, only to be devoured by the bacteria in the small intestine that loves them. Their sugar-eating frenzy is what produces intestinal gases, including the pungent ones.

2. Odorless gases make for about 99% of a single fart. It's the other one percent which gives sulfurous gases a bad rep!

3. Farts can blow at ten feet per second!

4. Flatulence is indeed flammable, and will burn blue if high on methane.

5. Their volume, expelling force, and tightness determine the many different sounds farts may achieve.

6. Though not bad for our health per se, holding flatulence in may seem polite, but is unnecessarily uncomfortable.

7. Jonathan Swift (1667-1735) and Benjamin Franklin (1705-1790) both penned essays on farting!

TAKING CARE OF BUSINESS

Some day the full history of the most human of inventions, the toilet, will be written, but in the meantime here are tidbits from its most notorious milestones across the centuries:

Egypt, 3,100BC: Rich Egyptians sat on limestone toilets, while peasants did so on wooden planks with holes.

Greece, 2,000BC: Cretans already had marble toilets flushed with water!

Rome, 800BC: Romans believed in communal toilets just as they swore by communal baths. They used to squat in large groups while passing a stick with a sponge on its tip to wipe their collective behinds.

England, 1596: Sir John Harington (1561-1612) published The Metamorphosis of Ajax, featuring a description of the modern flush toilet he had installed at his house, and later gifted on to Queen Elizabeth I (1533-1603).

Scotland, 1775: Among the many gifts bestowed upon modern civilization by Scotland is Alexander Cumming's (1733-1814) development of the S-trap, which uses the toilet's standing water to seal the outlet of the bowl, preventing the escape of foul air from the sewer down below.

Japan, 1980: Alongside many technological marvels from the land of the rising sun, the Washlet, a high-tech, fully-automated toilet, took that country by storm!

"AW, SHIIIIIIIIT!"
−ELVIS PRESLEY

Famous people die all the time, but no death is so undignified for a public figure as kicking the bucket while on the toilet.

Lenny Bruce (1925-1966): The popular comedian found an untimely death on the toilet, with a heroin needle stuck in his arm.

Judy Garland (1922-1969): Another drug-related Hollywood casualty, the beautiful and talented actress was found lifeless and slouched over her commode at age 47.

Elvis Presley (1935-1977): A drug cocktail overdose saw The King fall from the throne (pun intended) on a pool of his own vomit.

Don Simpson (1943-1996): A legendary *Flashdance* and *Top Gun* producer, he died on the toilet while reading a biography of director Oliver Stone, likely due to illegal prescription drug abuse.

Robert Pastorelli (1954-2004): Film and television actor with many important roles throughout his career, he was under investigation in connection to the 1999 shooting of his then-girlfriend, Charemon Jonovich, and was found dead on the toilet from a morphine overdose.

Powerful political figures who died—or were assassinated—while "releasing the kraken" include young Edmund Ironside (c.990-1016), Uesugi Kenshin (1530-1578), George II (1683-1760), Catherine the Great (1729-1796), and Jorge Rafael Videla (1925-2013).

LET IT MELLOW

Nothing improves the working man's morning like waking up earlier to take a leak, and then go back to bed to sleep another hour...

1. During your life, your kidneys will turn approximately one million gallons of water into urine.

2. Most people go pee between six and eight times a day, producing around 6.3 cups of urine a day.

3. Urine is 95% water, 2.5% urea, and a 2.5% combination of salt, hormones, nutrients, and creatine.

4. Urine tells a lot about a person's habits and diet, and even if that person is sick or not, but don't read too much into all its colors, unless it's dark yellow (dehydration), red (blood), or murky (kidney stones).

6. Urine may be used to fertilize the ground, make gunpowder and white phosphorus, whiten teeth, and even enhance the flavor of cigarettes.

7. Up to 10% of Americans suffer from *Paruresis*, "Shy Bladder Syndrome," a condition which prevents them from urinating in the presence of others.

8. 30-40% of adults pee in swimming pools. Red eyes are not caused by chlorine, but by chloramine, a combination of urine with the chlorine already in the pool!

FEARLESS ON MY BREATH

While writing this book you're now holding (possibly with rubber gloves), the world's caught in the grip of a pandemic, the size of which humans haven't seen in over a century: COVID-19, a.k.a. Coronavirus. But while unusual, there's a list of even stranger and deadlier illnesses out there just awaiting their moment in the spotlight.

Naegleriasis: Caused by the "brain-eating amoeba (*Naegleria fowleri*)," a shape-shifting little monster infects the brain suddenly, severely, and fatally, its mortality rate at 98.5%!

Noma (*Cancrum oris*): An aggressive infection starting off from the mouth or genitals, eating and mangling everything in its wake until nothing's left. It has a 90% mortality rate!

Madura foot (*Eumycetoma*): A horrible granulomatous fungal disease affecting mainly the limbs, and sometime the abdominal and chest walls, and even the head. It has no cure.

Münchmeyer disease (*Fibrodysplasia ossificans progressiva*): Popularly known as "Stone Man Syndrome," it is the bad boy of incurable genetic disorders, causing soft and connecting tissues to ossify. It is the only known condition in humans that changes our organ systems into something else.

Lewandowsky-Lutz dysplasia (*Epidermodysplasia Verruciformis*): Best known as the "Tree Man Syndrome," it's an extremely rare genetic disorder caused not by cellulose but by mutant, overgrowing warts which may be excised but not cured.

Hypertrichosis: This "Werewolf Syndrome" causes hair to grow abnormally, either on the whole body or a specific part of it (such as the face). The bread and butter of circus sideshows during the nineteenth and twentieth centuries, this genetic condition can be managed but not cured.

Nodding disease: Emerging from the mountains of Tanzania in the early 1960s, this rare sickness seems to target five to 17-year-old children. It starts with pathological nodding seizures, followed by complete and permanent brain damage. It's been speculated to be a byproduct of an immune reaction to the nasty parasitic worm *Onchocerca volvulus* (which also causes *Onchocerciasis*, or "River blindness"), but nobody knows for sure.

Elephantiasis: The "Dumbo" of hypertrophic diseases, it makes a person's body parts (including genitalia) massively swell and harden.

Elephantiasis nostras: Caused by longstanding chronic Lymphangitis.

Elephantiasis tropica (lymphatic filariasis): Caused by a number of parasitic worms, and affecting 120 million people in the developing world.

Nonfilarial elephantiasis (Podoconiosis): An immune illness attacking the lymph vessels.

Proteus syndrome: The condition suffered by Joseph Merrick (1862-1890), the "Elephant Man!"

CAN'T YOU SEE I'M BURNIN', BURNIN'?

In Western medical science "eponymity" and not anonymity is the standard when honoring the scientist who first identified, described or treated a given illness, disease, or condition.

Alzheimer's disease: Named after Alois Alzheimer (1864-1915), who first identified this chronic neurodegenerative scourge he labeled a "presenile dementia."

Parkinson's disease: Named after English surgeon James Parkinson (1755-1824), best known for his 1817 "An Essay on the Shaking Palsy."

Hodgkin's disease: Named after Thomas Hodgkin (1798-1866), a British physician and pathologist, known for writing the first account of this form of lymphoma in 1832.

Bell's palsy: Named after Scottish neurologist Sir Charles Bell (1774-1842), noted for describing this type of facial paralysis.

Corrigan's pulse: Named after noted Irish baronet and physician Sir Dominic John Corrigan (1802-1880), known for his observations on this particular aortic valve insufficiency.

Stokes-Adams syndrome: While the first description of the syndrome was published in 1717 by the Slovene physician Marko Gerbec (1658-1718), the cardiac and pulmonary treaties of Irishmen William Stokes (1804-1878) and Robert Adams (1791-1875) earned them the honor of having this condition named after them.

Ménière's disease: Named after Prosper Menière (1799-1862), a French doctor who first identified that the inner ear would be the source of a disorder which causes vertigo, hearing loss and ringing ears.

Addison's disease (a degenerative disease of the adrenal glands) and Addisonian anemia (pernicious anemia): Both named after Thomas Addison (1793-1860), the English physician who discovered them!

Korsakoff's syndrome and Wernicke–Korsakoff syndrome: Both named after Sergei Korsakoff (1854-1900) who studied the effects of alcohol and alcoholic psychosis.

Dupuytren's contracture: Named after Guillaume Dupuytren (1777-1835), a French surgeon who first described this condition, which bends fingers permanently.

Carrion's disease: Named after Daniel Alcides Carrión García (1857-1885), a Peruvian medical student who, in order to conclusively demonstrate the cause of the illness, fatally inoculated himself (with a little help from a friend) with the *Bartonella bacilliformis* bacteria in 1885.

BONUS FACT!

- "Bad Finger Boogie" was the original title of the Beatles' popular "With a Little Help from My Friends" song. British rock band The Iveys, at the time considered natural heirs to the Fab Four, renamed themselves "Badfinger" after that song.

LEGION

Parasites are nasty little creatures which live off of our body, and thrive to the detriment of our health. Forget bed bugs and scabies, here are some of the worst mankind has ever suffered!

Kissing bug (*Triatominae*):

Also known as "vampire bugs," these insects nest in our homes, feeding on our blood, and ultimately transmitting the *Trypanosoma cruzi* parasite onto us.

Trypanosoma cruzi:

These tentacled parasitic microorganisms dig into our tissues, feeding on blood and lymph, and causing the infamous Chagas disease, which generally doesn't show symptoms, but will kill you 30 years later via heart failure—like it did to none other than Charles Darwin (1809-1882)!

Paralysis tick:

Australia's arachnids are infamous for good reason, but this tiny bastard in particular will inject you with a neurotoxin strong enough to numb and even kill you from the allergic reaction to it. It is also know to transmit a form or typhus known as Rickettsial spotted fever.

Jigger flea:

Not to be confused with the Chigger mites, there are 13 species of this teeny tiny and very aggressive Latin American insect which has found its way to Africa. An adult female will infest your skin for the rest of her natural life, mating with traveling males, and embedding her

eggs in your soft tissue, all the while causing inflammation, severe pain, itching, and infected lesions, usually in your feet.

Loa Loa:

Don't let the quaint, Hawaiian-sounding name fool you. This is none other than the dreaded African eye worm, which unless treated will infest the inside tissue of your eyelids for up to 15 years!

Guinea worm:

The guinea worm infects humans when they drink water contaminated with fleas containing the worm's larvae, which are set free in the stomach and lodge themselves in the intestine walls where they grow 18 inches long before wriggling down to the host's legs and feet, sometimes coming out to see daylight.

Screw-worm Fly:

Literally the stuff of sci-fi nightmares like the *Alien* movie franchise, this fly will lay around 100 eggs in any open wound, which will hatch releasing spiky, toothy maggots which hungrily burrow into the human flesh, and dig deeper when removal is attempted. It has a mortality rate of 8%, and after being seemingly eradicated in the 1960s, it has seen a comeback on American soil since 2016!

BONUS FACT!

- Like something out of a *Conan* novel, the Skull Tower in Niš, Serbia, was constructed in 1809 by the Ottoman rulers using skulls from the Serbian rebels who defied their rule, and heroically immolated themselves during their first uprising.

VICTORY OR DEATH

Humanity doesn't sit idle against the threat of disease and illness. It's a fight to the death, and since the eighteenth century we have developed a new weapon to fight it off: vaccination!

1. Vaccines work by "training" the immune system by exposing it to a weakened version or small, noninfectious fragments of pathogens, prodding it to produce antibodies in a controlled environment, so if the real virus tries to get it, our organism will identify and kill it on the spot!

2. "Herd immunity" is the prevention of a disease spreading across an entire population, and is achieved only when the majority of said population has been inoculated.

3. A thousand years ago, India was one of the first civilizations to primitively vaccinate children in times of plague, by making a small incision into the child's arm and rubbing it with smallpox scabs.

4. The first modern vaccine was administered by English doctor Edward Jenner (1749-1823) for smallpox in 1796. The term vaccine is derived from *Variolae vaccinae* (smallpox of the cow), which used cowpox to combat its human-affecting cousin which, up until then, wiped out 10-20% of all Englishmen every year.

5. Jenner's smallpox vaccine was so successful than five years later, due to the lack of refrigeration technology at the time, Spain sent it around the world, stored in the bodies of 22 orphans. Their immune blood would be used to make vaccines for others! Edward Jenner wrote at the time: "I don't imagine the annals of history furnish an example of philanthropy so noble, so extensive as this."

6. Smallpox thus became the first disease to be eradicated, and is currently only stored in a handful of high-security labs, while the US government keeps a tremendous stockpile of vaccines against it.

7. Louis Pasteur (1822-1895) created the first vaccines for rabies and anthrax. It was such a high-risk job, the protocol stated that in the event he or anyone on the team got infected, they were to be gunned down on the spot!

8. A tuberculosis vaccine was invented in 1906 by the Pasteur Institute to be used on cattle, but as it turns out, it was successful in 1922 human trials as well!

9. Robert Koch (1843-1910), Emil Von Behring (1854-1917), and Kitasato Shibasaburō (1853-1931) are credited for developing antitoxins to treat diphtheria and tetanus. Shibasaburō is also remembered as the person who isolated and identified the infectious agent of both the bubonic plague and dysentery!

10. American virologist Jonas Salk (1914-1995) developed one of the first successful polio vaccines in 1952.

11. Considered "The Father of Modern Vaccines," biomedical scientist John F. Enders (1897-1985) and his team developed a successful measles vaccine. By 2008, measles-caused deaths had been reduced 78%!

12. According to the World Health Organization (WHO), vaccination saves 3 million lives a year, building our immunity against chicken pox, diphtheria, Hepatitis B, Hib disease, measles, mumps, rubella, pertussis, polio, rotavirus, smallpox, tetanus, and influenza!

OUTBREAK!

Zombies, cannibals, and vampires have taken over comics, video games, movies, and television, but what if we were only a mutated brain protein or a rogue bat virus away from total annihilation?

World War Kuru:

Eating members of one's own species may have devastating consequences! In Papua, New Guinea, the Urapmin tribe would eat their dead, while the Korowai was reportedly still devouring human flesh as of 2012!

The Fore tribe, on the other hand, used to cook and eat their dead, but when a village partook of the brain of a man who had died from neurodegenerative (means brain-rotting!) Creutzfeldt–Jakob disease, they too developed the illness which they called Kuru, which means "to shake." Akin to a zombie plague, "Kuru" became an epidemic of epic proportions, which only declined after the Fore stopped their cannibalistic funerary rites in the 1960s.

Cow Eat Cow:

Farmers in Europe had been using slaughterhouse meat and bone scraps to feed their cows since the 1840s. Something was bound to go wrong, and in 1986 the first case of "mad cow disease" (BSE) was confirmed in the United Kingdom. An estimated 400,000 BSE affected cows became part of the human food chain during that decade alone!

The scary part? When eating meat contaminated with BSE, a person may contract a version of "Kuru," called "variant Creutzfeldt–Jakob disease" (vCJD), which takes up to 50 years to show any symptoms, but only 13 months to kill you when it finally does!

Interview with the Fruit Bat:

The Ebola Virus Disease (EVD) reared its ugly head in two simultaneous 1976 outbreaks in South Sudan and the Democratic Republic of Congo (a village near the Ebola River).

When a human came into contact with the blood or secretions of natural Ebola virus carrying fruit bats, the highly infectious disease then propagated just as easily from human to human, and still does to this day! What starts as basic flu symptoms (fever, sore throat, muscular pain), gives way to diarrhea, vomiting, and a rash. At this point, when liver and kidneys start to fail, the infected start bleeding in and out, before dying in excruciating pain.

BONUS FACTS!

• The Hereford Cathedral (UK) contains a library of rare antique books (some of which date back to 800AD) which, in keeping with medieval tradition, have been chained to desks and pulpits since 1611!

• Joseph Stalin (1878-1953) refused the privilege of trading his eldest son, Yakov Iosifovich Dzhugashvili (1907-1943), who had been captured by the Nazis in 1941. Yakov would die in a concentration camp three years later.

• FBI Agent William Mark Felt Sr. (1913-2008) was revealed to be "Deep Throat," the Washington Post informant behind the Watergate scandal which caused Richard Nixon (1913-1994) to resign as President of the United States.

DR. HOOK &
 **THE MEDICINE SHOW**

Not only humans build up immunity, both individually and socially, against the diseases that plague us, bacteria does too … against the very antibiotics we use against them!

1. Mummies have been found to have their bones oozing with tetracycline (first isolated by modern science in the 1950s), which they got from drinking lots of beer, the beverage of choice for the working class at the time (not much has changed!). It would explain why disinterred mummies fetched high prices in the Middle Ages, when Egyptians sold them to European doctors to be grinded and mixed with ointments and other cures.

2. English botanist John Parkinson (1567-1650) was the first scientist to observe and document the use of molds to treat infections.

3. Having spent a holiday with his family, Scottish microbiologist and pharmacologist Alexander Fleming (1881-1955) returned to his untidy lab on September 3, 1928, to find one of his stacked bacteria cultures had grown a fungus which had obliterated all the staphylococci in it. In Dr. Fleming's own words:

"One sometimes finds what one is not looking for. When I woke up just after dawn on September 28, 1928, I certainly didn't plan to revolutionize all medicine by discovering the world's first antibiotic, or bacteria killer. But I suppose that was exactly what I did."

4. After Dr. Fleming's development of penicillin as a suitable drug (1941) came others, like Aminoglycosides (1944), Cephalosporins (1945), Chloramphenicol (1949), Tetracyclines (1950),

Macrolides/lincosamides/streptogramins (1952), Glycopeptides (1956), Rifamycins (1957), Nitroimidazoles (1959), Quinolones (1962), Trimethoprim (1968), Oxazolidinones (2000), Lipopeptides (2003), and Teixobactin (2016).

7. A growing health concern, 50% of the world's antibiotics production is used in meat and poultry production, while such application goes up to 80% in the US.

8. It was Dr. Fleming himself who, upon receiving his 1945 Nobel Prize, warned mankind about the rise of antibiotic resistance!

9. Every year, 500,000 cases of resistant tuberculosis are reported around the planet.

10. According to the 2019 CDC's *Antibiotic Resistance Threats in the United States* report, more than 2.8 million antibiotic-resistant infections occur in the U.S. each year, claiming more than 35,000 lives. A further 223,900 cases of Clostridioides difficile got 12,800 people killed. Urgent resistant bacteria threats include the aforementioned *C. difficile, E. Coli, Acinetobacter, Candida auris,* and *Neisseria gonorrhoeae*—yes, gonorrhea!

BONUS FACT!

- As reported by the *St. Louis Dispatch* in 1904, farmer Silas Perkins of Des Moines, Iowa, lost one of his eyes after his prize-winning duck exploded before him. Apparently, the fowl had been overindulging in yeast!

PENICILLIN PENNY

Fame, money, and power give celebrities plenty of advantages over regular folk, but no immunity against viral and bacterial sexually transmitted diseases. Rumored syphilitics (like Columbus, Lincoln, Lenin, and Hitler) aside, let's have a candid look at the confirmed STD cases among both the historically significant, and the more fatuous figures of recent decades.

Frederick the Great (1712-1786): Gonorrhea.

Napoleon Bonaparte (1769-1821): Syphilis.

Charle Baudelaire (1821-1867): Gonorrhea and syphilis.

Leo Tolstoy (1828-1910): Syphilis.

Scott Joplin (1868-1917): Syphilis.

Aleister Crowley (1875-1947): Gonorrhea and syphilis.

Al Capone (1899-1947): Syphilis.

Tallulah Bankhead (1902-1968): Gonorrhea.

John Dillinger (1903-1934): Gonorrhea.

Howard Hughes (1905-1976): Syphilis.

Evel Knievel (1938-2007): Hepatitis-C.

David Crosby (b.1941): Hepatitis-C.

Michael Douglas (b.1944): HPV

Steven Tyler (b.1948): Hepatitis-C.

Magic Johnson (b.1959): HIV

Tommy Lee (b.1962): Hepatitis-C.

Jim Carrey (b.1962): Gonorrhea and herpes.

Charlie Sheen (b.1965): HIV

Pamela Anderson (b.1967): Hepatitis-C.

Genital herpes' incidence in showbiz probably deserves its own book. In addition to baseball star Derek Jeter (b.1974) and his flings—Mariah Carey (b.1969), Jessica Alba(b.1981), and Jessica Biel (b.1982) to name a few—here's a list of its most notable carriers: Tony Bennett (b.1926), Liza Minnelli (b.1946), Billy Idol (b.1955), David Hasselhoff (b.1952), R.Kelly (b.1967), Brad Pitt (b.1963), Anne Heche (b.1969), Alyssa Milano (b.1972), Usher (b.1978), Katie Holmes (b.1978), Kristanna Loken (b.1979), Kim Kardashian (b.1980), Britney Spears (b.1981), Paris Hilton (b.1981), Scarlett Johansson (b.1984), and Rihanna (b.1988).

DOCTOR LOVE

Hippocrates of Kos (c.460-c.370 BC) was the physician who defined the ethical guidelines of medicine through an oath (the Hippocratic Oath) still recited, if not always practiced, or taken to heart, by graduates from many medical schools.

"I swear by Apollo the physician, and Aesculapius, and Health, and All-heal, and all the gods and goddesses, that, according to my ability and judgment, I will keep this Oath and this stipulation—to reckon him who taught me this Art equally dear to me as my parents, to share my substance with him, and relieve his necessities if required; to look upon his offspring in the same footing as my own brothers, and to teach them this Art, if they shall wish to learn it, without fee or stipulation; and that by precept, lecture, and every other mode of instruction, I will impart a knowledge of the Art to my own sons, and those of my teachers, and to disciples bound by a stipulation and oath according to the law of medicine, but to none others. I will follow that system of regimen which, according to my ability and judgment, I consider for the benefit of my patients, and abstain from whatever is deleterious and mischievous. I will give no deadly medicine to anyone if asked, nor suggest any such counsel; and in like manner I will not give to a woman a pessary to produce abortion. With purity and with holiness I will pass my life and practice my Art. I will not cut persons laboring under the stone, but will leave this to be done by men who are practitioners of this work. Into whatever houses I enter, I will go into them for the benefit of the sick, and will abstain from every voluntary act of mischief and corruption; and, further, from the seduction of females or males, of freemen and slaves. Whatever, in connection with my professional practice or not in connection with it, I see or hear, in the life of men, which ought not to be spoken of abroad, I will not divulge, as reckoning that all such should be kept secret. While I continue to keep this Oath unviolated, may it be granted to me to enjoy life and the practice of the art, respected by all men, in all times! But should I trespass and violate this Oath, may the reverse be my lot!"

"ONLY HUMAN"

Despite Hippocrates's best intentions, the medical profession has seen its share of incompetent physicians; enough so, that as of 2018 medical malpractice's death toll amounted to 250,000 people in the US alone (according to a study published by Johns Hopkins Medicine), making it America's third leading cause of death, behind heart disease and cancer!

1995: Admitted to University Community Hospital in Tampa (Florida), 51-year-old diabetic Willie King was supposed to have his right leg cut off below the knee, but woke to find the left one had been removed by Dr. Ronaldo Sanchez instead. Mr. King's right lower leg was later cut off at another hospital, while the subsequent lawsuit saw him net a $900,000 settlement.

2000: Comedian Dana "Garth" Carvey, 45 at the time, had the wrong artery in his heart bypassed, resulting in yet another surgery to unclog the right one, and repair the damaged one, which cost him two years of his life to recover from. His surgeon, Dr. Elias Hanna of Marin General Hospital (California), chalked it up to an "honest mistake." The movie star didn't abide, and the ensuing lawsuit made him $7.5 million richer.

2001: Diagnosed with degenerative spondylolisthesis, Arturo Iturralde was supposed to have titanium rods inserted in his spinal column at Hilo Medical Center (Hawaii). Finding those missing from the operating theater, Dr. Robert Ricketson decided to make do with screwdriver steel shanks, which broke, seing the 73-year-old Iturralde through three more procedures and a painful death two years later. A court awarded the family $5.6 million in damages, five years later.

2002: 67-year-old "Joan Morris" (real name withheld from the press) was recovering from a brain aneurysm at the San Francisco Medical Center (California), when she was mistakenly rushed for invasive cardiac testing. Surgeons had stopped and restarted her heart several times before realizing about the mix-up!

2003: After 17-year-old Jesica Santillan had been given a wrong-blood-type heart and lung transplant at Duke University Medical Center (North Carolina), a second transplant was decided upon, but the all-too-risky procedure put her in a coma. She was later declared brain dead and taken off life-support.

2006: 73-year-old Baptist minister Sherman Sizemore was admitted to Raleigh General Hospital (Virginia) for exploratory abdominal surgery, where the anesthesiologist and nurse anesthetist forgot to give him the anesthesia needed to render him unconscious until 16 minutes into the procedure! Ensuing trauma, nightmares, and excruciating pain drove the minister to take his own life two weeks later.

2007: 47-year-old Air Force veteran and father of four Benjamin Houghton was supposed to have his cancerous left testicle removed at the West Los Angeles VA Medical Center, but his right one was cut off instead, which meant they had to excise his metastatic left nut afterwards. Ironically, wrong testicle removal is a common malpractice feature the world over!

2009: Six days after being severely burned at the operating table, 65-year-old Illinois woman Janice McCall died at Vanderbilt University Medical Center (Tennessee). Apparently, surgical flash fires happen an estimated 550 to 600 times a year, but since they kill only about two people a year, they are promptly deemed "accidental."

DR. HECKYLL & MR. JIVE

Of course, medicine's own swindlers, crackpots, and psychos can make us long for plain incompetence, as they manage to hide their deviant ways behind the sheen of respectability the profession provides.

John R. Brinkley (1885-1942): The beloved "goat-gland doctor," this diploma-mill physician amassed great wealth transplanting goat testicles into human scrotums, as a means to cure erectile dysfunction. The lawsuits that ensued left him penniless shortly before his death.

Shiro Ishii (1892-1959): A microbiologist and the director of "Unit 731," a covert biological warfare unit of the Imperial Japanese Army responsible for the death of over 10,000 people subjected to heinous experiments. He was granted immunity alongside other unit members by the US Government in exchange for their research, and passed away in 1959, having converted to Catholicism.

Carl Clauberg (1898-1957): Of all the monsters bred at the Auschwitz concentration camp, this gynecologist stood out as he experimented with sterilization techniques on around 700 Jewish and Romani women. Aided by **Dr. Horst Schumann (1906-1983)**, he finally settled on using radiation to achieve his perverse goals.

Josef Mengele (1911-1979): Nicknamed the "Angel of Death," and by far the worst evil scientist in Auschwitz, Mengele sadistically experimented on 1,500 sets of imprisoned twins, most of them children, of which only 200 survived. On the run since the end of the war, he fled to Argentina, Paraguay, and finally died while vacationing in a Brazilian beach at age 67.

John Bodkin Adams (1899-1983): While a suspect in the murder of 163 of his patients, 132 of whom willed him huge sums of money, this general practitioner was finally acquitted of all murder charges due to the prosecution's mishandling of the entire case!

Walter Freeman (1895-1972): A neurologist on paper, he was essentially a legally sanctioned sadist, serially performing around 4,000 lobotomies (many in front of a cheering audience) on his patients over four decades, in 23 states. With as many as a hundred of his patients having died at the tip of his icepick, the death of Helen Mortensen after her third (!) lobotomy was deemed the last straw, and Freeman was finally banned from surgery.

James C. Burt (1921-2012): The "Love Doctor" never even tried to conceal his deranged views about women supposedly being "structurally inadequate" for intercourse. He even published a book purporting his theories, and worked for two decades as a licensed gynecologist, performing unnecessary hysterectomies and genital mutilations on his unsuspecting patients.

Harold Shipman (1946-2004): The demented "Dr. Death" is considered the most prolific serial killer in human history, with a death toll estimated at 250 victims, mainly elderly women, 15 of whom were enough to send him to jail for life, which he cut short by hanging himself in his cell four years later.

Paolo Macchiarini (b.1958): Considered a pioneer in the field of synthetic trachea transplants at Sweden's prestigious Karolinska Institute, after seven out of eight patients who got his plastic tracheas died, he was quickly dismissed in 2016.

SHE BLINDED ME WITH SCIENCE!

From humble beginnings, the Church of Christ, Scientist, founded on Mary Baker Eddy's (1821-1910) misguided principle of healing by faith and prayer alone, grew respectable through ingraining itself in American politics and the press. While Christian Science doctrine does not expressly forbid medical care, many Christian Science parents claim religious exemption from childhood vaccination and other treatments, with disastrous consequences.

1. Principia School (Missouri) and Principia College (Illinois) saw measles outbreaks in 1978, 1980, 1985 (100 infected, three dead), 1989 (100 infected), and 1994 (200 infected).

2. The church record on h-flu meningitis isn't much better, with at least 7 children dead in 1984 alone, several of their parents charged with child endangerment, neglect, and manslaughter, though in the end not all were convicted.

3. Christian Science has had a bad history with juvenile diabetes too. The deaths of Amy Hermanson (seven) in 1986, Ian Lundman (11) in 1989, and Andrew Wantland (12) in 1992 particularly stand out.

4. The deaths of 12-year-old Michael Schram (appendicitis, 1979), 13-year-old Kris Ann Lewis (bone cancer, 1981), nine-year-old Debra Ann Kupsch (diphtheria, 1982), and two-year-old Robyn Twitchell (peritonitis, 1986) should give us all pause as well.

5. In 1989, William Franklin Simpson, a professor at Emporia State University (Kansas), analyzed the death records of 5,558 people who graduated from Christian Science's Principia College (Illinois) from 1934 till 1983, and compared them to records from 29,858 University

of Kansas graduates during the same period. Not surprisingly, he found that the death rate among Principia graduates from cancer was twice the national average, and 6% of the overall deaths of Principia graduates were due to causes preventable by regular medicine.

6. Not content with the deaths of young people, Christian Science sanatoriums and nursing homes for the elderly have also been established, where no medical treatment is allowed to interfere with prayer. Legally deemed a Religious Non-medical Health Care Institution (RNHCI) in the US, they are even partly covered by Medicare.

BONUS FACTS!

- Most of the representatives signing the Declaration of Independence didn't do so until August 2, 1776!

- Since Nabisco lost the original recipes for the Babe Ruth and Butterfinger bars, they reverse-engineered them to make new formulas for both!

- There's a John Lennon (1940-1980) park, complete with a bronze statue of the musician in … Havana, Cuba!

- In 1822, a white stork was shot down near Mecklenburg, Germany, and found to have survived a previous attempt on its life: it had a 2.5 foot long African spear lodged in its neck!

SNAKE OIL

Outrageous cure-all remedies and treatments abound in human history, some even peddled by quacks to this day.

Bloodletting: Popular in every human culture since ancient times and up until the late nineteenth century, bleeding a person became the standard treatment for almost every ailment known to man, finally falling into disrepute in the twentieth century.

Mercury: Well recommended by Avicenna (980-1037) and Paracelsus (c.1493-1541), for centuries it was used as the best and only remedy for syphilis, and applied dermally, orally, and even vaporized and inhaled. Needless to say, unless used to treat initial sores, it resulted in the deaths by poisoning of many afflicted by the disease.

Tobbaco: Since Walter Raleigh (c.1552-1618) brought it to England from the Americas, it was used to treat cancer, headaches, respiratory problems, stomach cramps, head cold, hypothermia, intestinal worms, and somnolence. Across the channel, ambassador Jean Nicot (1530-1604), introduced snuff tobacco to French royalty and noblemen, as a cure for asthma, gout, labor pains, cancer and the bubonic plague!

Bezoars: King of European sixteenth century folk remedies, bezoars fell out of fashion after barber-surgeon Ambroise Paré (1510-1590) proved to King Charles IX (1550-1574) they were fake, by having a convicted felon on death row swallow one alongside his poison. Needless to say, it went bad for the thief. Paré is also gratefully remembered for proving castration does not cure inguinal hernia!

Enemas: Including the popular tobacco, baking soda, and coffee variations, clysters were used for treating the imaginary ailments of hypochondriac aristocrats for centuries, as well as the occasional real constipation.

Turpentine: This highly poisonous solvent distilled from pine resin used to be prescribed to treat bladder, gallbladder and kidney stones and intestinal parasites internally, and was even applied externally to kill lice. To this day, unscrupulous "natural medicine" swindlers still sell it online!

Opioids: In the nineteenth century, morphine and heroin were first issued to Civil War soldiers as painkillers, and then sold over-the-counter indiscriminately to deal with minor illnesses, such as colds and headaches, leading to a great addiction epidemic that left one in 200 Americans hopelessly addicted, 60% of which were women who used them to lessen ovary pains.

BONUS FACTS!

- Ants have five different noses attuned to different smells.

- "Hail to the Chief" was originally inspired by "The Lady of the Lake," an 1810 poem by Sir Walter Scott (1771-1832).

- The moving rocks of Racetrack Playa, California, remained a mystery until 2013, when they were photographed skidding under ice floes when pushed by strong winds.

REAL SNAKE OIL

Seemingly taken straight from some witch doctor's skin-bound grimoire, here are some of medicine's oddest cures that actually work!

Venoms: Formerly the stuff of fake medicines, testing for snake venom officially started with anticoagulant Arvin (from Malayan pit viper's venom) in 1968, and so far up to six groups of venom-derived drugs that have gotten FDA approval in the US, among which Captopril is one of the most successful against high blood pressure, and kidney problems caused by diabetes. Currently, snake venom is scientifically studied and used as an effective treatment against various types of cancer, while Cuban blue scorpion venom has shown promising trial results too. Wasp venom, on the other hand, is reportedly active against degenerative disorders including sclerosis, epilepsy, Parkinson's and Alzheimer's; and *Conus magus* snail venom is used to produce non-opioid anesthetic Ziconotide.

Honey: Antibacterial, hydrogen peroxide-rich honey has been used to treat infected wounds since ancient times, and recently proven to hinder pathogen growth as well.

Maggots: Using disinfected maggots (fly larvae) to clean out necrotic skin tissue allows wounds and ulcers to heal very effectively, and has been approved by the U.S. Food and Drug Administration (FDA) since 2004.

Leeches: Hirudotherapy (after the *Hirudo medicinalis* leech species) is an age old treatment which has seen a comeback since the seventies, mainly in reconstructive microsurgery. The leeches' bleeding as well as the anesthetizing, anti-inflammatory, and vasodilating properties of their saliva, help avoid postoperative venous congestion in

procedures which range from finger reattachment to varicose vein treatment, their use gaining FDA approval in 2004.

Fish: Ichthyotherapy is the use of West Asian "doctor fish" (*Garra rufa*) to palliatively clean up the outer skin layer of patients with psoriasis.

Petroleum Jelly: Robert Chesebrough (1837-1933) distilled a light-colored gel from crude oil, and marketed as Vaseline, an over-the-counter skin ointment of FDA-recognized effectiveness, which nonetheless became used as a cure-all used to fight toenail fungus, genital rashes (non-STD), nosebleeds, diaper rash, and chest colds. Spawning countless imitators, Mentholatum remains its most popular sibling.

Nitroglycerine: Originally called "pyroglycerine" by its inventor, Ascanio Sobrero (1812-1888), this explosive was later harnessed for practical use by inventor Alfred Nobel (1833-1869) who used it to make dynamite. For over a century, however, it's also been used as a powerful vasodilator for heart conditions, such as angina pectoris and chronic heart failure.

Arsenic: Synthesized from this highly toxic element by Alfred Bertheim (1879-1914) in 1907, Arsphenamine or Compound 606 later came to be commercialized as Salversan after Japanese bacteriologist Sahachirō Hata (1873-1938) discovered its antisyphilitic properties in 1909.

Stool transplant: Known as Fecal Microbiota Transplant (FMT), it is actually a very effective treatment to restore colonic microflora. How? By getting "healthy" feces from someone else into you, either anally or (ahem!) orally via a capsule containing freeze-dried feces. Talk about a medical breakthrough!

KICKING THE OXYGEN HABIT

Death accepts no excuses and no delays. Make no mistake, sooner or later you will see the other side of the grass!

1. Of the estimated 108 billion homo sapiens to ever have lived, seven billion are still alive.

2. In this day and age 150,000 people die every day around the globe, mainly from heart disease, cancer, respiratory disease, diabetes, and dementia, according to WHO.

3. Signs of impending death in yet-warm-blooded animals include no breathing and no pulse, no brain activity becoming the point of no return. Just imagine how many deaths could have been prevented before Cardiopulmonary resuscitation (CPR) was developed by James Elam (1918-1995) and Peter Safar (1924-2003) in the 1950s!

4. After death, the fresh corpse will undergo the following decomposition stages:

Eye clouding: From ten minutes (if you died with your eyes open) to 24 hours (if you died with eyes closed) after death, fluid and oxygen stop reaching the corneas and eyeballs flatten. Our hearing will be the last sense to go!

Pallor mortis: Paleness sets in 15 to 120 minutes after death. As decomposition progresses skin will go from pale to green, to purple, to black!

Algor mortis: Body temperature drops until it matches ambient temperature.

Rigor mortis: A.k.a., the stiff getting stiff. This is only temporary, as a day or two later the chemical bonds that made it possible will break down.

Livor mortis: Postmortem lividity when the blood accumulates in the lower portion of the body (say, in your back when at the coroner's table).

Putrefaction: Decomposition begins when, having nothing else to do, the enzymes and bacteria in our digestive system begin to digest us!

Decomposition: Enzymes and bacteria, doing what they do best, release pungent gases known as *putrescine* and *cadaverine*, which will swell a body like a balloon, all the while a repugnant bloody ooze will pour out through every hole in our body. If buried, animals such as worms and ants will help the process until nothing is left but our skeleton.

BONUS FACTS!

- The metal figure on the hood of Rolls-Royce cars is called "The Spirit of Ecstasy."

- Lightning bolts appear thicker because they glow, but in reality they are as thick as an average human thumb.

DEATH BY MISADVENTURE

Serious causes of death abound, but what about the pedestrian, the undignified, and the plain stupid set of circumstances that make us kick the bucket the wrong way?

Death by sexual intercourse: Dying while engaged in lovemaking may come about a number of ways, from asphyxiation to heart failure to … angry husband! At least two Catholic popes suffered the latter, while a long list of historically significant people have allegedly popped an artery while at it, including Attila the Hun (c. 406-453), French president Félix Faure (1841-1899), and America's forty-first vice president, Nelson Rockefeller (1908-1979).

Erotic asphyxiation, in turn, has claimed the lives of popular artists Vaughn Bodē (1941-1975), Albert Dekker (1905-1968), Michael Hutchence (1960-1997), and David Carradine (1936-2009).

Death by laughter: In rare instances, laughter not only isn't "the best medicine," but may bring about cardiac arrest or asphyxiation. Notable cases in history include Greek Stoic Chrysippus of Soli (c.279-c.206BC), Spanish King Martin of Aragon (1356-1410), Italian Renaissance author Pietro Aretino (1492-1556), and Scottish polymath Sir Thomas Urquhart (1611-1660).

Death by overeating: Gluttony has claimed its share of the self-indulgent, famously King Adolf Frederick of Sweden (1710-1771), America's twelfth president Zachary Taylor (1784-1850), British novelist William Thackeray (1811-1863), and T-Rex musician Steve Took (1949-1980). Less significant people, on the other hand, die regularly in eating contests all around the world!

Death by unusual floods: These include the London Beer Flood (October 17, 1814) in which the burst of a vat released 388,000 gallons of beer, killing eight people; and the Great Boston Molasses Flood (January 15, 1919) in which a tank burst, releasing 2.3 million gallons of molasses that killed 21 people.

Death by gliding: Floating in the air while sitting in a harness below a fabric wing sounds like a ton of free-flying fun, but according to the US Hang Gliding and Paragliding Association, 58 Americans lost their lives practicing these deadly sports between 2013 and 2018.

Death by vending machine: Shaking a malfunctioning—or a perfectly functional—vending machine might tip it over the person doing the shaking. It causes around 1,700 reported accidents, which lead to the deaths of two to three people in the US each year.

Death by shark: 64 unprovoked shark attacks were reported around the globe during 2019, but they resulted in only two deaths (the yearly average is four)—considering humans kill 11,417 sharks an hour, it's only fair sharks try to even the odds every now and then.

Death by stingray: While stingrays are mainly harmless, timid creatures, when stepped on or feeling threatened, they will defend themselves, causing two to three deaths a year on average, most recently Steve "Crocodile Hunter" Irwin (1962-2006), and Judy Kay Zagorski (1953-2008) only two years later!

Death by selfie: Accidents in pursuit of extreme selfies have claimed the lives of over 300 morons between October 2011 and January 2020!

IN THE NAME OF SCIENCE

Inventors will go to great lengths to prove a new contraption, even at the cost of their lives!

William Bullock (1813-1867): The inventor of the rotary printing press, he accidentally got his leg crushed while trying to repair it, the ensuing gangrene killing him shortly afterwards.

Otto Lilienthal (1848-1896): A pioneering hang glider, he fell and broke his neck, dying the next day.

Franz Reichelt (1878-1912): In a widely publicized and filmed stunt, this tailor and wingsuit pioneer jumped to his death from atop the Eiffel Tower!

Sabin Arnold von Sochocky (1883-1928): He invented, commercialized, and eventually died from exposure to his radium-based paint.

Karel Soucek (1947-1985): Dropped 180 feet inside a shock-absorbent barrel of his creation, the barrel spun and missed the center of the water tank which was supposed to break the fall by that much …

Ford Motor Company plant worker Robert Williams (1953-1979) became the very first human to be killed by a robot. His family sued Litton Industries, makers of the industrial robot arm, and was awarded ten million dollars. Decades later, Joshua Brown's (1976-2016) "intelligent" Tesla Model S vehicle failed to apply the breaks, smashing a tractor-trailer!

THE LIVING DEAD

Joining the "27 Club" has long been a staple of rock and roll culture, guaranteeing the infamous "they will live on through their music" cliche, which surely applies to inductees Robert Johnson (1911-1938), Brian Jones (1942-1969), Jimi Hendrix (1942-1970), Janis Joplin (1943-1970), Jim Morrison (1943-1971), Pete Ham (1947-1975), Kurt Cobain (1967-1994), and Amy Winehouse (1983-2011), but what about its lesser known members?

Alexandre Levy (1864-1892): Brazilian composer, conductor, and pianist.

Louis Chauvin (1881-1908): American ragtime musician.

Nat Jaffe (1918-1945): American swing jazz pianist.

Jesse Belvin (1932-1960): American rock and roll singer-songwriter and pianist.

Rudy Lewis (1936-1964): American rhythm and blues singer.

Joe Henderson (1937-1964): American R&B and gospel singer.

Rockin' Robin Roberts (1940-1967): American rock and roll singer.

Malcolm Hale (1941-1968): American pop guitarist.

Dickie Pride (1941-1969): British rock and roll singer.

Alexandra (1942-1969): German pop singer.

Arlester Christian (1943-1971): American funk singer and bassist.

Linda Jones (1944-1972): American soul singer.

Leslie Harvey (1944-1972): Scottish rock guitarist.

Cecilia (1948-1976): Spanish pop singer-songwriter.

Helmut Köllen (1950-1977): German prog-rock bassist and guitarist.

Zenon De Fleur (1951-1979): British rock guitarist.

Jacob Miller (1952-1980): Jamaican reggae singer.

D. Boon (1958-1985): American punk singer.

Alexander Bashlachev (1960-1988): Soviet rock singer-songwriter.

Dimitar Voev (1965-1992): Bulgarian new wave singer and guitarist.

Slađa Guduraš (1987-2014): Bosnian pop singer.

While not a musician, American graffiti artist Jean-Michel Basquiat (1960-1988) rose from homelessness to rock-star-level fame in the short seven years he spent as part of the modern art establishment, until his heroin addiction made him join the club.

HOLLYWOOD TOASTER BATH

The history of entertainment is ripe with cases where fame and fortune didn't guarantee longtime happiness for the poor souls who decided to kick the upside-down bucket.

Simone Mareuil (1903-1954): Forever immortalized by Luis Buñuel (1900-1983) in his 1929 surrealist film *Un Chien Andalou*, she walked to her town's public square, doused her body in gasoline, and burned herself to death.

Peg Entwistle (1908-1932): A talented and beautiful stage and screen actress, after various Broadway productions and a single film (1932's *Thirteen Women*), she threw herself off the top of the "H" of the "Hollywoodland" sign.

Lupe Vélez (1908-1944): A stage and screen actress, comedian, singer, dancer, and vedette during Hollywood's golden age, she reportedly had stormy relationships with many stars of her day, but finding herself pregnant with actor Harald Maresch's (1916-1986) baby, she decided to swallow 75 Seconal pills with a glass of brandy, instead of having an abortion.

Pedro Armendáriz (1912-1963): One of the best-known mid-century international movie stars, under great pain from terminal neck cancer, he shot himself in the chest with a gun he had smuggled into the UCLA Medical Center in Los Angeles.

Gig Young (1913-1968): An Academy Award winner (1969's *They Shoot Horses, Don't They?*), in 1978 he shot his wife and then killed himself, but the motive remains unclear.

George Reeves (1914-1959): Best known for playing Superman and Clark Kent in *The Adventures of Superman* (1952-1958), he died from a gunshot wound to the head, which was officially ruled a suicide, but theories suggesting otherwise abound.

Carole Landis (1919-1948): The voluptuous *One Million B.C.* (1940) film actress overdosed on Seconals, after an evening with her lover, British actor Rex Harrison (1908-1990), who refused to leave his then-wife, Lilli Palmer (1914-1986) for her. Harrison definitely had a type: his fourth wife, Rachel Roberts (1927-1980), also committed suicide after repeated attempts to win him over.

Anton Furst (1944-1991): Struggling with alcoholism and depression, the Academy Award-winning designer of the 1989 *Batman* film, jumped from an eight-story parking building, on the same day Freddie Mercury (1946-1991) and Eric Carr (1950-1991) also died!

Tony Scott (1944-2012): An enormously successful director of high-grossing action films like *Top Gun* (1986), and *Man on Fire* (2004), he jumped off the Vincent Thomas Bridge in Los Angeles, but there are contradicting accounts as to his underlying reason for taking the plunge.

Anthony Bourdain (1956-2018): He was an international celebrity chef and travel show host who hanged himself on an impulse, while shooting an episode of his TV show in France!

Chris Benoit (1967-2007): The Canadian WWE wrestler strangled his wife and son, and then hanged himself with the cord of a weight machine. It has been suggested that the years of wrestling brain trauma may have led to this fit of murderous rage.

"ROSEBUD"

Whether uttered in our final moments, spelled out in ink, or engraved in stone, our final statements need be chosen carefully, as they are likely to determine how we go down in history.

Last spoken words:

"A dying man can do nothing easy." —Benjamin Franklin (1706-1790)

"I'm so bored with it all." —Winston Churchill (1874-1965)

"I think I'll be more comfortable." —Lou Costello (1906-1959)

"Surprise me." —Bob Hope (1903-2003)

Last written words:

"Tell them I've had a wonderful life." —Ludwig Wittgenstein (1889–1951)

"It is stuffy, sticky, and rainy here at present—but forecasts are more favourable." —J. R. R. Tolkien (1892-1973)

"A life is like a garden. Perfect moments can be had, but not preserved, except in memory. LLAP." —Leonard Nimoy (1931-2015)

"Relax—this won't hurt." —Hunter S. Thompson (1937-2005)

Epitaphs:

"I am ready to meet my Maker. Whether my Maker is prepared for the great ordeal of meeting me is another matter." —Winston Churchill (1874-1965)

"I told you I was ill." —Spike Milligan (1918-2005)

"There goes the neighborhood." —Rodney Dangerfield (1921-2004)

"I will not be right back." —Merv Griffin (1925-2007)

Last wills:

"Upon the decease of my wife, it is my Will and desire, that all the slaves which I hold in my own right, shall receive their freedom." —George Washington (1732-1799)

"I hereby forgive any and all loans or indebtedness which may exist at the time of my death, whether in writing or otherwise, which may be owed to me by any of my children." —Frank Sinatra (1915-1998)

"If neither of my daughters survives me, I direct my executors to collect and destroy my 'personal diaries.'" —Richard Nixon (1913-1994)

"I give all my guitars made by DOUGLAS IRWIN, to DOUGLAS IRWIN, or to his estate if he predeceases me." —Jerry Garcia (1942-1995)

William Shakespeare (1564-1616) bequeathed his wife, Anne Hathaway (1556-1623), his "second best bed with the furniture," which some speculated a slight, but it was in fact customary at the time that the best bed in the house was reserved for guests, so the "second best" would have been their marital bed.

BONUS FACT!

- Statistically speaking, left-handed people have a three year shorter life span than right-handed people.

COUNTING WORMS

Tapophobia, or the fear of being buried alive, is by far one of the worst dreads a person may have, only matched by finding oneself, in fact, prematurely buried.

Thomas à Kempis (1380-1471): The Medieval German-Dutch author of *The Imitation of Christ* (c.1418) was denied canonization (sainthood) by the Catholic Church, after exhuming his body revealed he desperately scratched the coffin lid, instead of accepting his premature burial fate.

William Duell (1723-1805): Convicted as an accessory to rape and hanged, he woke up as he was about to be dissected by medical students. Sent back to prison, his sentence was revised to life exile, which he carried out in Boston, where he passed away forty-five years later.

Angel Hays (1918-2008): The famed inventor of a working "safety coffin" got his inspiration after surviving being buried alive himself, when a biking accident saw him knocked unconscious and declared dead in 1937.

Stephen B. Small (1947–1987): The Illinois businessman was kidnapped and buried alive in a homemade coffin with a breathing tube, which failed, causing him to die from suffocation.

Shakereh Khaleeli (1947-1991): Drugged asleep, placed on her mattress inside a box, and buried in the garden by her husband, her body was found clutching the mattress, and the box interior scratch-marked.

Noelia Serna (b.1965): After two consecutive heart attacks and not responding to CPR, the Colombian woman was pronounced dead. Hours later at the funeral home, when she was about to be injected with embalming fluid, an employee saw her move, which saved her life in the nick of time.

Sipho William Mdletshe (b.1969): With no signs of life after a serious car accident, this South African man was taken to the Johannesburg morgue, waking up two days and nights later. His ensuing screams prompted the morgue workers to take him out of the metal container he was in!

Neysi Pérez (1998-2015): Buried in her wedding dress at 16. The widower heard screams and punching noises coming from inside her tomb, but despite his best efforts, the young bride didn't make it out alive.

Essie Dunbar (1885-1955): When Essie's sister missed the funeral, and arrived late for the burial, the coffin had already been lowered six feet under , but she demanded to be given one last look at Essie anyway. To everyone's surprise, when the lid was opened, the 30-year-old woman sat up and smiled. The ensuing commotion saw three preachers fall in the grave themselves, as Essie tried to assure the stampeding mourners she wasn't a zombie!

BONUS FACT!

- The International Talk Like a Pirate Day is celebrated all around the world on September 19.

BUYING THE PINE CONDO

The final, legally accepted, and ritualized disposal of the remains of the deceased, as been well documented in certain mammals, most notably elephants and dolphins, but the wide variety of methods and practices in human culture is surpassed by none.

Burial: We've been burying our dead since our species sprung up in Africa. The practice gives ritual closure to family and friends, while saving them the discomfort of decomposition's pungent smell. 80% of the deceased are buried in the US, usually after being embalmed and put on display for a little while.

Preservation: First practiced by the *Chinchorro* of the Atacama desert 6,000 years ago, in Spain 5,000 years ago, and greatly developed in Egypt 3,500 years ago (mummies!). The embalming and three-week parade of Abraham Lincoln's (1809-1865) body greatly popularized this preservation method in America, where 5.3 million gallons of embalming fluid are used every year.

Cremation: Reducing the body to around eight pounds of ash and fragments via combustion is the second most popular method of final disposition. It came to prominence in ancient Rome, Scandinavia, and the far East, while it was traditionally rejected by Jews, Muslims, and Christians, though the latter have revised their stance since, as long as ashes don't get scattered. In modern times, nonbelievers who can afford it, like Gene Roddenberry (1921-1991), Timothy Leary (1920-1996), and Gerard K. O'Neill (1927-1992), may even get their ashes shot into space!

Alkaline hydrolysis: Known as flameless cremation, it is a process for dissolving remains using lye and heat. In it, the body is placed in a pressure cooker filled with a mixture of water and potassium hydroxide, and heated at 320°F, which will turn all soft tissue into a green goo, while the bones will be left as dust, for the next of kin to do as they wish.

Plastination: If you think the Swedish are weird, this preservation technique invented by German anatomist Gunther von Hagens (b.1945) takes the prize: the body or body part would first be fixed in formaldehyde, bathed in acetone to dehydrate it, boiling off the acetone in a vacuum, and then proceed to substitute all liquids and fat with a liquid plastic of your choice. The plastic then would need to be hardened by gas, heat or UV light, and while at it the body may suitably be posed to be exhibited.

In 2011 von Hagens announced he suffered from Parkinson's, and desired to be plastinated after death!

BONUS FACTS!

- The red-and-white-striped pole of the barbershop, still in use today, comes from Europe, where barbers also played surgeon and dentist. It literally means "blood and bandages!"

- A young George Clooney (b.1961) once relieved himself in his roommate's cat's litter box!!!

- When rats get entangled by their tail, they form a "Rat King" which, unable to move, is fed by other rats. It was thought to be a myth until a specimen was found in Nantes, France, in 1986.

SOYLENT GREEN

The rising eco-friendly alternative of final disposition, human body composting made headlines when legalized in the state of Washington, back in 2019.

1. Composting turns a man's soft tissue into soil conditioner by working a bit faster than nature, which usually takes weeks.

2. It is based on the ways we already compost livestock, only heating the remains to 131°F, killing off contagions to make the soil usable.

3. All in all, the process spends one-eighth of the energy used in cremation, while costing a little less.

4. The process was legalized in Washington, but not without considerable lobbying by the Recompose company, which offers the service.

5. A new Swedish method called "promession" freezes a corpse in liquid nitrogen, then vibrates it until turned to small icy grains which are then dried. After magnetically separating all metal particles (say, from teeth amalgams) the rest is used as fancy compost.

6. The Coeio company, on the other hand, offers a complement to standard casket burial in the form of the Infinity Burial Suit, a.k.a. the "mushroom suit," a full-body, biodegradable covering with a built-in "bio-mix" of mushrooms which supposedly accelerate ground decomposition. Actor Luke Perry (1966-2019) was reportedly buried in one.

GOING TO MEDICAL SCHOOL

For most of us, enrolling in medical school is a pipe dream, but joining post-mortem is open to almost everybody!

1. Back in the nineteenth century, there was such a shortage of bodies destined for medical research, anatomists and physicians had to hire the illegal services of "body snatchers," which sometimes led to murder, such as the infamous 1828 Burke and Hare Murders in Scotland.

2. In modern times, educational institutions, medical organizations, and research facilities all rely heavily on non-transplant body donations.

3. The Uniform Anatomical Gift Act governs individual body donation in the US yet, since the need for fresh corpses is so great and federal government enforcement of the act so little, the unregulated market has allowed the existence of "body brokers" who acquire cadavers (sometimes offering free partial cremation), resell them in part or in whole.

4. Legally, all it takes is an individual's signed donation consent form and no objections from the next of kin. Only bodies carrying infectious diseases are usually turned down. Unknown/unclaimed bodies may also be rejected on ethical grounds.

5. Seven university-run "body farms" dedicated to the study of human decomposition have been erected in the US since forensic anthropologist William Bass (b.1928) established the first one in 1971:

University of Tennessee

Western Carolina University

Texas State University

Sam Houston State University

Southern Illinois University

Colorado Mesa University

University of South Florida

6. Even in modern times, the corpses of the rich have been stolen to exact ransom on their families. This is quite common in Italy, notably the cases of entrepreneur Serafino Ferruzzi (1908-1979) and banker Enrico Cuccia (1907-2000), and TV host Mike Bongiorno (1924-2009). While the Cuccia and Bongiorno remains were later recovered, Ferruzzi's body is still missing.

BONUS FACTS!

- Contrary to popular belief, Mama Cass Elliot (1941-1974) did not choke to death on a ham sandwich!

- The Dragon's Breath chili pepper developed in the UK is so hot the anaphylactic shock resulting from eating one could kill you.

- The name "Jesus" is a Hebrew, to Greek, to Latin, to English derivation. If translated from Hebrew to English directly, our Savior's name would be "Joshua."

- Newborn babies don't have kneecaps.

REST IN PIECES

People will collect the oddest things, but none as odd as body parts from the historically relevant. While keeping relics became a religious staple, the secular world isn't without its share of bodily tokens.

1. Saint Anthony of Padua's (1195-1231) tongue apparently did not decompose along the rest of this body tissue, and was thus placed in a special reliquary, which rests in a separate nave of the saint's eponymous basilica.

2. Giovanni di Fidanza (1221-1274), a.k.a. Saint Bonaventura, was a Franciscan friar whose arm and hand have been preserved in a silver arm-shaped reliquary, in the parish church of St. Nicholas (Bagnoregio, Italy). St. Bonaventura is the one who placed St. Anthony of Padua's tongue in its reliquary.

3. The badly preserved body of Saint Francis Xavier (1506-1552) in Goa's Basilica of Bom Jesus (India), has been torn to pieces by relic hunters and mad pilgrims over the ages.

4. Galileo Galilei's (1564-1642) middle finger has been exhibited in different places since it was cut off from his corpse by Florentine antiquarian, Antonio Francesco Gori (1691-1757) in 1737.

5. The head of Austrian composer Joseph Haydn (1732-1809) was originally stolen by two phrenology aficionados. They kept the skull hidden amongst themselves, passing it down for generations, until it was finally returned to Haydn's grave in 1954.

6. Napoleon Bonaparte's (1769-1821) shriveled tiny penis belongs to Evan Lattimer of Englewood, New Jersey, who inherited it from his father, Dr. John Lattimer (1914-2007), a renowned urologist, author, and war memorabilia collector, who acquired it in Paris for $3,000.

7. Ludwig van Beethoven's (1770-1827) hair was shamelessly clipped by friends and visitors, before and after the composer's death. A particular lock, known as "The Guevara Lock," was purchased for $7,300 at Sotheby's (London), in December 1994 by the American Beethoven Society, and exhibited at the San Jose State University's Beethoven center until 2017.

8. Dr. Thomas Harvey (1912-2007) did the autopsy on Albert Einstein (1879-1955), but kept Einstein's brain, sliced in 170 pieces, in a jar for decades, without permission! He also gave Einstein's eyes to a Dr. Henry Abrams (Einstein's eye doctor) who has kept them in a safety deposit box ever since.

BONUS FACTS!

- Egypt's City of the Dead necropolis houses not only the deceased, but also 500,000 of the living who can't afford decent lodgings in Cairo.

- Comedian Larry David (b.1947) and politician Bernie Sanders (b.1941) are, in fact, distant cousins!

- The "Twisted Trees," a grove of creepy, gnarly aspens in Sasketchewan, Canada, is a single mutated organism!

MAX HEADROOM

Encased in our skull lies the brain, the incredibly complex "computer system" commanding our entire body, which has the ability to send and receive unbelievable amounts of information.

1. While the human brain weighs less than many other organs (around three pounds) it takes the longest to develop, and goes through more changes than other organs.

2. It burns through 20% of the body's oxygen and blood, generating up to 25 watts of energy (actually enough to power a light bulb).

3. Up to five minutes without oxygen will cause brain damage, while eight to ten seconds of blood loss will lead to losing consciousness.

4. It is made of 73% water, so a bare 2% dehydration will affect our cognitive skills.

5. Most of the remaining 27% is just fat. Without cholesterol it would die!

6. More than 100,000 complex chemical reactions take place in the brain each second.

7. Our brain comprises the cerebrum, the brainstem and the cerebellum, with our eyeballs and 19-inch spinal cord as direct physical extensions of it all.

8. The cerebrum has four interconnected ventricles in which about 0.625 cups of cerebrospinal fluid is produced, circulated, and replaced three to four times per day.

9. It contains roughly 100 billion neurons (10,000 different types of them!), which transfer 1,000 nerve impulses per second, at over 250 mph. And yet, surgical removal of almost half of our cerebrum is possible with little to no effect on personality or memory!

10. While it interprets pain signals sent to it, the cerebrum itself does not have pain receptors, and therefore cannot feel any pain. The tissue between it and the skull, however, does have those receptors, which explains headaches and migraines.

11. Our brain stops growing at age 18, begins to lose some memory and cognitive skills by the late twenties, and starts getting smaller after we reach middle age, eventually becoming unable to filter and remove old memories, hence preventing itself from remembering new things or embracing new ideas.

12. While "gray matter" is the name we give nerve cells, "white matter" are the fibers which connect them all and transmit information. Women have about ten times more white matter than men!

BONUS FACT!

- Around 534 professional Spanish bullfighters have died as a result of the sport in the past 300 years.

ENTER SANDMAN

The physical and psychological importance of sleep can't be overstated. Humans are the only creatures on Earth capable of delaying sleep on purpose, which may have life or death consequences.

1. Newborns sleep between 14 to 17 hours, teens around nine hours, and most adults between seven and eight hours a day.

2. Falling asleep typically takes from ten to 15 minutes. If it takes us less than five, it means we are sleep deprived.

3. While *insomnia* is the inability to fall asleep, *dysania* is lacking the power to get out of bed, both of which signal underlying conditions such as depression, anxiety, etc.

4. Sleeping people perceive fewer stimuli, but can still respond to loud noises and other extreme sensory events.

5. Deep-sleeping humans secrete bursts of growth hormone and prolactin hormone.

6. Sleep is divided into two types: non-rapid eye movement (NREM) sleep, and rapid eye movement (REM) sleep. NREM occurs during deep sleep, while REM sleep covers a smaller portion of sleeping time, when we experience dreams and nightmares.

7. We usually experience three to five dreams a night, taking two to three hours of the whole sleeping time, but we will only remember the dream that took most of that time.

8. 40% of people experience sleep paralysis during REM sleep, while the rest will go on sleepwalking, or mumbling during that time.

9. Most people experience sudden jolts in the lightest stage of sleep, either before falling into a slumber, or before waking up. These are known as "hypnic jerks."

10. Unborn babies and blind people dream too, but the nature of their dreaming revolves around touch and sound rather than images.

11. Dreaming prevents the brain from going psychotic, by consolidating all we have learnt in our memory, offering cognitive stimulation, allowing the unconscious mind to process complex stimuli, bringing balance and equilibrium to the mind.

12. Most people can't read a book, or the time, when dreaming, due to the entire language area of the brain being mainly inactive.

BONUS FACTS!

- An extinct carnivorous amphibian whale species, *Archaeoceti*, had feet and toes which it used to roam the land in northern Africa.

- Before becoming a modern progressive society, flaying the skin of a dead man from the waist down and wearing it to attract wealth (normally with a poor widow's coin tucked in the scrotum) was all the rage in Iceland.

DR. CALIGARI'S CABINET

The usual definition of free will is that of conscious mind over body, but it's been empirically proven the unconscious runs most of the show, building up the conscious mind's eagerness to do something, which in turn opens the door to seeing humans as programmable entities.

1. While the Greek root for hypnosis, *hypnos*, means "sleep," it has been proven hypnosis has nothing to do with slumber. On the contrary, it is a state of the mind involving focused attention, reduced peripheral awareness, and an enhanced capacity to respond to suggestion.

2. Hypnotists usually start with small suggestions on a willing subject, which will prime the subject to larger suggestions, while hypnotherapists will use of this technique to help a patient through trauma or a phobia.

3. Mentalists, on the other hand, are the stage version of a hypnotist, attempting to induce hypnosis on a subject for the amusement of a crowd.

4. Persian physician Avicenna (980-1037) documented hypnotic trance in 1027, but hypnosis didn't come to fashion until pseudoscientist Franz Mesmer (1734–1815) put "mesmerizing" back in the spotlight.

7. Dr. Jules Cloquet (1790–1883) operated on a woman with breast cancer, who reportedly felt no pain while under hypnosis, in 1829.

6. In the late nineteenth century serious psychologists such as Pierre Janet (1859-1947) and Sigmund Freud (1856-1939) developed hypnotherapy as we know it today, while Émile Coué (1857-1926) introduced the notion of autosuggestion or light self-hypnosis.

7. Day-dreaming, deep thinking, meditating or watching television states are akin to trance-like hypnosis.

8. Hypnotized people are not mindless automatons, nor are they helpless to refuse a suggestion if they so desire. Case in point, self-styled British hypnotist Timothy Porter (b.1973) tried to mesmerize a woman into becoming his sex-slave, but the woman called the police and Porter was sent to prison in 2013.

BONUS FACTS!

- Thought to be the oldest man in the world at age 111, in 2010 Katō Sōgen (1899-c.1978) was found to have been kept mummified for four decades by his family, in order to keep cashing his pension checks!

- The robber crab is the largest land-living arthropod in the world, known to drag stuff from tourists and beach goers, though it isn't fast enough to avoid being "caught in the act."

- John Adams (1735-1826) and Thomas Jefferson (1743-1826) died on the same day, exactly 50 years after the Declaration of Independence!

THE BRAIN THAT WOULDN'T DIE

Before the advent of psychology, a pseudoscience of the mind called phrenology claimed it could predict mental traits by measuring the contour of the skull, and detecting its "bumps."

1. It was founded by German physician Franz Josef Gall (1758-1828) in 1796, it name coined by Gall's colleague Johann Gaspar Spurzheim (1776-1832) who became its main proponent.

2. Spurzheim would systematize phrenology, creating its still remembered craniographical chart. He died amid an American tour, and was interred a hero, under a marble monument at Boston's Mount Auburn Cemetery.

3. Phrenology was used by racists and abolitionists alike to either justify slavery or paint black people as timid and tamable.

4. It was also used by the upper class to justify its dominance too, as well as demanded by employers as test proof of a perspective employee's reliability and good nature.

5. Phrenologists believed that by pointing out at a person's flaws, if said person had the disposition to change their behavior, it would alter the shape of their skull.

6. Thus phrenology introduced the concept of criminal rehabilitation, via the reorganizing of the brain through hard work and strict instruction.

7. Both "highbrow" and "lowbrow" are phrenology-coined terms, as is "shrink," now applied to psychotherapists, which used to mean reducing the bumps that produced undesirable traits!

8. While the phrenology practice began to vanish in America after the Civil War, it persisted in the UK until 1967, when the British Phrenological Society finally disbanded.

9. On *The Simpsons* **"Mother Simpson" episode (season 7), Mr. Burns is shown to still believe in phrenology:**

Joe Friday: "Are you sure this is the woman you saw in the post office?"

C.M. Burns: "Absolutely. Who could forget such a monstrous visage? She has the sloping brow and cranial bumpage of the career criminal."

Mr. Smithers: "Uh, sir, phrenology was dismissed as quackery a hundred-sixty years ago."

C.M. Burns: "Of course you'd say that, you have the brainpan of a stage coach tilter."

BONUS FACTS!

• Overtoun Bridge (Dumbarton, Scotland) has inexplicably lured hundreds of dogs to jump from it—about 50 have perished there since the sixties!

• Despite being Adolf Hitler's (1889-1945) nephew, William Stuart-Houston (1911-1987) joined the United States Navy during World War II, and was awarded a Purple Heart.

A DANGEROUS METHOD

Psychology, the "scientific study of behavior and mental processes" that replaced phrenology (already quite discredited in its time) as the method of choice to understand and heal the human mind, came to be after a very long trial and error process, rather than upon precise methodology.

1. Until the late nineteenth century psychology was a field of philosophy rather than a medical science.

2. Contrary to popular belief, it wasn't Sigmund Freud (1856-1939) who started it all but Wilhelm Wundt (1832-1920), who turned it into its own field of scientific study and called himself a psychologist for the first time ever!

3. Early pioneers of scientific psychology include Hermann Ebbinghaus (memory), William James (pragmatism), Ivan Pavlov (conditioning) and Hugo Münsterberg (psychology in the workplace).

4. Freud's breakthrough finally came with the implementation of "psychoanalysis," a method for understanding the unconscious mind, which may effectively be applied to treat mental-health disorders. This method was later developed by Alfred Adler (1870-1937), Carl Jung (1865-1971), and Erich Fromm (1900-1980), among many others.

5. Psychology advances led to the development of cognitive science in the late twentieth century, which proposes a wider, interdisciplinary study of the human mind, combining discoveries made by evolutionary psychology, linguistics, computer science, philosophy, behaviorism, and neurobiology, among other disciplines.

6. On the practical side, thanks to psychology there are many aspects of human thinking and behavior we now have a better understanding of, including:

- Decisions based on instinct are often better than educated ones, because the subconscious mind knows what's better for us before we understand it rationally.

- Communication affects mood, and not the other way around. For instance, men with deep voices are more attractive because they are perceived as reliable and non-aggressive.

- Bilingual people are more rational when thinking and speaking in their second language, which may unconsciously change their personalities.

- Most people willingly submit to authority figures, even if ordered to do things contrary to their own conscience.

BONUS FACTS!

- The exclusive Club 33, which charges an initial membership fee of $25,000, and another $10,000 annually, was established by none other than Walt Disney, and is hiding in plain sight, at Disneyland's New Orleans square.

- Up to 38% of people experience at least one precognitive dream in their lifetime. Abraham Lincoln (1809-1865) for one, was said to have dreamt his own assassination.

A DANGEROUS MIND

A permanent fixture of entertainment media, psychopaths are everywhere, but psychopathy is far more complex and not always as homicidal as portrayed on paper and screen.

1. Psychopathy is not a recognizable psychiatric or psychological disorder but rather an extension of antisocial personality disorder.

2. No brain imaging or biological test can identify a person as a psychopath. The most common device used to identify them is a personality traits and recorded behaviors checklist developed by Robert D. Hare (b.1934), which categorizes psychopathy according to interpersonal, emotional, lifestyle, and antisocial factors.

3. Psychopathy and sociopathy are hardly the same. Unlike sociopaths, psychos know how to blend in with the crowd and switch off empathy and remorse at will.

4. On a chemical level, the psychopathic brain craves dopamine a lot more than a regular person's, so they require constant stimulation and tend to take higher risks.

5. Psychopaths are always arrogant, charming and manipulative, but not always homicidal or physically violent, the traits that make them dangerous also making them highly successful in certain professions they find stimulating, according to British psychologist Kevin Dutton (b.1967).

6. Dutton's lists of professions that attract the highest and lowest number of psychopaths includes:

Higher:	Lower:
1. CEO	**1.** Care aide
2. Lawyer	**2.** Nurse
3. Mass media	**3.** Therapist
4. Sales	**4.** Craftsperson
5. Surgeon	**5.** Beautician/Stylist
6. Journalist	**6.** Charity worker
7. Police officer	**7.** Teacher
8. Clergy person	**8.** Creative artist
9. Chef	**9.** Doctor
10. Civil servant	**10.** Accountant

BONUS FACT!

- It takes from 364 to 411 licks to reach the center of a Tootsie Pop.

A PENNY A WORD

What do you get when a borderline psychopath starts his own religion?

1. In 1950, a college dropout and failed Navy officer, who dabbled as a science fiction writer and occasional con-man, L. Ron Hubbard (1911-1986) successfully managed to publish and commercialize a set of pseudoscientific self-help ideas about the relationship of mind and body, which he called "dianetics."

2. Appropriately, dianetics was first introduced as a series of articles in the pages of *Astounding Science Fiction*, and then collected and expanded with the publication of *Dianetics: The Modern Science of Mental Health*, which sold over 50,000 copies, and allowed Hubbard to abandon freelance writing to focus on his books and lectures, while establishing and running a foundation to manage it all (mostly from aboard a ship!).

3. At its core, dianetics purports mankind as intrinsically good, but hampered by trauma. Hence, it divides the mind intro three parts: analytical, reactive (subconscious), and somatic, aiming to cleanse, or "audit," the reactive mind via questions or commands intended to root out painful past experiences.

4. Despite being throughly discredited by the scientific community (and lambasted by the science-fiction community), dianetics gained cult-like traction, under Hubbard's leadership and charisma. However, when dianetics followers began to divide into factions, some of which did not recognize Hubbard's authority, and financial mismanagement saw the foundation close, Hubbard had learnt enough to take the next big step—coalescing it all into his own religious organization, The Church of Scientology!

5. Scientology therefore placed dianetics' pseudo-therapy practices within the framework of religious thought, all firmly under Hubbard's command, beyond scientific and IRS purvue.

6. Its belief system claims an evil being named Xenu exiled his planet's inhabitants, "thetans" to Earth, ultimately implanting their minds with false memories of historical events to keep them trapped. Obviously, their souls may be freed through dianetics "auditing," ultimately accessing psychic abilities, heightened senses, incredible intelligence, and other "Thetan" super powers.

7. Scientology is legally a religion in the United States, Spain, New Zealand, Portugal, Australia, Italy, South Africa, and the Netherlands, while Germany and France have so far refused to consider it as such, regarding it as an abusive scam.

8. It has shown little tolerance for any opposition to founder L. Ron Hubbard's teachings, and has often conducted a number of operations to expunge Hubbard's legal records ("Snow White") or harass its critics ("Freakout"). It also sued the Cult Awareness Network website into bankruptcy, and even spied on South Park cartoon creators Trey Parker (b.1969) and Matt Stone (b.1971). It has been banned from editing related Wikipedia articles, which it tried to embellish many times.

9. It also routinely interrogates ("security checks") its members, young and old, to determine their level of commitment.

10. Long a magnet for Hollywood celebrities, current members include Kirstie Alley (b.1951), Tom Cruise (b.1952), John Travolta (b.1954), Juliette Lewis (b.1973), Giovanni Ribisi (b.1974), Michael Peña (b.1976), and Elisabeth Moss (b.1982)!

A FOOL AND HIS SCIENCE

Of course, its aura of respectability doesn't exclude mainstream science from clinging to more than its share of well-meaning self deceit, which may lead to the general population pathologically maintaining these long-debunked theories and hypotheses despite all evidence to the contrary.

Aether: While considered the first modern chemist, Robert Boyle (1627-1691) sadly also proposed the hypothetical existence of aether, a conveniently invisible substance which didn't interact with physical objects, and was long thought to carry light itself. It was finally debunked in the early twentieth century.

Phlogiston: First conceived by physician Johann Joachim Becher (1635-1682), further theorized by chemist Georg Ernst Stahl (1659-1734), *phlogiston* (Greek for "burning up") was the element which enabled fire and combustion—combustible substances contained *phlox* (Greek for "flame"), and *dephlogisticate* (release phlox) when burned.

Élan vital: Just like phlogiston was supposed to be the all-explaining "element" of fire, Stahl also proposed an element of life itself, or "vital force" akin to the soul. This anima would control all physical processes within the body, as well as the direction and goals of the mind too.

N-Rays: When famed electromagnetic radiation researcher, French physicist Prosper-René Blondlot (1849-1930), announced the discovery of N-rays at the University of Nancy (hence, the "N" in "N-rays"), it caused quite the sensation in 1903. Unfortunately, while Blondlot's lab assistants and other French physicists all confirmed the results of his research, notable scientists everywhere else failed to

replicate its results, which led to further inquiry. As it turns out, rather than a new form of radiation, the French had stumbled into a new form of preconception—experimenter's bias!

Polywater: Developed by an obscure Soviet chemist, polywater was a form of water which appeared to have a higher boiling point and lower freezing point than normal water, and a consistency akin to syrup. As it turned out, it was just dirty water, but late 1960s mainstream media pushed the concept into the limelight so effectively, it had to be officially debunked.

Magnet therapy: All the new-agey belief in the health benefits of subjecting the body to weak magnetic fields (via magnets conveniently placed in bracelets, rings, etc.) generates, is billions of dollars in revenue for unscrupulous manufacturers and vendors to this day.

Subliminal advertising: According to legend, in 1957 James Vicary (1915-1977) conducted a "study" in which moviegoers were exposed to a millisecond Coca-Cola ad, leading to a significant sales boost at the theater's popcorn stand. This led to a media frenzy and several countries rushing to officially ban such ads. As it turns out, the famed experiment never really took place, but the public at large has chosen to continue believing the hoax.

BONUS FACT!

- The smell of real fresh Japanese wasabi is very effective at waking people up, and has been tested as a fire alarm.

AHEAD OF ITS TIME

Failure comes in many forms, not the least of which is the commercial one some inventions face when tested in real markets, sometimes against each other, vying for the preference of their intended users.

Polavision: An instant home movie system developed by Polaroid in 1977, it used film cartidges which recorded a mere three minutes of film to be seen in its own player, which put it at odds with then-new video systems which ran much longer. Its demise came a short two years later, and a $70-80 million loss for the company.

LaserDisc: Introduced in 1977, the first high-quality optical disc video format made inrods in affluent Asian markets like Japan or Singapore, which saw it endure until the late 1990s, when it was superseded by the smaller and much more affordable DVD.

Ford Pinto: A subcompact car made by the Ford Motor Company in 1971, as a response to similar cars introduced by Japanese brands, it was brought to an end a decade of fuel tank explosion-related accidents later.

AVE Mizar: What's worse than an exploding Ford Pinto? A flying Ford Pinto! The Mizar was all posed to take the market by storm in 1974, until a fatal 1973 test flight killed the men who invented it, dooming the AVE (Advanced Vehicle Engineers) venture altogether.

New Coke: Coca-Cola's 1985 reformulation, intended to capture the Pepsi youth market, led to a huge backlash from classic Coca-Cola consumers (and a 14% sales increase for Pepsi) which saw their preferred soda reinstated.

Pepsi AM: Anticipating the 2000s "energy drink" craze, Pepsi AM contained high levels of caffeine, but unsurprisingly failed after being marketed as a substitute for morning coffee, and was discontinued just a year later.

Twentieth Anniversary Macintosh: Or TAM, as it was known, it was an "All-in-One" LCD-based personal computer aimed at the wealthy executives who could afford the $7,500 price tag in 1997. Turns out execs showed a lot more sense than the current Apple fanbase and didn't. Steve Jobs (1955-2011) himself saw to discontinuing the product upon his return to Apple less than a year later.

Apple Newton: Another well-remembered Apple failure, the 1993 Newton Messagepad was a hand-held device with touch capabilities, a stylus, and handwriting recognition software licensed from a Russian company which, unsurprisingly, didn't work well. While this feature was certainly improved in later versions of its OS, it wasn't enough to prevent Jobs from discontinuing the product, which ironically is the precursor of both iPhone and iPad.

BONUS FACTS!

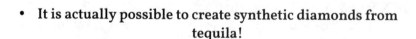

- It is actually possible to create synthetic diamonds from tequila!

- The world's biggest ball pit is the Ivanhoe Reservoir in Los Angeles, which was blanketed by 96,000,000 "shade balls" mainly to prevent sunlight from triggering unwanted chemical reactions.

INFOBAHN

The marvelous global system of interconnected computer networks we now call "the internet" didn't suddenly burst into existence, but was the result of continued development across continents, leaving a number of precursors along the way until it coalesced into its modern form; but these early forerunners are well worth looking at.

TELEGRAPH (1837): Using coded pulses of electric current through dedicated wires, it is considered the first fully digital communications system.

MUNDANEUM (1910): It was developed as an institution dedicated to data collection, classification, and management in Belgium by Paul Otlet (1868-1944) and Henri La Fontaine (1864-1943). When the amount of index cards amassed became too great, Otlet proposed a mechanical data cache accessed via interconnected telegraph wires, but sadly found no government support.

SABRE (1960): Standing for Semi-automated Business Research Environment, it is a computer flight reservation system developed by IBM for American Airlines, based on their SAGE (Semi Automatic Ground Environment) message relay project for the US Air Force.

AUTODIN (1966): The Automatic Digital Network System was a US Department of Defense data transmission project which linked more than 300 Air Forces bases, and remained operational until 1982!

ARPANET (1969): Also known as Advanced Research Projects Agency Network, its main purpose was connecting computers at Pentagon-funded research institutions and universities over telephone lines, which led to the development of applications like the FTP file transfer protocol , and the SMTP, or simple mail transfer protocol that was later nicknamed "e-mail."

CYCLADES (1971): An innovative French research network developed to allow for different types of university computer networks to connect to each other, until its shutdown ten years later.

CYBERSYN (1971): While the idea of a centralized socialist internet had been proposed early on by pioneering Soviet computer scientist Viktor Glushkov (1923-1982), it was actually implemented by British management theorist Stafford Beer (1926-2002) in socialist Chile, of all places, as a network of telex machines in state-run factories that would transmit and receive information through a central computer mainframe. The entire project was scrapped after a 1973 military coup backed by the CIA.

TELENET (1975): The first FCC-approved commercially available public data network, it charged companies a fee, while also offering free public dialup access to individuals across the USA.

MINITEL (1980): The world's most successful online service before the advent of the World Wide Web (WWW), or "the internet" as we know it. It allowed French home, office, and college users to purchase goods, make train reservations, check stock prices, search the telephone directory, chat, get e-mail, and even organize strikes! Also implemented in countries like Brazil, Finland, Germany, and Sweden, it was so efficient it remained operational until forcefully shut down in 2012!

TOO MUCH TIME ON MY HANDS

Universities, research facilities and individual scientists are all under extreme pressure to either justify their current funding or gain new sponsorships by showing results (what academia calls "publishing"). This has led to an increasingly alarming number of studies ranging from the obvious to the ridiculous, all of which mainstream media and social networks alike eagerly scoop up, to keep the rest of us clicking.

1. A 2005 Burnet Institute (Australia) survey concluded that 80% of their teaspoons disappear every month, and that the average "lifespan" of a teaspoon at the institute was 81 days.

2. A 2006 McGill University (Canada) study shockingly found women like porn as much as men do.

3. A 2007 National University of Quilmes (Argentina) uncovered that Viagra cures hamster jetlag.

4. A 2009 Guangdong Entomological Institute (China) accidentally observed that fruit bats love oral sex. This was confirmed and reconfirmed—not so accidentally—in 2010 and 2011.

5. A 2011 Louisiana State University (USA) study somehow arrived at the conclusion that people who eat candy and chocolates don't get as fat as people who do not.

6. A 2012 UC Berkeley (USA) study found that people with unfair advantages in the game of Monopoly become arrogant and ill-mannered towards other players.

7. A 2012 Detroit Medical Center (USA) study proved it is possible to stop nosebleeds by plugging a person's nose with raw, cured pork meat.

8. A 2013 University of Michigan (USA) study revealed that Facebook makes people unhappy.

9. A 2015 University of California (USA) study reached the conclusion that late-night snacks may cause brain damage.

10. A 2016 University of Cambridge (UK) study figured out Spider-Man couldn't possibly exist.

11. Last but not least, the 1998 Andrew Wakefield (b.1957) study linking vaccination to autism is widely considered the most damaging medical hoax of the twentieth century, as it gave rise to a new anti-vaccination movement, which has caused more measles epidemics than Christian Science!

BONUS FACTS!

- Humans cannot taste food without mixing it with saliva.

- The Portuguese man-of-war is a *siphonophore*, an animal made of four different polyp creatures working together.

- The last words Walt Disney (1901-1966) wrote on his deathbed were "Kurt Russell."

FREAKS AND GEEKS

It takes courage to be a nerd and change the world for good. The following list of exceptional, whimsical, and brave geniuses began shaping the world we live in today in 1801 ...

Joseph Marie Jacquard (1752-1834): The first computer wasn't a giant calculator, but rather an automatic loom which used punch cards, all invented by a man who only began receiving an education at age 13, and fought in France's revolutionary war alongside his own son.

Charles Babbage (1791-1871): The father of the first mechanical computer, or "Analytical Engine," was a British super-geek, then called a polymath, who mastered science, engineering, and the humanities, while also dabbling in paranormal investigation!

Ada Lovelace (1815-1852): This "poet-scientist," as she considered herself, saw potential for Babbage's Analytical Engine beyond calculation, and proceeded to write an algorithm for it, making her the first computer programmer in history.

Herman Hollerith (1860-1929): An early American computing genius took Jacquard's textile punch card system and applied it to a tabulating machine of his own creation, to process all the 1880 census data in just three years (saving the government millions of dollars in the process). His was the first data processing system!

Alan Turing (1912-1954): This brilliant British man made inroads into fields as diverse as biology, philosophy, and information systems analysis, and is considered the father of theoretical computer science and artificial intelligence, no less!

J. V. Atanasoff (1903-1995): An early boy genius by every account, he breezed through high school and college. At age 36, with the assistance of his top student, Clifford Berry (1918-1963), he would build the world's first electronic computer ... How's that for an achievement?

John Mauchly (1907-1980) and J. Presper Eckert (1919-1995): This physicist and engineer team, built the first universal "Turing machine": Electronic Numerical Integrator and Calculator (ENIAC) at the University of Pennsylvania, before going private and building the first UNIVAC (Universal Automatic Computer) for the US Census Bureau in 1951.

Bill Hewlett (1913-2001) and David Packard (1912-1996): The original Palo Alto duo, these longtime friends started their own empire, Hewlett-Packard (HP), from Packard's basement in 1939, originally to manufacture electronic measurement equipment for none other than Walt Disney Pictures. In the process of expanding into computing, they created Silicon Valley as we know it.

Jack Kilby (1923-2005): Up until 1958, computer engineers couldn't increase the performance of their machines without increasing the components involved, making computers bigger and bigger. Along came a young Texas Instruments engineer with a revolutionary idea: soldering circuits in a single piece of semi-conductor material, the first modern microchip!

Grace Hopper (1906-1992): Brilliant as she was courageous, as a computer scientist she developed the first machine-independent computer programming language, COBOL. Not content with that massive achievement, she also served in the US Navy, retiring a highly decorated Commodore (now Rear Admiral) in 1986!

III
JAMMING
HISTORY

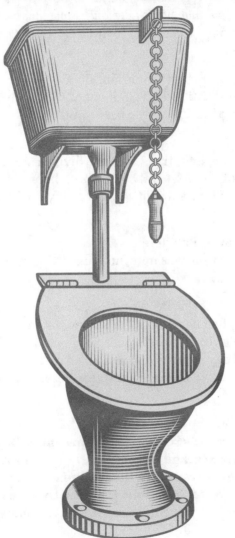

A BRIEF HISTORY OF TIME

While most scientists would argue nothing travels faster than light, most of us are well aware the effect of laxatives may easily surpass our ability to turn the light on. However, our inability to fully understand time hasn't stopped us from trying to measure it, if only for practical reasons.

7,000 years ago, ancient Sumerians divided hours into 60 minutes, and minutes into 60 seconds, not out of thorough calculation but because 60 was the base number they used.

1,500 years later, Egyptians began to divide each day into 24 parts, giving periods of daylight and darkness 12 hours each, but the length of these hours would vary according to the season.

1,200 years later, Babylonians figured out the Egyptian daylight savings time was nuts, making all 24 hours equal.

1,150 years later, in 46BC, Julius Caesar realized the Roman calendar had become out of step with the seasons, thus commissioning Greek astronomer Sosigenes a new one. Sosigenes proposed a 365 day solar calendar with an extra year every four years (our very first leap year).

1,600 years later (or some such), Pope Gregory XIII commissioned a correction of the previous, Julian calendar, shortening the average year by 0.0075 days to stop the drift of the calendar with respect to the equinoxes. This is the calendar used in most Western nations today, with the exception of the Orthodox Church, Berbers, and ... Anabaptists.

EMPEROR OF THE MONTH

All English names for the months of the year have Roman names, but while most relate to Roman festivals, numbers, and deities, two derive from historical figures.

January: Named after Janus, god of gateways!

February: Named after the festival of purification known as *Februa*.

March: Inspired by Mars, god of war.

April: After the ancient Aphrodite festival.

May: Celebrated Greek goddess of the earth, Maia.

June: After Juno, the goddess of marriage and wife to Jupiter.

July: Owes its name to none other than Julius Caesar, also to blame for the Western calendar.

August: The first emperor of the Roman empire, Augustus (63BC–14AD) had the Sextilis ("sixth") month named after himself.

On September, October, November, and December creativity apparently died in the Roman Empire, which named them Septem ("seven"), Octo ("eight"), Novem ("nine"), and Decem ("ten") respectively.

YOU SAY YOU WANT A REVOLUTION

The aims of the 1789 French Revolution went far beyond the political. As the movement radicalized it also tried to deeply subvert the country's cultural foundations, including the names of the months passed down since Roman times.

Vendémiaire (from *vendange*: grape harvest), starting in late September.

Brumaire (from *brume*: mist), starting in late October.

Frimaire (From *frimas*: frost), starting in late November.

Nivôse (from Latin *nivosus*: snowy), starting in late December.

Pluviôse (from *pluvieuse*: rainy), starting around January 20.

Ventôse (from *venteux*: windy), starting around February 20.

Germinal (from *germer*: germinate), starting around March 20.

Floréal (from *fleur*: flower), starting around April 20.

Prairial (from prairie), starting around May 20.

Messidor (from Latin *messis*: harvest), starting around June 20.

Thermidor (from Greek *thermon*: summer heat), starting around July 20.

Fructidor (from Latin *fructus*: fruit), starting on August 18.

Ironically, "Thermidor" survives as the designated term for the fall of the revolutionary French left, and in particular the end of the Reign of Terror with the guillotine execution of Maximilien Robespierre (1758-1794); "Thermidorian Reaction" standing for the undoing of all radical leftist measures and the return of traditional values, month names included!

DAYS OF OUR LIVES

While calendar years and months have pretty much been set in stone since the days of the Roman Empire, there seems to be no consensus as to the naming of the days of the week. The English language, however, has settled on the following.

Monday comes from old English *mon(an)dæg*, or day of the moon.

Tuesday comes from old English *tiwesdæg*, or Tiw's day—Tiw or Tyr being the old Germanic god of war.

Wednesday comes from old English *wodnesdæg*, or Woden's day—the eponymous Woden being the Anglo-Saxon's main god (akin to Odin).

Thursday comes from old Norse's *thorsdagr*, or Thor's day—the mighty Thor needs no introduction, does he?

Friday comes from the old English *frigedæg*, or Freya's day—after the German and Norse goddess of love.

Saturday, from old English *sæterdæg*, meaning Saturn's day, kept the Roman gods connection intact.

Sunday comes from the old English *sunnandæg*, or "day of the sun," and remains as such in almost every language. While most cultures rooted in Christianity keep it as a holiday, for Eastern cultures it is, in fact, the first day of the week!

WHITE RABBIT

The passage of time holds different meanings for different people and cultures, but almost all have devised mechanical contraptions allowing them to keep track of it—enter, the clock!

1. The earliest known sundials existed from ancient Babylon to the northern Black Sea (modern day Russia) around 1500BC.

2. The earliest written account of a sundial (700BC) may be found in the Bible (Isaiah 38:8 and 2 Kings 20:9)!

3. The oldest water clock dates to around 1417-1379BC, and it was located in the Temple of Amen-Re at Karnak, in Ancient Egypt.

4. Classical Greece was no stranger to complex mechanisms. Its *clepsydra* ("water thief") water clocks introduced indicator dials and pointers, and were often used to time conferences and speeches both in Greece and in Rome.

5. Faced with the problem of evaporation, which made water clocks unreliable, Ancient China experimented with liquid mercury (c.976AD) and sand (c.1360AD).

6. The first documented example of an hourglass being used dates from eighth century France, technological progress making them common use by the fourteenth century all over Europe, in particular aboard ships, where they were known as *horologes*.

7. The verge escapement (crown wheel) invention in thirteenth century Europe led to the development of the first all-mechanical clocks in the fourteenth century, which were called *horologia* ("to tell time" in Greek).

8. Gradually superceding *horologia*, the word clock comes from the Celtic *clocca* and *clogan*, which mean "bell," as early mechanical clocks are indeed placed mainly in church towers, to signal the timing of prayer and public religious events.

9. As it often happens with technology, in time mechanical clocks got smaller and more accurate. Christiaan Huygens's (1629-1695) invention of the pendulum clock in 1656 brought clocks indoors, while reducing lag from 15 minutes a day to only 15 seconds a day!

10. Canadian Warren Marrison (1896-1980) made the first quartz clock at Bell Telephone Laboratories in 1927, which quickly became the precision standard in science laboratories, and by 1969, Japanese company SEIKO began selling the "Astron"—the world's first commercial quartz wristwatch!

11. First theoretically proposed by American physicist Isidor Rabi (1898-1988), and later constructed by British physicist Louis Essen (1908-1997), Atomic clocks are currently the most accurate known to man, becoming the main standard for international time distribution, and global GPS navigation.

12. In 1999, the Commerce Department's National Institute of Standards and Technology activated the the NIST-F1 Cesium Fountain Clock, an atomic clock so accurate it will neither gain nor lose a second in 20 million years!

CONSTANT MOTION (PART 1)

The invention of writing is the invention of history, for writing allowed us to record human events in sequence, greatly helping us identify those pivotal moments when the whole of mankind's existence took a turn or changed track with lasting consequences for all.

c.7000BC: *Çatalhöyük*, the first city of the world is established in what we now call Turkey.

c.3500BC: Uruk and Ur, first modern city states, established in Sumeria (modern day Irak).

c.3000BC: Upper and lower Egypt kingdoms united.

c.2500-1500BC: Indus valley (modern day India) civilization rises and falls.

c.2371BC: The Akkadian Empire begins trading with India.

c.2065BC: Egypt and Crete start trade relations (which, among other things, would bring domestic cats to Europe).

c.1758BC: Hammurabi (c.1810-1750BC) publishes an extensive legal code, the first of its kind.

c.1580BC: Starting out as commercial middlemen between Egypt and Asia, Phoenicians trade all over the Mediterranean, establishing trading posts as far as Spain by 884BC. They spread their phonemic

alphabet, which became the basis for all western alphabets still in use today.

c.750-600BC: The Greeks colonize Italy and Sicily, spreading their language and culture all the way up to modern day France and Spain.

c.500BC: Democracy is firmly set in Athens. Other Greek city-states soon follow suit, while a republic is established in Rome.

c.530BC: Prince Siddartha Gautama's followers found Buddhism in India and spread it throughout Asia.

490-480BC: A first Persian invasion of Greece is defeated at Marathon, while a second one gets halted at Thermopylae by 300 Spartans. By 449BC Persians have no choice but to sign a peace treaty with the Greeks.

336BC: Alexander The Great (356-323BC) becomes king of Macedon, and proceeds to conquer Asia all the way to northern India. Without natural heirs, his empire fragments soon after his death.

c.325BC: Greek mariner and explorer Pytheas of Massalia (c.350-285BC) becomes the first to document visits to Britain, Ireland, and Iceland, describing the Arctic, polar ice, and tides.

163BC: The Maccabees successfully revolt against the Hellenistic (Greek-influenced) Seleucid Empire established after the division of Alexander's empire and secure an independent Judea.

27BC: Octavian Augustus (63BC-14AD) becomes sole ruler of the new Roman Empire.

JUGGERNAUT

While commonly depicted as relatively modern, mechanical devices powered to perform an intended action have been a staple of human invention since the dawn of time!

Abacus: First appearing around 2700BC in ancient Sumeria, this calculating device quickly made its way to Europe, China, and Russia.

Nebra Sky Disk: The oldest depiction of the night sky (1600BC) known to man, it was discovered and illegally dug out of a German prehistoric enclosure in 1999. It is made of bronze, with gold and copper inlays.

Trundholm sun chariot: Found in Denmark, this 1400BC Bronze Age metal sculpture of a horse towing a gilded disk on spoked wheels may have been used as an orbital calendar!

Antikythera mechanism: This ancient clockwork (37 gear wheels) computer was used in 87BC to follow the movement and orbit of the Sun and the Moon through the zodiac, as well as tracking the Olympic Games' cycles and other events.

Cotton gin: Handheld, rolling engines made to quickly and easily separate cotton fibers from seeds, have been in use at least since the fifth century in India.

South-pointing Chariot: This Chinese invention was used to used to pinpoint the southern cardinal direction without magnetism, it's earliest description on record dating back to the third century.

Vending Machine: Greek mathematician and engineer Hero of Alexandria (c.10-70AD) is credited for inventing a holy water dispenser for temples, which could be activated by dropping a coin into a slot.

Aeolipile: Hero also came up with this steam-powered turbine device made to propel chariots!

Quipu: Fashioned from cotton or llama fur strings, these were recording devices used by ancient Andean civilizations such as the Inca, for tax collection, census data, calendar information, and military supply management. They used a decimal numbering system encoded in knots!

Water-powered organ: The Banū Mūsā brothers from Baghdad invented this automatic hydraulic music machine in the ninth century, as well as an programmable steam-powered flute.

Automatons: Arab polymath Al-Jazari (1136–1206) engineered the first animatronic female servants which could serve drinks and pour water to wash a person's hands, as well as a band which could be programmed to play different musical compositions!

BONUS FACT!

- Despite ample evidence to the contrary, refusing to believe he could smell bad, Steve Jobs (1955-2011) would not bathe or shower while undergoing a strict vegetarian diet.

CONSTANT MOTION
(PART 2)

Greco-Roman rational thinking and Judeo-Christian ethic idealism would merge to shape the European world at large, while its contact and clashes with Asia expanded mankind's horizons down unforeseen paths.

c.0-40AD: Jesus of Nazareth is born, preaches to the Jewish people a new gospel of hope, and is crucified in Jerusalem (Judea). His followers begin spreading the new faith.

70-73AD: A Jewish revolt suppressed by Roman forces, which destroy the Jerusalem Temple. Masada, the last Jewish stronghold, would fall three years later.

122AD: Roman emperor Hadrian (76-138AD) halts the empire's territorial expansion, issuing an age of great prosperity.

306AD: Constantin the Great (c.272-337AD), proclaimed Roman emperor in York, England. He would found Constantinople (now Istanbul) 24 years later.

381AD: Theodosius I (347-395AD) establishes Christianity as the official religion, banning paganism completely in 391AD.

395AD: The Roman empire is forever split in two.

410-486AD: Italy invaded and plundered by successive waves of Visigoths, Huns, Vandals, and Franks.

622-711AD: Arab prophet Muhammad (570-632AD) and his followers begin to wage war against nonbelievers, conquering surrounding territories all the way to North Africa and Spain.

732AD: Charles Martel (c. 688-741AD) cuts the Muslim conquest short in Poitiers. His grandson, Charlemagne (748-814AD), would end up becoming Holy Roman Emperor in 800 AD.

c.780-1000AD: Scandinavian "Vikings" begin raiding, trading, and settling all over Europe, and even—briefly—across the Atlantic, in modern day Canada.

1096-1187: Norman and French crusaders help defeat the Turks in Constantinople, before freeing Jerusalem from Muslims, but it is ultimately retaken by Sultan Saladin (1137-1193).

1206-1223: Genghis Kahn (1162-1227) creates the second largest contiguous empire across Eurasia, which would bring the Silk road into one cohesive rule, enabling commerce between East and West.

c.1300: Marco Polo's (1254-1324) *Book of the Marvels of the World*, accounting his trade journeys to India, China, and Sumatra, becomes a medieval best-seller.

1338: Ashikaga Takauji (1305-1358) proclaims himself Shōgun (warlord), launching Japanese feudalism and military rule from Kyoto.

1347-1351: The bubonic plague ("Black Death") epidemic wipes out one-fourth of the entire European population.

DESTROYER OF WORLDS

Humanity's penchant for creation is only matched by its tendency to destroy, not only the planet it lives on, but also the fruits of the ingenuity, artistry, and hard labor of ages past.

Parthenon: Built around 432BC, this temple on the Athenian Acropolis (Greece) proudly stood in perfect shape for centuries, until Ottoman Turks used it as a gunpowder warehouse during the 1683-1699 Great Turkish War. Needless to say, a mortar blew it up, killing 300 people, and turning it into the picturesque ruin we see today. The remaining marble statues were promptly sent to England by the British occupying Greece during 1801.

Persepolis: The religious capital of the Achaemenid Empire was leveled and scorched by Alexander The Great (c.356-323BC) and his army, which held a large symposium (banquet) afterwards to celebrate it.

Artemision: Considered one of the ancient wonders of the world, the Temple of Artemis in Ephesus (modern day Turkey) was once destroyed by a flood and then rebuilt ... only to be torched by an arsonist named Herostratus in 356BC, who wished to be remembered by this (he got his wish). Fortunately, Ephesians managed to rebuild it, bigger and better than before, and it stood for hundreds of years (despite some Goths raiding it in 268AD), until its closure in later years saw it fall in disrepair and be vandalized until little of it was left.

Library of Antioch: Established circa 221BC, it was burned to the ground by Christian Emperor Jovian (331-364AD) in 363AD, but instead of gaining Christian favor, his act was deemed barbaric by both Christians and pagans living in the city.

Troy: This ancient city of Homer's *Illiad* (c.1260) was "sandwiched" in between nine other settlements piled on top of each other since time immemorial, but that didn't stop German businessman and amateur archeologist Heinrich Schliemann (1822-1890) from "digging" it up using dynamite.

Buddhas of Bamyan: These gigantic sixth century statues carved directly on sandstone cliffs in modern day Afghanistan territory, have been the target of repeated attacks by iconoclast Muslims, until *Taliban* radicals finished the job in 2001, over several weeks of artillery fire and finally blowing what was left to pieces.

Nohmul: Formerly an important Pre-Columbian site in the Yucatán Peninsula, it used to include a 250BC, 56 foot tall Mayan pyramid which was destroyed in 2013 by contractors looking for gravel to fill roads, which in itself would be sad if tearing down monumental archeology wasn't common practice in Belize at this point.

Mask of Tutankhamun: This world-famous gold mask from 1323BC was accidentally dropped by Cairo's Egyptian Museum employees in 2014 when taking it out of its display for cleaning. Its lapis lazuli beard falling off, the employees super-glued it back on … backwards. Fortunately, capable German restorers managed to get it fixed after two years of painstaking labor.

In 2020, a frenzy of iconoclasm shook the US, as misguided "activists" defaced and knocked down monuments deemed controversial, which ironically included statues of founding father George Washington (1732-1799), Ulysses S. Grant (1822-1885), the man who defeated the Confederacy, and Saint Junípero Serra (1713-1784) who, according to the *Washington Post*, "… died a beloved figure, mourned by indigenous people and Spaniards alike."

CONSTANT MOTION (PART 3)

The most significant invention since fire and writing, Johannes Gutenberg's (1400-1468) printing press would propel humanity into the future.

1455-1485: The War of the Roses wipes out the male lines of both Yorks and Lancasters, leaving the Welsh Tudors in charge.

1479-1492: In Spain, Isabella I of Castille (1451-1504) and Ferdinand II of Aragon (1452-1516) marry, and successfully manage to both rid Spain from Muslim rule, and fund the Christopher Columbus (1451-1506) expeditions across the Atlantic Ocean, which would result in the European discovery and colonization of the Americas.

1517: Martin Luther (1483-1546) mails his 95 Theses to Archbishop Albert of Mainz (1490-1545), while also nailing them to the door of the All Saints' Church in Wittenberg, a University custom to inspire public debate. It did way more than that, sparking the Protestant Reformation all over Europe.

1519-1521: Aided by locals and a smallpox epidemic, Hernán Cortés (1485-1547) defeats the Triple Alliance of Aztec city-states, notably Tenochtitlan (modern day Mexico City).

1519-1522: Ferdinand Magellan (1480-1521) leads an expedition to find a southward passage (the Magellan Strait) to the Pacific Ocean (which he named), eventually reaching the Philippines in Asia, where he died. The journey around the world is barely completed by Juan Sebastián Elcano (c.1476-1526) in one of the original five ships that originally set sail in 1519.

1532: King Henry VIII (1491-1547) of England defies the papacy by divorcing Queen Catherine of Aragon (1485-1536) and marrying Anne Boleyn (c.1501-1536), whom he crowned queen in 1533. The churches of Rome and England split as a result of this, the latter veering from Catholicism towards its own Reformation.

1533: Francisco Pizarro (c.1471-1541) reaches *Tawantinsuyu*, an advanced South American civilization already ravaged by a smallpox epidemic, which had spread south from Cortés's Mexico resulting in chaos and a civil war. Imprisoning and executing its young Inca (emperor), Atahualpa (c.1502-1533), Pizarro seizes the empire in a single stroke.

1618-1648: A deadly continental conflict known as the Thirty Years' War, which would engulf Europe from Spain to Sweden, is triggered when enraged Bohemian Protestants throw two Catholic governors out of a castle window in Prague.

1620: Puritan Separatists (later called Pilgrims) leave Plymouth, England, aboard the Mayflower, and found the Plymouth colony upon arrival to America, possibly atop an earlier Patuxet village, its original population already decimated by imported European smallpox.

1733: John Kay (1704-1779) patents the flying shuttle, a device which allowed for the mechanization of textile looms, speeding up production while cutting labor in half, starting the Industrial Revolution!

1775-1783: Emboldened by the ideals of the Enlightenment, the American Revolution led to the creation of a new independent nation, the United States of America, while inspiring similar revolutions all over the world.

CONSTANT NECK PAIN

A staple of human culture for tens of thousands of years, statues are free-standing sculptural representations of people, animals, or deities, which come in all sizes, from statuettes and figurines to the truly monumental, the biggest of which are listed below.

10. The Motherland Calls!: Unveiled in 1967, it is part of the "Heroes of the Battle of Stalingrad" monument in Volgograd, Russia. At 279 feet, it's the tallest in Europe, and the tallest female depiction in the world!

9. Dai Kannon: Yet another depiction of the Buddhist goddess, this one stands at 289 feet, and is Japan's third largest statue. It opened in 1989, in Hokkaido (Japan).

8. Grand Buddha: This 289 feet bronze celestial Buddha unveiled in 1996, towers over the town Wuxi (China).

7. Great Buddha: Sitting at 302 feet high by 210 feet wide, this gold-painted concrete Buddha was completed in 2008, and may be found in Ang Thong, Thailand.

6. Guishan Guanyin: An impressive bronze representation of Avalokitesvara (embodiment of the compassion of all Buddhas) stands with its many outstretched arms at 325 feet over the Weishan Township (China).

5. Sendai Daikannon: Yet another Kannon statue, this one is really tall at 330 feet, its massive concrete structure unveiled in Sendai (Japan) back in 1991.

4. Ushiku Daibutsu: Located in Ushiku, Ibaraki Prefecture, Japan, and standing 330 foot tall (390 feet, if counting its base and lotus-shaped platform), it houses a four-story museum, and was considered the world's biggest statue from 1993 till 2018.

3. Laykyun Sekkya: A 380 foot tall monumental statue of Buddha (him again?), located in the city of Monywa (Myanmar) it was unveiled in 2008.

2. Spring Temple Buddha: A 420 foot copper-plate Buddha, it stands above a monastery in Lushan (China), but its lotus platform and base bring it up to around 682 feet!

1. Statue of Unity: The world's biggest statue is a standing depiction of Deputy Prime Minister Sardar Vallabhbhai Patel (1875-1950) located in India. A modern concrete and steel marvel, it measures 597 feet and was built to withstand strong winds and even earthquakes.

Perhaps not the tallest but certainly the most influential, the Christ The Redeemer (98 ft) statue in Rio de Janeiro (Brazil), has inspired copycat versions in Bolivia, Indonesia, Peru, Philippines, Poland, and even a 67 foot tall "cousin" in the Ozarks!

BONUS FACT!

- Firmenich, Givaudan, Symrise, International Flavors and Fragrances (IFF), Frutarom, and Takasago International, are the companies currently making all the smells and flavors in the world, for everything we purchase including food, beverages, clothing, cosmetics, cars, and even sex toys!

CONSTANT MOTION (PART 4)

With unprecedented technological progress, rather than simple economics, the biggest conflicts in mankind's modern history would be sparked by ideological turmoil.

1861-1865: Civil War erupts in the US. Victory for the North is sour, as President Lincoln (1809-1865) is assassinated in its aftermath.

1867: Karl Marx (1818-1883) publishes the first volume of *Capital*, his influential analytical treatise on the relationship between society, economics, and politics, which split the world in half during the twentieth century, and is even debated to this day.

1881-1914: One of mankind's highest engineering achievements, the Panama Canal would open a new era of faster international trade.

1893: New Zealand becomes the first country to allow women to vote.

1900: Austrian neurologist Sigmund Freud (1856-1939) founds psychoanalysis.

1914-1918: Sparked by the assassination of Archduke Franz Ferdinand (1863-1914) by Bosnian radicals, World War I became one of the deadliest wars in history, reshaping the balance of power all over the world.

1917-1923: Weakened by World War I, Russian government was eventually overtaken by grassroots Marxist political organizations known as Soviets, which won over the armed forces.

The radical Soviet Bolshevik faction would ultimately seize control, and form a completely new country: the Soviet Union.

1918: The Spanish Flu Pandemic infected 500 million people, killing up to 100 million by some estimates. It was particularly deadly among young adults (most of whom were left in extremely dire living conditions after the end of the war).

1921-1943: While among the allied nations which had won WWI, an Italy demoralized by the conflict saw the birth of the ultra-nationalist, militaristic Fascist Party led by Benito Mussolini (1883-1945), which would impose its rule over the country while managing to successfully rebuild the economy.

1921-1945: Inspired by Mussolini's success in Italy, but giving it his own racist spin, Adolf Hitler (1889-1945) models his Nazi Party after the Fascists, seizing German power by 1933.

1925-1928: John Logie Baird (1888-1946) carries the first experimental wireless television transmission, and three years later the first one across the Atlantic.

1927: The fifth Solvay Conference in Brussels (Belgium) takes place, gathering the most notable and revolutionary physicists of the day, including Albert Einstein (1879-1955) and Neils Bohr (1885-1962).

1928-1933: The five-year development plan turns the USSR into the second most industrialized nation on Earth.

1929: A stock market crash triggers the Great Depression worldwide, severely striking down globalized Western markets.

THE LITTLE PRINCE

Thirty-six thousand years ago, humans began selectively breeding a now extinct species of wolf into what we now call dogs, thus beginning the domestication of the natural world around us, which would eventually bring agriculture and civilization about. Species created by mankind for the most varied uses, from sustenance to companionship, include:

Dogs: Two human skeletons and other bone remains were found in 1914 in a quarry at Bonn (Germany). The other remains turned out to be one of the first domesticated dogs on record at 14,500 years old!

Cats: The only feline species to be partly domesticated, house cats were kept around Asian households 7,500 years ago, possibly to hunt grain-eating rodents, but we only began to breed them about 200 years ago.

Poultry: Domesticating cliff doves into pigeons as a source of meat began 10,000 years ago, while domesticated chicken came much later, about 7,000 years ago. It has been found chicken were bred for cockfighting in China, as far back as 5,400BC!

Cattle: Aurochs were domesticated separately by different human societies in the near east (10,500 years ago), the far east and India (10,000 years ago), and Africa (8,500 years ago).

Llamas and alpacas: Domesticated from *guanacos* and *vicuñas* respectively, these grazing camelids were domesticated along the South American Andes mountain range between 7,000 and 5,500 years ago.

Horses: Domesticated as early as 3,500 years ago by the Botai culture in modern day Kazakhstan, and the Yamnaya culture in modern day Ukraine, the impact of the horse in the development of Eurasian civilization is simply immeasurable!

Bees: Partly domesticated by humans, which began collecting their honey 7,000 years ago, modern beekeeping became an institution around the eighteenth century, when people figured out a way to collect honey without destroying the hives and the insects themselves: the movable comb hive.

Plants: Plant domestication is thought to have begun with rye, 11,000 years ago in modern day Syria. 10,000-8,000 years ago the calabash gourd followed (it was a useful container bottle) all over the world (including the Americas), and 9,000 years ago, peas and wheat cultivation began in Mesopotamia.

Corn and potatoes: A high feat of sophisticated artificial selection, maize was domesticated by indigenous peoples in modern day Mexico over 10,000 years ago, and quickly spread through trade north and south of the Americas, becoming a staple of the pre-Columbian diet. The same happened to potatoes, which originated in modern day Peru, 7,000-10,000 years ago.

BONUS FACT!

- *Aphonopelma johnnycashi* is a species of tarantula discovered near Folsom Prison in 2015, and appropriately named after the legendary singer Johnny Cash (1932-2003).

LITTLE ANIMAL, BIG WORLD

Human trade and exploration first introduced exotic animal species into virgin ecosystems for profit, but nineteenth century voluntary acclimatization societies in particular sought to "terraform" the New World into something akin to Europe, with disastrous consequences.

1859: Thomas Austin (1815-1871) bred gray hares and domestic rabbits in his Melbourne estate as game for hunting parties. The offspring of said rabbits adapted so well to Australian soil they became a plague of Biblical proportions, destroying pasture, plants, and even trees! Desperate Australians have tried everything, from fences to viruses, to keep them at bay, with little effect.

1876: Not all invasive species came from the Old World to the New. The American eastern gray squirrel was brought to Britain where it quickly put the native red squirrel at risk, not only by competing for the same living space, but also through disease. In 1948, it was introduced to the continent and quickly spread across the Alps, all the way down to Italy!

1889: Argentinian nutria were first introduced to the US by American fur traders, but when that market tanked in the forties the orange-toothed rodents were released, quickly multiplying, and devastating wetlands all the way to California!

1890: Shakespeare aficionado Eugene Schieffelin's (1827-1906) initial release of 60 English starlings in Central Park (New York, USA), came at the cost of many native bird species who saw their tree niches reduced dramatically by the rapidly spreading invaders (which these days count over 200 million). Not happy with that, Schieffelin also imported bullfinches, chaffinches, nightingales, and skylarks to America!

1935: Released in Australia in hopes it would curb the cane beetle plague, South American burly and highly venomous cane toads created an even bigger pest problem, breeding like crazy and spreading all across the nation, which now houses 1.5 billion of them, killing off any predators (mainly snakes, goannas, and crocodiles) who make the mistake of ingesting them.

1946: Attempting to jumpstart a local fur industry, the Argentinian government imported 50 Canadian beavers, but having no natural predators in South America (bears!), they quickly spread all the way south to Tierra del Fuego and Chile, where they've destroyed an estimated 40,000,000 acres of native tree forests.

1956: When Warwick Estevam Kerr (1922-2018) imported bees from Tanzania to Brazil as part of a breeding experiment aimed at increasing honey production, he never suspected the 26 bees that escaped his lab would indeed crossbreed with every Western honey bee they came across, producing an aggressive new species of "killer bees" which would finally reach the US in 1985!

BONUS FACTS!

- Lenin's (1870-1924) embalmed body still on display in Moscow, is now made mostly of wax.

- John Stuart Mill (1806-1873) was intensively home-schooled by his Dad, who taught him Greek at three, Latin and geometry by the time he was eight, and logic at 12 years of age, all of which surely led to his nervous breakdown at 20!

CONSTANT MOTION (PART 5)

Seeing the success of thriving socialist and fascist economies, many western European countries trapped in the throes of deep financial depression, or civil war, would seek alliances with authoritarian regimes, or turn to increasingly strong forms of government themselves, leading to catastrophe.

1936-1939: Aided by Nazi Germany, Spanish Generalissimo Francisco Franco (1892-1975) overthrows the leftist republican government after a bloody civil war. Staying in power for decades, he would shrewdly keep Spain out of the ensuing World War II, while subsequently cozying up to the winning allied powers after it.

1939-1945: The deadliest conflict in human history at around 100 million casualties, World War II needs no introduction. Waged mainly between the militaristic authoritarian regimes of Italy, Germany, and Japan, a.k.a. the "Axis," which at first invade Ethiopia, China, and Poland. The slow response of a weakened League of Nations prompts further and more daring military invasions and overtaking of overseas colonies. Britain stands alone in its defiance for two years, until the US and the USSR join her two years later, finally squashing the Axis powers between them.

1945: Despite political division, the newly formed United Nations begins operations.

1947-1991: The Cold War, tense 50-year-period of rivalry, espionage, and proxy armed conflicts or coups, is staged between the two main powers left standing after WWII, the USA and the USSR. The idea of mutually assured nuclear destruction keeps them away from each other's throats, until the collapse of the Soviet Union in 1991.

1947: The General Agreement on Tariffs and Trade (GATT) paves the way for a new global market economy, leading to the formation of common markets in Europe, Africa, and South America between 1955 and 1970.

1947-1948: The European Jewish Holocaust survivors refugee crisis resulting from World War II leads Britain to finally abandon their mandate over the overflowing Palestine region in 1947, allowing leader David Ben-Gurion (1886-1973) to effectively organize and formally establish a new independent State of Israel the next year.

1949-1990: Perhaps the most terrible symbol of the new world order, Germany is divided into two countries, the Capitalist **Federal Republic of Germany**, and the Communist **German Democratic Republic**, with the city of Berlin literally divided by a wall built in 1961. The country would only reunite after the forced fall of said Berlin Wall in 1989.

1957-1969: Fueled by the Cold War, the space race begins with the USSR launching its first artificial satellite, Sputnik 1, followed by the first orbital human flight of Yuri Gagarin (1934-1968) in 1961, and Valentina Tereshkova (b.1937) in 1963. It climaxes with the 1969 American Apollo 11 moon landing which sees astronauts Neil Armstrong (1930-2012) and Buzz Aldrin (b.1930) become the first humans to ever walk on a surface not of planet Earth.

BONUS FACT!

- Ladybugs suffer from their own, widespread STDs.

THE FANTANAZIS

Surrounded by enemies, and struggling to maintain its territorial gains in Europe, Nazi Germany never stopped seeking a technological edge that would grant it victory despite its limited resources, which explains why some of its innovations were so ahead of its time.

Z3 Computer: Konrad Zuse's (1910-1945) line of electromechanical computers reaches its peak with the Z3, the world's first fully programmable universal (Turing-complete) digital computer, which was sadly lost to an Allied bombing in 1943, though a fully functioning replica was made in the 1960s.

Pernkopf Topographic Anatomy of Man: Also known as the Pernkopf Atlas, it is a fully illustrated anatomical treaty in two volumes. While currently out of print, used editions remain largely in use by many specialists today despite digital imaging supposedly rendering it "obsolete" (yup, its art is *that* good), despite its dissection subjects possibly being executed political prisoners of the regime (but not concentration camp inmates, according to the Simon Wiesenthal Center).

Paul Nipkow TV Station: The first public television broadcaster in the world, its coverage of the 1936 Berlin Summer Olympics made it very popular, despite TV sets not being common in German households at the time, so the state's propaganda machine had to set up *Fernsehstuben*, or television parlors, for people to gather around and watch transmissions, which were in fact cable-based rather than wireless!

Chemex: Chemist Peter Schlumbohm (1896-1962) invented what many consider the perfect coffe maker in 1941.

It's basically a conical hourglass, with a neck containing special filters, which is surrounded by a heat-proof wood collar. The product was so revolutionary it made the cover of the New York's Museum of Modern Art (MoMA) bulletin during wartime!

Rocketry and jet propulsion: Developed by leading scientists like Wernher von Braun (1912-1977) and Hans von Ohain (1911-1998) with considerable funding from both the government and the private aeronautic sector, Nazi Germany armed itself with the first long-range missiles (V-1 and V-2), turbojet fighter planes (He 178 and Me 262), and jet-powered bombers (Ar 234) the world ever saw.

***Vampir*:** The first portable infantry night-vision system, the Zielgerät ZG 1229 was introduced in 1944, but only saw combat in 1945. It weighed five pounds, of mainly the batteries which powered its infrared light and image converter.

Ink eraser: Chemical ink eraser was invented by German office and art supplies manufacturer Pelikan during the Nazi Reich, and reintroduced commercially several decades later.

Magnetophon K1: The first high quality magnetic tape recorder was unveiled by the BASF company in 1935. It was developed in cooperation with the *Reichs-Rundfunk-Gesellschaft* (RRG) public radio.

Fanta: Foreseeing a blockade which would render the German Coca-Cola subsidiary unable to obtain the beverage's secret syrup, director Max Keith (b.1903-?) developed Fanta in 1940. Originally an apple-flavored soft drink, it is still massively popular today!

NOBODY EXPECTS...

Few institutions in the history of mankind elicit as much dread as the Inquisition, but its existence has been fictionalized to the point nobody really knows what it was about, so the time is due to separate fact from myth!

1. It began in 1231 Germany, not Spain, when the priest Konrad von Marburg (1180-1233) was commissioned by the Pope to counter religious dissent from Albigensians. Von Maburg would recruit Dominican preachers to assist him and cover greater ground.

2. Originally, appointed Inquisitors would arrive to town unexpected (pun intended), announce their presence, and publicly denounce heresy. Open trials were conducted in secular courts, but punishments were largely symbolic (prayer, pilgrimage).

3. Soon the Inquisition practice caught on and spread throughout Europe. It became a permanent territorial institution, attending local matters (in France it fought the Waldensians, in the Netherlands the Beghards, and so on).

4. By the fourteenth and fifteenth centuries, the Spanish, Portuguese, and Roman Inquisitions were the biggest, most powerful of all.

5. In Spain and Portugal's case, their power extended to the New World as well.

6. Despite fearsome depictions in popular culture, by the fourteenth century an Inquisition trial was a lengthy and meticulous affair, subject to revisions, and appeals (even directly to the Pope himself).

7. The accused could not confront the witnesses against them (to avoid any acts of revenge) but they could also present witnesses in their defense. Accusing witnesses who lied were harshly punished, if anything, for wasting the Inquisition's time.

8. Even when the Inquisition judges (two of them) found someone guilty of heresy, they still needed the review and approval of both the bishop, and a council of clerics and laymen of good repute before passing sentence.

9. And yet, the sentence wasn't carried by the Inquisition itself, but by the State. Surprisingly, neither life imprisonment nor death penalty were the norm. It is estimated that only about a tenth of those judged guilty were subject to capital punishment. Galileo Galilei (1564-1642), for instance, got his life sentence commuted to house arrest, and was free to carry on with his work.

10. While Reformed Christians of the day used to point out the wrongs of the Inquisition, the Reformation did in fact apply a far harsher persecution of heresy in its domains, including the burning of "witches," which the Inquisition considered nothing but folk superstition.

BONUS FACTS!
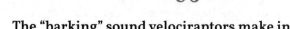

- The "barking" sound velociraptors make in the 1993 film, *Jurassic Park*, was taped from mating zoo tortoises.

- The word "robot," *robota*, was coined by Czech writer Karel Čapek (1890-1939), and means "forced labor."

CAN I PLAY WITH MADNESS

Bad things happen when certified nutjobs come to power. Hitler notwithstanding, here's some of the most notorious among demented rulers:

Emperor Qin Shi Huang (259-210BC): He was the first emperor of a united China, but sadly also suffered from extreme thanatophobia (fear of death), leading him on mad quests to find the "elixir of life," book-burning to have his best scholars exclusively focus on making him immortal, and sometimes scholar-burning too, if they failed to produce results.

Justin II (520-578AD): A vain, egotistical Byzantine emperor, Justin began to fall prey to schizophrenia when the house of cards he had built began to fall around him and his crumbling, indebted empire.

Charles VI (1368-1422): This French king went from being called "the Beloved" to "the Mad" for good reason: a psychotic outburst had him attack his own chamberlains and soldiers while on campaign, killing some and wounding others, until he was restrained and went catatonic for a while. Other episodes followed, ranging from claiming to be amnesiac, believing himself to be Saint George, or suffering from a popular collective hysteria at the time, known as the "glass delusion."

Eric XIV (1533-1577): A noted suitor of Queen Elizabeth I (1533-1603), the Swedish king had a strained relationship with the aristocracy which spiraled into full-blown paranoia, killing several noblemen he had imprisoned (one of them by his own hand) in the Uppsala Castle. Confronted by his tutor, he had him killed as well, before disappearing into a nearby forest. Later on he was found wandering a village, dressed in rags.

Brought back and nursed by his wife to an apparent recovery, a fit of rage saw him stab his secretary with a fire iron, which sparked a rebellion that ultimately deposed, imprisoned, and eventually executed him by poisoning.

Sultan Ibrahim (1615-1648): Suffering from strange migraines all his life, this eccentric Ottoman ruler had a fat fetish, making the biggest of his concubines Governor of Damascus. He was also noted feeding coins to fish. His extravagances got out of hand and so did his government, to the point his own mother, Sultan Kösem Sultan (c. 1589-1651) had to stage a coup against him!

Ferdinand I (1793-1875): Emperor of Austria, President of the German Confederation, and King of Hungary, Croatia and Bohemia among his many titles, Ferdinand the Finished was an epileptic, hydrocephalic inbred with a speech impediment. Lacking any talent to rule ("I am the Emperor, and I want dumplings!" seems to be his only remembered quote), he abdicated in 1848.

Saparmurat Niyazov (1940-2006): Known as *Turkmenbashi*, leader of the people of Turkmenistan, he was an eccentric despot, known to have banned opera, ballet, and the circus, along with makeup, music, and radios. He also renamed bread, and the month of April after his mother: Gurbansoltan!

BONUS FACT!

- Sunflowers are "hyper-accumulators" of toxic metals and therefore get planted around nuclear disaster sites to clean up irradiated soil.

POLITICAL ANIMALS

Local town elections lead to a number of extravagances, when reckless voters choose to satirize the whole process by electing non-human candidates.

Yo-yo (goat): 1922 city councilman of Fortaleza, Brazil.

Boston Curtis (brown mule): 1938 precinct committeeman for Milton, Washington.

Bosco Ramos (dog): 1981 honorary mayor of Sunol, California.

Clay Henry (goat): 1986 mayor of Lajitas, Texas—his grandson, Clay Henry III, was elected mayor in 2002!

Stubbs (cat): 1997 mayor of Talkeetna, Alaska.

Max II (dog): 2014 mayor (for life!) of Idyllwild, California.

Sweet Tart (cat): 2018 mayor of Omena, Michigan.

Lincoln (goat): 2019 mayor of Fair Haven, Vermont.

Rabbit Hash, Kentucky, has been electing dog mayors since Goofy Borneman-Calhoun was elected in 1996. He was succeeded by Junior Cochran in 2004, followed by Lucy Lou, who became the town's first female mayor in 2008. The people of Rabbit Hash would then elect pit bull Brynneth "Brynn" Pawltro as their current mayor in 2016.

REVILED POTUS!

Exceptional presidents may indeed be an exception, but what about the seedier end of the spectrum?

Andrew Johnson (1808-1875) succeeded Abraham Lincoln (1809-1865), but compares poorly to his predecessor. His lax, post-Civil War Reconstruction policies, his stubborn opposition to guaranteeing rights for African Americans, and his moves to remove from public service those who didn't see eye to eye with him, saw him impeached by the House of Representatives. He narrowly avoided conviction and removal from office, many thinking due to bribery means (a talent which may have proven useful when purchasing Alaska).

Theodore Roosevelt (1858-1919) had no shortage of notable detractors. Chief among them, writer Mark Twain (1835-1910) pulled no punches: "Mr. Roosevelt is the most formidable disaster that has befallen the country since the Civil War—but the vast mass of the nation loves him, is frantically fond of him, even idolizes him. This is the simple truth. It sounds like a libel upon the intelligence of the human race, but it isn't; there isn't any way to libel the intelligence of the human race."

William Gamaliel Harding (1865-1923) is usually ranked as the worst in US history. Bringing the infamous "Ohio Gang" of influence peddlers with him to Washington and the White House, his administration was mired by corruption (his interior secretary went to jail for letting private oil companies plunder the US Navy's petroleum reserves, while his attorney general was twice tried!).

Ronald Wilson Reagan (1911-2004) was loved by public opinion, but is also remembered as a supporter of friendly dictators overseas,

such as Saddam Hussein, Ferdinand Marcos, and Manuel Noriega (for a while). He also notably vetoed the Senate's Anti-Apartheid Act of 1986. At home, he opposed a farm credit bill that would have cut US farmers some respite from seeing their properties foreclosed, while also cutting funds on AIDS research. His administration saw over 130 officials (including cabinet members) investigated for, indicted for, or convicted of corruption crimes, many of whom he later pardoned.

Donald J. Trump (b.1946) has raised more than a few Democrat eyebrows since elected. Equally controversial out of the political arena, he has won The Golden Raspberry Award (or "Razzie") for his cameo in the film *Ghosts Can't Do It* (1989), as well as a double 2019 win for being featured in documentaries *Death of a Nation* (2018) and *Fahrenheit 11/9* (2018). He also made a cameo appearance in *Home Alone 2* (1992), and is a 2013 WWE Hall of Fame inductee!

BONUS FACTS!

- Cute elephants, pandas, koalas, hippos and gorillas are known to indulge in *coprophagia*—they eat feces!

- The three worst germ-ridden areas in hotel rooms include the bedspreads, carpets and hot-tub, in that order.

- The South African police has the only Occult Related Crimes Unit in the world, formed in 1992 to combat ritual murder.

- Tomatoes are actually berries!

IT'S A MISTAKE

War is waged for a variety of, or rather the accumulation of a number of excuses disguised as "reasons." But make no mistake, violent conflict is never rational, and may be sparked by the most absurd events.

The Jenkins' Ear War (1739-1748): When master mariner Robert Jenkins' (exact birth and death dates unknown) ear was cut off by boarding Spanish seamen in the Caribbean, the incident was used by British politicians and the British South Sea Company to pressure Spain into allowing slave trade in its domains. The following war soon engulfed other countries, and was finally resolved diplomatically, with Britain, thought to be unbeatable at sea, largely abandoning its Caribbean claims, and Spain's grasp on the area strengthened.

The Pastry War (1838-1839): The looting of French-owned shops in Mexico City, including a pastry shop whose owner raised a complaint directly to King Louis-Philippe I (1773-1850), caused the French Navy to seize the city of Veracruz, starting a blockade which was soon joined by the US, until a peace treaty was signed, and the Mexican government committed to pay 600,000 pesos as damages to French citizens … only it never did, leading to another French incursion in 1861.

The Pig War (1859-1874): This border war between the US and the UK took place in the San Juan Islands (between Vancouver and Washington), and began when an American farmer shot a pig owned by an Irish foreman, which he found eating his potatoes. The ensuing conflict between neighbors soon escalated into full-blown military intervention, which only ended when troops from both countries left the island 15 years later.

The Anglo-Zanzibar War (1896): At 38 minutes, it is the shortest war ever recorded. Apparently the Zanzibar Sultanate forgot to ask the British consul for permission after Sultan Khalid was elected to succeed Sultan Hamad. The resulting bombing of the palace saw Khalid quickly exiled, the consul's friend rapidly placed on the throne, and a score of 1,000 locals dead against a single British sailor casualty.

The Golden Stool War (1900): The war between the British and Ashanti empires in Africa began when Sir Frederick Mitchell Hodgson (1851-1925) demanded to take possession of the Golden Stool, considered the very soul of the Ashanti people, for Queen Victoria. He also saw fit not to be relegated to a normal chair but to sit on the stool himself. That's when all hell broke loose, and Hodgson had to be evacuated from Africa as a result.

The Soccer War (1969-1980): Fought briefly between Honduras and El Salvador over soccer 1970 FIFA World Cup qualifier matches, pushing both sore losers into severing diplomatic ties first, and their respective air forces to attack each other next. When a cease-fire was finally reached, 900 Salvadoreans and 2,250 Hondurans had been killed. It took them another decade to sign a formal peace treaty!

The Emu War (1932): An Australian farmer-instigated military operation to cull the emu population in that country surprisingly ended in humiliating human defeat, when emus proved to be far more resilient and tactical than previously thought. Their prolonged guerrilla war continued, leading farmers to request further military intervention (in 1934, 1943, and 1948), which was promptly denied. In the end, however, fences were far more effective than bullets in keeping the resourceful emu away from crops.

THE SWARM

Individuals are usually neurotic and rarely smart, but when two or more gather things can't get any dumber, as attested by the following cases of recent mass hysteria.

1980 Hollinwell Incident: It all began with a juvenile marching band on parade around Nottinghamshire, England, began collapsing on the street. Soon 300 children, and some very immature adults, began to similarly faint, suffering from nausea, headaches and other symptoms.

1983 West Bank Fainting epidemic: Similarly to the Hollinwell Incident, Palestinian schoolgirls and IDF female soldiers began to pass out in towns all over the area. Over 900 were hospitalized.

1988 San Diego Incident: 600 recruits started to breath heavily, leading the US Navy to hospitalize 119 of them, 117 of which were almost immediately released.

1994 Toxic Lady Scare: When Gloria Ramirez (1963-1994) passed from late-stage cervical cancer, various hospital workers who came in contact with her body either fainted, had trouble breathing, or experienced muscle spasms. Five of them were hospitalized, but no actual proof of any real bio-hazard was ever produced.

1995 Milk Miracle: When the "news" spread that a Hindu feeding Lord Ganesha milk in a temple had seen the milk mysteriously vanish, it sparked an idol milk-feeding frenzy among thousands of worshipers.

1999 Belgian Coca-Cola Panic: When 100 students complained to have been made sick by the beverage, it prompted Coca-Cola to recall 30 million units of its beverage from Belgium and northern France, but no evidence was found the product had been tainted in any way.

2001 Bin Laden Itch: In the months following the September 11 terrorist attacks, thousands of elementary school children became afflicted with skin rashes which were blamed on—what else?—terrorism!

2006 Strawberries With Sugar Virus: Another case involving schoolgirls, this time in Portugal, where 300 girls began to experience similar symptoms to a virus storyline in teen drama *Morangos com Açúcar*.

2017 Havana Syndrome: When US embassy officials began to report hearing loss, memory loss, and nausea in the recently reopened embassy in Cuba, it was speculated these symptoms were caused by a new kind of "sonic weapon," which caused a diplomatic row. Yet, when similar reports began to surface later in China, it became apparent the syndrome had "red scare" written all over it.

Recurring collective hysteria incidents include:

- **Tampered Halloween Candy: From razor-blade-filled apples to candy laced with whatever poison or drug imaginable, appropriately scary Halloween treat stories have been circulated among concerned parents since the 1960s.**

- **Day-care sex-abuse hysteria: Starting in the 1980s but continuing to this day, false charges brought upon day-care personnel (usually by a parent anxious about leaving a child with strangers) trigger an awful chain reaction within the whole community.**

SEDUCTION OF THE INNOCENT

No war more absurd, no hysteria greater, than the battle conservative culture has waged against pop culture over decades.

Chess: An 1859 article in the pages of *Scientific American* warned the public on the dangers the ancient board game known as chess posed, by making obsessed children sedentary and single-mindedly ill-fitted for other "healthier" pursuits—an argument applied almost verbatim to video games many decades later!

Paint by Number: When a hobbyist from San Francisco submitted an abstract Palmer Craft Master paint-by-number piece to a local art contest in 1952, and was awarded the third prize by unsuspecting judges, all hell broke loose among the art establishment (who cares about those things), which proceeded to lambast the highly popular kits.

Comics and cartoons: Intent on alerting parents of the effect violent imagery supposedly had on young and impressionable minds, reputed youth psychiatrist Fredric Wertham (1895-1981) wrote his 1954 book, *Seduction of the Innocent*, which led to a U.S. Congressional inquiry into the comic book industry, headed by Carey Estes Kefauver (1903-1963). While Kefauver's subcommittee found no evidence of any such impact, the outrage (which included public burnings of comic books in many towns) was used by some publishers like Marvel, DC, and Archie Comics to take their main competitors, EC Comics and Fawcett Publications, out of business.

Rock and Roll: Long before rock music, Baptist preachers would launch furious pulpit attacks on the blues, or "devil's music," as they called it, which drew crowds away from churches and into juke joints.

It didn't take long for similar accusations to reach the new popular music genre which sprung from blues. Not even The Beatles were safe from occasional public outbursts, while other musicians like The Rolling Stones, KISS, Ozzy Osbourne, and even Marilyn Manson relished the "satanic" (a.k.a. dangerous) reputation which made them a teen magnet for their respective generations.

Dungeons & Dragons: Before the rise of the internet gave overbearing parents something to keep busy with, this enormously popular board game came under scrutiny, triggered by the sensationalist media coverage around the suicide of American teenagers James Dallas Egbert III in 1979, and Irving Lee Pulling in 1982. Despite ample evidence of both kids struggling with depression, their mothers chose to blame D&D, which sparked a nationwide"Satanic Panic."

Harry Potter: The higher the popularity of a given product, the bigger the target on its back, and J.K. Rowling's (b.1965) teen wizard saga is no exception. With "Satanic Panic" back in full swing, early twenty-first century fundamentalists got a big new franchise to aim at, claiming it lures children towards witchcraft and the occult.

BONUS FACTS!

- A touch of the box jellyfish's ten-foot tentacles may cause eight hours of excruciating pain, and even death!

- In 2007, several ancient tombs from 220AD were bulldozed in Nanjing, China, to build an IKEA branch.

FRIENDLY FIRE

There's a simple truth every table games fan knows: the old ones are usually the best. There's a reason for that: mankind hasn't really changed that much since the dawn of civilization when, rather than chop themselves in half over every quibble, people chose to sort things out between them by engaging in scaled down simulacrum competitions of every sort.

Backgammon: One of the oldest games in existence, it bears a semblance of the famed Royal Game of Ur played in Mesopotamia over 6,000 years ago. It's a strategic game which requires each player to race 15 "men" (checkers) counter-clockwise out of the board in order to win. It's modern version dates back to the fourteenth and fifteenth centuries, with one all-American addition (possibly borrowed from Mahjong) from the 1920s: the doubling cube, which allows players to raise the stakes and gamble based on it.

Parcheesi: Dating back to the Pachisi game in India 5,500 years ago,"cross and circle" race games were played by royalty on palace grounds using people as pieces, this is a two to four player game in which each player has to move four pieces across a track from their own nest towards a central area known as "home."

Chess: Another Indian invention, *Chaturanga* was a four player 3,500 year old strategy board game, where pieces used to represent Indian army divisions (elephants, chariots, etc.), but upon reaching Europe through the Silk Road in the middle ages, Normans switched them to queens, rooks, bishops, and the like. Originally a throw of the dice decided which piece to move, but after doing away with that the game took its definitive form, which modern players agree just cannot be improved any further.

Checkers: Also know as Draughts in the UK, it is a two player strategy game with many, many local variations according to each country. Generally speaking, players take turns to move their men diagonally, capturing enemies. When a man reaches the farthest row forward (crownhead) it is crowned king by placing an additional piece on top of it, which gives it the ability to move backwards among other special powers.

Go: An abstract, "territorial" strategy board game for two players, it was invented in China about 2,500 years ago, and has suffered little changes since. It is played by two, on a 19 by 19 grid, where bi-convex stones are slid on to surround up to 361 line intersections and the opponent's stones in the process. Far more complex than chess, the game was slow to spread West, where it finally carved a niche mainly among scientists and intellectuals.

Dominoes: Like card games, dominoes is not a single game but a whole family of them, generally played by two people using a double six-pack of 28 tiles, each one divided in half, and each half featuring zero to six contrasting "pips." It originated in Ancient China around 800 years ago, and by the eighteenth century it had made its way up to Italy (brought either by tradesmen or Christian missionaries) from where it takes its current name, after the Venetian Carnival costume pattern.

Mahjong: Yet another tile games family from China, it is thought to have been developed in that country during the sixteenth century, where it used printed cards, until brought to the New World three centuries later. It was in America where the relatively simple "gin rummy" style game of the East increased its complexity by a number of special hands, elaborate scoring practices and even extra tiles, all 13 (for each player) of which are based on Chinese symbols. The game has many variations ranging from the local to the level of gambling required, but its rules have never been successfully unified.

Dice: Probably derived from knucklebones, these are faceted throwing devices used to generate random numbers, and therefore an element of chance, be them as their own game (Craps), or as an addition to many table games, both classic and modern. The Mesopotamian Royal Game of Ur used tetrahedron-shaped dice, while ancient Egyptians used up to twenty-sided die in their own games which wouldn't be out of place in modern Dungeons & Dragons sets. The modern cubic die, however, known back then as Tesserae, was probably invented in Ancient Rome, 2,000 years ago—while illegal, Romans enjoyed gambling with dice at every occasion they could (*aleam ludere*)!

BONUS FACTS!

- The Strelzyk and Wetzel families managed to escape East Germany (RDA) by building their own hot-air balloon in 1979.

- The Metrication of the United States received a severe blow in 1793 when the ship carrying the government-requested French artifacts that would be used to adopt the metric system was blown off course by a storm and captured by pirates!

- Oreos are perfectly vegan cookies, no trace of dairy found in their dough, nor in their "cream."

- Contrary to popular belief, the Library of Alexandria wasn't burnt, but gradually fell into neglect and disrepair, with no new memberships registered beyond 260AD.

THE OTHER WHITE MEAT

While taboo in most civilized cultures, the practice of partly or fully eating another person (popularly known as cannibalism) isn't just a feature of barbaric faraway cultures or individual deranged lunatics but has been well documented in modern times as well.

1918: Struck by lightning off the coast of Guam, the surviving crew members of the SS Dumaru were left with no choice but to eat the dead after their supplies ran out.

1930: Journalist William Buehler Seabrook (1884-1945) procured a slice of human meat from a Sorbonne hospital intern, which he roasted and ate in order to write an article about the whole culinary experience; he compared it to eating veal.

1939: Seeking to save her eldest son's life via human sacrifices, Leonarda Cianciulli (1894-1970) ritualistically baked the flesh of her victims into cakes she would feed others at tea parties.

1945: Japanese soldiers on Chichi Jima island ate at least five out of eight captured American airmen they had tortured and executed.

1972: The surviving members of Uruguayan high-school rugby who crash-landed and were trapped in the Andes for several months, resorted to eating their dead as a means to survive.

The same year, under similar circumstances but a hemisphere away in the Arctic, Canadian pilot Marten Hartwell (1925-2013), had no choice but to consume the flesh of one of the two passengers who died in the crash, which enabled him to survive until rescued.

1981: A vocational cannibal by his own admission, Issei "Pang" Sagawa (b.1949) killed and devoured a Dutch woman while studying at the Sorbonne. His rich dad apparently got him a great lawyer who got him declared insane, released from prison and deported back to Japan where he achieved celebrity status and, at least for a while, made a living as a writer until a 2013 aneurism put him under his brother's permanent care.

1988: Canadian performance artist Rick Gibson (b.1951) is known to have publically and legally eaten hors d'œuvres made with donated human tonsils and testicles.

2007: Marco Evaristti (b. 1963) is a controversial Chilean artist who served his dinner guests a meatball made from his own liposuction fat.

2011: Kidnapped and tortured by Irish criminals, Brendan Higginbotham (b.1990) was sadistically forced to eat half of his own right ear.

2012: Asexual Japanese chef Mao Sugiyama (b.1990) underwent genital-removal surgery, after which he cooked, garnished, and served his penis, testicles and scrotum to five people, charging 100,000 yen per meal!

BONUS FACT!

- Lucy, the popular *Australopithecus afarensis* found in Ethiopia, apparently fell asleep on a tree branch, and down to her death 3.2 million years ago.

MACHO MAN

A commendable fight for gender equality, feminism is irrefutably the original ideal of enlightened men. Male pioneers of this social movement include:

Plato (c.424-348BC): In his influential 375 dialogue, *The Republic*, he claimed women were as capable as men of ruling the people and fighting wars.

Heinrich Cornelius Agrippa (1486-1535): Rather than equality, the German polymath's 1509 cabalistic treatise, *On the Nobility and Excellence of the Feminine Sex*, argued for female superiority.

François Poullain de la Barre (1647-1723): This former Catholic priest authored two seminal feminist books, *On the Equality of the Two Sexes* (1673) and *On the Education of Ladies* (1674), proclaiming the human mind to be gender-less, and advocating equal education and employment opportunities for women.

Charles-Louis de Secondat, a.k.a. "Montesquieu" (1689-1755): In his *Persian Letters* (1721) satire, this French political philosopher reflects on the importance of both gender fluidity and equality as a key to unlock the fundamental value of any society.

Denis Diderot (1713-1784): A prominent figure of the Enlightenment, he wrote *Memoirs of a Nun* (1796), against the demeaning treatment of women by the Catholic Church.

Jeremy Bentham (1748-1832): As a jurist and social reformer, he advocated equal rights for women, the right to divorce, and even the decriminalization of homosexuality!

Charles Fourier (1772-1837): The reputed socialist thinker supported female individuality and liberation, as well as sexual diversity. He coined the term "feminism" in 1837.

Parker Pillsbury (1809-1898): Minister, abolitionist, and women's rights proponent, Pillsbury is well remembered for Pillsbury drafting the constitution of the American Equal Rights Association in 1865, and co-editing women's rights newsletter "The Revolution" (1868).

John Stuart Mill (1806-1873): Considered one of the most influential nineteenth-century philosophers, this social servant authored the 1869 essay "The Subjection of Women," defending women's emancipation and education, as the only true means for the advancement of society.

Frederick Douglass (1817-1895): An American statesman and social reformer, he reasoned African Americans could not accept the right to vote if women couldn't claim that right too, endorsing the women's suffrage movement.

William Moulton Marston (1893-1947): A writer, psychologist, and innovator, he is perhaps best remembered as the inventor of the polygraph "lie detector," and the creator of feminist icon Wonder Woman (1941), using her comic-book to divulge his liberal views on sexuality.

BONUS FACT!

- Gold and copper are the only metals which aren't colored silver-gray.

"ISMS"

Perhaps humanity's most distinctive trait, far from a dull "social-cultural structural beliefs system" the experience of the sacred we call religion works qualitatively, giving humanity a path, direction, and a sense of worth no other pursuit can match. About 10,000 distinct religions can be found in the world today, but here's a sampler of the ones gathering the most followers:

Christianity: 31.4% of the world currently calls itself Christian or aligns itself with inherited Christian values. Originally stemming from Judaism, it was spread by the followers of Jesus Christ (c.0AD-∞), but as it grew exponentially over centuries, so did its fragmentation along political and doctrinal minutiae, though most of its churches, the Roman Catholic Church being the biggest of them all, adhere to the same core beliefs and the writings of the Bible.

Islam: Spread mainly throughout the Middle East, Africa, and south eastern Asia, its believers make up 24.8% of the world's population, and follow the teachings of prophet-warlord Muhammad (c.570-632AD) and the Quran, their sacred text compiled by Muhammad's companions based on the former's revelations. It has also split over doctrinal differences, its largest denomination being Sunni Islam.

Hinduism: A wide range of religions, beliefs, deities, and philosophies practiced in the Indian subcontinent which began to merge around 500BC, some of its followers (15% of the world's population, but mainly Indian and Nepali) refer to it as *Sanātana Dharma*, or "eternal way." In spite of its diversity, its believers share common practices (yoga), cosmology concepts (karma and *Samsāra*), sacred sites and texts (such as the Vedas).

Buddhism: 7.1% of the world population, mainly in the Far East, Oceania, and North America, follow the teachings of prince Siddhartha Gautama (c.480-400BC), who came to be known as the Buddha, "enlightened one," some two centuries after his passing, his discourses and monastic codes compiled in Suttas by his followers in fifth century BC India, Theravada Buddhism being the oldest and most practiced school of Buddhist thought in the world today. While in the East it is perceived as orthodox, in the West (where it began spreading since the nineteenth century) it still has an aura of "progressive cool" around it.

Chinese folk religion: While China is officially a Communist nation, enough of its people (including immigrants and their descendants) keep a hodgepodge of unified traditions inherited from Buddhism, Taoism, Confucianism, and even Catholicism or Hinduism, to consider it a major religion. Grounded in kinship and belonging rather than belief, and practiced by 5.9% of the world's population—while Judaism, Bahá'í, Sikhism, and Jainism only gather a mere 1% of the world's population between them!

BONUS FACTS!

- Research shows that dressing small kids in superhero outfits improves their perseverance and resilience. It's called the "Batman Effect!"

- As a young man, author Graham Greene (1904-1991) would seek adrenaline rushes by playing "Russian roulette" with a gun he found at home.

BOONDOCK SAINTS

Largely a working-class religion (after all its founder and his followers all applied themselves to distinct known trades to make a living), Christianity adopted saints as protectors of specific crafts and occupations, no job being too small, nor too questionable, not to have its godly patron.

Actors: St. Genesius of Rome (third century AD)

Advertising executives: St. Bernardino of Siena (1380-1444)

Arms dealers: St. Adrian (c. 637-710AD)

Barbers: St. Martin de Porres (1579-1639)

Bartenders: St. Amand (c. 584-679)

Beekeepers: St. Ambrose of Milan (c. 340-397)

Chess players: St. Teresa of Ávila (1515-1582)

Coffee makers and baristas: St. Drogo of Sebourg (1105-1185)

Comedians: St. Lawrence (225-258AD)

Environmentalists: St. Kateri Tekakwitha (1656-1680)

Gamblers: St. Cajetan (1480-1547)

Ice sketers: St. Lidwina of Schiedam (1380-1433)

Murderers: St. Julian the Hospitaller (seventh century AD)

Pawnbrokers: St. Bernardine of Feltre (1439-1494)

Programmers: St. Isidore of Seville (c.560-636AD)

Publishers: St. John Bosco (1815-1888)

Translators: St. Jerome of Stridon (c.347-420AD)

Undertakers: St. Joseph of Arimathea (first century AD)

Woodcarvers: St. Wolfgang of Regensburg (c.934-994AD)

Saint Nicholas of Myra (270-343AD), a.k.a. Santa Claus, was originally the patron saint of thieves and prostitutes!

BONUS FACT!

- Painter Raphael (1483-1520) had a fatal heart attack at 37, during a rowdy, wild night with his mistress, Margarita Luti, a.k.a. *La Fornarina* ("The baker's daughter").

LOVE FOOLOSOPHY

Named by Pythagoras of Samos (c.570-495BC), philosophy (literally "love of wisdom") is the search of truth about the fundamental questions of human existence, branching into aesthetics (beauty), epistemology (knowledge), ethics (morality), logic (reasoning), metaphysics (reality), politics, law, and society. Its most influential schools of thought include:

Dialectics: Meaning "dialogue" in Greek, it is indeed a form of reasoning based on arguments and counter-arguments, espoused by Socrates (c.470-399BC) and his disciple Plato (c.424-348BC), it was picked in the Middle Ages by Thomas Aquinas (1225-1274) and William of Ockham (c.1287-1347), and later influenced Hegelianism, Marxism, and Existentialism.

Platonism: A student of Socrates, Plato's belief in unchanging absolute ideas which model our world, is a major influence in both the modern political system of government, Christianity via St. Augustine (354-430AD), and even feminism!

Aristotelianism: Also known as the Peripatetic school, it was founded by Aristotle (384-322BC), the father of logical reasoning and scientific thought, who influenced Rationalism, Cartesianism and American Objectivism.

Cynicism: Purported by the controversial Diogenes (c.404-323BC), a man who scorned conventional values in favor of virtuous poverty, urging for a return to austere self-sufficiency in balance with nature, greatly influencing Stoicism, early Christianity, Empiricism, American Transcendentalism, and even modern environmentalism.

Taoism: Dating as far back as the fourth century BC, this Chinese philosophical and religious school of thought, generally attributed to the semi-mythical sage Laozi, emphasizes balance and flow in life through flexibility and spontaneity, and is considered a permeating influence on Zen Buddhism, martial arts, Chinese medicine, and even Confucianism.

Confucianism: A system of political thought developed by Confucius (551-479BC) in ancient China, it seeks the achievement of social harmony as the supreme good of mankind, through humanist education and communal effort. Confucius's *Analects* are thought to have influenced Western philosophers Gottfried Wilhelm Leibniz (1646-1716) and Voltaire (1694-1778).

Utilitarianism: Founded by Jeremy Bentham (1748-1832), it's a progressive school of though which asserts the importance of action directed at ensuring individual and collective happiness and well-being. It may be considered an influence on Marxism, modern Humanism, and American Pragmatism.

Darwinism: Rather than a philosophy, it is the scientific theory of biological evolution developed by Charles Darwin (1809-1882) in his massively influential nonfiction book *On the Origin of the Species by Means of Natural Selection, or the Preservation of Favored Races in the Struggle for Life* which, despite its horribly long title, managed to sell out on publication day in 1859, burning through five more editions by 1872!

BONUS FACT!

- Judge Charles Lynch (1736-1796) was known to informally execute British Loyalists—that's where "lynching" comes from!

PHILOSOPHICALLY INCORRECT

Philosophers, of course, have left us with memorable quotes ... none of which are included here.

"Women and people of low birth are very hard to deal with. If you are friendly to them, they get out of hand, and if you keep your distance, they resent it."

—Confucius (551-479BC)

"Trust not a woman when she weeps, for it is her nature to weep when she wants her will." **—Socrates (c.470-399BC)**

"Torture is a kind of evidence which appears trustworthy, because a sort of compulsion is attached to it." **—Aristotle (384-322BC)**

"When you die, it will not be because you are sick, but because you were alive." **—Seneca (c.4BC-65AD)**

"As regards the individual nature, woman is defective and misbegotten, for the active force in the male seed tends to the production of a perfect likeness in the masculine sex; while the production of woman comes from a defect in the active force or from some material indisposition, or even from some external influence."
—Thomas Aquinas (1225-1274)

"The condition of man ... is a condition of war of everyone against everyone." **—Thomas Hobbes (1588-1679)**

"A woman can keep one secret: the secret of her age."
—**Voltaire (1694-1778)**

"Nature herself has decreed that woman, both for herself and her children, should be at the mercy of man's judgment."
—**Jean-Jacques Rousseau (1712-1778)**

"In short, all of these factors account for the origin of the Negro, who is well-suited to his climate, namely, strong, fleshy, and agile. However, because he is so amply supplied by his motherland, he is also lazy, indolent, and dawdling." —**Immanuel Kant (1724-1804)**

"What is the worldly religion of the Jew? Huckstering. What is his worldly God? Money." —**Karl Marx (1818-1883)**

"Nobody is more inferior than those who insist on being equal."
—**Friedrich Nietzsche (1844-1900)**

"Organized people are just too lazy to look for things."
—**Bertrand Russell (1872-1970)**

BONUS FACTS!

- Sugarhill Gang's "Rapper's Delight" (1979) was the first truly massive hip hop single, and was specially popular in Canada and the UK.

- 672 is Antarctica's international telephone area code.

QUESTIONABLE PRACTICE (PART 1)

Seeing himself nicknamed "The Merchant of Death" broke Alfred Nobel's (1833-1896) heart. Determined to change his legacy, he destined his vast fortune to the establishment of the Nobel Prize to celebrate the best of human progress. Sadly, no prize has ever been exempt from controversy, and the Nobels are no exception. Let's begin with the science one!

Robert Koch (1843-1910): Awarded the 1905 Nobel Prize in Physiology or Medicine for the development of a promising new drug, *tuberculin*, to treat tuberculosis, but when the drug started to kill patients, the scandal was so great the Nobel Foundation judges had to quit their seats.

Philipp von Lenard (1862-1947): He won the Nobel Prize in Physics in 1905 for his work on cathode rays, was also a fierce anti-Semite (and future Nazi) who lobbied at the Royal Swedish Academy of Sciences to keep Albert Einstein from winning the prize for his colossal theory of relativity. The Academy finally awarded Einstein the prize in 1921 for the law of the photoelectric effect … Lenard's own area of research.

Frederick Banting (1891-1941) and John Macleod (1876-1935): Both men received the Nobel Prize in Physiology or Medicine in 1923 for the discovery of insulin, which was followed by a long, unseemly feud over credit and the splitting of the reward money, which saw both men never speaking to each other again.

Johannes Fibiger (1867-1928): Awarded the 1926 Nobel Prize in Physiology or Medicine for his discovery of a roundworm parasite which caused cancer in rats, his conclusions were proven to be completely wrong later on, causing yet another scandal.

Irène Joliot-Curie (1897-1956): Daughter of prize winners Pierre Curie (1859-1906) and Marie Curie (1867-1934), died from leukemia caused by the same research she was awarded the 1935 Nobel Prize in Chemistry for (discovery of artificial radioactivity), same as her mother!

Otto Hahn (1879-1968): Considered the true father of the atomic bomb, after being nominated for the Nobel Prize in Chemistry and Physics over 35 times, he was finally awarded the 1944 Nobel Prize in Chemistry for the discovery of nuclear fission. However, since he had been detained by the Allied forces' Operation Epsilon, he could not attend the ceremony, nor cash the reward until much later.

BONUS FACTS!

- In 2017, the World Taekwondo Federation (WTF) shortened its brand name to World Taekwondo (WT), to avoid the negative connotation of its former initials!

- In 1964, Zambia began its own mock space program which planned to send a teenage girl and two cats to the Moon, and later Christian missionaries to Mars!

- A slender, white root originating in Persia (modern-day Iran), the modern orange carrot was developed by the Dutch during the seventeenth century to honor William of Orange (1533-1584).

- Orcas are not whales at all, but the largest species of sea dolphin in the world.

LOST

Some endeavors are doomed from the start. The most ill-fated discovery expeditions in human history include:

1. A Portuguese navigator in the service of Castile, Juan Díaz de Solís (1470-1516) launched the first journey to find a southern route across the newly discovered America to the Pacific, and ultimately Asia. Thinking he had found it, he sailed up the Río de la Plata (which he dubbed Mar dulce or "Sweat Sea") in 1516. Invited ashore by seemingly friendly natives, he set foot with some of his men in modern-day Uruguay only to find he was dinner; the surviving crew aboard his ship quickly sailed back to Spain.

2. Overshadowed by the super successful Hernán Cortés (1485-1547), Pánfilo de Narváez (c.1473-1528) managed to convince Charles V (1500-1558) to fund his 1527 expedition to Florida with 600 men and women. By the time they reached Cuba from Spain, he had already lost several ships and 350 people to a storm. Courageously, he proceeded with the remaining 250 survivors to modern-day Tampa Bay and northward to the Gulf Coast where another storm drowned most of his people near Galveston Island. Only four of the remaining 80 men survived during the next six years, by journeying to Mexico on foot! Pánfilo de Narváez was never heard from again, to this day his first name becoming a synonym of "dumbass" in Spanish.

3. Don Pedro de Mendoza y Luján (1487-1537) founded modern day Buenos Aires (Argentina) in 1536, but constant struggle with the natives saw him sail back to Spain to seek help, and he died during the voyage. While some settlers managed to escape by sailing up the Paraná river, by the time help arrived in 1580, the original Buenos Aires was completely deserted, and nobody knows for sure what happened to the rest.

4. Modern day Chile was discovered in stages by *conquistadores* who didn't get along well with Francisco Pizarro (1478-1541) up in Perú. Pizarro had just conquered the Inca empire, and wasn't keen on any form of competition. The first to leave (around 1533) was Gonzalo Calvo de Barrientos (d.1538), whose ear had been publically cut off by Pizarro. With the aid of fellow prisoner Atahualpa (c.1500-1533), the last Inca, Calvo de Barrientos would find refuge among the locals, who renamed him Gasco, adopting the indigenous lifestyle until the arrival of Diego de Almagro (c.1475-1538) in 1536. Almagro had fallen out with Pizarro over a number of issues, so he decided to try his luck south, but his native guide and translator, loyal to Pizarro, turned his voyage into a living nightmare, forcing him to return to Perú.

5. If you think Puerto del Hambre, or "Port Famine," an uninviting name, you're probably right. It was founded as Rey Don Felipe by explorer-poet Pedro Sarmiento de Gamboa (1532-1592) in 1582, hoping to fortify the Magellan Strait against the British, but by the time Thomas Cavendish (1560-1982) arrived there in 1587, he found only the desiccated remains of the original 300 settlers among ruins, and renamed the place "Port Famine."

6. Sir John Franklin's (1786-1847) lost expedition in 1845 is called lost for good reason. Like Magellan before him, but far less successfully, he sought a northwest passage to the Pacific, but both his ships, the HMS Erebus and HMS Terror, became stranded on Arctic ice in the Victoria Strait. Franklin and his crew disappeared without a trace until Canadian expeditions found the wrecked Erebus in 2014, and the Terror in 2016. It is thought all 130 men died either from exposure to the elements or starvation within two years, while trying to reach the Canadian mainland on foot.

SOMETHING BORROWED

Lingua franca of the modern world, English is borrowed from many sources beyond Anglo-Saxon, all of which add to its linguistic versatility and strength.

Anglo-Saxon: Freedom, life, love, night, old, what, when, where, who, year.

Norse: Anger, awe, clumsy, crooked, fog, husband, law, ransack, skill, wrong.

Norman French: Beauty, court, crown, dress, joy, justice, marriage, peace, people, prayer.

Modern French: Ballet, coup, elite, espionage, garage, menu, police, pajamas, regime, soup.

German: Angst, diesel, fest, gesundheit, hamburger, kindergarten, kitsch, noodles, snorkel, spiel.

Latin: Auditorium, circus, etcetera, exit, focus, invention, manufacture, refrigerator, status, trivia.

Greek: Alphabet, cemetery, dialogue, dinosaur, idiot, metaphor, metropolis, planet, technology.

Italian: Concert, diva, duo, falsetto, finale, maestro, mandolin, piano, soprano, tempo.

Dutch: Aardvark, aloof, bamboo, bazooka, blink, booze, brandy, cashier, cookie, cruise.

Spanish: Alligator, bodega, buckaroo, cockroach, desperado, lasso, pronto, ranch, rodeo, taco, vanilla.

Arabic: Alcohol, algebra, almanac, assassin, cipher, crimson, cotton, genie, ghoul, sofa.

Taíno: Barbecue, cannibal, canoe, hammock, hurricane, iguana, maize, mosquito, savannah, tobacco.

African languages: Banana, banjo, chimpanzee, cola, ebony, jazz, jive, mojo, safari, tote.

Isolated in the western Pyrenees region between northern Spain and southwestern France, Basque (*Euskara*) is an indigenous language predating Indo-European dialects, but no matter how strange, English has managed to borrow a few words from it as well, including *anchovy* and *bizarre!*

BONUS FACT!

- Polish environmental group EcoLogic got a $2,650 phone bill in 2018, after a GPS tracker they had attached to the back of a stork named Kajtek to track its migration got stolen in Sudan, and someone used its SIM card to make calls … lots of them!

QUESTIONABLE PRACTICE (PART 2)

Often tainted by the politics of the day at the Swedish Academy, rather than literary accomplishment, what the Nobel Prize in Literature rewards is idealism, as originally requested by Alfred Nobel himself.

René Prudhomme (1830-1907): The Swedish Academy had originally chosen Leo Tolstoy (1828-1910) to be the first writer ever to receive the award in 1901, but the anti-Russian sentiment of some of its members forced them to settle for Prudhomme, who was praised for the "lofty idealism" of this poetry.

Bjørnstjerne Bjørnson (1832-1910): Chosen in 1903 for being Alfred Nobel's favorite writer over playwright Henrik Ibsen (1828-1904) who they criticized for his "lack of idealism."

Selma Lagerlöf (1858-1940): Swedish playwright, novelist, poet, essayist, and painter August Strindberg (1849-1912) was supposed to win the award in 1909, but being hated by the prime minister, and frowned upon by the Swedish public at large (who considered him to be an womanizing alcoholic), the jury chose Lagerlöf instead after an internal tug-of-war, rehashing the "lofty idealism" praise they used with Prudhomme years earlier.

Knut Hamsun (1859-1952): Widely considered a world-class innovative stylist, the 1920 winner of the prize was also a Teutophile (German lover) who welcomed the Nazis into his country, eulogizing Adolf Hitler (1889-1945) as "a preacher of the gospel of justice for all nations." Hamsun was trialed as a collaborator, pleaded ignorance, and in the end all he got was a reduced fine on account of his advanced age.

Jacinto Benavente y Martínez (1866-1954): A celebrated playwright and satirist, Benavente was awarded the 1922 prize when the academy passed over influential Irish novelist James Joyce (1882-1941) author of the controversial *Ulysses* (1922), which raised more than its share of eyebrows the world over.

W.B. Yeats (1865-1939): Following the snub to Joyce, the ensuing Irish lobby locked Yeats, a favorite poet of King Gustaf V (1858-1950), to an easy win.

Gabriela Mistral (1889-1957): She was virtually unknown in Sweden, and to most judges but one, poet Hjalmar Gullberg (1898-1961), who personally translated and read her work to the rest of the academy members, completely derailing then-favorite Herman Hesse's (1877-1962) bid in favor of the Chilean poet.

Pablo Neruda (1904-1973): Also having an academy champion in fellow communist poet, and personal translator Artur Lundkvist (1906-1991), Neruda would receive the prize in 1971, despite his constant refusal to condemn repression of dissident writers in the USSR.

Bob Dylan (b.1941): Continuing its policy of choosing "idealism" over literary merit, the American singer was awarded the prize in 2016, over the likes of Haruki Murakami (b.1949) and Don Delillo (b.1936), causing quite the stir in highbrow circles. On top of it all, Dylan did not return the Academy's calls for weeks, nor did he attend the official ceremony, but finally did accept the prize in a very private event. He was quoted saying:

"If someone had ever told me that I had the slightest chance of winning the Nobel Prize, I would have to think that I'd have about the same odds as standing on the moon."

AMERICA, F*CK YEAH!

Far from the untouched, primeval wilderness romanticized by nineteenth century writers, the ancient Americas before the arrival of Europeans were a thoroughly landscaped, civilized land, where trade, culture, and politics flourished beyond imagination!

1. According to up-to-date archeological evidence, the Americas were populated by Siberians well before originally thought (at least 32,000 years ago) in three main waves. Most modern indigenous nations, however, seem to descend from the second wave.

2. The Inca (modern-day Peru) and Aztec (modern-day Mexico) civilizations had earlier precedents. Wari and Tiwanaku cultures in the Andes (modern-day Peru and Bolivia respectively) developed extensive fishing industries as well as terrace agriculture to grow cotton and potatoes, well before the Olmecs, Toltecs, Mixtecs, and Maya genetically engineered maize (corn), and subsequently began to urbanize Central America.

3. Land and sea trade must have flourished between South, Central, and North America, which explains why Andean potatoes and cotton, Mesoamerican maize and tobacco, and Amazonian mandioc and sweet potatoes made their way all across the land, from Canada to southern Chile!

4. Far from nomadic, around 1000AD the Mississippian culture built important religious and trading centers along the Mississippi basin while up northeast, five independent agricultural nations founded the Haudenosaunee Confederacy, an egalitarian and politically sophisticated parliamentary league (not unlike the modern-day UN) which extended all the way up to Canada.

5. The lush Amazon forest as we know it today was developed by the Beni (modern-day Bolivia), and Xingu (modern-day Brazil) who built ponds, bridges, canals, and even artificial islands to inhabit, around 1250AD, after domesticating and planting around 138 plants and trees which fed them, and make up about 12% of the basin's flora.

6. Contrary to popular belief, Europeans initially arriving to the Americas didn't consider natives to be inferior in any way, neither racially (they were described as portly and beautiful), nor technologically (moccasins and other garments, as well as local crops being quickly adopted by conquistadores, frontiersmen, and pilgrims alike).

7. Down in the Andes a binary notation and calculation device, *Quipu*, based on knotted wool and cotton strings of different colors was invented early on to keep precise historical and numerical state records. It baffles scientists to this day!

BONUS FACTS!

- The word "checkmate" used in chess comes from the Persian *shāh māt*: "the king is helpless."

- Michael Jackson (1959-2009) reportedly paid $150,000 to a witch doctor, to put a curse on *Hook* director Steven Spielberg (b.1946)!

- Pavement would need to be at 158°F to fry an egg on it, but only gets up to 145°F.

LAW & ORDER

The creation of permanent human settlements all over the world meant people had to regulate individual and group behavior through laws and codes to ensure peaceful and prosperous living.

1. One of the earliest known legal texts, the Ur-Nammu clay stele from around 2100BC, dealt mainly with compensation for workplace injuries!

2. Covering crime, marriage/divorce, slave rights, inheritance, and debt settlements, the code of King Hammurabi (c.1810-1750BC) established harsh, yet impartial punishments throughout its 282 paragraphs carved in a stone pillar.

3. Roman Emperor Justinian I (c.482-565) commissioned the creation of a legal system based in Roman thousand-year-old jurisprudence, and was the scaffold of European civil law everywhere until Napoleon came along in the eighteenth century.

4. English Common Law stemmed from the court system established after the eleventh-century Norman conquest, and institutionalized in 1154 by the first Plantagenet king, Henry II (1133-1189). Centuries later, the British Empire would spread it to its colonies, many of which retain versions of this system to this day.

5. The Napoleonic Code, enacted and written in a large degree by the man himself, Napoleon Bonaparte (1769-1821) took Justinian's Roman Law and leftover Feudal customs, and refined all into a clear legal system that would become the norm in much of Continental Eurasia, Canada, and Latin America.

6. Perhaps the biggest difference between Common Law and Napoleonic Law is the former works from the bottom up, while the latter does so from top to bottom, which explains in part the controversial departure of Britain from the European Union on January 20, 2020: a country ruled by Common Law would find it difficult to comply with European laws imposed from Brussels.

7. The people of the English Channel Islands may still invoke the aid of Rollo (c.860-930AD), first Duke of Normandy, by falling to their knees in the presence of witnesses and calling out:

Haro! Haro! Haro! À l'aide, mon Prince, on me fait tort. **("Hear me! Hear me! Hear me! Come to my aid, my Prince, for someone does me wrong.")**

Which is followed by the Lord's Prayer and Grace in French.

Notre Père qui est aux cieux. Ton nom soit sanctifié. Ton règne vienne. Ta volonté soit faite sur la terre comme au ciel. Donne-nous aujourd'hui notre pain quotidien. Et nous pardonne nos offenses, comme nous pardonnons à ceux qui nous ont offensés. Et ne nous induis point en tentation, mais délivre-nous du mal.

La Grâce de Notre Seigneur Jésus Christ, la dilection de Dieu et la sanctification de Saint Esprit soit avec nous tous éternellement. Amen.

The *Clameur de Haro*, as it is known, guarantees any dispute will be given 12 months to be properly settled in court, and is worth being remembered by anyone visiting Jersey and/or Guernsey.

THE DA VINCI CODE

Considered a genius in his lifetime, Italian Renaissance polymath, Leonardo di ser Piero da Vinci (1452-1519), a.k.a. Leonardo da Vinci, remains to be regarded as such in modern times, and for good reason!

1. Born in Tuscany out of wedlock but still supported by both of his parents and their families, Leonardo apprenticed at Andrea del Verrocchio's (c.1435-1488) emerging as a master painter in his own right seven years later.

2. One of the greatest painters and draftsmen in history, of his 15 surviving masterpieces, his *Mona Lisa* painting, his *Last Supper* mural, and his *Vitruvian Man* ink-on-paper drawing are possibly the most reproduced works of art in history.

"A beautiful body perishes, but a work of art dies not." —LdV

3. However, having many ideas but little time, most paintings were left unfinished by the artist, who chose to focus his efforts on design and engineering projects for wealthy patrons.

"It had long since come to my attention that people of accomplishment rarely sat back and let things happen to them. They went out and happened to things." —LdV

4. Some of his engineering projects, jotted down in many notebooks, were so ahead of their time, they remained unattainable until modern times, including the tank, the machine gun, the helicopter, the hang glider, the parachute, and even the bicycle chain!

5. For Leonardo, who had little interest in literature or history, science and art informed each other, so he had no qualms about dissecting corpses to learn more about anatomy. His accurate organ drawings are some of the first illustrations of their type ever, as were his many studies of birds' anatomy and flight capability, while his geological observations were depicted in many of his paintings.

"I have been impressed with the urgency of doing. Knowing is not enough; we must apply. Being willing is not enough; we must do."
— LdV

6. Leonardo's surviving notebooks (codexes) reveal a curious habit of reversing his handwriting (mirror script). Long thought to be a secretive habit of his, the reality is much more pedestrian: a lefty, he hated to smear still-wet ink while writing. It is thought he also sketched this way for the same reason.

7. If not secretive, Leonardo was indeed a sensitive and very private man. So much in fact, after being charged—and later acquitted—with sodomy at 24, he withdrew from the public eye for two whole years!

"You do ill if you praise, but worse if you censure, what you do not understand." —LdV

8. Leonardo's 36 page Codex Leicester which collects some of his scientific output, was purchased by Bill Gates (b.1955) in 1994 for $30,802,500.

"I have offended God and mankind because my work did not reach the quality it should have." —LdV

THE NAKED GUN

While aircraft, missiles, tanks, submarines and other inventions usually steal all the attention, wars are still largely fought by gun-totting land infantry. The most successful guns of the twentieth and twenty-first centuries include:

AK-47: Easy to use, durable, and relatively cheap, the *Avtomat Kalashnikova* was designed by Mikhail Kalashnikov (1919-2013) in 1947, and became the standard issue assault rifle of the USSR Army. With 100 million units currently carried by armies in 106 countries, its production is licensed by Russia to China, Israel, India, Egypt, Venezuela, and Nigeria. Particularly popular in Africa, we can find it emblazoned in the flag of Mozambique, as well as the coats of arms of Zimbabwe, Burkina Faso (1984-1997) and East Timor, where parents sometimes name their babies "Kalash" too!

M-16: The second most widely used firearm in the world, the AR-15 was originally designed in 1959 by Eugene Stoner (1922-1997) and Leroy James Sullivan (b.1933) at the California ArmaLite company. The military didn't like it at first sight, but the Colt company did, marketing it as an assault rifle and a competition gun. Tested and loved by army Rangers in South Vietnam, by 1964 it had entered US Army service, and fully deployed in Vietnam, re-christened as the M-16. Over eight million units have been sold to this day, and it has been adopted by NATO armies as well.

M-240: Also in use by the US Army (the "M" designation gives it away), NATO, and the armed forces of 80 other countries, including now defunct Rhodesia (1965-1979), this gas-operated machine gun was invented in 1954 by Belgian Ernest Vervier (1909-c.1974), chief designer at gun manufacturer FN Herstal, which licensed its

production to Argentina, Canada, Egypt, India and the United Kingdom. Far more durable than the M-60, it may handle shooting 100 to 600 rounds per minute without overheating.

PK: Extensively exported and licensed to manufacturers worldwide, the *Pulemyot Kalashnikova* ("Kalashnikov's machine gun") was the 1961 Soviet answer to the M-240, and is usually found wherever AK-47s are shot. It has an excellent accuracy of up to 2,600 feet, and may be used as an anti-aircraft gun when mounted on a tripod. A modern modified version known as the PKP (*Pulemyot Kalashnikova Pekhotny*), "Pecheneg," is said to be more accurate due to a fixed air-cooled barrel and haze-dissipating handle.

QBZ-95: A short-barreled ("bullpup") automatic assault rifle designed and manufactured by Norinco in China, it has been the service rifle of that country's People's Liberation Army, and several of its law enforcement agencies, as well as many other armies in southern Asia since 1995. QBZ stands for *Qīng Wǔqì Bùqiāng Zìdòng*, meaning "light automatic rifle." Highly versatile, it has spawned many local and international variants, including a grenade-launching version.

Meanwhile, the twenty-first century has seen the rise of an arsenal which incorporates advances from smart phone and drone technology:

EXACTO: The "EXtreme ACcuracy Tasked Ordnance," is a .50 BMG sniper rifle which basically fires smart guided bullets that never miss their target. It was developed for DARPA (Defense Advanced Research Projects Agency) by Lockheed Martin.

PHASR: Standing for "Personnel Halting And Stimulation Response," this mean-looking, non-lethal rifle is designed to blind and disorient using laser beams no less!

XM-25: This semi-automatic grenade launcher with programmable ammo, has a laser rangefinder system which quadruples its accuracy and effective range, compared to regular launchers.

iP1: A smart semi-automatic pistol by Armatrix, it works in conjunction with a smart watch which ensures it may only be fired by its user, while keeping a record on every fired shot.

BONUS FACTS!

- Pringles don't have enough potato to be considered potato chips, potato crisps, potato sticks or potato puffs.

- Movie star and former singer Mark Wahlberg (b.1971) has admitted to having three nipples!

- Founded in 1923 Vienna, Interpol (International Criminal Police Organization) was fully absorbed by the Gestapo in 1938.

- There is no anti-venom for Australia's blue-ring octopus bite, which may cause paralysis and even death from respiratory failure.

- The skeleton of utilitarian philosopher Jeremy Bentham (1748-1832), an early advocate of body donation to science, was covered in wax, dressed in his best clothes and wig, and put on display at London's University College, where it silently presided over many a college meeting for decades!

BLOODBATH

Every war pays a high price in human lives, and the carnage of particular battles may particularly be staggering. The following list ranks the bloodiest military campaigns in human history which, unsurprisingly, finds all of them either within either of the early twentieth century World Wars.

10. Operation Typhoon (1941-1942): A two-fold offensive by German forces which intended to take the city of Moscow, but was ultimately thwarted by the capable Soviet counter-offensive, despite a high body count of 1,000,000 dead.

9. Siege of Leningrad (1941-1944): The German and Finnish siege of the Soviet city of Leningrad took 1,110,000 million lives over a period of 872 days.

8. The Somme (1916): This WWI battle between British, French and German forces marked the defeat of the Second German Army, but wiped out 1,120,000 civilians and soldiers in the process.

7. Operation Ichi-Go (1944): A Japanese forces attempt at opening a land route to French Indochina, taking control of the railroad between Beijing and Hong Kong, and capture several American air bases in southeast China via three main battle operations, claimed the lives of 1,300,000 people.

6. Fall of Berlin (1945): The last major offensive in WWII's European theater, the Soviet capture of Berlin was staged to launch on Adolf Hitler's (1889-1945) birthday on April 20, and ten days later 1,300,000 people had been killed, including the Führer himself, who committed suicide.

5. Operation Bagration (1944): A codename for the fifth deadliest campaign on the European theater, the Soviet Belorussian Strategic Offensive Operation, inflicted what many consider the biggest blow to German armed forces in WWII, but the toll was high at 1,430,000 casualties.

4. German Spring Offensive (1918): Intending to destroy the Allied forces before the US fully joined WWI, Germany launched a series of attacked along the Western Front during that spring, resulting in 1,550,000 deaths.

3. Battle of the Dnieper (1943): A major offensive involving 4,000,000 troops from both sides along that river (870 miles), it was one of the costliest of WWII campaigns, killing 1,580,000 men.

2. Brusilov Offensive (1916): 1,600,000 dead was the result of the victorious attack General Aleksey Brusilov (1853-1926) laid waste to the Austro-Hungarian Fourth Army over several months.

1. Battle of Stalingrad (1942-1943): A sad record, the German offensive which began with extensive Luftwaffe air-raids, and quickly devolved into cutthroat close-quarter fighting, snuffed out the lives of 2,500,000 people.

BONUS FACT!

- While comedian Jim Carrey (b.1962) was paid $7,000,000 for his role in *Dumb and Dumber*, his colleague, renowned career actor Jeff Daniels (b.1955), only got $50,000.

SHAKEN, NOT STIRRED

Espionage has be a useful military tool since ancient times, but only became to be highly regarded by society during the twentieth-century Cold War, when it stormed mass media and public imagination.

1. Macedonian king Alexander the Great (356-323BC) would encourage his men to write letters home, only to intercept them and use their contents to weed out dissent from his ranks.

2. Cyrus the Great (c.600-530BC) recruited discontented Babylonian priests to allow his forces to enter the city without fighting, and bring down king Belshazzar with a single stroke.

3. Military strategist Sun Tzu (544-496BC) recommended espionage as a valuable source of information about the enemy which would lead to victory in the pages of his *Art of War* magnum opus.

4. Sir Anthony Standen (c.1548-?) is said to have infiltrated Phillip II's court at the behest of Elizabeth I's spymaster Sir Francis Walsingham (c.1532-1590), intercepting plans for the Armada's invasion.

5. Set up by none other than George Washington (1732-1799) himself, and led by spymaster Benjamin Tallmadge (1754-1835), the Culper Ring supplied valuable intelligence during the American Revolution, including Benedict Arnold's (1741-1801) treason, and was so good at its job, the identities of its members weren't revealed until two centuries later!

6. Arnold had been turned by none other than British spymaster

John André (1750-1780). A refined man of considerable artistic skill, André was fluent in four languages, but was eventually caught while attempting to pass through US lines in disguise. A gentleman to the end, he reportedly put the noose around his own head on the day of his execution.

7. Famed detective Alan Pinkerton (1819-1884) served as Union Intelligence Service (UIS) for two years, thwarting an early assassination attempt on president Abraham Lincoln, and often went undercover behind enemy lines, as a Confederate "Major E.J. Allen." The UIS counter-intelligence is considered a precursor to modern neutralizing of enemy spies.

8. The head of Austro-Hungarian Army counter-intelligence unit, the Evidenzbureau, Alfred Redl (1864-1913) is considered an innovator in the use of spy technology, which he used to spy for … the Russians. Soon after being exposed by a colleague, he committed suicide.

9. Executed by a French firing squad, "Mata Hari," the stage name of Dutch exotic dancer Margaretha Geertruida MacLeod (1876-1917), is perhaps the best known real-life femme fatale spy archetype, working for Germany during World War I.

10. Fluent in Arabic and Malay languages, Dutch scholar Christiaan Snouck Hurgronje (1857-1936) faked being a Muslim to infiltrate and dismantle anti-colonial resistance in Indonesia, resuming his academic career upon his return to the Netherlands in 1909.

11. The original "Black Panther," famed international German spy and saboteur during both World Wars, South African Boer Frederick Joubert Duquesne (1877-1956) is perhaps most famous for leading a wide Nazi spy ring on US soil until caught by the FBI in 1941 and sentenced to 18 years in prison.

12. Established by President Harry S. Truman (1884-1972) in 1947, the Central Intelligence Agency (CIA) is the successor of WWII's Office of Strategic Services (OSS) created by FDR (1882-1945) during WWII at the behest of the British government. Trained in Canada by the British Security Co-ordination (BSC), OSS agents carried multiple operations during the war, including intelligence, counter-intelligence, sabotage, and the training of resistance guerillas, all tasks carried on into the Cold War by the CIA.

13. Too tall for the US Women's Army Corps, and a couple of decades before she became a celebrated TV chef, Julia Child (1912-2004) joined the OSS in 1942, serving in Ceylon (modern-day Sri Lanka) and China!

14. Another OSS "catch" (pun intended) was MLB catcher Moe Berg (1902-1972), who despite not being a great ballplayer, had a college education, photographic memory, and spoke several languages, traits he made use of while on spying missions to the Balkans, Italy, and Switzerland.

15. Kim Philby (1912-1988) became a high-ranking counter-intelligence agent at MI6's Section Five, while in reality he was an undercover agent for the Soviet Union, and a member of the infamous Cambridge Spy Ring, until being exposed and defecting to Russia in 1963.

16. As Syrian-Argentinian businessman "Kamel Amin Thaabet," Mossad spy Eli Cohen (1924-1965) successfully infiltrated the upper echelons of Syrian society, politics and military from 1961 to 1965, when he was uncovered and publically hanged in Damascus. His exploits were made into a 2019 Netflix series, *The Spy*, starring distant relative Sacha Baron Cohen (b.1971).

17. A former spy for MI5 and MI6, David John Moore Cornwell (b.1931) became a best selling author of spy novels under pen name John le Carré, his term for an agent who successfully infiltrates another agency, "mole," crossing over to become widely used in real-life.

18. Perhaps the most famous spy of fiction, Ian Fleming's (1908-1964) James Bond is thought to be based mainly in two real-life spies, Dušan "Duško" Popov (1912-1981), a.k.a. "Tricycle," who Fleming had met while a British Naval Intelligence officer during his 1941 stay in Portugal at Casino Estoril (the basis for "Casino Royale"), and Sidney Reilly (c. 1873-1925), the "Ace of Spies," who worked for the Foreign Section of the British Secret Service Bureau (precursor of the MI6) to bring down the Bolshevik regime in the USSR, where he was apprehended and executed by the OGPU (*Obyedinyonnoye gosudarstvennoye politicheskoye upravleniye*) secret police.

Needless to say, Soviet counter-intelligence agency SMERSH featured in early James Bond novels was also inspired by the very real *СМЕРШ*, an umbrella for three different counter-intelligence KBG agencies founded by the man himself, Josef Stalin (1878-1942), to end German infiltration in the Red Army.

BONUS FACTS!

- Child labor, as legislated in the UK in 1802, allowed nine-year-olds to work eight hours a day, and 14-year-olds up to 14 hours a day.

- Irving Berlin (1888-1989), the composer of the patriotic anthem "God Bless America," was born in Russia!

DEAD SERIOUS

While current Commander-in-Chief Donald J. Trump (b.1946) currently nabs all media attention for his outrageous statements, he certainly isn't the first American president to intentionally or accidentally sucker punch the unsuspecting public with the wrong choice of words.

"Within twenty years we can peacefully colonize the Negro ... under conditions in which he can rise to the full measure of manhood."
—Abraham Lincoln (1809-1856)

"If blacks were given the right to vote, that would place every splay-footed, bandy-shanked, hump-backed, thick-lipped, flat-nosed, woolly-headed, ebon-colored in the country upon an equality with the poor white man." —Andrew Johnson (1808-1875)

"I have a strong feeling of repugnance when I think of the Negro being made our political equal. And I would be glad if they could be colonized, sent to heaven, or got rid of in any decent way."
—James Garfield (1831-1881)

"Criminals should be sterilized and feeble-minded persons forbidden to leave offspring behind them." —Theodore Roosevelt (1858-1919)

"Uncle Will says that the Lord made a white man from dust, a nigger from mud, then he threw up what was left and it came down a Chinaman. He does hate Chinese and Japs. So do I. It is race prejudice, I guess. But I am strongly of the belief that Negroes ought to be in Africa, yellow men in Asia and white men in Europe and America."
— Harry S. Truman (1884-1972)

"When the President does it, that means it is not illegal."
—Richard Nixon (1913-1994)

"Well, I learned a lot ... I went down to (Latin America) to find out from them and (learn) their views. You'd be surprised. They're all individual countries." —Ronald Reagan (1911-2004)

"For seven and a half years I've worked alongside President Reagan. We've had triumphs. Made some mistakes. We've had some sex ... uh ... setbacks." —George H. W. Bush (1924-2018)

"It all depends on what the meaning of the word 'is' is."
—Bill Clinton (b.1946)

"Our enemies are innovative and resourceful, and so are we. They never stop thinking about new ways to harm our country and our people, and neither do we." —George W. Bush (b.1946)

"If you got a business, you didn't build that, you didn't make it on your own." —Barack Obama (b.1961)

BONUS FACT!

- One of the most successful movie stars of all time, Adam Sandler (b.1966) saw his five-movie deal with Netflix expanded to another four films and a stand-up comedy special, after his movies became the streaming service's most watched ever.

QUESTIONABLE PRACTICE
(PART 3)

The Norwegian Nobel Committee is a five-member committee appointed by the Parliament of Norway to grant the Nobel Peace Prize, which certainly doesn't make them infallible.

Theodore Roosevelt (1858-1919): This exceptional American president was awarded the 1906 prize for negotiating the end of the Russo-Japanese War. Backstage, however, it was widely reported the US government's official recognition of an independent Norway in 1905 had more to do with it.

Cordell Hull (1871-1955): Secretary of State from 1933 to 1944, he was awarded the prize for his role in the creation of the United Nations, despite his role forcing FDR to deny entry to the SS St. Louis, which damned over 250 of the 950 Jewish refugees on board to die in concentration camps back in Europe.

Henry A. Kissinger (b.1923) and Le Duc Tho (1911-1990): The American Secretary of State and the Vietnamese general were both awarded the 1973 prize for the Vietnam War ceasefire at the Paris Peace Accords. Kissinger accepted it with humor, still ordering further bombings in Laos and Cambodia, while supporting military coups in South America. Tho had the decency to turn it down.

Anwar Sadat (1918-1981) and Menachem Begin (1913-1992): While awarded for "for the Camp David Agreement, which brought about a negotiated peace between Egypt and Israel," Sadat was a known autocrat, and Begin had allegedly taken part in a plot to assassinate German president Konrad Adenauer (1876-1967).

Rigoberta Menchú (b.1959): As an indigenous feminist and human rights activist, Ms. Menchú was awarded the 1992 prize despite well-founded accusations of misrepresenting her life and achievements in her 1983 *I, Rigoberta Menchú* autobiography.

Yasser Arafat (1929-2004): Despite engaging in active terrorism most of his life, he was awarded the prize in 1994 alongside Israeli Prime Minister Yitzhak Rabin (1922-1995) and Israeli Foreign Minister Shimon Peres (1923-2016) for the Oslo Peace Accords.

Barack Obama (b.1961): In 2009, just nine months into his first term, the American president was awarded what many candidly interpreted as the "we like you better than George W. Bush" award.

Already awarding anti-Semites, warmongers, terrorists, and frauds, the Nobel Committee went a step further giving the 2012 Nobel Peace Prize to a non-human entity, the European Union (EU) ... which happens to be one of the largest weapons manufacturers in the world!

BONUS FACTS!

- The Xi'an Stele is a limestone block inscribed in both Chinese and Syriac, which describes the existence of Nestorian Christian communities in northern China back in 781AD.

- Colombian race driver Tatiana Calderón (b.1993) purposefully increased her neck's length by 3.5 in, in order to cope with Formula One racing g-force.

IT'S THE LAW OF THE WEST

Nothing excites the imagination like that mythical spot in time and space that was the open border we now call the Old West, where facts were often stranger than fiction!

1. Technically speaking, the first group of Mormon pioneers to arrive in the Salt Lake Valley in 1847 were illegals, as the area which later came to be known as Utah was still very much part of Mexico.

2. America's third gold fever, the California Gold Rush (1848-1855), brought an estimated influx of 300,000 people to the west.

3. Samuel Colt's (1814-1862) 1836 revolutionary revolver invention was spread out West by the Texas Rangers, who placed a large order for it during the Mexican-American War (1846-1848).

4. Reasoning southwest desert had to be very similar to the Arabian Peninsula, the US Army imported camels in 1856. The program was a success, but after the Civil War (1861-1865) the US Camel Corps was disbanded, and the animals let loose—the last Texan feral camel was seen in 1941!

5. The famous Pony Express mail service only lasted 18 months, from April 3, 1860 to October 24, 1861. It was financially insolvent, and was finally put to pasture once the building of the transcontinental telegraph was complete.

6. Not far from the home of Laura Ingalls Wilder (1867-1957) and her family, the reclusive Bender family had turned theirs into an inn,

where they slaughtered at least 12 people, before seemingly vanishing off the face of the Earth!

6. Long a staple of the Old West, tumbleweeds (*Kali tragus*) were in fact imported from Russia in 1870, and have long since become impossible to get rid of!

7. The 1881 O.K.Corral gunfight between Wyatt Earp (1848-1929) and his lawmen, and the Cochise County Cowboys outlaws lasted only 30 seconds, and didn't take place in the corral but at a street intersection behind it.

8. While the real "Wild West" was coming to an end, popular literature had catapulted it to new heights of fame, so having made a name for himself as a scout and bison hunter, William "Buffalo Bill" Cody (1846-1917) founded the "Buffalo Bill's Wild West" performing show in 1883, with which he toured America and Europe. The troupe was joined by an aging Sitting Bull (1831-1890) in 1881.

9. The original Miss Kitty's Long Branch Saloon of Dodge City, Kansas, famously portrayed in the *Gunsmoke* TV show (1955-1975) burned down in 1885. It was rebuilt much later as a tourist attraction.

10. While the train-robbing outlaws known as Butch Cassidy's Wild Bunch successfully operated for a period of less than three years (1899–1901) in America, with the Pinkerton Agency hot in pursuit, Butch Cassidy (1866-1908), Sundance Kid (1867-1908), and Etta Place (c.1878–?) decided to try their M.O. down in Argentina, but were much less successful due to a combination of factors which kept them on the run, and ultimately gunned down in Bolivia, though their deaths over there continue to be somewhat disputed.

BLACK BLACK WEST

The Wild West wasn't made only by vanilla white folks, but by half a million courageous African Americans looking to make their own luck away from servitude and discrimination.

Bill Pickett (1870-1932): From African-American and Cherokee heritage, Pickett became a ranch hand as a fifth-grade kid, his bulldogging (grabbing cattle by the horns and wrestling them to the ground!) technique gave birth to modern rodeo steer wrestling. After a stint performing in the 101 Ranch Wild West Show as "The Dusky Demon," he starred in two silent-era westerns before retiring.

Robert Lemmons (1848–1947): Born a slave, he gained his freedom at age 17, at the end of the Civil War, and found work with Duncan Lammons, who gave him his last name and tech him to herd cattle. Lemmons excelled at catching wild mustangs and made a small fortune from it, which allowed him to buy his own ranch, marry, and learn to read and write.

Nat Love (1854-1921): A young slave in Tennessee, Love learned to read and write. Finding he had a gift for breaking horses, he headed west at age 16, where he became a noted cowboy, making side money in rodeos, and even being captured by Indians according to his successful 1907 autobiography *Life and Adventures of Nat Love*.

Crawford Goldsby (1876-1896): Known as "Cherokee Bill," Goldsby was an outlaw. Alongside the notorious Cook Gang, he terrorized Indian Territory for two years before his capture and execution by hanging, before which he uttered his famous last words: "I came here to die, not make a speech."

Mary Fields (c.1832-1914): The formidable "Stagecoach Mary," held many jobs until landing the star route contract for the delivery of US mail at age 60, becoming a respected public figure in Montana until her retirement at age 71. In 1992, asteroid "7091 Maryfields" was named after her.

Addison Jones (c.1845-1926): Achieving recognition in his lifetime as one of the greatest Texas and New Mexico cowboys who ever lived, little is known about Jones's childhood other than having been born in Gonzales County, Texas. As a cowboy, he led a crew of all-black herdsmen and became a noted breaker of wild broncos, keeping at it until well into his seventies.

Charley Willis (1847–1930): Freed after the Civil War, Willis headed farther west at age 18, finding work as a breaker of horses first, and later on herding cattle across the Chisholm Trail into Wyoming. A talented musician, his "Good-bye, Old Paint" song composed while on the trail is well remembered to this day.

Bass Reeves (1838-1910): Considered one of the greatest lawmen of all time, Reeves was born a slave but fled west during the Civil War, to live among Cherokee, Creeks and Seminoles, learning their languages. This knowledge led to being recruited as deputy US marshal (the first African American marshal west of the Mississippi!). Over his long career in law enforcement, he arrested over 3,000 felons (including one of his own sons)!

BONUS FACT!

- "Q" is the only letter not appearing in any US state name.

'NAM IN A NUTSHELL

The second longest armed conflict America ever faced (1955-1975), the Vietnam War was a costly affair which spilled to neighboring Laos and Cambodia, and ultimately ended in defeat for a demoralized US, and the firm establishment of communism in all of Vietnam.

1. France is to blame: Colonial rulers of Vietnam, Laos, and Cambodia since the mid-nineteenth century, WWII Japanese occupation saw the rise of the nationalist Viet Minh, which fought the new invaders and sought an independent Vietnam, when France tried to reassert its rule in the area. In 1954, with the country firmly divided between a French South supported by the US, and a communist North supported by the USSR and China, the French decided to quit altogether, leaving the US out in the cold, to continue its financial and military support for the South Vietnamese state.

2. The communists took advantage early on: The Viet Minh up north and the Viet Cong insurgent guerillas down south soon began their bid to reunite the country in 1955, which prompted President Dwight D. Eisenhower (1890-1969) to organize the presence of troops in South Vietnam. Military action quickly escalated during John F. Kennedy's (1917-1963) presidency.

3. Lyndon B. Johnson (1908-1973) used the manufactured Gulf of Tonkin incident in 1964: Granted power by Congress to aid any Southeast Asian country in peril from communist intervention, he used it to wage open war against both North Vietnam and the Viet Cong insurgents in South Vietnam.

4. The death count was staggering: Throughout the war, 2,594,000 US soldiers served in Vietnam, 58,220 of which died during the

conflict, and 2,646 were captured or went missing—as of 2019, around 1,600 were still unaccounted for. North Vietnam and the Viet Cong lost an estimated 849,018 soldiers, while South Vietnam lost 313,000. Vietnam as a whole los 627,000 civilians to the war.

5. America sprayed of 20,000,000 gallons of toxic herbicide "Agent Orange": It resulted in 400,000 deaths, and 500,000 children subsequently being born with defects. Many veterans were affected too.

6. It was an international war: Armies from South Korea, Australia, New Zealand, Thailand and the Philippines fought alongside the US, while forces from the USSR, China, and North Korea fought for the North.

7. The US actually managed to beat the Viet Cong guerillas: But North Vietnam had invaded Laos and Cambodia, despite US air superiority and heavy bombardment, while the morale of American armed forces and the public back home was seriously compromised after years of never-ending offensives, which cost then-President Johnson the primary, and eventually led Republican Richard Nixon (1913-1994) to win the presidential election over vice president Hubert Humphrey (1911-1978).

8. Nixon and his National Security Advisor Henry Kissinger (b.1923) initially devised the "Vietnamization" strategy: While continuing to support the South Vietnam's armed forces, they would gradually slink away from the whole mess. By 1972 American ground forces were all but gone, but aerial bombings in Vietnam, Laos, and Cambodia went on unhindered, despite signing the Paris Peace Accords with North Vietnam in 1973.

9. North Vietnam's Spring Offensive would grant them victory: By May 3, 1975, the South Vietnamese government had officially capitulated, after the fall of Saigon on April 30.

10. Many evaded the draft: Two-thirds of American soldiers volunteered for duty, while the rest were drafted, mainly from poor and working-class families. 125,000 of them chose to evade the draft, some crossing the borders to either Canada or Mexico. In 1977, President Jimmy Carter (b.1924) officially pardoned the draft-dodgers, but almost half chose to never return home.

BONUS FACTS!

- The word "hipster" goes all the way back to the 1930s, when it was used to define someone who was part of the jazz scene.

- Twitter's bluebird mascot's official name is "Larry the Bird," after the NBA's Larry Bird (b.1956)!

- Female bedbugs may only be inseminated if males drill a hole in them with their pointy little penises!

- Zebroids are the steriles offspring of zebras and other equines. For instance, a "zorse" is born from zebra stallion and a horse mare, while "zonies" are the the result of breeding them with ponies, and "zonkeys" with, well, donkeys!

  - People whose *amygdala* has been removed can't feel fear.

FLOWERS BY IRENE

Known throughout the world for their portrayal in fiction, the Federal Bureau of Investigation (FBI) is America's principal federal law enforcement agency since 1935. With jurisdiction over 200 crimes, it also conducts domestic intelligence and counter-intelligence operations, some of which have gone well beyond its originally intended scope.

1. In charge of the Bureau (then known as the BOI) since 1924 until his death (48 years!), director J. Edgar Hoover (1895-1972) built it into what we know today, while amassing a great deal of power which he had no qualm using against political enemies, from movie stars to presidents! After his passing, the US Congress cautiously limited future directors' tenure to ten years.

2. As with any government agencies, the FBI has a conservative, "stick with what works" attitude towards scientific and technological developments—it took them until 2012 to ditch paper files and go fully digital! Its Scientific Crime Detection Laboratory officially opened 1932, in a single room, with a single agent, Charles Appel (1895-?), and a borrowed microscope. It worked, and grew from analyzing 200 pieces of evidence a year to 600 a day today.

3. Similarly other units had humble beginnings or were finally established once the workload became problematic, including the Serial Crime Unit (which profiles psycho killers), the Trace Evidence Unit (which collects hair samples), the Forensic Document Examiners Unit (which tapes shredded papers together), and even an Art Theft Unit established in 2004.

4. In spite of its huge workload and relatively small manpower for a government agency (around 35,000 employees), it also allocated

years of its time in investigating potential pop culture threats, including Richard Berry's (1935-1997) allegedly "obscene" 1955 song *Louie Louie*, 1946 movie classic *It's a Wonderful Life*, 2006 mockumentary film *Borat*, and the 2005 theft of a pair of ruby slippers from *The Wizard of Oz*, which took them a decade to find!

5. The Bureau also kept detailed files on a number of celebrities, most famously Albert Einstein (1879-1955), Hellen Keller (1880-1968), Charlie Chaplin (1889-1977), Ernest Hemingway (1899-1961), Lucille Ball (1911-1989), Frank Sinatra (1915-1998), Arthur Miller (1915-2005), Jackie Robinson (1919-1972), Truman Capote (1924-1984), Rock Hudson (1925-1985), Marilyn Monroe (1926-1962), Martin Luther King Jr. (1929-1968), George Steinbrenner (1930-2010), Phil Ochs (1940-1976), John Lennon (1940-1980), John Denver (1943-1997), Steve Jobs (1955-2011), and Whitney Houston (1963-2012). FBI celebrity informants included Walt Disney (1901-1966), and Ronald Reagan (1911-2004), of course!

BONUS FACTS!

- The Royal Canadian Mint made a 2011 series of legal tender, $20 silver coins engraved with Bugs Bunny, USS Enterprise, and Superman motifs!

- Caskets are rectangular, while coffins are six-sided!

- In 1995, Saddam Hussein (1937-2006) had his *Fedayeen* elite guards wear black uniforms designed by his son Uday (1964-2003), a huge *Star Wars* fan, who naturally had them wear Darth Vader helmets!

PUBLIC ENEMY #1

When a reporter asked J. Edgar Hoover for the names and descriptions of the worst bad guys currently on the run, his article got so much publicity, Hoover decided to create an official FBI's Top Ten Most Wanted Fugitives campaign in 1950. It was, and still is, a success: 488 of the 523 criminals who have made the top ten since have been apprehended, but let's set our sights on those criminals who, for better or worse, pioneered the catalog.

Thomas James Holden (1896–1953): The list's first inductee, he headed the Holden-Keating Gang of bank robbers, together with Francis Keating (1899-1978), not to mention killing his wife and her two brothers in 1949. After being spotted thanks to the list, he spent the rest of his natural life in prison.

Henry Randolph Mitchell (1895-?): The fourth of the first list inductees, Mitchell, a bank robber with a serious gambling habit, was the first to successfully escape the Bureau's grasp, staying on the list until 1958.

Nick George Montos (1916-2008): A career criminal, this Chicago gangster earned the dubious honor of being placed twice on the list in 1952 and 1956, dying in prison aged 92.

Charles Lee Herron (b.1938): One of four black power activists charged for the murder of two Nashville officers in 1968, he managed to avoid capture for 18 years, hiding in the criminal underworld until being finally arrested in 1986. His record has currently been surpassed by Victor Manuel Gerena (b.1958), on the list since 1984 and still at large.

Ruth Eisemann-Schier (b.1942): Born in Honduras, she became the first female inductee of the list in 1968, along with her American boyfriend Gary Stephen Krist (b.1945), for the kidnapping of heiress Barbara Jane Mackle (b.1948), who they buried alive, but fortunately survived the ordeal. Eisemann-Schier served four years in prison, and was then paroled and deported to Honduras in 1973.

Susan Edith Saxe (b.1949) and Katherine Ann Power (b.1949): The first same sex couple to ever be placed in the list in 1970 for bank robbery, arms robbery, and the killing of a police officer. Radical feminists from Brandeis University, Saxe was finally apprehended in 1975 and served seven years in prison, while Power eluded capture for 23 years until she finally turned herself in 1993, doing six years of prison time.

Wai-Chiu "Tony" Ng (b.1956): The first Asian criminal on the list, "Tony" was part of a gang which bound, robbed and then shot 14 people at a Seattle casino in 1983. He fled to Canada where he was finally arrested and deported back to the US in 1984, serving prison time until paroled and deported to Hong Kong in 2013.

BONUS FACTS!

- The Seuss in Theodor "Dr. Seuss" Geisel (1904-1991) is actually pronounced "soice."

- In Alaska, it is illegal to hunt moose using an airplane to spot them!

FACT VS. FICTION

A 2008 study conducted in the UK uncovered that one fifth of young British people believe historical figures Richard the Lionheart (1157-1199) and Winston Churchill (1874-1965) to be fictional, while fictional characters like King Arthur and Sherlock Holmes are deemed to be historical. Other than expose serious flaws within the UK's education system, it also revealed how blurry the line between myth and reality is within the human mind.

1. Fictional characters deemed real:

WILLIAM TELL:

Don't tell the average Swiss this, but according to Scottish folklorist Sir James Frazer (1854-1941) in his seminal 1890 book, *The Golden Bough*, their national hero from the middle ages, his son, his crossbow, and the apple were all borrowed from ancient Persian and German lore!

CAROLYN KEENE & FRANKLIN W. DIXON:

Like Laura Lee Hope and Victor Appleton before them, the creators of the "Nancy Drew" and "Hardy Boys" series were nothing but an umbrella pen name for the many ghostwriters employed by the Stratemeyer Syndicate.

BETTY CROCKER:

Once the second-best known woman after Eleanor Roosevelt (1884-1962), only Ms. Crocker happens to be a fictional persona invented in 1921 by General Mills to respond to consumer queries in a personal and friendly manner.

2. Real people deemed fictional:

CHEF BOYARDEE:

Italian immigrant Ettore Boiardi (1897-1985) anglicized his name, becoming a renowned chef at the Plaza Hotel in New York city, a restaurateur, and by 1938 a canned food industry entrepreneur.

COLONEL SANDERS:

After a number of dead-end jobs, Harland David Sanders (1890-1980) found his calling at 40, selling pressure-fried chicken at his roadside service station and lunchroom during the Great Depression. In the 1950s he began to franchise it, expanding the business until he sold it, famous secret recipe and all, for $2,000,000 in 1963, while staying on board as a paid KFC ambassador.

THE GIRL FROM IPANEMA:

Heloísa Eneida Paes Pinto Mendes Pinheiro (b.1945) was a local beauty in Rio de Janeiro (Brazil), who happened to stroll down the beach one day, catching the eye of bossa nova pioneers Antônio Carlos Jobim (1927-1992) and Vinicius de Moraes (1913-1990) in 1962.

3. Fictional characters based on real people:

COSMO KRAMER AND THE SOUP NAZI:

Both stemming from the Seinfeld (1990-1998) TV sitcom, Kramer is based on former standup comedian Kenny Kramer (b.1943), while the Nazi is based on restaurant chain owner Al Yeganeh (b.?), who reportedly still hates Jerry Seinfeld's (b.1954) guts.

"DIRTY" HARRY:

Inspector Harold Francis Callahan, the film character played by Clint Eastwood (b.1930) in several films, was based mainly on San Francisco PD detective Dave Toschi (1931-2018), who became publicly known for tackling the Zodiac Killer case from 1966 to 1978.

"ROCKY" BALBOA:

At this point, no one can deny Sylvester Stallone (b.1946) saw the 1975 boxing match between Muhammad Ali (1942-2016) and Charles Wepner (b.1939). Wepner wasn't expected to last as long as he did against "The Greatest," but that's what he did, and the 1976 film *Rocky* was all the better for it!

BONUS FACTS!

- Inventor Donald Weder (b.1947) of Highland, Illinois holds a total of 1,397 US patents, including synthetic grass, more than Thomas Alva Edison (1847-1931) ever did!

- *Octotroph* is the hashtag symbol's (#) real name!

- Malicious nineteenth-century journalists gave Chicago its "windy city" moniker when criticizing the city's elite as "full of hot air!"

- Rather than just five senses, people may have up to 21 senses, including balance, intuition, and proprioception (the sense of space).

NOSTRADAMUS

The art of forecasting is the extrapolation from today combined with a touch of imagination, but sometimes even supposed "experts" lack both, and are therefore unable to see beyond their own nose!

"The telephone has too many shortcomings to be seriously considered as a means of communication." —William Orton (1826-1878)

"Airplanes are interesting toys, but of no military value."
—General Ferdinand Foch (1851-1929)

"(When) music can be heard in the homes without the labor of study and close application, and without the slow process of acquiring a technique, it will be simply a question of time when the amateur disappears entirely, and with him a host of vocal and instrumental teachers, who will be without field or calling."
—John Philip Sousa (1854-1932)

"How will youths of 20 be able to compete in the professions or business against vigorous men still in their prime at 120, with a century of experience on which to draw?" —F.E. Smith (1872-1930)

"There will be no C, X, or Q in our everyday alphabet. They will be abandoned because unnecessary." —J. Elfreth Watkins Jr. (1875-?)

"The (atomic) bomb will never go off. I speak as an expert in explosives." –Admiral William Leahy (1875-1959)

"(In the future) cooking as an art is only a memory in the minds of old people. A few die-hards still broil a chicken or roast a leg of lamb, but the experts have developed ways of deep-freezing partially baked cuts of meat." —Waldemar Kaempffert (1877-1956)

"Cinema is little more than a passing fad. It's canned drama. What audiences really want to see is flesh and blood on the stage." —Charles Chaplin (1889-1977)

"Man of the next century will revolt against shaving and wear a beautiful beard. His hat will be an antenna snatching radio out of the ether. His socks—disposable. His suit minus tie, collar, buttons. His belt will hold all his pockets ever did." —Gilbert Rohde (1894-1944)

"Television won't last. It's a flash in the pan." —Mary Somerville (1897-1963)

"(The woman of the future) will wear a size 11 shoes, have shoulders like a wrestler, and muscles like a truck driver." —Dorothy Roe Lewis (1904-1985)

"Stick to driving a truck, because you'll never make it as a singer." —Eddie Bond (1933-2013) to Elvis Presley (1935-1977)

"It will be years—not in my time—before a woman will become prime minister." —Margaret Thatcher (1925-2013)

"There is no reason anyone would want a computer in their home." —Ken Olsen (1926-2011)

IV
CLOGGED
CULTURE

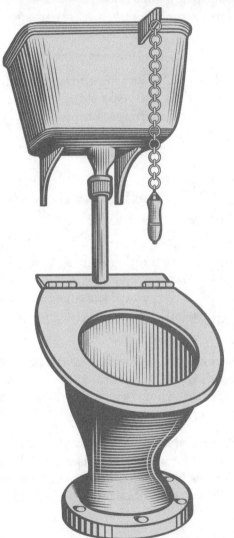

ENCINO MAN

Homo sapiens is a creative species. Be it for adorning itself or its surroundings, as well as expressing thoughts and emotions, mankind has been creating art, and therefore culture, possibly since the species sprung from Africa 300,000 years ago.

44,000-35,000BC: Oldest cave paintings made in Sulawesi, Indonesia. The oldest (44,000 years old), a stick-figure depiction of what appear to be boar-hunting anthropomorphic creatures (which scientists call *therianthropes*) was found in 2019.

35,600BC: Forever etched on the walls of the Altamira caves were the ochre and charcoal pictures of bison, and horses which would have made Picasso green with envy. Hand-prints too!

25,000BC: Adorned with hunting scenes, capibaras, and trees, the rock escarpments at *Serra da Capivara* National Park in Brazil, prove mankind not only had populated the Americas sooner than most thought possible, but also the creativity of "paleo-Indians."

18,000BC: The caves of Las Geel in Somalia feature sophisticated ritual abstract paintings of domesticated cattle in what are thought to be robes, domesticated dogs, a giraffe, and well dressed people!

17,000BC: While made later than others, the beautifully naturalistic cattle (including a 17 foot wide bull!), bison, and felines, among other animals and a single human painted on the Lascaux Caves, prove French art's illustrious beginnings!

13,000BC: Art was popular in India early on, as the Bophal (India) animal paintings on rock shelters attest. Red and white abstract paintings of tigers, bison, wild boar, rhinoceros, monkeys, elephants, and many more adorn these walls. Around the same time early inhabitants of southern Argentina were stenciling their hands on what came to be called *Cueva de las manos* ("Cave of Hands"). They also depicted the sun, abstract patterns, local fauna, and even hunting scenes of humans using what seems to be an early forerunner of bolas!

6,000-5,000BC: *Grotta dei Cervi* ("Deer Cave") is located in Otranto, Italy. Its enigmatic parietal scenes are thought to represent Neolithic creation myths, possibly rendered by ancient shamans.

40,000-35,000BC: Not all prehistoric art is 2D! The *Löwenmensch* ("Lion man") ivory figurine is the oldest sculptural representation of an anthropomorphic feline. Possibly the oldest "action figure" ever, it was found in a cave in Germany, surrounded by ancient artifacts, such as bone tools, antlers, and jewelry (pendants, beads, and perforated animal teeth)!

BONUS FACTS!

- In 1976, an unidentified woman sued Disneyland because one of the Three Little Pigs groped her.

- Peanuts, walnuts, almonds, cashews, and pistachios aren't really nuts, but seeds!

- 3% of Antarctica's glaciers are made of penguin urine!

THE BLACKLIST

We've all heard academia refer to cinema as "the seventh art," but few know those expressions are rooted in G.W.F. Hegel's (1770-1831) influential philosophy of art, which listed all arts known to eighteenth century people, nor the lists that preceded it, which used to categorize then-culturally acceptable art forms, at least in Europe.

1. In antiquity the arts were considered to be inspired by the Muses (Greek inspiration goddesses). Disciplines related to making physical objects (sculpture, architecture) or the pursuit of knowledge (science, philosophy) were considered lowbrow, or at the very least not purely creative. Art, therefore, was the conjuring of ideas "out of thin air" by divine inspiration:

First art: Epic verse (Calliope)

Second art: History (Clio)

Third art: Lyric poetry and song (Erato)

Fourth art: Music (Euterpe)

Fifth art: Stage drama (Melpomene)

Sixth art: Rhetoric (Polymnie)

Seventh art: Singing and dancing (Terpsichore)

Eighth art: Comedy (Thalia)

Ninth Art: Astronomy (Urania)

2. The Muses long forgotten, during the Middle Ages the distinction between science and art was erased, instead drawing the line between "liberal arts" and "applied arts" still used by many:

Liberal Arts:

First art: *Trivium* or the three arts of language: rhetoric, grammar, dialectic.

Second art: *Quadrivium* or the four sciences of numbers: arithmetic, geometry, astronomy, and music.

Applied Arts:

First art: Architecture

Second art: Sculpture

Third art: Painting

Fourth art: Metalworking

Fifth art: Textiles

Sixth art: Glass making

Seventh art: Herbal medicine

3. Then came Hegel's rediscovery of the Classical Greek listing, which has been further expanded to include new modern art forms as they appeared on the scene:

First art: Architecture

Second art: Sculpture

Third art: Painting

Fourth art: Music

Fifth art: Poetry

Sixth art: Performance

Seventh art: Cinema

Eighth art: Media (Radio, Television, Photography)

Ninth art: Comic books

DIFF'RENT STROKES

It is common knowledge that visual arts stopped evolving in the 1970s, and from them on all we get, if we are lucky, are regurgitated (a.k.a. "Postmodern") versions of tried and true major art styles, which may be summarized as follows.

Gothic: Western Christian art stemming from Byzantine (Greek or "Eastern") art, which involved elongated figures in long robes. Encompassing sculpture, panel painting, stained glass, fresco and illuminated manuscripts, it developed between the late Middle Ages to the late Renaissance.

Renaissance: Delving deeper into Greek and Roman history, fifteenth-century art abandoned modestly dressed stylized subjects in favor of naturalistic human nude figures, while never fully ditching the religious component, if only because the Catholic Church and its members were its main patrons.

Baroque: Long associated with the Catholic counter-reform movement, it flourished in architecture, music, dance, painting, sculpture between the seventeenth and eighteenth centuries. Extravagant and decorative, it took Renaissance art for a spin, shrouding its naturalistic nude figures with overflowing robes.

Rococo: The flamboyant, decadent late-eighteenth-century French offshoot of Baroque, Rococo was all about pastel hues, soft but plentiful curves and volutes, rosy cheeks, and even the occasional Chinese or Japanese motif (cherry blossoms included), which lives on in wedding cakes everywhere.

Pre-Raphaelite: Created by a close-knit community of Victorian

artists, poets and critics, theirs was deemed a return to early fourteenth and fifteenth century Italian art sans its religious aspects. Romantic, colorful, and highly symbolic, pre-Raphaelite art delved in German and Scandinavian Middle Ages lore instead.

Art Nouveau: At the turn of the century, this truly international movement embraced by both the fine and the applied arts revolutionized the way the world looked between 1890 and 1910, drawing on Baroque and Pre-Raphaelite influences, with a decidedly egalitarian spin—like the pre-Raphaelites, it concerned itself with the ugliness of forced and widespread industrialization, but rather than break the machine it sought to embellish it, and use it to spread its aesthetic ideas.

Impressionism: Yet another late-nineteenth-century movement, Impressionists focused almost exclusively on painting, though later branching out to literature and music. They rebelled against what they saw as the crass commercialism of Art Nouveau, as well as the rigid constraints of academic fine arts, while embracing light, freedom, spontaneity, and the acute observation of everyday subjects. As the pursuit of self expression went wilder, post-impressionism emerged with the likes of Paul Cézanne (1839-1906) and Vincent van Gogh (1853-1890).

Expressionism: Undoubtedly influenced by French post-impressionists, a young cadre of German painters started a new "total art" movement (meaning it encompassed both the arts, the applied arts, and even new media like film) at the dawn of the twentieth century. It would eventually spread beyond German borders, while surviving two World Wars!

Cubism: Pioneered by Georges Braque (1882-1963) and Pablo Picasso (1881-1973), while enamored with post-impressionism, it

subdued its color palette and emphasized a fragmented perception. It wasn't about the illusion of depth and volume, but a smashing of the glass through which people see reality.

Abstract: An undercurrent of Cubism, when some of its artists began to deconstruct shapes into geometrical shapes. The more mathematically precise these shapes and compositions got, the more "pure" the abstraction, while the more subjective and less defined they got, the more expressionistic it got. The early century Soviet bloc (and therefore, left-leaning European and Latin American artists too) would embrace the former in the form of Constructivism, while post-WWII America would turn to the latter, giving birth to something new: Abstract Expressionism.

Art Deco: The successor of Art Nouveau with an abstract streak, it would seek yet another marriage between fine and applied arts, while streamlining its predecessor's features, reducing its pattern load significantly. Seeking elegance above all, it also looked for inspiration in Gothic art's sleek representation of the human figure, while incorporating a degree of pre-Raphaelite symbolism.

Surrealism: Embracing the discoveries of psychoanalysis regarding the unconscious dreamscape, it was originally only a literary movement headed by the controversial, mercurial André Breton (1896-1966), which would grow beyond its original scope during the Jazz Age, to incorporate artists like Salvador Dalí (1904-1989), and film makers like Luis Buñuel (1900-1983).

Social realism: With the 1929 crash and ensuing Great Depression the party was over. Many artists turned from the gaiety of the surreal towards the depiction of the struggles of the poor and the working classes. It would reach its maximum scope in Mexican murals by artists like Diego Rivera (1886-1957), David Alfaro Siqueiros (1896-

1974), and José Clemente Orozco (1883-1949), while America's Edward Hopper (1882-1967) would give it a distinct voice in the US.

Pop Art: Recycling "lowbrow" applied art and design from comic books, advertising, and packaging, while taking advantage of print media and industrial production, some American artists would create this new form of art in the late 1950s and 1960s. As the sixties rolled along, Pop Art would incorporate Art-Nouveau influenced psychedelia, giving rise to artist-entrepreneurs like Andy Warhol (1928-1987) and Peter Max (b.1937).

BONUS FACTS!

- Timothy Ray Brown (b.1966), a.k.a. "The Berlin Patient" was cured of HIV in 2002 by receiving a bone marrow transplant from someone with immunity to the disease.

- The human eye is so keen, it can see a candle burning 1.6 miles across a flat landscape at night.

- By law, all pandas, even those born in foreign zoos, are a loaned property of the Chinese state.

- Rather than an agent, comedy legend Bill Murray (b.1950) reportedly has an equally mythical 1-800 number where prospective employers may leave him a message.

- The belief that duck quacks don't echo has, in fact, been disproved by science.

RENAISSANCE FAIR

If you think "Ninja Turtles" every time you hear Leonardo, Michelangelo, Raphael, and Donatello, here are the most relevant facts you need to know about those Renaissance artists not immortalized as cartoon super heroes.

Giotto (1267-1337): The ten-year old son of a blacksmith, Giotto di Bondone was sketching sheep on a flat stone when late middle-ages Florentine painter Cimbaue, Cenni di Pepo (1240-1302), happened to stroll by. Recognizing the boy's natural talent Cimbaue took the young lad under his wing. The rest as they say, is history, as Giotto soon surpassed his master (he could reportedly draw flies so realistic people would try to swat them, and hand-draw perfect circles), becoming a direct influence on Michelangelo (1475-1564) himself.

Leon Battista Alberti (1404-1472): The prototypical Renaissance man, Alberti didn't excel in all of the fields he tried his mind and hands on, but was a pioneering author of instructional "how-to" books, such as *De statua* ("On sculpture"), *De re aedificatoria* ("On Architecture"), *De cifris* ("On Ciphers" … yes, he did puzzles too!), and many others. His seminal 1435 *De pictura* ("On Painting"), became the first truly modern book dealing with linear perspective, and Alberti himself an influence on another polymath, Leonardo da Vinci (1452-1519).

Jan Van Eyck (1390-1441): In addition to being sent on diplomatic and spying missions by rulers as dissimilar as John the Pitiless (1374-1425) and Philip the Good (1396-1467), by the time he completed his naturalistic 1432 "Adoration of the Mystic Lamb" altarpiece, he had established oil painting as a reputable artistic medium over egg tempera, forever changing Renaissance painting.

Albrecht Dürer (1471-1528): This German artist achieved early fame by taking advantage of a new invention, the printing press, effectively becoming the first multi-media celebrity via his 1515 Rhinoceros woodcut print, which caused a sensation to the point of licensing it for various merchandise, including porcelain figurines!

Titian (c.1488-1576): Tiziano Vecelli was and is regarded as the most important painter of late Italian Renaissance. It is said while he was painting his famous "Equestrian Portrait of Charles V" he accidentally dropped the brush, which the lantern-jawed Emperor promptly stooped down to pick! Ironically, Tiziano's own prominence during this time, which trickled down to other painters as well, in part triggered a new rise of virulent iconoclasm which led to the destruction of art in churches and public places.

Paolo Veronese (1528-1588): In a scene which may have inspired Monty Python's famous "Last Supper" skit, starring a fictional Michelangelo, Venetian painter Veronese was in fact interrogated by the Inquisition with regard to his own 1573 *Last Supper* commission featuring dwarves, buffoons, animals, and even German soldiers! Unmoved by Veronese's plea regarding his need to fill such a large canvas with everything and anything he could muster, the Inquisition finally agreed to the painting being retitled "The Feast in the House of Levi."

BONUS FACT!

- Far from nice, "Positive Giants" are lightning bolts so powerful they may strike 20 miles away from the storm that birthed them, often under clear skies!

MUSIC AND LYRICS

Perhaps the most democratic of art forms, humanity has made music, sung, and danced since the dawn of time, and continues to do so!

1. There's a long list of kings who, not content with simply being a patron of the arts, have crossed to the other side and become performers themselves, including Biblical kings David and his son Solomon, Henry V (1386–1422) and Henry VIII (1491-1547), and Frederick the Great (1712-1786).

2. As dear to the crown, music has always been close to the cloth as well. Notable composer-priests include Tomás Luis de Victoria (c.1548-1611), Gregorio Allegri (c. 1582-1652), Gaspar Sanz (1640-1710), and Antonio "The Red Priest" Vivaldi (1678-1741).

3. While best known for his *Four Seasons* series of violin concertos, while employed at the *Pio Ospedale della Pietà* ("Devout Hospital of Mercy") orphanage in Venice, Vivaldi was expected to write two concerti a month (and five rehearsals) for the children's orchestra. He reportedly did 140 concerti at said institution, and over 400 more on his own!

4. Persecuted for eloping with an underage girl, Giuseppe Tartini (1692-1770) sought sanctuary at a Franciscan monastery, where he took up playing the violin. Dissatisfied with his progress, one night he dreamt of the devil playing the instrument at his bedside, and the next morning proceeded to replicate what he had heard. The resulting *Il trillo del diavolo* ("The Devil's Trill") sonata is considered to be fiendishly hard to play, even by modern standards. Tartini would become a music teacher and scholar of repute, and the first known owner of a Stradivarius violin in 1715!

5. Perhaps the most famous composer of all time, and an international celebrity during his own lifetime, Wolfgang Amadeus Mozart (1756-1791) died at 35 after a long illness—despite Salieri's (1750-1825) claim to have poisoned him! While it has long been stated that Mozart had a pauper's burial in an unmarked grave, the truth is he died neither poor nor forgotten. The Viennese custom at the time for non-royalty ("commons") was a modest funeral in graves subject to excavation after a decade ("common graves").

6. Composer William Crotch (1775-1847) was a child prodigy akin to Mozart, who at age two would play church hymns at a home-made organ, and later taken to London to play for King George III (1738-1820) himself. Becoming a renowned organist, unlike Mozart he lived a long fruitful life.

7. Necessity being the mother of invention, also spurs musical geniuses. Frederic Handel (1685-1759), said to have composed his *Messiah* oratorio in 24 days. Giacomo Rossini (1792-1868) finished the comic opera *Il barbiere di Siviglia* ("The Barber of Seville") in 19 days. Gaetano Donizetti (1797-1848) did his *L'elisir d'amore* ("The Elixir of Love") in less than a month. Mozart? Well, he wrote the overture for his *Don Giovanni* in less than 48 hours!

8. Ludwig van Beethoven (1770-1827) began to lose his hearing at 28. Completely deaf by the time his Ninth Symphony premiered in Vienna in 1824 to thunderous applause, ovation, and even feet stomping, he remained oblivious to it all and had to be turned around by co-conductor Michael Umlauf (1781-1842) to notice how well the "D minor, Opus 125" had been received by its original audience.

VIDEO KILLED
THE RADIO STAR

Music was and still is affected by technological developments which allow it to be recorded and transmitted like never before. Propelled from concert and popular venues to everyone's homes and pockets, the development of music as an industry and big business rapidly took to specialization as well as the setting, marketing, and following of trends from both sides of the musical aisle.

1. In 1864, Scottish scientist James Clerk Maxwell (1831-1879) theoretically stated air wave transmission was possible. It would be experimentally made possible by German physicist Heinrich Rudolf Hertz (1857-1894) only in 1888!

2. Engineer Elisha Gray (1835-1901) created the "Musical Telegraph," considered the first modern synthesizer, in 1874. Two years later, he pioneered electronic music transmission, creating a machine that sent music over telephone lines!

3. Thomas Alva Edison (1847-1931) innovated into many fields, but none more than music when inventing the phonograph in 1877. He used paraffin soaked paper strips to record and play sounds, which by 1978 he had replaced with tinfoil, and in 1886 he developed wax cylinders to replace tinfoil. Now anyone who could afford it, could record their own voices!

4. In 1887, Emile Berliner (1851-1929) patented his gramophone, which played a flat rubber disc with a spiral groove etched on its surface, which would eventually phase wax cylinders out. Rubber would eventually be completely replaced by sturdier shellac, and much cheaper Polyvinyl chloride (PVC) later on, but the record industry was born and would dominate the entire twentieth-century music scene.

In 1948, the first vinyl LP (long-playing) was finally unveiled by Columbia Records, ushering what has been called the "Album Era." Then in 1957, a small company called Audio Fidelity Records marketed the first stereo vinyl.

5. Originally wrapped in brown paper sleeves, album cover art was introduced by designer Alex Steinweiss (1917- 2011) at Columbia Records in 1938. It was a—ahem!—resounding success, and other companies immediately followed suit.

6. Building on an electrical wireless transmission patent purchased from his friend, Thomas Edison, Italian inventor Guglielmo Marconi (1874-1937) was able to build the world's first working radio, which he patented in Britain two years later.

By 1954, the newly developed semiconductor technology which would revolutionize computing, led to the transistor radio. A year later, a new company in Japan, SONY, marketed its very first pocket radio, the TR-55!

7. Perfected by Nazi Germany, magnetic tape recording had been available in the US since the late 1940s, but it was inventor Bill Lear (1902-1978) who made it accessible for the average American consumer via his eight-track tape, becoming a mass market success when Ford incorporated eight-track players into several of their cars. Originally developed for dictation devices, the portable and customizable compact cassette (developed by Phillips in 1963) would eventually outgrow the eight-track, sparking the rise of the mix-tape, as well as a whole independent scene of self-made DJ, hip-hop, and garage-rock artists.

8. On August 1, 1981, a new Viacom-owned cable channel called MTV (Music Television) exploded onto the TV, record, and music scene, airing music video clips on shows hosted by "video jockeys."

While music films (not to be confused with musicals) had long been a staple of rock and pop music since the Beatles decided to stop touring altogether, MTV turned the whole industry on its ear, forcing it to go visual, and catapulting the careers of new music stars who so far had had little success in the radio waves and record store aisles.

9. Developed from LaserDisc technology, which thrived only in Asia, the Compact Disc (CD) was a joint venture by Philips and Sony. Storing music (in a thin aluminum sheet sandwiched in clear plastic) with a level of quality previously unheard of, while immune to scratches, static, and dust (but not humidity), the first commercial CD, a Chilean pianist Claudio Arrau (1903-1991) concert, was produced in 1982, followed by *The Visitors*, a new ABBA album for the pop-music crowd. Eventually this technology turned more affordable and spread all over the world, widely surpassing cassette and vinyl record sales. Even the original Playstation games had their game music set as CD audio and could be listened to from a regular CD player—some games even had secret tracks that could only be listed to this way!

10. With computer hard drives and processors gradually becoming more powerful, and cloud-dominated internet music streaming becoming the norm, CD sales finally began to decline in 2010. Strangely enough, nostalgia around "analog" vinyl resurrected an industry in the brink of extinction, from an all-time low $35 million yearly revenue in 2005, to an estimated $500 million by 2019, according to the RIAA US Sales Database!

BONUS FACT!

- Only Dominica and Nicaragua use purple in their flags.

LISTEN TO THE MUZAK

As dull as it sounds, non-entertaining, unintrusive, functional background music designed to either energize or tranquilize the general population was and still is a revolutionary idea, regardless how it may come to be derided by the uninformed masses.

1. It all began when soldier-inventor Major General George Owen Squier (1865-1934) laid the theoretical groundwork for what he called "Wired Entertainment," which basically consisted in piggybacking radio signals on utility lines. That's where cable originally comes from, but in the 1920s wireless radio almost got him out of business, so he came up with the Muzak concept (the name itself is a contraction of music and invented word "Kodak"), which he wired to retail stores and other public companies.

2. The Muzak company grew exponentially, reaching a peak from the 1950s to the 1970s, when president Dwight D. Eisenhower (1890-1969) installed Muzak speakers in the White House, NASA used it to relax the Apollo program astronauts, and Lyndon B. Johnson (1908-1973) even owned a franchise out of Austin, Texas! Muzak was everywhere—even in police stations in Japan!—but all good things must come to an end, and a series of mergers and bankruptcies saw the company's demise in 2011, with different, smaller providers quickly filling its gap.

3. Background music is usually found on retail stores, and for good reason, as it increases sales by 34% according to a 1982 study which has been repeatedly confirmed. Classical and Jazz style "muzak" played at a slower tempo stimulates higher spending in retail and restaurants alike!

4. In office environments, where productivity needs to be stimulated, background music is also designed "not to be," its tempo increasing in the most lethargic work hours. Familiar music, such as hit songs, even when re-mixed tends to distract (via dopamine) the working drone.

5. In 2015, Belfast (Ireland) Police used nursery rhymes to successfully defuse teenage rioting!

6. Of course, the same principle applied to "elevator music" can be reverse-engineered to inflict pain and disturb the enemy mind in psychological warfare, most famously:

- **Van Halen's "Panama" made General Manuel Noriega (1934-2017) surrender to US forces after ten days back in 1989.**

- **During the 1991 Gulf War, Richard Wagner's (1813-1883) "Ride of the Valkyries" was used against Iraqi forces by US military, as a way to evoke the 1979 film *Apocalypse Now*.**

- **"The Real Slim Shady" by rapper Eminem (b.1972) tortured Guantanamo prisoners during the early War on Terror, while in the Afghan front, songs by Metallica, Thin Lizzy, and The Offspring were blasted against the Taliban.**

- **When Russia annexed Crimea in 2014, broadcasting propaganda on loudspeakers, the defiant Ukranian military responded with music by Cher, though it appears to have been surprisingly ineffective ...**

GOD GAVE ROCK AND ROLL

There's no bigger treasure trove in music history than rock and roll, and here are the facts to prove it!

1. Lynyrd Skynyrd's name was inspired by coach Leonard Skinner (1933-2010), who had a zero-tolerance policy towards long hair at Robert E Lee high school in Jacksonville. Another man who clearly didn't like long-haired men was the farmer who shot drummer "Artimus" Pyle (b.1948) while seeking help after the 1977 plane crash that killed most of the band's original lineup!

2. Though much has been said about Axl Rose, the stage name of William Bruce Rose Jr. (b.1962), being an anagram for "oral sex," the truth is he adopted his first band's name, AXL, as his own, before forming Guns N' Roses.

3. Paul David Hewson (b.1960), a.k.a. "Bono," got his stage name from Dublin's Bonavox hearing aid store, but originally wanted to be called "Steinhegvanhuysenolegbangbangbang," which obviously didn't pan out. Regardless, Bono has somehow managed to be nominated for Grammys, Oscars, Golden Globes, and even the Nobel Peace Prize!

4. While The Beatles have been featured on the cover of Rolling Stone magazine more than any other band (30 times!), Dr. Hook & the Medicine Show made it there only after their song "The Cover of Rolling Stone" was a hit. Apparently the magazine was so reluctant to include such a lowbrow band, they decided to use a caricature instead of a photo, under a sardonic "What's-Their-Names Make the Cover" title!

5. For years, ZZ Top's drummer Frank Beard (b.1949) ironically remained clean-shaven. The other band members reportedly turned down a one million dollar offer from razor-blade brand Gillette to shave off their beards in one of their ads!

6. Leo Fender (1909-1991), the 1992 Rock and Roll Hall of Fame inductee, and maker of the iconic electric guitars played by many rock legends, never actually learned to play the instrument!

7. If you listen very carefully to The Beatles' 1968 "Hey Jude," just before the "na-na-na-na-na-na," Paul McCartney (b.1942) on the piano utters a loud curse after making a mistake. Years later, that same piano would be played by none other than Freddie Mercury (b.1946-1991) when recording "Bohemian Rhapsody!"

9. Underage groupie Lori Maddox (b.1958) lost her virginity to David Bowie (1947-2016), tried some BDSM with Mick Jagger (b.1943), and later had a long relationship with Led Zeppelin's Jimmy Page (b.1944). Statutory rape isn't a new thing in rock and roll by any means, its "lolicon" stars including pioneers Chuck Berry (1926-2017), Elvis Presley (1935-1977), and Jerry Lee Lewis (b.1935), who infamously married his 13 year-old cousin, while many musicians even flaunt their exploits in tunes like Iggy Pop's "Look Away," Red Hot Chilli Peppers' "Catholic School Girls Rule," Ted Nugent's "Jailbait," Billy Joel's "Only the Good Die Young," and The Commodores' "Young Girls Are My Weakness!"

BONUS FACT!

- Grapes are poisonous to dogs and cats!

TOP OF THE POPS

Widely considered one of the greatest guitarists in history, Peter Frampton (b.1950) rose to mega-stardom with his 1976 Frampton Comes Alive! *live album, which sold 8,000,000 copies in the US and yet, it doesn't even come close to scratching the following RIAA-certified list of all-time best selling albums.*

15,000,000 units sold: Bob Marley's *Legend*, Bruce Springsteen's *Born in the U.S.A.*, Journey's *Greatest Hits*, and Pink Floyd's *Dark Side of the Moon*.

16,000,000 units sold: Led Zeppelin's *Physical Graffiti*, Bee Gees' *Saturday Night Fever*, Metallica's *Metallica*, and Alanis Morissette's *Jagged Little Pill*.

17,000,000 units sold: Boston's *Boston*, Elton John's *Greatest Hits*, and Garth Brooks's *No Fences*.

18,000,000 units sold: Guns N' Roses' *Appetite for Destruction*.

19,000,000 units sold: The Beatles' *The Beatles*, and Whitney Houston's *The Bodyguard*.

20,000,000 units sold: Fleetwood Mac's *Rumours*, and Shania Twain's *Come on Over*.

21,000,000 units sold: Garth Brooks's *Double Live*, and Hootie & The Blowfish's *Cracked Rear View*.

22,000,000 units sold: AC/DC's *Back in Black*.

23,000,000 units sold: Billy Joel's *Greatest Hits Volume I & Volume II*, Led Zeppelin's *Led Zeppelin IV*, and Pink Floyd's *The Wall*.

26,000,000 units sold: Eagles' *Hotel California*.

33,000,000 units sold: Michael Jackson's *Thriller*.

38,000,000 units sold: Eagles' *Their Greatest Hits 1971-1975*, which so far makes it the best-selling album in history!

To win a "gold record" RIAA certification in the US, an album needs to sell 500,000 units, a "platinum record" is given after selling 2,000,000, and a "diamond record" after cracking the 10,000,000 barrier! Money, of course, is a different question. Artists usually make around 6.6% per unit, while producers net 2.2%, songwriters 4.5%, distributors 22%, manufacturing 5%, retailers 30%, and record labels 30% (after the advance paid to artists is recouped). You do the math!

BONUS FACTS!

- President Abraham Lincoln's (1809-1865) grandfather, Captain Abraham Lincoln (1744-1786), was also shot dead!

- American basketball player Shaquille O'Neal (b.1972) only made one three-pointer in his entire NBA career, back in 1996.

HI-YO, SILVER! AWAY!

Before television became king of home entertainment (a throne it never relinquished), radio was queen of the airwaves. Pioneering many formats, including drama, sitcom, soap opera, super-heroes, western, game, and cooking, some of its serials would even successfully transition to TV shows down the road.

The Lone Ranger: Created by Francis "Fran" Striker (1903-1962), the first few episodes of the serial broadcast locally at Buffalo's WEBR in 1932, before moving to George Trendle's (1884-1972) WXYZ in Detroit. The show was so successful over its almost 3,000 episodes, it crossed over to comics, animation, TV, and the movies, while spinning off to the much less successful "The Green Hornet."

The Adventures of Superman: Based on the 1938 comic book, it was a long running serial (1940-1951), perhaps its most famous episode ever is the one where Superman/Clark Kent fights the evil Knights of the White Carnation, an obvious Ku Klux Klan reference, in a cover effort by the Anti-Defamation League to denounce and ridicule the Klan's perverse ideology. It worked, and the episode's ratings skyrocketed!

Perry Mason: Broadcast on CBS Radio from 1943 to 1955, the show was inspired by Erle Stanley Gardner's (1889-1970) novels featuring the title character. It was so successful, CBS immediately went ahead not with one, but two TV adaptations: the eponymous prime-time courtroom drama starring Raymond Burr (1917-1993), and daytime mystery soap opera "The Edge of Night," which remained on air for 30 years!

The Saint: From 1945 till 1950, the adventures of Simon Templar, the charming anti-hero created by author Leslie Charteris (1907-1993), was broadcast intermittently from coast to coast. Interpreted by different actors, notably Vincent Price (1911-1993) throughout its

run, it would appeal to a whole new generation from 1962 to 1969, on a TV show starring Sir Roger Moore (1927-2017).

Dragnet: Widely considered the most influential police procedural in history, it ran from 1949 to 1957 on NBC Radio, the serial was the brainchild of Jack Webb (1920-1982), who both produced and starred it as Sargent Joe Friday. Webb insistence on verisimilitude and realism paid off, and the show was even commended by the Detroit Police Officers' Association, which praised it for increasing public esteem and awareness of police work. Needless to say, it made a seamless transition to television from 1951 to 1959, returning again in the late 1960s.

Gunsmoke: A gritty western set in post-Civil War Dodge City, Kansas, it was developed at CBS Radio by John Meston (1914-1979) and Norman Macdonnell (1916-1979), running from 1952 till 1961. Its popularity saw it adapted (almost to the letter) to television shortly after it began airing. The TV show that would outlive the original, becoming the longest-running live-action series of the twentieth century— it ended in 1975!

Lassie: Adapted from Eric Knight's (1897-1943) 1940 novel, *Lassie Come Home*, it was initially broadcast on ABC Radio, and then moved to NBC Radio between 1947 and 1950. Lassie was already a household name and the star of a previous 1943 MGM film adaptation, Lassie would translate well to television, where it became the fifth longest-running U.S. primetime television series ever (1954-1973) on CBS.

Truth or Consequences: A pioneering live game show originally broadcast by NBC Radio from 1940 to 1957, and hosted by Ralph Edwards (1913-2005). In 1941, it was once experimentally aired at the WNBT New York TV station, becoming the first-ever televised game show. Successfully relaunched on TV in 1950, it was broadcast until 1988!

Take It or Leave It: A CBS Radio game show from 1940 to 1947, it is now mainly remembered for being the basis of the "$64,000 Question" TV game show which began in 1955 and ended in 1958, amid a rigging scandal which inspired the 1994 *Quiz Show* film.

Young Doctor Malone: Created by the multi-talented Irna "Queen of the Soaps" Phillips (1901-1973) and produced by Betty Corday (1912-1987), it was a long-running soap opera which began in 1939 and ended in 1960, alongside other CBS Radio soap serials. However, two years earlier it had made the jump to television, where it remained until 1963.

The Abbott and Costello Show: A 30-minute comedy segment which took advantage of it's starring duo vaudevillian talents from 1940 till 1949, and from 1947 till 1949 alongside "The Abbott and Costello Children's Show." Already film celebrities at the time, Bud Abbott (1897-1974) and Lou Costello (1906-1959), made a quick transition to television, until their popularity waned due to overexposure in the mid-1950s. In spite of Costello's passing, Abbott managed a return of sorts, on the 1966 Hanna-Barbera "The Abbott and Costello Cartoon Show."

War of the Worlds: Perhaps the most famous radio serial episode of all time, on October 30, 1938, Orson Welles's (1915-1985) straight-faced, "1930s news bulletin" style adaptation of the 1898 H.G. Wells (1866-1946) novel for an episode of "The Mercury Theatre on the Air" scared the daylights out of casual listeners, if not the serial's usually small audience of hard-core sci-fi aficionados.

BONUS FACT!

- Pre-sliced bread was invented in 1929 Missouri.

FEAST OR FAMINE

There's more to a writer's life that meets the eye...

David Hume (1711-1776): Of modest means, Hume had no academic credentials, and was therefore barred from teaching at the university of Edinburgh. Undeterred, he got a job there as a librarian instead, and then as a private tutor, while writing his influential treatises and essays.

Walt Whitman (1819-1892): Working since age 11, the celebrated poet not only wrote his seminal *Leaves of Grass* (1855), but also handled its first and subsequent editions' typesetting and design. Used to hardship, during the Civil War (1861-1865), he volunteered as a hospital nurse, caring for wounded soldiers!

Joseph Conrad (1857-1924): The home-schooled son of Polish political activists, who would become the masterful author of *Heart of Darkness* (1899), *Lord Jim* (1900), and *Nostromo* (1904), Conrad only began to learn English after joining the British merchant navy in his early twenties. Quitting life as a sailor at age 36, he embarked on a literary career which would only begin to bear fruit 19 years later, with the publication of his novel *Chance* in 1913.

Raymond Chandler (1888-1959): While not a pauper, Chandler failed as a journalist in Britain, and held a number of odd jobs in the US, before landing a job as a bookkeeper at an oil company. He soon climbed up the company ladder and was made its vice president in 1931, but his alcoholism, depression, and promiscuity soon saw him fired. Finding himself unemployed during the Great Depression, he turned to writing detective pulp-fiction, becoming wildly successful.

Francis McCourt (1930-2009): Brought up in squalor and indigence, McCourt worked odd jobs after leaving school at age 13, until he had saved enough to migrate to the US. Drafted for the Korean War, after his discharge he used his G.I. Bill to study and graduate from the New York University, becoming a public school teacher, a job he kept for 30 years, until his 1996 memoir *Angela's Ashes* allowed him to pursue a full-time writing career.

Chuck Norris (b.1940): Beyond the popular tall-tale "facts," this American actor and martial artist has written six non-fiction books and two fiction novels, in between his many jobs and charity work: *Winning Tournament Karate* (1975), *Toughen Up! The Chuck Norris Fitness System* (1983), *The Secret of Inner Strength: My Story* (1987), *The Secret Power Within: Zen Solutions to Real Problems* (1996), *Against All Odds: My Story* (2004), *The Justice Riders* (2006), and *A Threat to Justice* (2007).

Steven Pressfield (b.1943): Before breaking in as a novelist with his 1995 novel *The Legend of Bagger Vance: A Novel of Golf and the Game of Life*, and *Gates of Fire* (1998), Pressfield struggled as a copywriter, schoolteacher, truck driver, bartender, mental hospital attendant, fruit-picker, and screenwriter.

Stephen King (b.1947): Grinding his teeth as a school teacher, while his pregnant wife worked in Dunkin' Donuts, King wrote three rejected novels from his trailer home, until striking gold with a fourth one, *Carrie* (1973), he based on a short story his wife fished out of the trash can after he had scrapped it!

BONUS FACT!

- Monowi, NE, only has one resident, Ms. Elsie Eiler (b.1934).

THE PHANTOM

When established authors are not able to keep up with the public's demand, and public personalities "have a book inside," but not the means nor the training to put it on paper, ghostwriting became a big part of the publishing business. The practice has two basic modes:

Uncredited: *When a writer is legally bound to maintain confidentiality and relinquish all rights to a given work.*

Alexandre Dumas (1802-1870): Akin to a modern day TV show producer, the legendary author of *The Count of Monte Cristo* and *The Three Musketeers*, both of which were originally serialized in newspapers for many years, had a production company with a stable of writers, including his own son Alexandre Dumas fils (1824-1895). These writer would work on stories based on Dumas's basic outlines, which he would later polish before sending then to the presses.

Ian Fleming (1908-1964): A chain-smoking alcoholic with cardiac problems, Fleming relied heavily on Kingsley Amis (1922-1995) during the second half of his career, when Bond's fame put a heavy workload on his shoulders.

R.L.Stine (b.1943): The "Stephen King" of children's horror, Stine relies on a number of freelance ghostwriters to sustain his long-lived book series, including *Goosebumps* and *Fear Street*.

Francine Pascal (b.1938): Not unlike Stine, Pascal also employs a small army of writers to keep her *Sweet Valley High* series running, alongside spin-offs such as *The Unicorn Club* and *Sweet Valley University*.

Ulysses S. Grant (1822-1885): Going through serious financial problems in the latter part of his life, America's eighteenth president was helped by none other than Mark Twain (1835-1910) who wrote and published the *Personal Memoirs of Ulysses S. Grant*, with tremendous success.

John F. Kennedy (1917-1963): When he was still a US Senator, JFK won the 1956 Pulitzer Prize for *Profiles in Courage*, a nonfiction book reportedly written by his speech writer, Ted Sorensen (1928-2010).

Partially credited: *When a celebrity of some sort lends their name as the main sales hook, while the name of the person who actually does the writing appears beneath it, usually to the financial benefit of both parts.*

James Patterson (b.1947): America's highest-paid, best-selling author's output of over 12 books a year wouldn't be possible without many co-authors including Andrew Gross (b.1952), Mark T. Sullivan (b. 1958), and many, many, many more!

Lee Iacocca (1924-2019): Among other ghostwriters, the influential automobile executive worked with William Novak (b.1948), who also wrote Nancy Reagan's *My Turn: The Memoirs of Nancy Reagan* (1989), and Magic Johnson's *My Life* (1993).

Chris Gardner (b.1954): The influential businessman memoir, *The Pursuit of Happyness* (2006), was written with Quincy Troupe (b.1939), who also wrote the autobiography of Miles Davis, *Miles* (1990).

Donald J. Trump: (b.1946): Certainly not the first president, nor business mogul to share author credit with ghostwriters including Tony Schwartz (b.1952), Kate Bohner (b.1967), and particularly Meredith McIver (b. c.1950).

THE SHAWSHANK REDEMPTION

Real writers don't wait until they're perfectly comfortable at the studio with a steaming coffee mug at their side. Indeed, some of the most enduring and influential literary works of every type and genre were written in the worst of circumstances, imprisonment, by writers who understood there's no time like the present!

Paul the Apostle (c.5-67AD): Credited for spreading the Gospel to the Gentiles, the Christian saint wrote four of his seminal Epistles while in prison (Ephesians, Philippians, Colossians, and Philemon), before his execution in Rome.

Marco Polo (1254-1324): While he didn't put pen to paper by himself, Polo dictated his journeys to a fellow prison inmate, which would then be compiled as *Il Milione*, or "The Travels of Marco Polo."

Miguel de Cervantes (1547-1616): The "one-armed man from Lepanto" began writing what is considered to be the first modern prose novel (before it, everything was verse), *El ingenioso hidalgo Don Quijote de la Mancha* ("Don Quixote") while in jail.

John Bunyan (1628-1688): Jailed for his Puritan teachings, Bunyan wrote the influential theological fiction book *The Pilgrim's Progress*, as well as the autobiographical *Grace Abounding to the Chief of Sinners*.

John Cleland (1709-1789): While in debtor's prison, the author finished his 1748 erotica classic *Fanny Hill: or, the Memoirs of a Woman of Pleasure*, which became a best-seller, though its success landed the author another stint in prison!

Voltaire (1694-1778): While his satirical writings got him an 11-month sentence at the infamous Bastille prison, François-Marie Arouet used that time to keep writing, emerging from imprisonment as "Voltaire!"

O. Henry (1862-1910): William Sydney Porter got his first 14 short stories published under pen name "O. Henry" while serving a five-year sentence for embezzlement!

Bertrand Russell (1872-1970): Sometimes, people get locked up for the right reasons, as was the case for Russell's two prison sentences resulting from his active pacifism during WWI, which he used to work on his *Introduction to Mathematical Philosophy.*

Adolf Hitler (1889-1945): Far from a pacifist, the German dictator wrote his *Mein Kampf* ("My Struggle") manifesto while serving nine months in prison after his failed coup d'état in Munich, known as the Beer Hall Putsch in 1923.

Erich von Däniken (b.1935): The Swiss author of several pseudoscientific books dealing with extraterrestrial phenomena, Däniken began to write his best selling *Chariots of the Gods?* (1968) while serving prison time for embezzlement, but the books was published only after an extensive rewrite by its editor, Utz Utermann (1912-1991), working under pen name "Wilhelm Roggersdorf."

Rubin "Hurricane" Carter (1937-2014): Convicted for a murder he didn't commit, the middleweight boxing champion wrote his best-selling *The 16th Round: From Number One Contender to Number 45472* (1975) in a bid to gather public support for his release, which finally took place a decade later.

HIDDEN FIGURES

Almost everyone is familiar with the rhetorical tools such as alliterations, metaphors, euphemisms, puns, and irony, but what about the lesser-known yet widely-used figures of speech?

Antimeria: Using one part of speech as another, as when using nouns as verbs, e.g. "Let's book that flight."

Antimetabole: The reverse repetition of words in successive clauses, e.g. "When the going gets tough, the tough get going."

Dehortatio: The complete opposite of an exhortation, it is used to demotivate, e.g. "You've got to ask yourself one question. 'Do I feel lucky?' Well, do ya, punk?" —*Dirty Harry* (1971)

Dysphemism: Polar opposite to a euphemism, a dysphemism substitutes a not-so-bad term for a harsher one, e.g. "Snail mail."

Enallage: Deliberately dismissing grammatical rules, e.g. "Thunderbirds are go!"

Epanorthosis: Also known as correctio, it is a speech device used to correct one's mistakes, e.g. "Maybe there is a beast. . . . What I mean is . . . maybe it's only us." —William Golding (1911-1993).

Epitrope: When permission is ironically granted to someone to do what they propose to do, e.g. "Go ahead, make my day." —*Sudden Impact* (1983)

Euphony: A combination of beautifully sounding words, e.g. "Cellar door."

Homograph: Words which are identically written while having different meaning, e.g. "Bear" (both "to carry a load," and Ursidae mammals).

Hypozeuxis: When every clause in a sentence has its own subject and predicate, e.g. "We shall fight on the beaches. We shall fight on the landing grounds. We shall fight in the fields and in the streets. We shall fight in the hills." —Winston Churchill (1874-1965)

Litote: Understating a negative to ironically affirm a positive, e.g. "not too bad."

Paradiastole: Sarcastically representing a vice as a virtue, e.g. "You should have seen how wisely I proceeded—with what caution—with what foresight—with what dissimulation I went to work! ... Oh, you would have laughed to see how cunningly I thrust it in!" —Edgar Allan Poe (1809-1849)

Paronomasia: Also known as a malapropism, it happens when we unwittingly replace a word with a similarly sounding but incorrect word, e.g. "I am a person who recognizes the fallacy of humans." —George W. Bush (b.1946)

Sine dicendo: An obvious, superficial comment which doesn't add anything to a conversation, e.g. "Dogs are loyal."

Spoonerism: Switching syllables between two words in the same sentence, e.g. "Don't pet the sweaty things." —George Carlin (1937-2008)

COMMON SENSE

Behind every popular expression in the English language there is a history which explains how it came to be used.

Not One Iota of Difference: Arius (c.250-336AD) was a Libyan priest in Alexandria, Egypt, was the source of a Christian doctrine which stated the Father and the Son (Jesus Christ) were separate entities: *Homoi-ousion*. Arianism was staunchly opposed by Christians who believed the Father, the Son to be one: *Homo-ousion*. So while technically the only thing separating both beliefs was a single Greek *iota*, Arianism was promptly declared a heresy in 325AD.

Rock of Ages: Originally a 1775 Christian hymn composed from a hastily written verse ("Rock of Ages, Cleft for Me") by Reverend Augustus Montague Toplady (1740-1778) while accidentally stranded by a storm in the gorge of Burrington Combe (Mendip Hills, England).

Hip Hip Hooray!: "Hip" is thought to be derived from the Middle Ages "Hep," an abbreviation of *Hierosolyma est perdita*, or "Jerusalem is fallen." "Hooray," on the other hand, came from *Hu-raj*! ("To Paradise!"). How this Crusader war-cry came to be adopted as a toast in Georgian Britain is anybody's guess!

OK: The last surviving intentional misspelled abbreviation from the 1830s, which included KC ("Knuff Ced"), KY ("Know Yuse"), and OW ("Oll Wright"), it is the neutral affirmative expression "Oll Korrect," meaning everything's in order. Outgrowing the Boston youth fad that gave birth to it, it began to appear in the press, and was popularized nationwide by America's eighth president, Martin van Buren (1782-1862), a.k.a. "Old Kinderhook!"

Happy Birthday: While ancient Roman men used to get a birthday celebration cake when they reached 50 (considered a senior citizen those days), "Happy Birthday" only became a standard greeting after a retooled version of a song titled "Good Morning to All" began to substitute the more generic "For He's a Jolly Good Fellow" in the early 1900s. The company that copyrighted "Happy Birthday to You" was later acquired by Warner Music, which began to prosecute anyone who used it without paying for the privilege, until officially declared it to be in the public domain in 2016.

Home Sweet Home: Credited to American playwright John Howard Payne (1791-1852), "Home Sweet Home" was an emotional ballad written to a tune composed by Henry Rowley Bishop (1787-1856), where the former was living as an expatriate. Years later, while Payne found himself a US ambassador in North Africa, Bishop would become the first musician ever to be knighted.

Kilroy Was Here: American shipyard inspector James J. Kilroy (1902-1962) used to chalk the inscription next to rivets he had checked. When WWII sailors began to find the inscription in sealed areas within those same ships, they began to use it as graffiti overseas, which grew its legend exponentially.

BONUS FACTS!

- Hippos kill around 500 people every year, more than cows, lions, sharks, and wolves combined!

- Perfectly pure water with no side ions wouldn't be able to conduct electricity in any way.

THE BRAVE AND THE BALD

It's on everybody's scalp: bald is the new black! While the ego of insecure men everywhere apparently rests on the length of their hair, strong role models baldly go where no hipster has gone before.

THE GOOD:

Gandhi (1869-1948): His successful non-violent resistance against British colonial rule over India inspired Rev. Martin Luther King Jr.'s (1929-1968) Civil Rights Movement and the 1989-1991 Singing Revolution in Estonia, Latvia, and Lithuania which brought down the USSR!

Pope Francis (b.1936): While keeping with the Catholic Church's doctrine, since elected as pope in 2013, Cardinal Jorge Mario Bergoglio has done his utmost to raise public consciousness on the plight of the poor, climate change action, and the high cost of over development. He's also allowed access to Communion for the divorced and remarried, and generally showed greater tolerance and compassion that his predecessors.

Phil McGraw (b.1950): The good doctor is a psychologist and host of his eponymous TV show, dealing with various self-improvement, relationship, and family issues, which Dr. Phil also addresses in his many best-selling books.

THE BAD:

Dick Cheney (b.1941): Quiet, unassuming, and driven, the forty-sixth vice president of the United States, was also the most powerful man in the country during the first decade of the twenty-first century. Launching the still-ongoing War on Terror, he made America

regain its predominant place at the world stage, while keeping federal government on a tight leash.

Rupert Murdoch (b.1931): From relatively humble beginnings in Australia, the media tycoon took a single newspaper and grew his business into a multinational mass media corporation known as News Corp., which even acquired Twentieth Century Fox back in 1985, and sold it to Disney in 2019 for a staggering $71.3 billion!

Jeff Bezos (b.1964): As of 2020, the richest man in the whole wide world (and the closest to comic book character Lex Luthor), in addition to owning the world's biggest online store and internet company, Amazon, he also launched aerospace company Blue Origin, which plans to reach the moon by 2024!

THE BADASS:

Telly Savalas (1922-1994): Over a memorable 40-year career in film, which included *The Greatest Story Ever Told* (1965), and *The Dirty Dozen* (1967), Savalas will forever be remembered as the lollipop-wielding Lt. Theo Kojak, from TV series "Kojak" (1973–1978), one of the best cop shows ever!

Ving Rhames (b.1959): The Julliard School graduate career actor has played many iconic roles in his career, including Luther Stickell in the *Mission: Impossible* film franchise and Marcellus Wallace in *Pulp Fiction* (1994), but playing iconic bald cop Theo Kojak in the excellent 2005 series remake earned him a spot in this list.

Samuel L. Jackson (b.1948): Did someone say *Pulp Fiction*? While his breakthrough role in that film secured his career, Jackson, a former member of the Black Power movement, made "bald badass" his

trademark in subsequent films, particularly his recent rendition of Nick Fury, Agent of S.H.I.E.L.D., in the Marvel cinematic universe.

THE BRAVE:

Hulk Hogan (b.1953): While currently semi-retired, Terry Gene Bollea rose to the heights on wrestling fame in the 1980s, and hasn't climbed down since. Winning five WWF (now WWE) Championships and two consecutive Royal Rumble matches, somehow he also found time for a Hollywood movie and TV career which includes *Suburban Commando* (1991), *Mr. Nanny* (1993), and *Thunder in Paradise* (1994).

Dwayne Johnson (b.1972): Grandson of wrestler Peter Maivia (1937-1982), and son of wrestler Rocky Johnson (1944-2020), he became one of the most popular wrestlers of all time before achieving Hollywood mega-stardom. His films said to have grossed over ten billion dollars worldwide!

Jesse Ventura (b.1951): Formerly a part of the US Navy's Underwater Demolition Team (UDT), and while achieving fame as a WWF superstar, as well as flirting with movie success in films like 1987 Predator, Ventura had public service in mind, serving as mayor of Brooklyn Park, Minnesota, from 1991 to 1995, and as governor of Minnesota from 1999 to 2003! Since then he has written several books, including *Sh*t Politicians Say* (2016) and *Jesse Ventura's Marijuana Manifesto* (2016).

THE FUNNY:

Larry David (b.1947): King of the uncomfortable, and real-life inspiration behind *Seinfeld* character George Constanza, David breaks all the rules on HBO's *Curb Your Enthusiasm*, a show he stars in, produces, and writes! He has won two Emmys and a Golden Globe.

Dave Chappelle (b.1973): Not content with his two Emmy Awards and three Grammy Awards, the groundbreaking stand-up comedian, and proud Ohio resident, also won the Mark Twain Prize in 2019, while his starring role in cult comedy film *Half-Baked* (1998) earned him a spot on this list!

Louis CK (b.1967): A kind-yet-flawed middle-aged man both in his award-winning show *Louie*, and in his real life, sex scandals aside, Louis Székely is also one of the funniest bald men alive!

THE RUSSIANS:

Yul Brynner (1920-1985): Russia has given America many good things, Vladivostok-born Yuliy Borisovich Briner being atop that list. The French-speaking guitarist and circus trapeze acrobat, took to American showbiz naturally, his roles in films like *The Ten Commandments* (1956), *The Magnificent Seven* (1960), and *Westworld* (1973) securing his silver screen immortality.

Mikhail Gorbachev (b.1931): The eighth and last leader of the USSR from 1985 till 1991, his glasnost ("openness") policy enhanced freedom of speech and improved relations with the West, but his government-decentralizing perestroika ("restructuring") destabilized and ultimately brought the Soviet Union to its end.

Vladimir Putin (b.1952): The former KGB agent and alternating President or Prime Minister of the Russian Federation being the epitome of the "in America you turn the corner, in Russia the corner turns you" quip, there's nothing funny about Russia's most powerful modern leader, who could fill a book of facts all on his own—you will have to settle for the next couple of pages though!

GO HARD LIKE...

His last name may rhyme with "pudding," but there's nothing squishy about Mr. Vladimir Putin!

1. The grandson of Spiridon Ivanovich Putin (1879–1965), chef for Lenin (1870-1924) and Stalin (1878-1953), Vladimir Putin took on learning martial arts to defend himself from bullies. By the time he turned 18, he had become a Judo black belt. Nowadays he is known to practice Sambo, Russia's own martial art, as well as being very good at hockey.

2. Joining the KGB in 1975, Putin was posted in East Germany from 1985 to 1989, but while made Lieutenant Colonel, he ended up resigning in 1991, not wanting part in the failed August coup.

3. Knowing of Angela Merkel's (b.1954) cynophobia (fear of dogs), he brought Koni, his black labrador, to a 2007 commerce meeting with her in Sochi.

4. In 2008, while on a televised visit to a natural reserve, Putin saved a television crew from the attack of a Siberian tigress.

5. While overseeing zoological research, in 2010 Putin attached a tracking device to the neck of a polar bear, two Siberian tigers, and a snow leopard, all of which were released into the wild.

6. Later during another 2010 scientific expedition, Putin enjoyed shooting sample-taking darts at a gray whale, apparently missing three times, but striking it with the fourth dart.

7. Also in 2010, Putin took a 1,300 mile promotional road trip aboard a yellow Lada "Kalina" from the far eastern city of Khabarovsk to beautiful Chita, in Siberia.

8. At a 2012 Kremlin youth camp, Putin indulged in artificial climbing, without any safety harness or helmet, arm-wrestled, and even tried bending a frying pan with his bare hands!

9. Putin enjoys fishing bare-chested, and was filmed catching a 46-pound pike during a 2013 Siberian fishing trip in Siberia.

10. After a swift military intervention in 2014, Putin annexed the Black Sea's Crimean peninsula, possibly in retaliation for the Ukrainian insurrection which saw pro-Russian president Viktor Yanukovych (b.1950) removed from office.

11. Just off the recently-acquired Crimean coast, Putin explored a Byzantine shipwreck 200 feet underwater, aboard a nifty mini-sub in 2015.

12. Putin gave Russian citizenships to actors Gérard Depardieu (b.1948) and Steven Seagal (b.1952), and granted asylum to NSA whistleblower Edward Snowden (b.1983).

13. Russian motorcycle club, The Night Wolves, Putin's biggest fans, work closely with him in a paramilitary and propagandistic capacity.

14. Putin's face and name can be seen on t-shirts, comics, calendars, vodka (*Putinka*), caviar (*Gorbusha Putina*), spy beluga whale "Hvaldimir" (caught by Norwegian fishermen in 2019), and even inspired the hip-hop song "Go Hard Like Vladimir Putin!"

SPANGLISH

Something definitely gets lost in translation when American movies cross the border into Mexico and the rest of Latin America!

One Hundred and One Dalmatians (1961) became the incomprehensible *La noche de las narices frías* or "The Night of the Cold Noses."

The Sound of Music (1965) became the absurd *La novicia rebelde* or "The Rebel Postulant."

Midnight Cowboy (1969) became a ridiculous *Perdidos en la noche* or "Lost at Night."

Jaws (1975) became a prosaic *Tiburón* or "Shark."

Alien (1979) became the ludicrous *El octavo pasajero* or "The Eighth Passenger."

Airplane! (1980) became "¿Dónde está el piloto?" or "Where Is the Pilot?", used as the basis for the title of every comedy starring Leslie Nielsen (1926-2010), case in point **The Naked Gun** (1988) became *¿Dónde está el policía?* or "Where Is the Police Officer?"

Sixteen Candles (1984) became an obvious *Se busca novio* or "Boyfriend Wanted."

Home Alone (1990) became the ironic *Mi pobre angelito* or "My Poor

Little Angel."

Thelma & Louise (1991) became the spoilery *Un final inesperado* or "An Unexpected Ending."

A Few Good Men (1992) became *Una cuestión de honor* or "A Matter of Honor," the default title for a number of other military drama and action films.

The Nightmare Before Christmas (1993) became an odd *El extraño mundo de Jack* or "Jack's Strange World."

Pulp Fiction (1994) became the generic *Tiempos violentos* or "Violent Times."

The Green Mile (1996) became a casual *Milagros inesperados* or "Unexpected Miracles."

City of Angels (1998) became the descriptive *Un angel enamorado* or "An Angel in Love."

Napoleon Dynamite (2004) became *Un verano de locura* or "A Crazy Summer," yet another generic title used for practically every comedy ever made.

Walk the Line (2005) became the soapy *Johnny y June, pasión y locura* or "Johnny and June, Passion and Madness."

The Founder (2016) became the political *Hambre de poder* or "Hunger for Power!"

AND THE OSCAR GOES TO...

One of the most important bald men in the world since 1929, Oscar, also known as the Academy Award, has had its own long history well worth reading about.

1. Academy Awards are considered property of the Academy of Motion Picture Arts and Sciences, and forbidden to be sold by winners to third parties before notifying the Academy, which has the right to purchase it back for just one dollar! Oscars awarded before 1950 are exempt from this, but used to be made of plaster.

2. Designed by MGM art director Cedric Gibbons (1890-1960), and sculpted by George Stanley (1903-1970), the statuette itself is a 13.5-inch-tall ArtDeco depiction of a knight thrusting a crusader's sword into a film reel, its "Oscar" moniker attributed to Academy librarian Margaret Herrick (1902-1976), who mentioned it reminded her of her uncle Oscar!

3. The 1929 Oscars were a private affair for a small crowd of industry insiders, the ceremony becoming televised for the first time decades later in 1953.

4. German actor Emil Jannings (1884-1950) was the very first to win the Academy Award for Best Actor in 1929, but found he had been the Academy's second choice. The first? German Shepherd Rin Tin Tin! Jannings's thick accent meant he had to return to Germany with the advent of sound, where he became a star of the Nazi film industry.

5. Songwriter Oscar Hammerstein II (1895-1960) was the only man named Oscar to have won the Oscar (twice)!

6. Liza Minnelli (b.1946) won the Academy Award for Best Actress in a Leading Role for *Cabaret* (1972), becoming the first winner whose parents both earned Oscars—her father Vincente Minnelli (1903-1996) won Best Director for *Gigi* (1958), while her mother, Judy Garland (1922-1969) had won a special honorary Oscar awarded to young performers in 1939.

7. Lionel (1878-1954) and Ethel Barrymore (1879-1959) are the only siblings to both win Academy Awards for their performances in 1931 and 1944 respectively.

8. Not counting Shirley Temple's (1928-2014) honorary award in 1934 at age five, Tatum O'Neal (b.1963) won Best Supporting Actress in 1974 at age ten, making her the youngest person to ever have won, followed by Anna Paquin (b.1982) grabbing the Best Supporting Actress statuette in 1994 at age 11.

9. Christopher Plummer (b.1929) is the oldest gentleman to have won the Academy Award for Best Supporting Actor at age 82 in 2010, while Jessica Tandy (1909-1994) was the oldest lady to receive hers in 1989 at age 80, for *Driving Miss Daisy*.

10. Sound engineer Kevin O'Connell (b.1957) had been nominated 20 times, before finally winning his first Academy Award for *Hacksaw Ridge* (2016) in 2017.

11. The Oscar was once awarded to an institution instead of a person, when the British Ministry of Information got it for their 1941 *Target for Tonight* documentary.

12. One of the rules for any film to be Oscar-nominated used to be it had to be screened for paid admission in Los Angeles for at least

seven days. Since the 2020 Covid-19 pandemic, however, that norm has been relaxed to include films screened via internet streaming.

13. Bob Hope (1903-2003) hosted the most Academy Award ceremonies, 18, while Billy Crystal (b.1948) comes second with eight ceremonies, and Johnny Carson (1925-2005) third, having done so five times.

14. *Ben-Hur* (1959), *Titanic* (1997), and *Lord of the Rings: Return of the King* (2003) may have won 11 Oscars each, but Walt Disney (1901-1966) won 26 during his lifetime!

15. Award manufacturer R.S. Owens & Company of Chicago, Illinois, makes the 24-karat gold plated Oscars which currently cost $500 each. They also make the Emmys, the Rock & Roll Hall of Fame trophies, and many more!

16. The whole mystique attached to the Oscars makes them valuable collector's items. In 1999, Michael Jackson (1958-2009) paid a million dollars for David O. Selznick's (1902-1965) award. Two years later, Oscar winner Steven Spielberg (b.1946) acquired Bette Davis's (1908-1989) own statuette for $578,000, while Orson Welles's 1941 Oscar for *Citizen Kane* was sold to an anonymous bidder for $861,542 in 2011.

BONUS FACT!

- Hoping to achieve eternal youth through blood transfusions, Soviet physician Alexander Bogdanov (1873-1928) died after taking the blood of a student suffering from malaria!

REGRETTABLE LINES

Let's face it: putting intentionally nonsensical Top Gun *and* Showgirls *on the list is almost unfair to the rest of them...*

"At least he won't be using heroin-flavored bananas to finance revolution." —*Goldfinger* (1964)

"What's the matter, boy? I bet you can squeal. I bet you can squeal like a pig. Let's squeal. Squeal now. Squeal!" —*Deliverance* (1972)

"I want somebody's butt, I want it now!" —*Top Gun* (1986)

"Kenner, just in case we get killed, I wanted to tell you. You have the biggest dick I've ever seen on a man." —*Showdown in Little Tokyo* (1991)

"Honey, you could never handle me with all these wrinkles of fat." —*Showgirls* (1995).

"How do you write women so well?" "I think of a man, and I take away reason and accountability." —*As Good As It Gets* (1997)

"Are you a Mexi-CAN or a Mexi-CAN'T?" —*Once Upon a Time in Mexico* (2003)

"I'm pretty sure that only counts when you're kissing a human." —*Man of Steel* (2013)

JEWS IN SPACE

Arriving in California from shtetls and ghettos, a band of Jewish outcasts built Hollywood into their own promised land, and gave birth to the American Dream through their films.

Carl Laemmle (1867-1939): The grandaddy of American film immigrated to the United States from Germany in 1884. He began buying nickelodeons (early twentieth century movie theaters) in Chicago, later going into movie distribution with his company Laemmle Film Service, and film production with Universal Film Manufacturing Company, both of which he would be merged into **Universal Pictures**.

Adolph Zukor (1873-1976): The stocky Hungarian arrived to America in 1891, successfully going into the fur business, and then investing in a movie theater chain in Buffalo, New York, creating the Famous Players Film Company to distribute imported silent-era French films, before merging it with Jesse L. Lasky's (1880-1958) Feature Play Company, to form what we now call **Paramount Pictures**.

William Fox (1879-1952): Born Vilmos Fuchs in Hungary, when his father abandoned his mother and siblings to their own devices, young Vilmos quickly took to working in everything and anything, his entrepreneurial spirit leading him to purchase his first nickelodeon in 1904, which 11 years later would grow into the Fox Film Corporation, which would eventually become **Twentieth Century Fox**.

Louis B. Mayer (1884-1957): Born in Russia, his family emigrated to Canada where his father owned a junkyard. A rebellious teen,

Louis would eventually move to Boston to set up his own salvage operation, later purchasing various vaudeville venues in town. Teaming up with Irving Thalberg (1899-1936) in California, they would end up founding **Metro-Goldwyn-Mayer.**

Harry (1881-1958), Albert (1884-1967), Sam (1887-1927), and Jack Warner (1892-1978): Accustomed to pooling in their resources from a young age, to try their hand at different business ventures, the brothers eventually bought a used film projector to run their own chain of nickeodeons, which they sold to get into film production as **Warner Bros.** in 1910.

Martin Beck (1868-1940): Originally from Slovakia, he became a vaudeville impresario, giving Harry Houdini (1874-1926) his first big break in showbiz, becoming the escapist's friend and agent. Together with fellow Jewish theater entrepreneur David Sarnoff (1891-1971), and Benjamin Franklin Keith (1846-1914), they formed Keith-Albee-Orpheum (KAO) in 1928, which would merge with Radio Corporation of America a few months later, the resulting company being named Radio-Keith-Orpheum, RKO Pictures, the pioneering studio of classics *King Kong* (1933), *Citizen Kane* (1941), and *It's a Wonderful Life* (1946)!

BONUS FACTS!

- The original orange fruit was a green tangerine-pomelo hybrid developed in southeast Asia.

- Female ferrets die if they don't procreate for more than 12 months!

VIDEODROME

In its long, checkered history, television has made and unmade presidents, recorded human history, and served as a vehicle for every human aspiration, changing people's lives, and molding their self-perception like no other medium before or since.

1897: Nobel Prize winner Ferdinand Braun (1850-1918) may have invented the cathode-ray tube in Germany, but it was Russian scientist Boris Rosing (1869-1933) who realized its picture making potential, using it to produce basic shapes on a screen.

1908: It wold be Scottish engineer Alan Archibald Campbell-Swinton (1863-1930) who would come up with yet another application for the tube, as a transmitter of pictures rather than just a receiver.

1923: Russian inventor Vladimir K. Zworykin (1888-1982) manages to put Rosing and Campbell-Swinton's theories to use by creating a transmitting and receiving system employing cathode ray tubes. Image quality was blurry, but it was a start.

1926: Another Scotsman, John Logie Baird (1888-1946) makes a working color TV set in London, capable of transmitting and receiving television signals over a short distance. Two years later, he would figure out a way to transmit television across the Atlantic using radio transmitters!

1929: Herbert E. Ives (1882-1953) leads the Bell Laboratories team that develops a working color TV screen using RGB (red, green, and blue) pixels. Not content with that, he goes on to invent the fax machine, and proving Einstein's General Theory of Relativity to be experimentally correct!

1931: Modern, working television systems are developed in three countries practically at the same time but the aforementioned Vladimir K. Zworykin in the USSR, Isaac Shoenberg at EMI (1880-1963) in the UK, and Philo Farnsworth (1906-1971) in the USA. EMI's system takes the lead when the BBC choses it to begin its first broadcasts in 1936, while it would take Farnsworth a decade-long lawsuit against the Radio Corporation of America (RCA) to be recognized for his own contribution to the field, and earn some royalties from it. The National Broadcasting Company (NBC) would begin its first TV transmissions in 1938.

1950: While postwar Britain's BBC continues to transmit at 405-line definition, and France has opted for a far sharper 819 lines, the rest of Europe settles on a common 625 lines. Across the Atlantic, however, America uses a 525-line standard, while perfecting color cameras, and a coding signal allowing for both color and black and white transmissions. At the same time, commercial transmission of content using coaxial cables, takes its first steps.

1956: The Ampex Corporation produces the very first working videotape recorder, allowing stations to, well, record their shows and retransmit them without significant picture quality loss.

1960: Semiconductors make possible the manufacturing of portable TV sets at Japanese company SONY. By 1979, the first flat screen pocket TV set is patented by PANASONIC in Japan. Four years later, SONY would start selling its own gadget.

1962: The Telstar satellite makes international relay of TV programming possible!

1986: Japan's Nippon Telegraph and Telephone (NTT) and the

Ministry of Posts and Telecommunication (MPT) first propose a digital television "Integrated Network System," but it would only be made possible in the early 1990s when high performance computers at affordable prices, and the World Wide Web, our modern-day internet, become available.

2006: Luxembourg is the first country to completely switch over from analog to digital TV, while the US is expected to finish its own by 2021.

BONUS FACTS!

- Back in 1567, the man who held the record for the longest beard in the world fatally tripped over it while running away from a fire.

- Originally wearing human hair wigs, judges and lawyers in Britain these days use horsehair and even nylon ones.

- A "Megadeath" is, in fact, the unit of measurement of hypothetical millions of deaths caused by a nuclear explosion!

- Living in Paris during Nazi occupation, and in spite of being a handicapped gypsy who befriended blacks and Jews, jazz guitarist Django Reinhardt (1910-1953) had such a large fanbase among the Nazi higher ups, he was considered untouchable!

- Crows are smart creatures with long memories, and the capacity to hold a grudge for many years!

EVERLAST

Continually striving to hook audiences up by any means necessary, TV shows, be they air-waved or online-streamed, are one of the most addictive forms of entertainment around the world, some of which have seemingly gone on forever!

Agriculture: *Krishi Darshan* (since 1967), DD National, India.

Animated: *Sazae-san* (since 1969), Fuji TV, Japan.

Annual beauty pageant: *Miss Universe* (since 1952), Various, US.

Annual song contest: *Sanremo Music Festival* (since 1955), RAI, Italy.

Automotive: *Top Gear* (since 1977), BBC, UK.

Children's: *Blue Peter* (since 1952), BBC, UK.

Christian: *Le jour du Seigneur* (since 1949), France 2, France.

Cooking: *Today's Cooking* (since 1957), NHK, Japan.

Documentary: *Teleenciclopedia* (since 1965), TVR1, Romania.

Game: *Des chiffres et des lettres* (since 1965), France 3, France.

Live music: *Top of the Pops* (since 1964), BBC, UK.

Medical drama: *General Hospital* (since 1963), ABC, US.

News show: *Meet the Press* (since 1947), NBC, US.

Newscast: *Evening News* (since 1948), CBS, US.

Police procedural: *Tatort* (since 1970), Das Erste, Germany.

Reality: *America's Funniest Home Videos* (since 1989), ABC, US.

Science fiction: *Dr. Who* (since 1963), BBC, UK.

Soap Opera: *Coronation Street* (since 1960), ITV, UK.

Sportscast: *The Championships, Wimbledon* (since 1937), BBC, UK.

Talk show: *The Tonight Show* (since 1954), NBC, US.

Runner-ups include British finance show *The Money Programme* (1966-2010), and Chilean variety show *Sábado Gigante* (1962-2015), which are no longer with us.

BONUS FACT!

- In 2016, a disturbed former employee of a care home for the disabled in Sagamihara, Japan, stabbed 19 patients to death, and wounded another 26.

BEAM ME UP!

Boldly going where no man has gone before since 1966, Star Trek *has grown from a humble three-season TV show into a worldwide multimedia franchise with a cult following of millions of devoted fans.*

1. Set roughly in the 2260s, "The Original Series" was conceived as a science fiction western by LAPD officer-turned-scriptwriter Gene Roddenberry (1921-1991), and submitted to Lucille Ball's (1911-1989) production company (Desilu Productions) which, after considerable retooling (including two pilots!), managed to get it on air, and keep it there for three years. It was an instant hit among college science nerds and not much else, but its fanbase has kept on growing since, their first convention held in 1972, and even fully developing fictional extraterrestrial Klingon and Vulcan languages!

2. "The Original Series" followed the adventures of William Shatner's (b.1931) Captain James Tiberius Kirk and his multiracial, multi-color shirt crew (including ubiquitous and very vulnerable "redshirts") aboard the USS *Enterprise*, a 953.7-foot-long (three football fields) exploration starship. Teleportation was used as a special effects budget-saving device which allowed the starship not to ever land, so by *The Next Generation*, the ship's D model had grown to a staggering 2,103 feet.

3. The *Enterprise* travels through space and time using a "warp drive." In the series' mythology, this engine was first invented by the Vulcan race, which proceeded to contact humans after an inventor named Zefram Cochrane developed it on Earth. Federation starships may travel from warp speed 1 to 9.2, but warp 10, according to the *Voyager* series, turns humans into reptiles! In real life the concept was first envisioned by writer and editor John W. Campbell (1910-1971)

in his *Islands of Space* (1931), and found to be theoretically possible by Mexican physicist Miguel Alcubierre (b.1964) in 1994—all we lack now is the technology to make it real!

4. Originally played by Leonard Nimoy (1931-2015), the cold and rational Spock became the breakout character of "The Original Series" despite the network wanting Roddenberry to ditch the character completely. Enduring well beyond the original show, his pointy ears were worn by Jet Propulsion Laboratory scientists while monitoring the Mariner 5 probe's 1967 journey to Venus, but neither William Shatner, nor Zachary Quinto (b.1977) are physically able to do the Vulcan salute Spock popularized.

5. In "The Original Series" and several movies, Nichele Nichols (b.1932) plays Lieutenant Nyota Uhura (which means "freedom" in Swahili), protagonist of the first interracial kiss on television! It's been reported that while considering leaving the show for a Broadway career, Ms. Nichols was talked into staying by none other than Dr. Martin Luther King Jr. (1929-1968). Nichols went on to work as a recruiter for NASA.

6. Among the many celebrities playing supporting characters on *Star Trek* over the years, actors Majel Barrett-Roddenberry (1932-2008), James Cromwell (b.1940) and Kurtwood Smith (b.1943) stand out for portraying multiple characters across different Trek shows and films, while world-famous physicist Stephen Hawking (1942-2018) played himself (in hologram form) in a 1993 episode of *Star Trek: The Next Generation*.

7. So far, Star Trek's TV series include *The Original Series* (1966-1969), *The Animated Series* (1973–1974), *The Next Generation* (1987-1994), *Deep Space Nine* (1993–1999), *Voyager* (1995–2001), *Enterprise* (2001–2005), *Discovery* (2017-persent), and *Picard* (2020-present).

8. *The Next Generation* enjoyed the highest ratings of all *Star Trek* shows!

9. Most *Star Trek* films are part of the original series timeline, while the latest three (as well as, presumably the *Discovery* and *Picard* shows) take place in a parallel universe known as the "Kelvin timeline." The former include *The Motion Picture* (1979), *The Wrath of Khan* (1982), *The Search for Spock* (1984), *The Voyage Home* (1986), *The Final Frontier* (1989), *The Undiscovered Country* (1991), *Generations* (1994), *First Contact* (1996), *Insurrection* (1998), and *Nemesis* (2002), while the latter include *Star Trek* (2009), *Into Darkness* (2013), and *Beyond* (2016). The highest-grossing film in the franchise is the 2009 reboot!

BONUS FACTS!

- Having blue eyes is a mutation which has been traced to a single human living 6,000-10,000 years ago!

- Seven US presidents who died in office, were elected in 20 year intervals: Harrison in 1840, Lincoln in 1860, Garfield in 1880, McKinley in 1900, Harding in 1920, Roosevelt in 1940, and Kennedy in 1960!

- Romanian Irina Margareta Nistor (b.1957) courageously distributed over 3,000 banned Western films, dubbing every character with her own shrill voice!

- At room temperature, there are only two liquid elements: bromine and mercury.

I WAS IN JEOPARDY, BABY

Think fast—the clock is ticking! Game shows (which include quiz shows, panel shows, audience participation shows, and reality shows) have been giving away prizes of every sort, including billions of dollars, since the dawn of American radio and television, and while some have faded into oblivion, the very best continue to provide audiences with some very real TV magic.

Hollywood Squares: Premiering on NBC in 1965 and running until 2004, this panel show featured different celebrities sitting in a three by three "tic-tac-toe" cubicle stack. Its format was successfully exported to countries all over the world, from Argentina to Vietnam!

Jeopardy!: A Merv Griffin (1925-2007) 1964 creation in which all clues are presented as "answers" while responses need be phrased as questions. While originally presented by Art Fleming (1924-1995), the current daily syndicated version has been broadcast continually since 1984, hosted by Alex Trebek (b.1940).

Wheel of Fortune: Yet another Merv Griffin brainchild, this 1975 show is based on the popular "hangman" guessing game, and has been hosted by Chuck Woolery (b.1941), Pat Sajak (b.1946), Rolf Benirschke (b.1955), and Bob Goen (b.1954).

Family Feud: An airwaves classic, it has seen three separate runs: 1976 to 1985 presented by Richard Dawson (1932-2012) on ABC, 1988 to 1994 presented by Ray Combs (1956-1996) on CBS, and the ongoing 1999 version presented by various hosts, the latest being Steve Harvey (b.1957).

The Price Is Right: This quintessential audience participation show

based on having contestants come down to accurately guess merchandise price tags, premiered in 1972 and has aired well over 9,000 episodes. It is currently presented by comedian Drew Carey (b.1958).

Survivor: Based on Swedish reality game show *Expedition Robinson* (1997–2003), *Survivor* has been airing for 40 seasons and counting, despite current pandemic-related delays. In it, a group of strangers is placed in an isolated location to fend for themselves, when not too busy back-stabbing each other out of the game.

Who Wants to Be a Millionaire?: Dark, dramatic, and developed in the UK, "Millionaire" revolutionized game shows the world over since its 1998 debut. In the US, it remained on air, both as a primetime and a daily show for twenty years, until cancelled in 2019, only to be rebooted in 2020. In the late 1990s and early 2000s, it was revealed an international community of contestants had formed to help each other cheat their way to major winnings, including a Major Charles Ingram (b.1963), who won (but was never awarded) the top prize.
A decade and several other shows later, Ingram lost three toes in a freak lawnmower accident!

BONUS FACTS!

- Harry S. Truman's (1884-1972) "S" is not a name but just that letter of the alphabet!

- Flamingo feathers are grayish white, their pink hue acquired later through their fish and algae diet.

WORD CRIMES

An American original, the modern crossword puzzle has had a rich, long history, from its humble origin as a newspaper fillers to an American national craze during the appropriately roaring twenties.

1. Arthur Wynne (1871-1945) is credited with creating the first crossword for the Sunday FUN page of the New York *World* in 1913, but the *World's* editorial department took little notice of the feature's growing popularity.

2. A decade later, piano salesman Richard L. Simon (1899-1960) noticed the popularity of the puzzle among his family, and associated himself with copy editor M. Lincoln Schuster (1897-1970) to publish the very first crossword puzzle collection (which included its own pencil) of 50 New York *World* puzzles. Its 3,600 copies sold quickly, the "Plaza Publishing Company" later being renamed Simon & Schuster!

3. 1924 was a big year for crosswords. In Pittsburgh, a Reverend George W. McElveen, a pastor of the Knoxville Baptist Church, came up with a crossword challenge for his congregation, which resulted in the church overflowing with crossword aficionados. Later that year, a mob stormed that city's Carnegie Library demanding a solution to a particular definition, while prison inmates got into fights for the same reason. When the Baltimore & Ohio Railroad began to provide dictionaries to passengers, as did other rail lines, high demand meant a significant rise in dictionary sales by that year's Christmas season.

4. As 1925 began, crosswords began to catch on internationally, with both Queen Mary and the British Prime Minister counting themselves as crossword fans, while the President of the British

Optical Association denounced the puzzle for the eye-strain it supposedly produced. Back in America, the *New York Times* and the *New Republic* lambasted the new hobby in articles and cartoons, while black and white square patterned dresses became all the rage among flappers. At the end of the year, it was reported that a New York Telephone company employee had shot his wife, and then himself, over her refusal to help him with a puzzle solution!

6. In 1930, crossword puzzles still raged on everywhere in spite of the *New York Times* claiming they were "past their prime." In the UK, crossword solving got more competitive on every front. Puzzlers, for one, introduced quirky, witty, and downright cryptical clues, while puzzlists began to track down and figure out the puzzlers' true identities (they traditionally worked under pen names), and clock how long it took to solve a given crossword. Publishers, on their end, just couldn't keep up with the demand and continued to undercut each other. In continental Europe, on the other hand, took hold a type of crossword which included very short clues (usually synonyms) within the grid itself.

7. It took until 1942 for the last anti-crossword bastion, the *New York Times*, to fall. It began to publish a Sunday crossword, until finally adopting it in its daily edition. By 2018, its payment rates for accepted Sunday crosswords had gone up to $2,250, while dailies could reach $750!

BONUS FACT!

- Greek-born Canadian cook Sam Panopoulos (b.1934) is credited for inventing the Hawaiian pizza in 1962, by sprinkling it with chunks of pineapple ... a South American fruit!

MONEY FOR NOTHING

Some people insist that advertising wasn't as pervasive in "the old days" as it is today, but that is utter nonsense!

1. A 3,000 BC clay sign was unearthed in the ruins of Thebes, Egypt, offering a reward for a runaway slave. Similar "lost and found" papyrus posters and earthen signs can be found in almost every ancient Western civilization polis that we know of.

2. In eleventh century BC China, print ads were already a thing, advertising everything from bamboo flutes, to needles, and even medicinal concoctions!

3. During the European Middle Ages, a low literacy rate meant both sign-boards (say, a big horseshoe at the blacksmith's or a giant fish at the fishmonger's) and town criers in farmer's markets became the norm. Recognizable trademarks also came into existence back then!

4. The advent of print meant that by the sixteenth and seventeenth centuries, daily newspapers and weekly gazettes were already in circulation, which naturally carried ads to reduce publication costs. A 1622 ad on Britain's "Weekly News" paper offered a reward for a stolen horse, while in 1630 the first ad placement agency opened in Paris, and in 1666 London the "London Gazette" began printing its first classified ads! By the 1670s, a higher literacy rate meant print flyers and trade cards for particular businesses and shops also became the norm.

5. In the eighteenth century, every major metropolitan area was already covered in signs and posters. One of the industries taking full

advantage of the new medium was tobacco, of course, but false advertising and quackery were widespread too. In the colonies, newspapers such as the "Boston News-Letter," which already ran classifieds in 1704, and Benjamin Franklin's (1706-1790) "Pennsylvania Gazette," which carried ads for books, stationery, and soap as early as 1729, did very well. Franklin would make a fortune selling his own stove invention over other brands of "inferior quality." Even Paul Revere (1735-1818) would publish ads for the dentures he manufactured! The American Revolution itself also wouldn't hesitate to also run political and enlistment ads, and by the time it ended the new country would already have 43 newspapers in circulation.

6. During the nineteenth century, print was still king, posters and labels reaching unseen levels of design sophistication. By the 1840s the first advertising agency was set up in Philadelphia by Volney B. Palmer (1799-1864), a real state man with a coal business, who bought and resold ad space in newspapers, and did the copy-writing of ads which he the commissioned artists to design and illustrate. In 1869 N.W. Ayer & Son was founded in New York. They would acquire Palmer's agency and went on to create entire campaigns (a military term they applied to advertising) such as Morton Salt's "When it rains it pours," and Camel cigarettes' "I'd walk a mile for a Camel," changing the game forever! In 1882, the first glowing signboard was erected in London. It used 2,000 bulbs and was an immediate sensation.

7. With Northwestern University setting it as an academic discipline in 1900, by that first decade of the twentieth century advertising had become a firmly established profession, and companies were already expected to allocate part of their budget for ads. By the 1910s, most agencies' revenue came from the food and beverage, automobile, soap, tobacco, and garment industries, in that order. In the 1920s radio broadcasting began to sell spot time for ads, thus beginning a new era of electronic advertising which continues to this day.

I'D LIKE TO BUY THE WORLD A COKE

If advertising has proven anything through the ages is that ideas are a dime a dozen, but good ideas are the product of hard, professional labor. The ten greatest campaigns of all time include:

A Diamond is Forever:

If longevity is one of the marking of a successful campaign, this one by the De Beers diamond-mining group has been around since 1947, and is credited for popularizing the diamond engagement ring custom in America.

Marlboro Man:

Created by the Leo Burnett Company in 1954, the rugged cowboy as used as a symbol of manliness to sell filtered cigarettes to men, which up until then, had been considered a feminine product. The ads and commercials, which initially featured professional male models, soon hired real-life rodeo men and ranchers to boost authenticity to an almost mythical proportion. By 1957 Marlboro sales had quadrupled, and the campaign became one of the world's most enduring ones.

Old Enough to Know, and Young Enough to Do:

The highly telegenic John Fitzgerald Kennedy (1917-1963) would win the 1960 election on the shoulders of an upbeat ad campaign which included a folksy jingle, cartoons and photo stills of smiling people. His successor, Lyndon Baines Johnson (1908-1973) would also drive his nomination home with contrastingly bleak-but-powerful "girl with daisy obliterated by nuclear explosion" ads in 1964.

Think Small:

In another killer campaign from the sixties, the DDB agency went the

opposite direction of American car maker ads of the day by focusing on the advantages of owning a Volkswagen Beetle in a big city, in a series of appropriately minimalistic monochrome magazine ads, which didn't shy away from the Beetle's odd shape either, labeling it a "lemon" with productive and thriving connotations. This campaign would inspire Apple Computer's own "Think Different" three decades later.

I'd Like to Teach the World to Sing (In Perfect Harmony):

Conceived by Bill Backer (1926-2016) at the McCann Erickson agency, it is also known as the "Hilltop" Coca-Cola campaign, and portrayed an ethnically diverse chorus of people singing the wholesome song, composed by folk music band The Hillside Singers. Its Christmas version remained in use throughout the world until well into the 1980s!

Great Taste, Less Filling:

Introduced in 1975 via an extremely effective campaign, also conceived by Bill Backer, featuring the great Bubba Smith (1945-2011) to market it among adult male consumers, Miller Lite became America's favorite beer by the end of that decade and remained so until Bud Light (introduced in 1982) took over that spot in 1994.

Absolut:

Struggling during the 1970s, the Swedish vodka brand finally made big by targeting the creative community in 1981 with a campaign by the TBWA agency, which essentially is still used today, and whimsically plays with the "absolute" concept in every possible way, through striking, artful photos of customized bottles.

Mr. Spleen:

In 1981, FEDEX unveiled this humorous campaign starring

John "Motormouth" Moschitta, Jr. (b.1954) as a fast-talking executive serviced by a fast-delivering courier company. Moschitta, who, at 586 words per minute, is considered one of the world's fastest talkers, would become a superstar of the advertising world, and also be featured in the well-remembered Micro-Machines toy brand campaign.

1984:

A rarity in advertising history, this influential and enduring original Apple Macintosh computer commercial aired only once, during the 1984 Super Bowl, but people haven't stopped talking about it since! It featured several omnipresent motifs of its decade, including the fear of all-powerful nation-states controlling people through mass media, and the importance of fitness and athletics to break through the everyday lag, all ironically focused on selling a product which makes consumers sedentary and compliant!

The Man Your Man Could Smell Like:

The over-the-top, hilarious Old Spice Body Wash 2010 campaign became a sensation overnight. Developed by the Wieden+Kennedy agency, it clearly targets the wife of the potential consumer (studies showed women make most purchasing decisions of household hygiene products), but went on to revitalize the venerable brand as a whole, turning football receiver and actor Isaiah Mustafa (b.1974) into the one and only "Old Spice Man," and an instant celebrity.

BONUS FACT!

- The Vatican's Swiss Guard still wears the same colorful uniforms designed by Michelangelo (1475-1564) in 1506!

BUT WAIT, THERE'S MORE!

An alternative to end-of-the-day signing-off, infomercials, also known as paid programming, are a staple of late night television, and the most popular form of direct response marketing, by providing a toll-free phone number or website for their audience to reach the announcer and make their purchase without any middlemen.

1. Soap companies pioneered this approach across both print and electronic media in the early twentieth century. Their creation or sponsorship of daytime drama television series is the reason those shows are called "soap operas" in the first place!

2. Turkish Taffy in particular, was behind children's show "The Magic Clown" on NBC, from 1949 to 1954, predating the wave of animated cartoons made to advertise toy lines during the 1980s and 1990s.

3. Best known for his now-defunct company Ronco Teleproducts, Ron Popeil (b.1935), went from selling wares in open air markets to buying spare TV time slots at local stations to promote his products in the early 1950s, pioneering the late night infomercial format we know today and selling millions of novelty household gadgets (usually under the "O-Matic" suffix) in the process!

4. During the late 1950s, Federal Communications Commission (FCC) regulations relegated sponsors to the background, and saw infomercials effectively ostracized to late-nights, but these were completely lifted by 1984, which led to a paid programming extravaganza, which went from kitchenware to televangelists raiding the airwaves the world over. Since then, American broadcasters have come to a point of replacing syndicated television series reruns and movies with infomercials during non-revenue-generating time slots, a trend which greatly increased during and after the 2007-2008 global financial crisis.

5. Notably, due to the termination of its 18 year lease with 4Kids Entertainment, in 2008 Fox replaced its entire Saturday morning children's programming with an infomercials block called "Weekend Marketplace." It was widely considered the last nail in the "Saturday Morning Cartoons" coffin.

6. World heavyweight boxing champion George Foreman's (b.1940) lifetime earnings from his entire career in the sport amount to $17.5 million, while the eponymous grill he promoted on infomercials has sold over 100 million units, netting the champ around $200 million on royalties alone, not to mention he was paid another $138 million just for the use of his name on the product.

7. The infomercial culture of the internet age has given rise to unlikely heroes, like Phil Swift (b.1944) who alongside his brother Alan (b.1961) runs Florida-based adhesive company Swift Response, makers of the Flex Seal product line which Phil sells with great, er, zeal! Phil's good nature and energetic demeanor have gone viral since 2014, being recognized by celebrities like Daniel Tosh (b.1975) and Jerry Seinfeld (b.1954).

8. Infomercials are low cost but highly lucrative. While most of the products they peddle fail, the ones that sell usually cut around 400% profits, later making it into brick-and-mortar retail stores. Production-wise, an infomercial costs $138 per second to make, while regular national commercials may cost up to $12,000 per second. Broadcasting-wise, TV stations may charge around $50,000 to broadcast a 30-second commercial, but for that kind of money, an infomercial product company may purchase ten 30-minute spots, so it's no wonder why these days the infomercial market is worth around $250 billion—more than twice the entire US television business!

THE HUDSUCKER PROXY

Toys have been used since prehistory, cavemen's children playing with people and animal figures, not to mention tiny make-believe weapons and tools, and wheeled toys later becoming popular in ancient Greek, Asian, and Mesoamerican civilizations. Yet, since the dawn of the twentieth century, new technologies allowing the manufacturing of new materials like plastics brought forth the most popular toys still selling today, some of which also happen to be adaptations of ancient toys!

Plasticine: An 1897 invention of Bath (England) art teacher William Harbutt (1844-1921), it was patented and manufactured commercially by Harbutt and his family-run company in 1900, until acquired by another brand in 1983. The material saw many other applications, including stop-motion animation (dubbed "claymation"). Its most successful heir, Silly Putty, was originally invented by James Wright (1874-1961) in 1943, while charged by the U.S. War Production Board with finding an inexpensive substitute for synthetic rubber, as South Pacific suppliers were under Japanese control. His "nutty putty" didn't fly with the government, but overtime became the number-one plasticine in America, until the advent of colorful Play-Doh, invented by Noah McVicker (1905-1980) in 1956 to clean coal stains off wallpaper!

Meccano: Englishman Frank Hornby (1863-1936) invented the Meccano system to teach his kids the basics of mechanics in 1900. Also known as "Mechanics Made Easy," this toy construction system predated equally popular, plastic-based brands like LEGO and Playmobil. Hornby and the company he created would also pioneer the invention of model railways and Dinky Toys, the die-cast miniature vehicles which inspired brands like Matchbox, Majorette, and Hot Wheels!

Crayons: In 1885, chemists Edwin Binney (1866-1934) and C. Harold Smith (1860-1931) founded Binney & Smith to produce shoe polish. The company eventually expanded to ink manufacturing, and school supplies including powder-less chalk and slate pencils. The stage was set then for the invention of crayons in 1903. Brand name "Crayola" was created by Binney's wife by combining the French word for chalk (*craie*), and "oily." Its first box contained black, brown, blue, red, purple, orange, yellow, and green crayons, and sold for five cents.

Yo-Yo: The idea of looping a string around an axel joining two wheels to make them spin back and forth is as old as mankind. Ancient Greeks and Chinese had this toy and culturally spread it all over Eurasia. By the nineteenth century, the British imported it back from Asia, and called it the "bandalore," but it wasn't until Filipino entrepreneur Pedro Flores (1896-1964) began to market his own modern version, which he named using the Filipino word for it, *yoyo*, in the late 1920s, that the toy really caught on in America.

Frisbee: Connecticut's Frisbie Pie Company originally made pies packaged in tin saucers, which college students delightedly threw at each other. The trend was picked by LA building inspector Walter Morrison (1920-2010) (in fact, a distant cousin of movie legend Marion Morrison, a.k.a. John Wayne), who began to market his light plastic disc in 1937, selling it to the Wham-O toy company in 1957, and it was Wham-O that gave the saucer its "Frisbee" name that year.

Slinky: When in 1943, American naval engineer Richard T. James (1914-1974) accidentally dropped one of the springs he was testing for use aboard navy ships, he realized he had a successful toy in his hands—the Slinky! His wife Betty (1918-2008) would head the company they created around the toy until selling it in 1998. She was responsible for the Sinky Dog toy which helped turn the company's fortune around after sales began to decline in the 1960s.

Mr. Potato Head: Children used to insert sticks to make dolls out of potatoes for ages, but it was inventor George Lerner (1922-1995) who saw an opportunity in plastic pushpin body parts children could insert into fruits and vegetables back in 1949. Originally a promotional cereal box toy, Lerner finally sold his product to Hassenfeld Brothers (now HASBRO) for $7,000 in 1951, the first Styrofoam spud-included Mr. Potato Head kits hitting shelves in 1952.

Hula-Hoop: Inspired by the Frisbee's success, Wham-O company founders Richard Knerr (1925-2008) and Arthur "Spud" Melin (1924-2002), came up with the modern, plastic version of this ancient Greek toy in 1958, its new brand-name derived from the hip-twisting dance of Hawaii. Current hula-hoop world records include the fastest spun (245 rpm) by American Gregory Sean Dillon in 2012, the most waist-spun hoops (200) by Australia's Marawa Ibrahim in 2015, the largest (52.8 feet diameter) single hoop ever spun by Japan's Yuya Yamada in 2017, and the longest-ever spin (100 hours) by American Jenny Doan in 2019!

Barbie: Everybody in the world knows Barbara Millicent Roberts, a.k.a. Barbie! The somewhat-realistically proportioned adult woman mannequin doll was commissioned to Mattel's design team by company manager Ruth Marianna Handler (1916-2002) after coming across the originally nippled, German "Bild Lilli" doll during a trip to Europe in 1958. Mattel would shrewdly buy the Lilli trademark in 1964, and immediately halt its production, clearing the way for Barbie to conquer the fashion doll market.

Ball pit: Considered the "father of the modern play area" we now see in most city parks, Eric McMillan (b.1942) is the English-Canadian industrial designer who invented the ball pit, a popular fixture in shopping malls all over the world, in the early 1970s.

AND YET IT MOVES

Popularly known as "the cartoons" after its print sibling, the animation artform and industry remains in good health after well over a century, but its rich and ever-expanding global history is well worth an exhaustive look.

1. Predating American animation by decades, French pioneer Charles-Émile Reynaud (1844-1918) was already projecting his *Pantomimes Lumineuses* in 1892 Paris, ahead even of the Lumière brothers' first live-action filming and exhibition of an arriving train in 1895! Three years later, German company Gebrüder Bing was already selling its toy cartoon reel film projector in stores. By 1900, animation reached America for the first time thanks to British film producer J. Stuart Blackton's (1875-1941) *The Enchanted Drawing* film. On the other side of the world, the granddaddy of "anime," 1907's *Katsudō Shashin* ("Motion Picture"), is a three-second Japanese animated film fragment rediscovered in 2005.

2. Starting in 1911, newspaper cartoonist Winsor McCay (c. 1866-1934) premiered his own hand-drawn animation short, adapting his popular "Little Nemo" comic strip to film, followed by his seminal 1914 *Gertie the Dinosaur* short film. Since McCay drew every single animation frame of his cartoons, he grew tired of it all and by 1921 had returned to newspapers full-time.

3. Canadian animator Raoul Barré (1874-1932) quit Edison Studios in 1914 to start his own. The Barré-Nolan Studio became the first large-scale professional animation studio, inspiring several others to ditch the experimental McCay approach and embrace chain production. To make it easier and cost-effective Barré pioneered the two-peg system to align drawings on top of each other, and reusing backgrounds and non-moving elements on each frame.

4. South of the border, Argentinian animator Quirino Cristiani (1896-1984) created the world's first two animated feature length films, *El Apóstol* in 1917 and *Sin dejar rastros* the following year, though he worked single-handedly, using characters made of articulated paper and leather clippings he then shot frame by frame.

5. Otto Messmer (1892-1983) created the enduring Felix the Cat for Pat Sullivan Studios in 1919. The first cartoon character to be fully merchandised, Felix popularity began to wane after studio owner Pat Sullivan (1885-1933) refused to adopt sound into his films, setting the market to be taken over by the creation of a young and innovative Walter Elias Disney (1901-1966), Mickey Mouse. Felix, however, would later become the first image to be transmitted by RCA during its initial experiments with a new medium, television!

6. Poland-born Max Fleischer (1883-1972), who had patented "rotoscoping" in 1917 and went on to produce a number of animated films both in the US and abroad, established Fleischer Studios, Inc. in 1929 and went on to produce some of the best-known, most ground-breaking cartoon serials of the 1930s including *Betty Boop*, *Popeye*, and largely-rotoscoped *Superman*. Fleischer Studios notable alumni would include future "Fantastic Four" and "Avengers" co-creator Jack Kirby (1917-1994), and Argentinian comics artist Dante Quinterno (1909-2003), who would build a small empire around his "Patoruzú" comic book, which he would live to see published in the US, and turned into a 1942 animated color short (Argentina's first).

7. While Max Fleischer's Inkwell Studios had been producing animated pictures with synchronized sound throughout the 1920s, it would be upstart Walt Disney's 1928 *Steamboat Willie*, that would put the nation in a Mickey Mouse frenzy. Disney had only two animators working for him at the time, notably Ub Iwerks (1901-1971), but by the time his very first $1.4 million color film, Snow White, had hit theaters in 1937, his artists' stable had grown to 600 people.

Color animation, both short and feature-length was big business, and soon every major Hollywood company wanted a slice of the Disney pie, most notably Warner Brothers, which would eventually churn out Porky Pig (1935), Daffy Duck (1937), Bugs Bunny (1938) and Sylvester the Cat (1939), displaying its own brand of zanny humor.

8. Disney's success also inspired animators internationally. The Soviet Union's Soyuzmultfilm was founded in 1936, would produce around 20 films per year, and is still making cartoons today. The man who invented the signature Japanese comics ("manga"), and animation ("anime") style, Osamu Tezuka (1928-1989), would seek to imitate the Disney storytelling and style, first as a comic-book artist, and then as head of his own animation studio, Tezuka Productions. *Bambi* (1942), in particular, made a lasting aesthetic impact on Tezuka, who began to draw characters with big, shiny eyes, after seeing that film for the first time.

9. World War II brought many pains to the American animation industry by limiting its international audience, and drafting talent away. While it eventually redirected its efforts toward propaganda films, those productions were never profitable in the scale studios were used to, and ever-low salaries brought problems with its labor force, most of it lacking a proper union until the Screen Cartoonists Guild (SCG) came to the rescue. Prominently, the SCG organized strikes against the Fleischer and Disney studios. Walt, in particular, took matters into his own hands by firing 18 "agitators," which included legendary animator Art Babbitt (1907-1992), creator of Goofy, who Disney also had arrested under false charges. As tension escalated, and picket lines grew, Walt dug his heels deep and refused any mediation offers. The company, however, would take advantage of Walt's propaganda trip to Latin America, to finally settle and end the strike, but when he returned unmoved and determined to keep firing "troublemakers," talent such as Babbitt ended up leaving the company in their own accord to find work elsewhere.

Some of those left soured by the whole industry eventually revolutionized other mediums such as print comic strips, including duck-men Al Taliaferro (1905-1969) and Carl Barks (1901-2000), and influential cartoonists Walt "Pogo" Kelly (1913-1973), and Hank "Dennis the Menace" Ketcham (1920-2001).

10. In the decades following World War II, the ensuing cultural shift from the silver screen onto the small one, saw the animation industry adapt itself away from the movie studios (most of which unceremoniously shut their animation departments following the strikes) and theaters, and into home entertainment and advertising. Disney exiles John Hubley (1914-1977), David Hilberman (1911-2007), and Stephen Bosustow (1911-1981) founded ground-breaking United Productions of America (UPA), its modernistic *Mr. Magoo* and *Gerald McBoing-Boing* taking full advantage of the new medium. MGM exiles William Hanna (1910-2001) and Joseph Barbera (1911-2006) founded Hanna-Barbera Productions, Inc., the most prominent supplier of cartoon shows in twentieth-century television, with hits such as *The Huckleberry Hound Show*, *The Flintstones*, *The Yogi Bear Show*, and *Scooby-Doo, Where Are You?* They didn't shy away from the money-making power of advertising either. Case in point, *The Flintstones* were originally sponsored by the Reynolds Tobacco Company, which meant Fred Flintstone and Barney Rubble had to smoke on the show!

11. While the 1980s FCC deregulation saw the return of "cartoons as advertising," this also meant the rise of visually stunning, license-based animated shows. Smaller studios such as Filmation and Ruby-Spears Productions rose to prominence by being quicker on their feet in landing the rights to produce shows based on *He-Man and the Masters of the Universe*, and *Mister T*, among a great many other properties, while in Canada and Japan, direct-to-video adult animation made great quality strides as well, epitomized in films like *Rock & Rule* (1983), and *AKIRA* (1988).

CAT CHASES MOUSE

By sheer number of viewers since their first TV inception, the ten most popular cartoon shows to ever grace the otherwise-idiot box around the world are:

1. Tom & Jerry: Originally created in 1940 by William Hanna (1910-2001) and Joseph Barbera (1911-2006) for MGM, they brought it with them and into television, amassing around **450,000,000** worldwide viewers since 1965!

2. Looney Tunes: One of the biggest cartoon brands on the planet, its shorts featuring Daffy Duck, Bugs Bunny, and so many others have gained an international audience of around **420,000,000** people.

3. Rick and Morty: A relative newcomer, this harsh science fiction sitcom created by Justin Roiland (b.1980) and Dan Harmon (b.1973) has taken the world by storm since 2013, its viewership amounting to **390,000,000** people.

4. The Simpsons: Shows #3, 5, 6, 8, and 9 on this list wouldn't exist without "The Simpsons" breaking the TV mold in 1989-1990. The brainchild of American cartoonist Matt Groening (b.1954) is loved by approximately **390,000,000** loyal fans.

5. SpongeBob Squarepants: The nutty children's cartoon show created by the late Stephen Hillenburg (1961-2018) has been watched by **390,000,000** kids and adults since first airing in 1999.

6. Gravity Falls: This unusual (for a Disney cartoon, anyway) limited series by Alex Hirsch (b.1985) has gained **350,000,000** fans.

7. Scooby Doo: The successful animated franchise's many series has gathered almost **340,000,000** viewers over the last 50 years.

8. Steven Universe: Another newcomer, this warm and fuzzy "Rick and Morty" polar opposite has a growing audience of **325,000,000** people since introduced to Cartoon Network by creator Rebecca Sugar (b. 1987).

9. Futurama: Conceived to replace "The Simpsons" in 2000, it never quite lived up to its original expectations, but still has a not-at-all-negligible viewership of around **280,000,000** people.

10. South Park: The acerbic creation of Trey Parker (b.1969) and Matt Stone (b.1971) continues to satirize the issues of the day since 1997, with 270,000,000 viewers worldwide.

BONUS FACTS!

- Running low on ideas, artist Andy Warhol (1928-1987) offered to pay $50 to anyone who would suggest a suitable subject for him to paint. Gallery owner Muriel Roberta Latow (1931-2003) suggested Campbell's Soup Cans—needless to say, she got the money!

- *Get Smart* debuted on TV in 1965, ran for five seasons, and aired a total of 138 episodes. The show was special for two reasons: each episode worked like a whole stand-alone spy movie, and its star, comedian Don Adams (1923-2005) agreed to a lesser salary in exchange for a stake in the show, which made him a rich man!

STARRY-EYED

For many, cartoon characters are as real as people, or even more so. Adequately, the Hollywood Walk of Fame in Los Angeles honors not only flesh and blood, but "ink on paper" creations deemed culturally relevant as well.

Mickey Mouse: Awarded in 1978, on his fiftieth anniversary. Minnie Mouse, on the other hand, got it much later on her ninetieth, in 2018.

Bugs Bunny: Debuting in the 1938 film Porky's *Hare Hunt*, and voiced by Mel Blanc (1908-1989), Bugs got this star in 1985.

Woody Woodpecker: Also voiced by Blanc, this Walter Lanz (1899-1994) creation from 1941 was awarded his own star in 1990.

The Simpsons: Back in 2000, the Matt Groening (b.1954) show got his star just in time for its tenth anniversary.

Rugrats: Also in time for their tenth anniversary, the Klasky-Csupo and Nickelodeon animated show for children, also got a star in 2001.

Snoopy: Created by cartoonist Charles Schulz (1922-2000), who also got a Walk of Fame star, Charlie Brown's beagle dog from the "Peanuts" comic strip (successfully adapted into TV animation specials since 1965) got a star back in 2015.

Alvin and the Chipmunks: The cartoon chipmunk band created for a Ross Bagdasarian (1919-1972), a.k.a. David Seville, for his 1958 novelty record, got theirs in 2019!

THE PARENT TRAP

Keeping the happiest, most magical places on Earth continually open comes at a cost, with both Disneyland and Disney World theme parks seeing their share of casualties over the years.

DEATH AT DISNEYLAND:

May 19, 1964: Mark Maples (1949-1964) stood and fell from the Matterhorn Bobsleds, becoming the park's first casualty since opening in 1955.

June 8, 1966: Thomas G. Cleveland (1947-1966) climbed onto the monorail track and was fatally struck by the speeding train.

August 21, 1967: Ricky L. Yama (1951-1967) tried jumping from one PeopleMover car to another while inside a tunnel, but fell and was run over by the following train.

June 20, 1973: Bogden Delaurot (1955-1973) drowned trying to swim across the Rivers of America, carrying his younger brother on his back.

July 8, 1974: Park employee Deborah G. Stone (1956-1974) was crushed to death at the America Sings attraction.

June 7, 1980: Gerardo Gonzales (1965-1980) pulled a "Ricky Yama" aboard the PeopleMover.

March 7, 1981: Mel C. Yorba (1963-1981) was stabbed to death in Tomorrowland.

June 4, 1983: Philip Straughan (1965-1983) drowned in the Rivers of America ride while piloting a rubber emergency boat from Tom Sawyer's Island he had stolen while on drugs.

January 3, 1984: Dolly Young (1936-1984) fell from a Matterhorn Bobsled and was decapitated by the following one.

September 14, 1985: Jennifer F. Reid (1978-1995) was run over by a bus.

March 7, 1987: Salesi Tai (1972-1987) was shot dead by another teen.

December 24, 1998: Computer programer Luan D. (1964-1998) was slain by a metal cleat falling from the Sailing Ship Columbia hull, which also disfigured his wife (Lieu V.).

September 1, 2000: Newlywed Cristina Moreno (1977-2000) died from a cerebral aneurysm caused by the Indiana Jones Adventure ride.

April 22, 2003: Stage technician Christopher Bowman (1967-2003) fell to his death from atop a Hyperion Theater catwalk.

September 5, 2003: Marcello Torres (1981-2003) perished after the Big Thunder Mountain Railroad roller coaster derailed.

January 26, 2009: Brandon Zucker (1996-2009) passed after being left with life-long disabilities and brain damage back in 2000, when he fell under Roger Rabbit's Car Toon Spin.

October 17, 2010: A 61-year-old unnamed man jumped from the

Mickey & Friends parking structure.

April 2, 2012: A 23-year-old unnamed man presumably jumped from the Mickey & Friends parking structure.

July 14, 2015: An unnamed three-year-old boy drowned in a pool at Disney's Art of Animation Resort.

November 26, 2016: A 40-year-old unnamed man also jumped to his death from the Mickey & Friends parking structure.

March 13, 2019: Park construction worker George W. Grimes (1961-2019) fatally fell at EPCOT.

August 29, 2019: Park construction worker Javier Jimenez (1981-2019) died from injuries after being crushed by a steel plate.

The Disneyland Hotel has recorded three suicides in 1994, 1996, and 2008, and an unsuccessful attempt in 1998!

DISNEY WORLD DEMISES:

August 11, 1977: Joel Goode (1973-1977) drowned in the moat surrounding Cinderella Castle.

June 13, 1982: One-year-old Cassandra Lusinski died after falling from a tram in the parking lot.

September 12, 1992: Deranged Allan Ferris (1955-1992) killed an

EPCOT guard and took two others hostage before taking his own life.

February 14, 1999: Park custodian Raymond Barlow (1934-1999) died after accidentally falling from a Fantasyland Skyway station ride.

November 5, 2000: An unnamed 37-year-old man was hit and killed by a Splash Mountain vehicle while attempting to jump off from the vehicle he was on.

February 11, 2004: Javier Cruz (1966-2004) was run over while in his Pluto outfit by a Beauty and the Beast float.

November 27, 2007: Park employee Karen Price (1944-2007) died after falling off the Primeval Whirl platform, and fatally hitting her head.

July 5, 2009: Monorail Purple pilot Austin Wuennenberg (1988-2009) died after crashing with Monorail Pink.

August 6, 2009: Park employee Mark Priest (1962-2007) slipped on a stage puddle and hit his head on against the wall, passing four days later.

April 1, 2010: An unnamed 9-year-old boy was fatally by a bus at Disney's Fort Wilderness Resort & Campground.

March 13, 2011: Park employee Russell Roscoe (1959-2011) also died from injuries sustained after a fall from the Primeval Whirl.

The countless people who have died at Disney World from "pre-existing heart conditions" could fill an entire book!

STOMP

Trampling Tokyo since 1954, the embodiment of nuclear horror known as Godzilla has become a cultural icon all around the world, starring in more movies that James Bond!

1. Its Japanese name, *Gojira*, is a portmanteau of *gorira* ("gorilla") and *kujira* ("whale"), and used to be the nickname of a Toho publicity department employee!

2. Inspired by Ray Harryhausen's (1920-2013) Rhedosaurus from *The Beast from 20,000 Fathoms* (1953), in Japanese films *Gojira* is a huge, wild, prehistoric amphibious dinosaur awakened and empowered by nuclear radiation.

3. However, in Roland Emmerich's (b.1955) 1998 *Godzilla* film, the first to be produced completely in Hollywood, "Godzilla" is in fact a mutated, tuna-eating iguana (a product of French nuclear testing in Polynesia), a surviving Japanese fisherman happens to compare to the original "Gojira!"

4. While wrongly colored green in comics, cartoons, movie posters, and films starting in the 2000s, the original *Gojira* was charcoal grey with bone-white dorsal plates.

5. *Gojira* doesn't like human meat, and prefers to eat radioactive waste instead, the resulting blue atomic breath laying waste to cities and enemies alike. Its iconic roar was created by composer Akira Ifukube (1914-2006) rubbing a tar-coated leather glove along the strings of a bass and then slowing down the playback!

6. Godzilla has more weird powers and abilities than 1950s Superman, including, but not limited to electro magnetic pulse (*Godzilla vs. King Gidorah*), magnetism (*Godzilla vs. Mechagodzilla*), precognition (*Godzilla vs. Biollante*), fireballs ("Godzilla: Destroy All Monsters Melee" video game), electric bite (Godzilla pachinko), super-speed ("Ryūsei Ningen Zone" TV show), heat-vision (1978 "Godzilla" cartoon), flight (*Godzilla vs. Hedorah*), talking (*Godzilla vs. Gigan*), and even dancing (*Ghidorah, the Three-Headed Monster*).

7. Its only weakness? Ice!

8. The monster's size changes through all its films, cartoons, and comic-books according to the needs of the script, and the size of its enemies, but sometimes its enemies size changes too, like in *King Kong vs. Godzilla* (1962), though considering the giant prehistoric ape had been resized in its own American movies, doing so wasn't such a stretch either.

9. Godzilla has had children too! An adopted son, Minilla, appeared in *Son of Godzilla* (1967), in an effort to make Godzilla more appealing to Japanese home-makers. *Godzilla vs Mechagodzilla 2* would mark the appearance of Baby Godzilla. The eponymous (yet much, much tamer) Hanna-Barbera "Godzilla" cartoon, which aired from 1978 to 1981 on NBC, gave "Godzooky" a prominent role. In Emmerich's 1998 film, the parthenogenesis-capable male mutant iguana, had many offspring!

10. Godzilla has starred comic books both in its native Japan, as well as in the US—notably Marvel's 1977-1979 *Godzilla, King of the Monsters* series, which saw it fight the Avengers and the Fantastic Four!

11. There are three well-known Gojira landmarks in Tokyo. The best known is the lifesize statue towering over Shinjuku's Toho movie theater complex atop Hotel Gracery roof terrace (it's actually about half the monster, its atomic breath activated every evening). The second one is a man-sized bronze outside the Toho Studios building in Setagaya. The third, a mid-sized Shin Godzilla at Yurakucho Station in Hibiya.

12. **The recipient of a 1977 song by American rock band Blue Öyster Cult, a Hollywood Walk of Fame star, and an MTV Lifetime Achievement Award, Godzilla was been seen endorsing Dr. Pepper in 1985, Nike in 1992, Subway in 2006, and Snickers candy in 2014.**

BONUS FACTS!

- A proctologist by trade, Edwin Katskee (1903-1936) gave himself a lethal injection of cocaine, intending to document its symptoms!

- While coaching the *Estudiantes de la Plata* (Argentina) soccer team during the late 1960s, Carlos Bilardo (b.1938) infamously encouraged his players to cheat in every way imaginable, from nails in their socks, to itching powder!

- A light cavalry mercenary force in the service of the Habsburg monarchy, the *Crabats* used to wear a strip of neckcloth which became known as *cravat*, our modern necktie!

I LOVE IT WHEN A PLAN
COMES TOGETHER

A staple of 1980s American television, The A-Team ran on NBC from 1983 to 1987, it's characters and tropes becoming an integral part of popular culture worldwide, but how well do we really know that show? Let's find out! (Answers on page 383)

1. What other show did Frank Lupo and Stephen J. Cannell create together?

a) *Magnum P.I.*

b) *Riptide*

c) *Knight Rider*

2. Which popular series of novels did Stephen J. Cannell write after retiring from television?

a) Travis McGee series

b) Matt Helm series

c) Shane Scully series

3. What does the "A" in A-Team stand for?

a) Alpha

b) Avenger

c) Astonishing

4. Tim Dunigan played Lt.Templeton "Faceman" Peck, on the series pilot, but was replaced for looking …

a) Too tall

b) Too dashing

c) Too young

5. What other leading TV role was George Peppard known for before playing Col. John "Hannibal" Smith on *The A-Team*?

a) Jim Rockford

b) J. R. Ewing

c) Thomas Banacek

6. Why was Colonel John Smith nicknamed "Hannibal?"

a) After the fictional psychopath

b) After the Carthaginian general

c) After the American trumpeter

7. Who composed *The A-Team's* original opening theme?

a) Haim Saban and Shuki Levy

b) Stu Phillips and Glen A. Larson

c) Mike Post and Pete Carpenter

8. Who originally ordered the A-Team to rob the Bank of Hanoi in 1972?

a) Colonel Decker

b) Colonel Morrison

c) General Stockwell

9. How much money did they steal?

a) 100,000,000 yen

b) 100,000,000 dong

c) 100,000,000 riel

10. What is Mr. T's real name?

   a) Louis Thomson

   b) Lawrence Tureaud

   c) Terrence Lambert

11. Which ancient culture did he model his hairstyle on?

   a) Mohawk

   b) Mandinka

   c) Maya

12. Where did Mr. T's "I pity the fool!" catchphrase come from?

   a) *Penitentiary 2*

   b) *Rocky 3*

   c) *D.C. Cab*

13. Which animation company produced the 1983 *Mr. T* cartoon show?

   a) Ruby-Spears

   b) Hanna-Barbera

   c) Nelvana

14. How many issues of *The A-Team* comic did Marvel publish in 1984?

   a) Six

   b) Four

   c) Three

15. Who did B. A. Baracus fight in the second issue of the Marvel comic series?

a) The Sumo

b) The Ninja

c) The Samurai

16. Who wrote the first six officially licensed *The A-Team* novels?

a) Harold Robbins

b) Charles Heath

c) Donald Hamilton

ANSWERS:

16. b) Charles Heath

15. a) The Sumo

14. c) Three

13. a) Ruby-Spears

12. b) *Rocky III*

11. b) Mandinka

10. b) Lawrence Tureaud

9. a) 100,000,000 yen

8. b) Colonel Morrison

7. c) Mike Post and Pete Carpenter

6. b) After the Carthaginian general

5. c) Thomas Banacek

4. c) Too young

3. a) Alpha

2. c) Shane Scully series

1. b) *Riptide*

BONUS FACT!

- Elvis Presley (1935-1977) loved collecting guns and police badges!

ON THE JAZZ

Think you ain't getting in no plane? Think again with this A-Team *season one quiz! (Answers on page 406)*

Episode 1-2 (Pilot): "Mexican Slayride"

1. Who directed the pilot episode?
a) Rod Holcomb
b) Stephen J. Cannell
c) Michael Preece

2. Reporter Al Massey is kidnapped in which Mexican town?
a) Playa del Carmen
b) San Sebastian Bernal
c) San Rio Blanco

3. Which California newspaper does Amy Amanda Allen work for?
a) *Los Angeles Times*
b) *L.A. Courier Express*
c) *The Sacramento Bee*

4. What 'B' movie character is Col. John "Hannibal" Smith playing?
a) The Aquamaniac
b) The Creature from the Black Lagoon
c) Godzilla

5. Col. Lynch has been pursuing the A-Team since they escaped from where?

a) Fort Carson
b) Fort Bragg
c) Fort Sill

6. What is written on "Howling Mad" Murdock's t-shirt in the asylum?

a) Caesar
b) Mussolini
c) Napoleon

7. Where does Murdock tell Amy to meet the team?

a) At the alley behind the Kozy Kat in Hollywood at 2:00 a.m.

b) At the parking lot behind Dan Tana's in Hollywood at 3:00 a.m.

c) At the Formosa Café next to the Samuel Goldwyn studio in Hollywood at 4:00 a.m.

8. Under which guises does "Hannibal" meet Amy Allen before introducing himself in person?

a) An informant, and Dr. Chiang
b) A pizza delivery guy, and Officer Wang
c) A hobo, and Mr. Lee

9. What does Bosco "B. A." Baracus fear the most?

a) Snakes.
b) Flying.
c) Confrontation.

10. What is the tail number of the Gulfstream jetplane the team steals to go to Mexico?

a) N236MJ

b) N707JT

c) N8000J

11. What film does the team pretend to be shooting in fictional Punta Arenas?

a) 20th Century Fox *Boots and Bikinis*, starring Farrah Fawcett, Bo Derek, Loni Anderson

b) 20th Century Fox *9 to 5*, starring Jane Fonda, Lily Tomlin, and Dolly Parton

c) 20th Century Fox *3 Women*, starring Shelley Duvall, Sissy Spacek and Janice Rule

12. What bar do "Hannibal," and B.A. get beaten up at?

a) El Chato Chaparro

b) El Toro Loco

c) El Rebelde Sin Causa

13. What's the name of the Mexican bandit who kidnapped Al Massey?

a) Pancho Villa

b) Manuel Noriega

c) Malavida Valdez

14. What do Murdock and "Faceman" spray the marijuana crops with?

a) Cyanide

b) Ammonia

c) DDT

15. What does the A-Team build to defeat the Malavida gang?

a) A submarine

b) A catapult

c) An armored bus

16. What reward does "Hannibal" ask for after saving the day?

a) $25,000

b) A cold beer

c) A Cuban cigar

Season 1. Episode 3: "Children of Jamestown"

1. This episode marks the debut of which A-Team vehicle?

a) White (with a red stripe) Cheverolet Corvette

b) Black and metallic grey (with a red stripe) GMC Vandura

c) Olive green AMC CJ5 Jeep

2. Who replaced Tim Dunigan as Templeton "Faceman" Peck from this episode onward?

a) Dirk Benedict

b) Kent McCord

c) Barry Van Dyke

3. Who does the team rescue at the beginning of the episode?

a) Amy Allen

b) Sheila Rodgers

c) Tawnia Baker

4. What is painted on the back of "Howling Mad" Murdock's jacket?

a) A dragon

b) An eagle

c) A tiger

5. Who plays the main villain, Reverend Martin James, in this episode?

a) John Saxon

b) Rick James

c) Michael Ironside

6. While imprisoned at the compound, it is revealed the A-Team has learned to ...

a) Accept failure

b) Make any kind of weapon

c) Accept death

7. How many vehicles, boarded by how many henchmen pursue the team from the compound?

a) Two pickup trucks, boarded by five henchmen each

b) Three jeeps, boarded by three henchmen each

c) Four dune buggies, boarded by two henchmen each

8. During this episode "Faceman" loses two …

a) Guns

b) Crowns

c) Boots

Season 1. Episode 4: "Pros and Cons"

1. What is "B. A." Baracus teaching at the day-care center?

a) Gymnastics

b) Arts and Crafts

c) History

2. "Hannibal" is trying to land a role for himself (by playing his own agent) in which movie?

a) *The Golden Voyage of Sinbad*

b) *Sinbad and the Eye of the Tiger*

c) *Sinbad Goes to Mars*

3. What does "Hannibal" send Amy and "Faceman" to find at the Public Library?

a) A recent book on prison reform

b) A Hoyle guide to patience games

c) A Green Berets survival manual

4. How does B.A. know Jase Tataro?

a) They did time in prison together

b) They were in the same Vietnam unit

c) They grew up in the same neighborhood

5. Who does "Faceman" pretend to be?

   a) Dr. John Pemberton

   b) Dr. Caleb Bradham

   c) Dr. Dwight Pepper

6. What is the team's GMC Vandura license plate number?

   a) S967238

   b) D853850

   c) J211077

7. Where does the team drive cross-country to?

   a) Blountstown, Florida

   b) Strikersville, Florida

   c) Jasper, Florida

8. What crime do Baracus, Murdock, and Smith commit to get sent to prison?

   a) Bank robbery

   b) DUI

   c) Assaulting a police officer

Season 1. Episode 5: "A Small and Deadly War"

1. Who wrote this episode?

   a) Stephen J. Cannell

   b) Frank Lupo

   c) Bill Nuss

2. The rogue SWAT unit threatens the lives of Inspector Maloney's ...
a) Mom and dad
b) Wife and daughter
c) Bowling team

3. Where did Maloney originally wait for the A-team?
a) At the Long Beach pier
b) At the Brand Park
c) At the Old Plaza Firehouse

4. Which comic strip and which TV show did "Faceman" love as a kid in the orphanage?
a) Buck Rogers and *Captain Video*
b) Red Ryder and *Gunsmoke*
c) Dick Tracy and *Dragnet*

5. Amy and "Faceman" pretend to be exterminators working for...
a) Drop Dead Pest Control
b) Vamonos Pest
c) Vexcon Animal and Pest Control

6. What's Captain Stark's girlfriend called?
a) Debbie
b) Bonnie
c) Lizzie

7. Where does the final showdown take place?

a) An empty parking lot

b) A closed amusement park

c) An abandoned movie studio

8. How much money did Maloney originally pay the team?

a) $25,421

b) $14,602

c) $9,563

Season 1. Episode 6: "Black Day at Bad Rock"

1. Where has B.A. been shot?

a) The leg above the knee

b) The gut below the waist

c) The arm below the elbow

2. What was B.A. shot with?

a) .30 Carabine

b) .40 S&W

c) .50 BMG

3. What type of blood do B.A. and Murdock share?

a) O+

b) AB−

c) AB+

4. What card game do "Hannibal" and "Faceman" play at Mo Sullivan's?

a) Poker

b) Bridge

c) Gin Rummy

5. What rank did Mo Sullivan hold in Vietnam?

a) Sargent

b) Lieutenant

c) Captain

6. When was the Redwood Café established?

a) 1949

b) 1954

c) 1972

7. "Hannibal" tells Dr. Sullivan he doesn't make any …

a) Plans

b) Mistakes

c) Passes

8. What watch brand does "Hannibal" wear?

a) Baylor

b) Zodiac

c) Seiko

Season 1. Episode 7: "The Rabbit Who Ate Las Vegas"

1. Where did Professor Bruce Warfel teach?

a) California Institute of Technology

b) Arizona State University

c) Princeton University

2. Who is the bikini girl in the photo?

a) Richard Romanus's wife

b) Templeton Peck's sister

c) Gianni Christian's girlfriend

3. Who's performing at the Riviera?

a) Bob Newhart, Bernadette Peters, and the Dick Palombi orchestra.

b) Tony Bennett, Joey Heatherton, and Pete Barbutti

c) Paul Anka, Andy Williams, and the Lennon Sisters

4. What suite do "Hannibal," B.A., and Murdock get at the Xanadu hotel?

a) The Dean Martin suite

b) The Sammy Davis Jr. suite

c) The Elvis Presley suite

5. What is Murdock watching on TV at the Motel?

a) Wally Gator

b) Woody Woodpecker

c) Yogi Bear

6. What bounty does the mob offer for the A-Team?

a) $100,000

b) $1,000,000

c) $10,000,000

7. "Hannibal," "Faceman," and Murdock take the secret elevator to …
a) The heliport
b) The lobby
c) The garage

8. Where is "Howling Mad" Murdock at the end of the episode?
a) Tucson International Airport
b) Dallas-Fort Worth Airport
c) Los Angeles International Airport

Season 1. Episode 8: "The Out-of-Towners"

1. What does Nicky do for a living?
a) Bellhop
b) Paperboy
c) Shoeshiner

2. "Hannibal," B.A, and Murdock fly to New York via …
a) American Airlines
b) United Airlines
c) Delta Air Lines

3. Which magazine classifieds does "Faceman" use to buy guns and explosives?
a) *Soldier of Fortune*
b) *Guns & Ammo*

c) *Mercenary Quarterly*

4. What business front does the team set up?
a) A hot dog stand
b) A candy store
c) A used electronics store

5. What symbolic fee does the team accept for their services?
a) $3.68
b) $25.00
c) Absolutely nothing.

6. What is the goons car license plate number?
a) 682 VYT
b) 65C TPV
c) 30F IVQ

7. The protection racket is run by the owner of the ...
a) *Wetlands Preserve*
b) *Limelight*
c) *Sugar Hill Club*

8. Where does Amy's old boyfriend work?
a) The *New Yorker*
b) *The New York Times*
c) The New York *Post*

Season 1. Episode 9: "Holiday in the Hills"

1. Where does the action begin?
　　a) Nicaragua
　　b) Panama
　　c) Guatemala

2. What plane is Murdock flying?
　　a) Beechcraft C-18 S
　　b) Lockheed C-60 L
　　c) Douglas B-18 B

3. What song are "Hannibal" and "Faceman" singing to mask the plane noise from B.A.?
　　a) "I'm So Lonesome I Could Cry"
　　b) "You Are My Sunshine"
　　c) "Folsom Prison Blues"

4. Aboard the plane, "Hannibal" berates "Faceman" for failing to …
　　a) Paint the church
　　b) Bribe the military
　　c) Dynamite the bridge

5. What's the name and occupation of the unconscious man the team saved?
　　a) James McDonald, County Surveyor
　　b) Kenneth MacFarlane, County Secretary
　　c) Alan Digby, County Commissioner

6. What does the team build to take the unconscious man out of the valley?

a) An ultralight airplane

b) A hot-air balloon

c) An airboat

7. What does Lou Ann lend "Faceman?"

a) A lawnmower's oil filter and belt

b) A seeder's engine and wheels

c) A combine's blades and drum

8. Where does the team hide from the Military Police?

a) Inside a bus

b) Inside a helicopter

c) Inside Amy's car trunk

Season 1. Episode 10: "West Coast Turnaround"

1. What picture does the episode begin with?

a) A grazing cow

b) A trotting horse

c) A braying donkey

2. What's the brand name on the watermelon crate?

a) Colton & Wood

b) DePalma

c) Mr. Fresh

3. Farmer Penhall is a veteran from which conflict?

    a) World War II

    b) The Korean War

    c) The Vietnam War

4. In Vietnam "Hannibal" Smith was a ...

a) Lieutenant colonel in the Fifth Special Forces Group

b) Colonel in the Nineteenth Special Forces Group

c) Major in the First Special Forces Group

5. What is Murdock's imaginary dog's name?

    a) Mikey

    b) Billy

    c) Sparky

6. The team hijacks two trucks belonging to which company?

    a) Heitz Trucking Inc.

    b) Matheson Inc.

    c) Lone Horse Trucking

7. Amy's new car is a ...

    a) Renault 5

    b) Fiat Uno

    c) Peugeot 205

8. What market price did "Faceman" manage to get for the Penhall watermelons?

a) $33.60/bushel

b) $42.50/bushel

c) $25.40/bushel

Season 1. Episode 11: "One More Time"

1. "Hannibal" had been acting in broad daylight under which alias?

    a) Smith

    b) Lynch

    c) Patton

2. What's the name of Templeton Peck's girlfriend?

    a) Melinda

    b) Yolanda

    c) Rhonda

3. In this episode, Colonel Lynch manages to …

    a) Frame Amy Allen

    b) Commit Murdock to a mental hospital

    c) Capture the A-Team

4. What does Mr. Perry threaten Col. Lynch with?

    a) Packing parachutes in Utah

    b) Peeling potatoes in South Carolina

    c) Pushing daisies in Arlington

5. What vehicle does Murdock steal to get to Amy?

a) Mr. Softee's Ice-Cream truck

b) Sandy's Bakery truck

c) California Tacos truck

6. When Murdock parachutes out of the plane he starts …

a) Yodelling

b) Whistling

c) Screaming

7. What does Rashaad want from General Ludlam?

a) The maps to the CIA's secret base

b) The codes for the NORAD satellites

c) The plans to the NATO missile sites

8. B.A feels uneasy about …

a) Being drugged and waking in strange places

b) The team making newspaper headlines

c) "Hannibal" Smith smoking cigars in the van

Season 1. Episode 12: "Till Death Do Us Part"

1. Where was Jackie headed to before being abducted?

a) Houston

b) Dallas

c) Austin

2. What disguise is "Hannibal" using when he first appears?

a) Truck driver
b) Bus driver
c) Cab driver

3. What is "Adrian's Catering" service's phone number?
a) 555-5576
b) 555-5126
c) 555-5236

4. Who does Murdock pretend to be at the wedding?
a) The chef, and the bride
b) A waiter, and the groom
c) The pastor, and the best man

5. Who marries "Faceman" and Jackie?
a) Colonel John "Hannibal" Smith
b) Reverend Allen Allensworth
c) Justice of the Peace Joe Birnie Jr.

6. Who will receive Templeton Peck's inheritance if he dies?
a) The A-Team
b) The orphanage
c) The Catholic Church

7. What does Calvin Cutter smash?
a) Jackie's framed picture
b) The TV screen
c) The wedding video tape

8. "Hannibal" buys burgers for everyone at …
    a) Keller's Drive-In
    b) Dirty Martin's Place
    c) Captain Bellybuster's Burger Heaven

Season 1. Episode 13: "The Beast from the Belly of a Boeing"

1. What's the Beller Air employee driving inside the hangar?
    a) A Harlan baggage tractor
    b) A Moto EV4 golf cart
    c) A Suzuki shuttle

2. What's the name of the terrorist group hijacking the plane?
    a) Volksfrei Movement
    b) National People's Army
    c) United People's Resistance

3. What's printed on Murdock's t-shirt?
    a) The Flintstones
    b) Fat Albert and the Cosby Kids
    c) The Jetsons

4. Who does "Hannibal" pretend to be, to get the hostages released?
    a) President Ronald Reagan
    b) President Edward Beller III
    c) Governor George Deukmejian

5. After failing to jump from the aircraft before takeoff, B.A. becomes …

a) Enraged

b) Hysterical

c) Catatonic

6. What the Beller Air slogan?

a) "You Can't Beat the Experience"

b) "First in the Sky, Second to None"

c) "Airlines are the Same. Only People Make the Difference"

7. Where is the plane headed for?

a) The Yucatán Peninsula

b) The Baja California Peninsula

c) The Alaska Peninsula

8. How much of the $50,000 is the team left with after various deductions and fees?

a) $236.00

b) $23.60

c) $2.36

Season 1. Episode 14: "A Nice Place to Visit"

1. This episode begins with a chase scene recycled from which previous episode?

a) Episode 4

b) Episode 6

c) Episode 7

2. The A-Team is on its way to …
a) A wedding
b) A funeral
c) A bachelor party

3. What had B.A. done to a traffic officer?
a) Eat his parking ticket
b) Punch him in the nose
c) Chew his badge

4. What's the Watkins Brothers towing service's phone number?
a) 555-5615
b) 555-5165
c) 555-5651

5. What did Ray Brenner did for "Faceman" in Vietnam?
a) Gave him his helmet
b) Dragged him to the medevac
c) Help him blow up a bridge

6. How much do the Watkins Brothers charge per towing mile?
a) $15.00
b) $25.00
c) $35.00

7. Amy drove back Harold Watkins using a…

a) Frying pan

b) Kettle with boiling water

c) Fire extinguisher

8. What is Ray's headstone inscription?

a) "Brave in Spirit, Strong in Love"

b) "Lest We Forget"

c) "His Duty Done, His Honor Won"

ANSWERS:

Episode 1-2 (Pilot):
1. a) Rod Holcomb
2. c) San Rio Blanco
3. b) L.A. Courier Express
4. a) The Aquamaniac
5. b) Fort Bragg
6. c) Napoleon
7. a) At the alley behind the Kozy Kat in Hollywood at 2:00 a.m.
8. c) A hobo, and Mr. Lee
9. b) Flying.
10. c) N80001
11. a) 20th Century Fox Boots

Season 1, Episode 3:
1. b) Black and metallic grey (with a red stripe) GMC Vandura
2. a) Dirk Benedict

and Bikinis, starring Farrah Fawcett, Bo Derek, Loni Anderson
12. b) El Toro Loco
13. c) Malavida Valdez
14. b) Ammonia
15. c) An armored bus
16. b) A cold beer

3. b) Sheila Rodgers

4. c) A tiger

5. a) John Saxon

6. c) Accept death

7. b) Three jeeps, boarded by three henchmen each.

8. b) Crowns

Season 1. Episode 4:

1. b) Arts and Crafts

2. c) *Sinbad Goes to Mars*

3. a) A recent book on prison reform

4. c) They grew up in the same neighborhood

5. c) Dr. Dwight Pepper

6. a) S967238

7. b) Strikersville, Florida

8. b) DUI

Season 1. Episode 5:

1. b) Frank Lupo

2. b) Wife and daughter

3. a) At the Long Beach pier

4. c) Dick Tracy and Dragnet

5. a) Drop Dead Pest Control

6. b) Bonnie

7. b) A closed amusement park

8. b) $14,602

Season 1. Episode 6:

1. a) The leg above the knee

2. c) .50 BMG

3. b) AB-

4. c) Gin Rummy

5. c) Captain

6. b) 1954

7. c) Passes

8. a) Baylor

Season 1. Episode 7:

1. b) Arizona State University

2. c) Gianni Christian's girlfriend

3. a) Bob Newhart, Bernadette Peters, and the Dick Palombi orchestra.

4. c) The Elvis Presley suite

5. b) Woody Woodpecker

6. a) $100,000

7. c) The garage

8. a) Tucson International Airport

Season 1. Episode 8:

1. c) Shoeshiner

2. b) United Airlines

3. c) *Mercenary Quarterly*

4. c) A used electronics store

5. a) $3.68

6. b) 65C TPV

7. c) Sugar Hill Club

8. b) The *New York Times*

Season 1. Episode 9:

1. c) Guatemala

2. a) Beechcraft C-18 S

3. b) "You Are My Sunshine"

4. c) Dynamite the bridge

5. a) James McDonald, County Surveyor

6. a) An ultralight airplane

7. b) A seeder's engine and wheels

8. a) Inside a bus

Season 1. Episode 10:

1. c) A braying donkey

2. a) Colton & Wood

3. c) The Vietnam War

4. a) Lieutenant colonel in the Fifth Special Forces Group

5. b) Billy

6. c) Lone Horse Trucking

7. a) Renault 5

8. a) $33.60/bushel

Season 1. Episode 11:

1. b) Lynch

2. c) Rhonda

3. c) Capture the A-Team

4. a) Packing parachutes in Utah

5. b) Sandy's Bakery truck

6. a) Yodeling

7. c) The plans to the NATO missile sites

8. b) The team making newspaper headlines

Season 1. Episode 12:

1. b) Dallas
2. c) Cab driver
3. b) 555-5126
4. a) The chef, and the bride
5. c) Justice of the Peace Joe Birnie Jr.
6. b) The orphanage he was raised in
7. a) Jackie's framed picture
8. c) Captain Bellybuster's Burger Heaven

Season 1. Episode 13:

1. a) A Harlan baggage tractor
2. c) United People's Resistance
3. c) The Jetsons
4. b) President Edward Beller III
5. c) Catatonic
6. b) "First in the Sky, Second to None"
7. b) The Baja California Peninsula
8. a) $236.00

Season 1. Episode 14:

1. c) Episode 7
2. b) A funeral
3. a) Eat his parking ticket
4. a) 555-5615
5. a) Gave him his helmet
6. b) $25.00
7. c) Fire extinguisher
8. b) "Lest We Forget"

BONUS FACT!

- The world's oldest rose bush has been covering an outer wall of the Hildesheim Cathedral (Germany) since 815AD, surviving even a bombing in 1945!

V
BURSTING
SPORTS

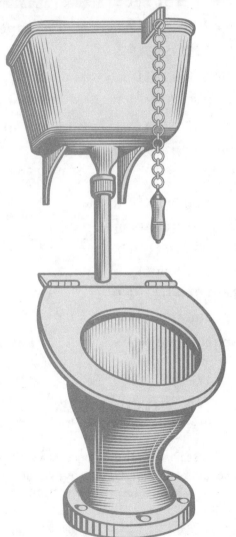

OLYMPUS HAS FALLEN
PART 1

The antediluvian origin of sports is tied to ritual play, warfare enactment, and hunting training, which mankind brought from the cave dwellings it used to inhabit, into the permanent settlements which would eventually turn to ancient cities.

1. 15000BC Lascaux (France) cave depictions show wrestling and sprinting competitions, while 7000BC cave paintings from Bayankhongor (Mongolia) show not only early wrestling matches, but the cheering crowds surrounding them.

2. Sumerian civilization in modern day Iraq left plenty of evidence for early wrestling and boxing both in the form of bronze figurines and cuneiform literature (*Epic of Gilgamesh*) dating as far back as 3000BC.

3. 4,000 year old Egyptian hieroglyphs aplenty, describe the rules of varied sports which included wrestling, weightlifting, javelin, high jump, long jump, swimming, rowing, archery, athletics, and even ball games.

4. Ancient Persia had its own *pahlevani* and *zourkhaneh* rituals; forms of wrestling, fencing and jousting still in vogue today in modern day Iran.

5. Gymnastics and calisthenics are, of course, Greek inventions of the Minoan culture, as is bullfighting (Minoans loved their bulls), thousands of years before it became a thing in Spain, while Mycenaean Greece's penchant for celebrating funeral games has been well known since *The Iliad*.

6. Instituted formally in the Peloponnese town of Olympia in 776BC, the Olympics grew from a single sprinting event, to include boxing, wrestling (*pankration*), chariot racing, long jump, javelin, and discus. It was so important an event, that peace among usually warring Greek city-states was declared for its duration, which in turn fostered tourism and commerce among them.

6. Naturally, other *polis* took notice, quickly instituting their own game celebrations, including the Isthmian games, the Nemean Games, the Pythian Games, Athens's *Panathenaia* of Athens (which included musical ceremonies not unlike those of modern Olympics), and women's own Heraean Games, also held in Olympia.

BONUS FACTS!

- The *Friends* (1994-2004) starring cast negotiated to receive a percentage (2%) of the revenue from reruns, which nets a nifty $20 million to each one of them every year!

- The Marsili family in Siena, Italy, has a hereditary pain insensitivity which apparently makes them nigh impervious to most injuries.

- Cecil B. DeMille's (1881-1959) City of the Pharaoh, built for the 1923 film *The Ten Commandments* in the Colorado Desert, was dismantled after filming and buried in the sand, where it remains to this day.

KEEP IT ROLLING

For millennia, ball games and human civilization have gone hand in hand.

No Human Sacrifice, No Gain!

As early as 1600BC, ancient inhabitants of a land stretching from Arizona to Costa Rica, where making rubber balls to play with, which evolved into *Ōllamaliztli,* what we now call Mesoamerican ballgame. According to the "Popol Vuh," the sacred book of the K'iche tribe from Guatemala, the game recreates a conflict between the gods of light and darkness. In order to settle the dispute, it is believed the end of each game was celebrated with a fitting human sacrifice!

Tonight We Play in Hell!

A thousand years earlier, on the coast of the Mediterranean Sea, ancient Spartan civilization played yet another ball game, akin to modern rugby and American football. It was called *episkyros* ("commonball"), and involved getting a ball past the opposing team's back line using interceptions, fumbles, tackles, and every tactic you can think of. Episkyros eventually reached the Italian Peninsula and Romans made it their own, an even more violent version called *harpastum* ("snatch"), using a smaller round ball (the size of a softball), which had a pattern made of hexagons and pentagons (similar to modern soccer balls). Each team would try to keep it on their side of the field, while the other would use every manoeuver to snatch it for themselves.

Kung-Fu Soccer

Centuries later, during the Han Dynasty (202BC-9AD) in China, a game called *cuju* ("kickball") was invented where the use of hands was not allowed.

While not connected to the genesis of modern soccer in nineteenth century Britain, FIFA now recognizes it as the oldest form of the sport. Much like its modern counterpart, *cuju* generated clubs, professional players, fans, ever-improving equipment, and widespread celebrations which took Asia by storm for 1500 years, until the "fad" died away.

Ball for Vendetta

Possibly evolving from Roman *harpastum*, sixteenth century *calcio fiorentino* ("Florentine football"), also known as *calcio storico* ("historic football"), was fittingly described by Henry III (1551-1589) as "too small to be a real war and too cruel to be a game." Combining "mixed martial arts," or simple brutality, with passes aiming to get the ball into an opponent's goal area, or *caccia*, *calcio friorentino*'s 50-minute sand field matches pit two 27-player teams, checked by referees armed with swords. In the old days, the winning prize used to be a cow, but that has been replaced with a free dinner. Benito Mussolini (1883-1945) made it into an officially sanctioned Italian sport in 1930, and it continues to be eagerly played today, while still guarded by sword-wielding referees!

BONUS FACTS!

- Erik Satie's (1866-1925) *Vexations* holds the record for being both the longest and the shortest of musical compositions ever. A piano piece lasting less than a minute, it is supposed to be repeated 840 times nonstop over 14 hours.

- When something moves faster than the speed of light, it emits a blue glow known as Cherenkov Radiation.

THE ENGLISH GAME

In Medieval England, jousting and indoor tennis were the sports of the rich, while peasants and townsfolk used to engage in drunken kick-ball games, which continued to grow in popularity until adopted by the very gentry which used to despise them. By the nineteenth century, colonial England would disseminate its codified sports worldwide, modern association football (soccer) chief among them. Currently played by 265 million people (4% of the world's population), soccer has become the most popular and lucrative sport of all!

1. Modern association football in itself has existed since its initial 1848 Cambridge Rules (established by Eton, Harrow, Rugby, Winchester and Shrewsbury) were set in mid-nineteenth century England, as a means for achieving a standard code of play among the elite British colleges and schools.

2. However, under the elites' noses, public schools were also forming football clubs and club associations (notably Sheffield's) with their own sets of rules, which led to the legendary Freemasons' Tavern meetings of 1863, with the subsequent formation of an all-encompassing Football Association (FA), and the formulation of a comprehensive body of rules to regulate this new English game, now played by prince and pauper alike. Said code would eventually give way to the Laws of the Game, which regulate the sport today.

3. But not everyone in the FA was happy with the new rulebook, which forbade grabbing the ball, and kicking opponent players in the shins, among other forms of rough play. The clubs that split from the FA in 1871 would form its own Rugby Football Union, giving birth to an entirely new sport—can we guess its name?

4. The original English FA was comprised of 12 clubs nationally.

Its example led to the formation of similar soccer associations in Wales, Scotland, and Ireland, their first international matches beginning in 1872. In 1904, the spread of the game to Belgium, Denmark, France, Germany, the Netherlands, Spain, Sweden, and Switzerland, saw the formation of the Fédération Internationale de Football Association (FIFA) in Paris, with British and South African associations joining in not much later. By 1914, Argentina, Chile, Canada, and the US had joined too.

5. As mentioned earlier, Victorian England promptly and eagerly spread soccer worldwide, either by its many colonies or its itinerant business ventures and workforce. The game took particular root in 1880s Uruguay, brought over by English and Scottish railroad company workers. By 1881 the small country had established its first club named—what else?—the Albion FC, and many more followed.

6. Before FIFA's first World Cup, its tournaments had been incorporated into the new, rebooted Olympic Games, starting with the 1908 London Olympics, and by the 1924 Summer Olympics held in Paris, 22 national teams which included the US, Egypt, Turkey, and tiny Uruguay were present. The Uruguayans, who arrived to Paris traveling third class, and pretended to be clumsy players while training, made it to the final match undefeated, and beat then-favorite Switzerland 3-0, to win their Olympic gold. Naturally, the first FIFA World Cup in 1930 was held in Uruguay, who kept that cup at home after beating Argentina 4-2.

BONUS FACT!

- Selfie sticks have been banned by Disney parks since 2015!

MONEYBALL

In spite of little evidence that hosting sports tournaments ever pays off for the countries involved, for many governments they provide priceless prestige, so the FIFA World Cup being the most-watched sporting event on the planet has sadly led to many an opportunity for graft and malfeasance.

1. From its humble 1904 beginnings FIFA moved from Paris to Zürich in 1932, and by 2016 its member states had grown to 211 (more than the UN's 193), split into regional confederations UEFA (Europe), CONMEBOL (South America), CONCACAF (North America, Central America, and the Caribbean), AFC (Asia), CAF (Africa), and OFC (Oceania), with a yearly working budget of approximately one billion dollars!

2. Since each FIFA country member has an equal right to vote in its presidential elections, acting presidents wouldn't hesitate to bribe reelection votes from confederation executives of smaller, poorer countries, and given everyone in FIFA get an equal cut from its revenues (which include ever-growing corporate sponsorships and media rights sales), everyone has plenty of incentive to fall in line!

3. In 2002, while allegations of corruption were swiftly swept under the rug (along those who dared to make them), South Korea suspiciously reached the Korea-Japan World Cup semifinals, defeating stronger teams like Italy and Spain.

4. Years later, support from Africa's CAF secured FIFA President Joseph "Sepp" Blatter (b.1936) reelection, who in turn saw it that South Africa won the right to host the World Cup in 2010. That year, it was reported Russia and Qatar had also bribed their way into their respective tournaments of 2018 and 2022.

5. Meanwhile in New York, the FBI would arrest general CONCACAF secretary Chuck Blazer (1945-2017), on accounts of fraud, money laundering, and tax evasion. To avoid prison Blazer agreed to become an FBI informant. He wasn't the only one, as the feds found another mole in Chile's football association president Sergio Jadue (b.1979).

6. On May 27, 2015, the US Department of Justice (DOJ) finally arrested seven FIFA high-ranking executives in Zurich, including vice presidents Jeffrey Webb (b.1964) and Eugenio Figueredo (b.1932), from New Zealand and Uruguay respectively. A following DOJ indictment would see another 16 CONCACAF and CONMEBOL executives in chains by the end of that year.

7. In spite of everything, a newly reelected Blatter remained untouchable, and tried to save face by having the arrested executives banned by FIFA's "Ethics Committee," yet it wasn't enough. In the end, not DOJ nor the FBI took FIFA's all-powerful president down, but combined pressure from sponsors Coca-Cola, McDonald's, Visa, and Budweiser!

BONUS FACTS!

- On August 6, 2013, the Mars Curiosity rover played "Happy Birthday" to itself, making it the first human song ever played on another planet!

- Charles Dickens's (1812-1870) beloved pet raven, Grip, was included in his 1841 novel *Barnaby Rudge*, which in turn influenced Edgar Allan Poe's (1809-1849) 1845 poem "The Raven."

THE OTHER ENGLISH GAME

The rough offspring of Victorian English football, rugby football is also the father of gridiron football (which includes American and Canadian football), and has had a life of its own, remaining very popular beyond the UK, in southern hemisphere countries like Argentina, Australia, New Zealand, Fiji, and South Africa.

1. Rugby football is named after its birthplace, the Rugby School, an English boarding school for boys located in Rugby, Warwickshire, England.

2. Modern rugby balls (originally called a *quancos*) may be oval shaped, but in the old days they were plum shaped as they were made out of the bladder of pigs, encased in leather by their inventor, English leatherworker Richard Lindon (1816-1887), who ran a leather shop in the town of Rugby, and by the mid-1800s began to be flooded with ball and shoe orders coming from the boarding school.

3. Balls became oval shaped as bladders were substituted with more sanitary rubber tubes to prevent the people who used to blow them by mouth from catching diseases, after Mr. Lindon's own wife passed away due to a lung infection!

4. The first time a national anthem that was ever sung before sports was that of Rugby, in a match between Wales and New Zealand back in 1905. When the New Zealand team began to perform their famous *Haka* (a Maori war dance/cry meant to intimidate an opponent), the Welsh spontaneously responded by singing their national anthem, "*Hen Wlad Fy Nhadau*" ("Land of My Fathers"), which caught on among the crowds as well.

5. Rugby football was an official Olympic Games sport between 1900 to 1924. The winning team of the 1924 Olympic tournament was the USA!

6. Rugby sevens (which pits teams of seven players playing seven-minute halves, as opposed to standard rugby with 15 players playing 40-minute halves) was introduced to the Olympics at the 2016 Rio de Janeiro Summer Games. The men's tournament was won by Fiji, while the women's was won by Australia.

7. The Rugby World Cup, organized by World Rugby, was first held in New Zealand and Australia in 1987. The 2019 Rugby World Cup took place in Japan, with South Africa taking the trophy home.

8. Every Rugby World Cup tournament is kicked off by blowing the whistle a Welsh referee named Gil Evans blew to kick off match between England and New Zealand in 1905. It was also used at the final 1924 Paris Olympics match by Evans himself, and was donated to the New Zealand Rugby Museum in 1969.

BONUS FACTS!

- Bernard Herrmann's (1911-1975) salary on *Psycho* was doubled after Alfred Hitchcock (1899-1980) saw the famous shower footage with Herrmann's score.

- 34 years after TV series *MacGyver* (1985-1992) aired, the term "MacGyvered" (meaning "adapted or improvised in an ingenious or expedient way") was finally added to the *Oxford English Dictionary*.

THIS MEANS WAR

Rugby's most famous offspring, gridiron football, is played both in America and Canada, but their differences became apparent as early as 1874, when a match between Harvard and McGill university teams revealed each side of the border to be playing their own bespoke "rugby."

CANADA:

Playing field: 110 by 65 yards

End zones: 20 yards

Goal posts: At the goal line

Players: 12 per side

Offense: Two slotbacks

Defense: Two halfbacks

Downs: Three

Scrimmage zone: One yard

Scrimmage movement: Unlimited

Fair catch: Penalized

Snap motion: All offensive players

Time: 20 seconds from whistle, penalty or timeout.

Clock: Stops after every play.

Delay penalty: Ten yards.

Period: Ends with final play.

AMERICA:

Playing field: 100 by 53 1/3 yards

End zones: Ten yards

Goal posts: At the end line

Players: 11 per side

Offense: One tight end

Defense: One strong safety

Downs: Four

Neutral zone: 11 inches

Offensive movement: Restricted

Fair catch: Allowed

Snap motion: One offensive player

Time: 40 seconds from the end of previous play, 25 seconds from penalty or timeout.

Clock: Runs after in-bound tackle. Stops after incomplete pass or out-of-bounds tackle.

Delay penalty: Five yards.

Period: Ends when time expires.

CANADA:

Receiver blocking: Within one yard of the scrimmage lines.

Open field kick: Allowed

Overtime: "Kansas Playoff" rules

Penalty flags: Orange

Season: Late June to late October (18 games)

AMERICA:

Receiver blocking: Up to five yards from the line.

Open field kick: Penalized

Overtime: 15-minute sudden-death period (NFL)

Penalty flags: Yellow

Season: Mid-September to late December (16 games)

Despite all their differences NFL and CFL have one thing in common: the football's size. While CFL ball dimensions were historically larger than its American counterpart, the CFL adopted the NFL football specifications in 2018, yet retaining their standard one inch white stripes around the ball—NFL balls have none!

BONUS FACTS!

- Scotland's entrancing Fingal's Cave was created by lava cooling down so slowly it broke into hexagonal basalt pillars.

- Perry Como (1912-2001) received the very first RIAA gold record in 1958, while Paul McCartney (b.1942) got his eighty-first gold record in 1997!

- According to the *New England Journal of Medicine*, on May 7, 2020, a 38 year-old man walked into a Sao Paulo (Brazil) hospital complaining about a lower back hernia, but a tomography revealed the presence of three kidneys!

GONE TOO SOON

Death, it would appear, never takes a holiday, not even to spare our favorite sportspeople from falling while still in pursuit of their passion.

Pheidippides (c.530-490BC): The Athenian soldier and herald was sent running from the Marathon plain to Athens, with news of the Greek victory over the Persians. After delivering his message, he collapsed on his bloodied feet and died.

Frank Hayes (1888-1923): The jockey, or rather his horse, famously won a steeplechase race despite dying from a hart attack halfway through it!

Ray Chapman (1891-1920): The Cleveland Indians shortstop took a lethal pitch to the head, and event which prompted the MLB to make umpire helmets mandatory.

Lou Gehrig (1903-1941): The legendary New York Yankees first baseman saw his career cut short by Amyotrophic Lateral Sclerosis (ALS), now commonly referred to as "Lou Gehrig's disease."

Al Blozis (1919-1945): The New York Giants offensive tackle joined the US Army and was killed in action during World War II.

Ed Sanders (1930-1954): The Olympic gold winning heavyweight boxer fell on the ring during a friendly sparring contest.

Roberto Clemente (1934-1972): The beloved Pittsburgh Pirates right fielder was killed in a plane crash while on a mission to help

earthquake victims in Nicaragua.

Bill Masterton (1938-1968): The Minnesota North Stars center became the only NHL player to die on the ice, after falling backwards and smashing his head, yet it took the NHL another 11 years to establish mandatory helmet use (fortunately no casualties registered on the interim).

Brian Piccolo (1943-1970): The Chicago Bears running back passed at age 26 from aggressive testicular cancer.

Chuck Hughes (1943-1971): The Detroit Lions wide receiver died from a heart attack (brought on by an advanced arteriosclerosis) while playing, thus becoming the first NFL player to ever die on the turf.

Thurman Munson (1947-1979): The New York Yankees catcher broke his neck in a plane crash.

Steve Prefontaine (1951-1975): The Pan American Games gold medallist runner who broke several long-distance records, died in a car accident at age 24.

Dale Earnhardt (1951-2002): The NASCAR race driver and seven-time Winston Cup Series champion, died in a crash during the Daytona 500.

Payne Stewart (1957-1999): The winner of 11 PGA Tours, Stewart was killed in a plane crash.

Ayrton Senna (1960-1994): The three time Formula One World

Drivers' Champion from Brazil fatally crashed his vehicle during the 1994 San Marino Grand Prix.

Dražen Petrović (1964-1993): The Croatian basketball player who made it into the NBA's New Jersey Nets perished in a car accident at age 28.

Reggie Lewis (1965-1993): The Boston Celtics player died from cardiac arrest during off-season practice at age 27.

Andrés Escobar (1967-1994): The Colombian national soccer team defender was shot by three irate soccer fans, as payback for the own goal he made during the 1994 FIFA World Cup, which gave the US the lead to win that particular match.

Darryl Kile (1968-2002): The St. Louis Cardinals pitcher became the second MLB player after Thurman Munson to die during season, on account of a heart attack caused by undiagnosed arteriosclerosis.

Pat Tillman (1976-2004): The Arizona Cardinals safety and all-around American hero who joined the Army Rangers in the aftermath of the 9-11 attacks, was killed in Afghanistan by friendly fire.

Kobe Bryant (1978-2020): The Los Angeles Lakers superstar died at age 41 in a helicopter crash along with his 13-year-old daughter.

Sarah Burke (1982-2012): The X Games gold winning skier suffered injuries followed by a cardiac arrest while still on the slope, passing nine days later.

Sean Taylor (1983-2007): The Washington Redskins free safety was tragically shot by a burglar.

Caleb Moore (1987-2013): The X Games professional snowmobile racer died as a result of injuries sustained during a race.

While unusual, sometimes entire teams have been killed, particularly in the history of soccer:

- **In 1958, eight Manchester United soccer team players were killed in a plane crash over Munich, while flying back home from Yugoslavia.**

- **In 1998, the entire Bena Tshadi (Democratic Republic of the Congo) football team was struck dead by a lightning bolt while playing!**

- **In 2016, only three players of the Brazilian Chapecoense soccer team survived a plane crash en route to Medellín, Colombia.**

BONUS FACTS!

- The only US presidents to have written their own books without the aid of ghostwriters are Thomas Jefferson (1743-1826), and Theodore Roosevelt (1858-1919).

- While married with two children, Florida radiologist Carl Tanzler (1877-1952) fell madly in love with tuberculosis patient Elena Milagro de Hoyos (1909-1931), to the point of stealing her dead body in 1933, and keeping it at home (encased in wax and plaster) to have sex with it, until found out, and arrested in 1940!

OLYMPUS HAS FALLEN
PART 2

Held in honor of Zeus, the original Olympic Games of Ancient Greece continued into the Christian era, when a series of natural disasters and barbarian invasions saw them decline until officially cancelled by emperor Theodosius I (347-395AD) in 393AD.

1. Inspired by ancient history Baron Pierre de Coubertin (1863-1937) led to the foundation of the International Olympic Committee (IOC) in 1894, followed by a revival of the Olympic Games in 1896 Greece.

2. Originally only intended for amateur athletes, the IOC began to allow professionals, and expanded the games' reach with the creation of the Winter Olympics, held in Chamonix, France, for the first time in 1924; the Paralympic Games, held in Rome, Italy for the first time in 1960; the Youth Olympic Games (YOG) held for the first time in Singapore, in 2010; and the World Games, first held in Santa Clara, USA, in 1981, to accommodate "lesser" but equally widespread sports not included in the Olympics, such as powerlifting, squash, billiards, and water skiing.

3. Greek composer Spyridon Samaras (1861-1917) and lyricist Kostis Palamas (1859-1943) were commissioned to compose the official Olympic Hymn in 1896.

4. Originally crowning athletes with an olive wreath in the spirit of Ancient Greece, the IOC began the gold, silver, and bronze medals tradition in the 1904 Olympic Games held in St. Louis, Missouri, in the US. Medals used to be made of solid gold, silver, and bronze, until 1912, when they began to be simply plated with said metals.

5. The 1908 London Olympic Games was the first to establish a proper opening ceremony, complete with an athletes procession, which traditionally is always led by Greece's athletes, followed by every other country in alphabetical order, except the host country which enters the arena last.

6. First flown in 1920, the Olympic flag designed by de Coubertin contains five interconnected blue, yellow, black, green, and red rings on a white background, symbolizing the five continents and their friendship during the event.

7. In 1920, de Coubertin also developed an Olympic motto ("Swifter, Higher, Stronger"), an oath ("In the name of all competitors, I promise that we shall take part in these Olympic Games, respecting and abiding by the rules that govern them, in the true spirit of sportsmanship, for the glory of sport and the honor of our teams"), and a creed ("The most important thing in the Olympic Games is not to win but to take part, just as the most important thing in life is not the triumph but the struggle. The essential thing is not to have conquered but to have fought well"), which continue to define good sportsmanship.

8. Johnny Weissmuller (1904-1984) the *Tarzan* movie serials actor, won Olympic three Olympic gold swimming medals in the 1924 Games held in Paris, and another two in the 1928 Amsterdam Olympics—a record smashed in the 2000s by swimmer Michael Phelps's (b.1985) 23 Olympic gold medals!

9. From 1912 till 1948, the Olympics also included competitions in painting, sculpting, writing, and music, which were awarded gold, silver, and bronze medals like any sport!

10. Inspired by the ancient Greek Olympics, the modern version rekindled the lighting of the Olympic flame in the 1928 Amsterdam Games. The torch relay, which symbolizes the continuation of Olympic tradition, was devised for the first time in Nazi Germany, for the 1936 Berlin Summer Olympics (the first Olympic Games to be televised!). In modern times, the unlit torch has even been flown up to space several times!

11. Barely making it through civil war, two large scale global wars, and Stalin's purges, the Soviet Union (USSR) finally managed to enter the Olympic Games in 1952 Helsinki, discus thrower Nina Ponomaryova (1929-2016) winning their first gold medal that year, while skier Lyubov Kozyreva (1929-2015) would win that nation's first Winter Olympics gold in 1956.

12. While World War I and World War II saw the Olympics cancelled in 1916, 1940, and 1944, the Covid-19 pandemic has managed to postpone the 2020 Tokyo Olympics until 2021 at the very least!

13. People with disabilities could compete at the Olympic Games, before the Paralympics were established, remarkably:

- **American gymnast George Eyser (1870-1919), who despite the loss of his left leg went on to win three gold and two silver medals in the 1904 Summer Olympics.**

- **Hungarian shooter and right-arm amputee Károly Takács (1910-1976) competed in the 1948 and 1952 Summer Olympics, winning the respective gold medal for each 25 metre rapid fire pistol event he participated in.**

- **Permanently paralyzed from polio, Danish equestrian Lis Hartel (1921-2009) won the 1952 dressage silver medal ... competing against men!**

STICKS AND STONES

Originating as a children's game in medieval England, and spread throughout the world by the British Empire in the nineteenth century, cricket is one of the many "club ball" sports in existence today (baseball, golf, hockey, and tennis, to name a few), and certainly one of the most interesting.

1. Its name comes from the Saxon word *cryce* (pronounced "cricc") meaning a crutch, stick, or staff.

2. The earliest mention of the game being played by adults comes from 1611 Sussex, where parishioners Bartholomew Wyatt and Richard Latter failed to attend church on Easter Sunday over a cricket game, both men being fined 12 pennies each, and given a penance.

3. Jasper Vinall (c.1590-1624) was the first cricketer known to have died from being accidentally struck on the forehead with a cricket bat during a game.

4. Persecuted during Oliver Cromwell's (1599-1658) Commonwealth years (1649-1660), it naturally resurfaced after the Royalists' triumph in 1660, firmly establishing itself as a major sport by the end of that century.

5. During the eighteenth century, cricket matches attracted large, normally gambling crowds, while the "single wicket cricket" two-players-only variant of the game, became very popular among the elites. Since pitching a ball through the air was considered normal, that is the century when the bat went from being curved to the flat one still used today.

6. Considered to be cricket's "golden age," the late nineteenth and early twentieth centuries saw the rise of legendary players like W. G. Grace (1848-1915), who despite being an "amateur," in his lifetime made more money from the sport than anyone else.

7. Cricket's most famous tournament, The Ashes began in 1882. It is named after its trophy, a terra cotta urn containing the ashes of a burnt cricket ball! The sport has its own international competition, of course, the ICC Cricket World Cup beginning in 1975, two years after the ICC Women's Cricket World Cup was first instituted.

8. Cricket's longest match took place in 1939 between England and South Africa, but after 14 days of continued play it was decided to end it with a tie!

9. England's cricket team is the only team in history to have lost a 60 over final (1979 World Cup), a 50 over final (1992 World Cup), and a 20 over final (2013 Champions Trophy) in ICC tournaments!

10. Perhaps a tribute to its early farm days, it is still considered legal to suspend the game if an animal enters the field, and there have been several instances of such interruptions.

BONUS FACT!

- During the failed Bay of Pigs invasion of Cuba, a time zone mishap meant the two American B-26B bombers sent to obliterate Havana arrived an hour before their planned jet fighter escorts got there, so both bombers were immediately shot down.

NOT CRICKET

Considered a form of "lawn billiards," akin to golf or hockey, croquet aims at hitting a ball not at wickets but through them, and rather than using a bat, its weapon of choice is a mallet, so it is far more entertaining a sport than it sounds—specially if you're a toddler or an eighteenth-century aristocrat!

1. It is thought to have been imported to England from France by merry king Charles II (1630-1685) who called it *paille-maille* ("ball and mallet") or pall-mall.

2. Croquet is considered the first sport to embrace equality, allowing both men and women to play the game on an equal footing.

3. Originally made from wood, croquet balls are now made with a cork or nylon core, encased in very hard plastic.

4. Its heyday took place during the 1860s and 1970s. Lewis Carroll (1832-1898) featured the game in his *Alice's Adventures in Wonderland* 1865 novel, the Queen's soldiers using a flamingo as the mallet, and a hedgehog ball, while it seemed to be a favorite pastime in *Anna Karenina*, the 1878 novel by Leo Tolstoy (1828-1910).

5. In 1900, croquet was accepted, and quickly dropped from the Olympics, but to this day it doesn't have enough international players and fans to be readmitted, nor be included in the alternative World Games.

6. However, contrary to popular belief, croquet isn't just played by small children at birthday parties, but an internationally regulated

version of the sport, known as "association croquet," is also played by adult men in World Croquet Federation (WCF) tournaments, with Chris Clarke (b.1971), Robert Fulford (b.1969), and Reg Bamford (1967) considered the sport's top players.

7. In 2005, scientists played croquet in Antarctica, at the Amundsen–Scott South Pole Station telescope, but penguins were reportedly unimpressed.

8. Croquet lives on in Japan's gateball, a fast-paced, strategic team sport invented by a Suzuki Kazunobu in 1947 Hokkaido, which would successfully spread to China, South Korea, Taiwan, Hong Kong, Macau, Singapore, and the Philippines, during the 1980s.

BONUS FACTS!

- A stuffed baby bear doll was developed in 1902 by Morris Michtom (1870-1938), its "Teddy" moniker derived from America's own twenty-fifth president, Theodore "Teddy" Roosevelt Jr. (1858-1919), who reportedly refused to shoot a bear cub during a hunting trip in Mississippi, and allowed his nickname to be used by Mitchom.

- French King Louis III (863-882) died by bashing his head on the lintel of a low door, while in lascivious pursuit of a damsel!

- In order to prove the accuracy of the Bible, scholar Robert D. Wilson (1856-1930) learned 45 languages and dialects!

A DIAMOND IS FOREVER

Evolving not from cricket, and certainly not from croquet, but from a Tudor-era children's game called "rounders," America's favorite pastime, baseball, is popularly believed to have been adapted by Major General Abner Doubleday (1819-1893) in the US, begetting a rich sporting history of its own.

1. While his claim of inventing baseball has been disputed, Major General Abner Doubleday (1819-1893) undoubtedly did invent and patent the San Francisco cable car railway system, still in use today.

2. Not only did Alexander Cartwright (1820-1892) found one of the first baseball clubs in history, the New York Knickerbockers Base Ball Club, he also organized the first game played under modern rules, on June 19, 1846, between his New York Knickerbockers and the New York Nines.

3. Holding MLB records for the most career wins (511), innings pitched, games started, and complete games, pitcher Cy Young (1867-1955) also holds the record for most career losses (315), proving you have to lose some to win some!

4. Regarded as one of the greatest American heroes of all time, Babe Ruth (1895-1948) started out as a great pitcher, but became baseball's best known outfielder, breaking several records like career home runs (714), runs batted in (2,213), bases on balls (2,062), slugging percentage (.690), and on-base plus slugging (1.164). Commensurately, his salary reached $80,000 in 1930, the equivalent of a little over $1.1 million today!

5. With a professional career spanning 19 seasons, and seven teams,

catcher Rollie Hemsley (1907-1972) played most games completely drunk, and made no attempts to hide it!

6. Giant among basemen, Lou Gehrig (1903-1941) played 2,130 games for the New York Yankees, beginning in 1925 and never missing a game until 1939.

7. Formerly a professional second baseman, American gangster John Dillinger (1903-1934) never made it to the major leagues, turning instead to a life of crime.

8. World War II grenades were designed by the military to be the size and weight of a baseball, so young American men should be able to properly throw it!

9. Former WWII riveter, at three feet and seven inches, the St. Louis Browns' Eddie Gaedel (1925-1961) remains the smallest MLB player ever, and possibly the one with the shortest career ever at just one plate!

10. Despite being born without his right hand, MLB pitcher Jim Abbott (b.1967) played ten seasons (1989-1999) for the California Angels, New York Yankees, Chicago White Sox, and the Milwaukee Brewers!

11. Grip is very important in baseball. All MLB baseballs are rubbed in Lena Blackburne Baseball Rubbing Mud (said to come from the New Jersey side of the Delaware River), while many an outfielder has admitted to have peed on their own hands to improve their clasp on the bat!

12. Considered the greatest catcher in the history of the sport, Cincinnati Reds exclusive Johnny Bench (b.1947) was able to hold seven baseballs in one hand!

13. Iconic relief pitcher Rollie Fingers (b.1946) grew his iconic handlebar mustache to get a $300 bonus from Athletics owner Charles O. Finley (1918-1996), as part of a Father's day mustache wax promotional stunt.

14. The first black MLB player in history, Jackie Robinson (1919-1972) would also become first African-American vice president of a major corporation (coffee company Chock Full o' Nuts), and a founding investor of the Freedom National Bank.

15. An ankle injury thwarting his college baseball career, Todd McFarlane (b.1961) went on to become a renowned comic book artist, the founder of his own toy company, and a famous collector of baseballs, reportedly paying $2,600,000 for Mark McGwire's seventieth home run ball, $175,000 for Sammy Sosa's sixty-sixth home run ball in 1998, and $517,500 for Barry Bonds's seventy-third home run ball in 2003!

BONUS FACTS!

- American stuntman Bobby Leach (1858-1926), the second man to go over Niagara Falls on a barrel, died after the amputation of the leg he had broken by slipping on an orange peel.

- The accordion is North Korea's most popular musical instrument, and it was once compulsory to learn to play it!

- In 2015, Indonesian police intoxicated the population of an entire town by burning 3.3 tons of confiscated marijuana!

IF YOU BUILD IT...

Baseball has inspired some of the best American films ever, the best ten of which are listed below.

The Pride of the Yankees (1942): Rather than a plain biopic, this Gary Cooper (1901-1961) starring classic about the life of the legendary Lou Gehrig (1903-1941), lays it closer to a hagiography (a flattering biography of a religious saint), which stands out thanks to cameos of real-life Yankees Babe Ruth (1895-1948), Bob Meusel (1896-1977), Mark Koenig (1904-1993), and Bill Dickey (1907-1993)!

The Bad News Bears (1976): A comedy classic, starring award-winning actors Walter Matthau (1920-2000) and Tatum O'Neal (b.1963), with Matthau in his usual grouchy self as the alcoholic coach of a team made of young rejects. Back in the day it did so well, it had two film sequels, a TV show, and a 2005 remake not good enough to be featured here.

The Natural (1984): Based on Bernard Malamud's (1914-1986) 1952 novel, this film is as highbrow as a baseball film can get. Impeccably directed by Barry Levinson (b.1942), with charming performances by Robert Redford (b.1936) and Glenn Close (b.1947), it was nominated to four Academy Awards, but the fireworks ending alone is worth a standing ovation.

Bull Durham (1988): Considered by many to be the best baseball film of all time (which would be true, if it weren't for *Field of Dreams*), this romcom is based on writer/director Ron Shelton's (b.1945) life as a minor league infielder, and stars legendary actor/director Kevin Costner (b.1955), alongside Tim Robbins (b. 1958), and Susan Sarandon (b.1946).

Major League **(1989):** In perhaps the opposite end of the spectrum compared to *The Natural* lies this screwball (pun intended) blockbuster comedy starring an admittedly steroids-pumped Charlie Sheen (b.1965), about the Cleveland Indians assembling the worst possible team ever to force relocation to Miami, but going on to win anyway. It spawned two sequels!

The Sandlot **(1990):** A cult-comedy classic, *The Sandlot* is baseball childhood nostalgia in its purest form, with a splendid cast, and a flawless, well-rounded story we all wish had been replicated in the awful direct-to-video sequels!

A League of Their Own **(1992):** A Geena Davis (b.1956) and Madonna (b.1958) dramedy vehicle—with Tom Hanks (b.1956) in the backseat—about the short-lived All-American Girls Professional Baseball League (AAGPBL) inspired an equally short-lived CBS series the following year, the film itself doing better on cable than at the box-office, amassing its own cult following.

Mr. Baseball **(1992):** A modest-yet-effective film about Jack Elliot, a fictional, declining Yankees first baseman played by Tom Selleck (b.1945), who gets traded to a Japanese team, with all the "stranger in a strange land" trouble that follows. While vastly superior to *A League of Their Own*, it went largely, and unjustly unnoticed by the public at large, but always makes for a satisfying movie night.

Moneyball **(2011):** Based on the Michael Lewis (b.1960) nonfiction book, this acclaimed Brad Pitt (b.1963) starring drama about Billie Beane's (b. 1962) struggles to make the Oakland Athletics competitive again takes a seemingly arid subject and turns it on its head for a touching film, which landed six Academy Award nominations.

Field of Dreams (1989): Iowa corn farmer Ray Kinsella (Kevin Costner) struggles with the memory of his deceased father. Walking in his field one night he hears a whisper, "If you build it, he will come," and has a vision of a baseball diamond in the cornfield, which he builds in the face of certain financial ruin. Once finished, the field is magically populated by baseball-playing ghosts from the Black Sox scandal era, Ray's father included. The two make amends, while crowds of people begin arriving to watch the game. Hands down the best baseball film ever!

BONUS FACTS!

- Lawmaker Draco (c.600-650BC) of Athens was reportedly smothered to death by cloaks and hats showered upon him by a cheering crowd!

- The September 1859 geomagnetic storm (also known as the Carrington Event) was powerful enough to disrupt telegraph systems all over the world.

- The Egyptian Empire lasted for so many centuries that some Pharaohs actually commissioned archeological excavations to uncover the secrets of their predecessors!

- In 2014, a live snake that fell from a Disney World tree and bit an eight-year-old boy involuntarily killed the boy's grandmother, who died two days later from the ensuing cardiac arrest she suffered.

TRADEOFF

A turn-of-the-century promotional product of newspaper, candy, and tobacco companies reaching its peak during the 1980s, baseball trading cards are one of the biggest and most enduring collectibles in history, still fetching exorbitant prices in the auction market, case in point:

#1: Honus Wagner | Year: 1909-1911 | Series #: T206 | Dimensions: 1 7/16" by 2 5/8" | Manufacturer: American Tobacco Company | Est. PSA Value: **$1,000,000** (PR) to **$4,000,000** (VG-EX)

#2: Mickey Mantle (Yankees) | Year: 1952 | Series #: 311 | Dimensions: 2 5/8" by 3 3/4" | Manufacturer: The Topps Company | Est. PSA Value: **$2,500,000** (NM)

#3: Babe Ruth (Rookie) | Year: 1916 | Series #: M101-5/151 | Dimensions: 1 5/8" by 3" | Manufacturer: Sporting News | Est. PSA Value: **$1,350,000** (NM-MT)

#4: Babe Ruth (Rookie) | Year: 1916 | Series #: M101-4/151 | Dimensions: 1 5/8" by 3" | Manufacturer: Sporting News | Est. PSA Value: **$1,350,000** (NM-MT)

#5: Ty Cobb | Year: 1909-1911 | Series #: T206 | Dimensions: 1 7/16" by 2 5/8" | Manufacturer: American Tobacco Company | Est. PSA Value: **$1,000,000** (VG-EX)

#6: Babe Ruth (Orioles) | Year: 1914 | Series #: 9 | Dimensions: 4 1/2" by 6" | Manufacturer: Baltimore News | Est. PSA Value: **$925,000** (VG-EX)

#8: Mickey Mantle (Rookie) | Year: 1951 | Series #: 253 | Dimensions: 2 1/16" by 3 1/8" | Manufacturer: Bowman Gum Company | Est. PSA Value: **$700,000** (MT)

#9: Sherry Magee (misspelled "Magie") | Year: 1909-1911 | Series #: T206 | Dimensions: 1 7/16" by 2 5/8" | Manufacturer: American Tobacco Company | Est. PSA Value: **$660,000** (NM-MT)

#10: Joe Jackson (Rookie)| Year: 1909-1911 | Series #: E90-1 | Dimensions: 1 1/2" by 2 3/4" | Manufacturer: American Caramel | Est. PSA Value: **$600,000** (NM-MT)

#11: Joe Jackson (Pelicans)| Year: 1910 | Series #: T210 | Dimensions: 1 1/2" by 2 5/8" | Manufacturer: Old Mill | Est. PSA Value: **$600,000** (VG+)

#12: Babe Ruth (yellow background) | Year: 1933 | Series #: 53 | Dimensions: 2 3/8" by 2 7/8" | Manufacturer: Goudey Gum Co. | Est. PSA Value: **$600,000** (MT)

#13: Joe Doyle ("N.Y. Nat'l") | Year: 1909-1911 | Series #: T206 | Dimensions: 1 7/16" by 2 5/8" | Manufacturer: American Tobacco Company | Est. PSA Value: **$550,000** (VG)

#14: Willie Mays (Rookie) | Year: 1951 | Series #: 305 | Dimensions: 2 1/16" by 3 1/8" | Manufacturer: Bowman Gum Company | Est. PSA Value: **$500,000** (MT)

#15: Leroy Paige (yellow background) | Year: 1948 | Series #: 8 | Dimensions: 2 3/8" by 2 7/8" | Manufacturer: Leaf Trading Cards | Est. PSA Value: **$400,000** (NM-MT)

#16: Joe Jackson (red background) | Year: 1915 | Series #: NA | Dimensions: 2 5/8" by 3 3/4"| Manufacturer: Cracker Jack | Est. PSA Value: **$350,000** (MT)

#17: Ty Cobb (red background) | Year: 1915 | Series #: NA | Dimensions: 2 5/8" by 3 3/4" | Manufacturer: Cracker Jack | Est. PSA Value: **$350,000** (MT)

#18: Babe Ruth (full body) | Year: 1933 | Series #: 144 | Dimensions: 2 3/8" by 2 7/8" | Manufacturer: Goudey Gum Co. | Est. PSA Value: **$350,000** (MT)

#19: Babe Ruth ("Sport Kings Gum") | Year: 1933 | Series #: 2 | Dimensions: 2 3/8" by 2 7/8" | Manufacturer: Goudey Gum Co. | Est. PSA Value: **$350,000** (MT)

#20: Jackie Robinson (yellow background) | Year: 1948 | Series #: 79 | Dimensions: 2 3/8" by 2 7/8" | Manufacturer: Leaf Trading Cards | Est. PSA Value: **$350,000** (NM-MT)

#21: Mickey Mantle (Yankees) | Year: 1953 | Series #: 82 | Dimensions: 2 5/8" by 3 3/4" | Manufacturer: The Topps Company | Est. PSA Value: **$325,000** (MT)

#22: Roberto Clemente (Pirates) | Year: 1955 | Series #: 164 | Dimensions: 2 5/8" by 3 3/4" | Manufacturer: The Topps Company | Est. PSA Value: **$325,000** (NM) to **$480,000** (MT)

#23: Ty Cobb (bat off shoulder) | Year: 1909-1911 | Series #: T206 | Dimensions: 1 7/16" by 2 5/8" | Manufacturer: American Tobacco Company | Est. PSA Value: **$315,000** (MT)

#24: Ty Cobb ("Tyrus R. Cobb") | Year: 1902-1911 | Series #: W600 | Dimensions: 5" by 7.5" | Manufacturer: Sporting Life | Est. PSA Value: **$300,000** (G)

#25: Babe Ruth (red background) | Year: 1932 | Series #: 32 | Dimensions: 2 1/2" by 3" | Manufacturer: US Caramel | Est. PSA Value: **$300,000** (MT)

The world's biggest collection of baseball cards (31,000) is currently kept at New York's Metropolitan Museum of Art.

BONUS FACTS!

- Perpetually drunk Ottoman Sultan Murad IV (1612-1640) died from cirrhosis in Constantinople at age 27.

- Despite being exposed to vast amounts of radiation which destroyed him from the inside out, 1999 Tokaimura nuclear disaster victim Hisashi Ouchi (1964-1999) was kept alive and studied for 83 days, in spite of the man's repeated appeals to be taken out of his misery.

- In 2010, a four-year-old Isaiah Harris's face was severely burned by hot nacho cheese at Disney's Magic Kingdom.

- The USS *Tang* (SS-306) was an American submarine sunk by her own torpedo during World War II. Its nine survivors were taken as prisoners of war by the Japanese.

EASY LIKE SUNDAY MORNING

Originally an MLB outfielder with the Chicago White Stockings (which would become the Chicago Cubs) at the turn of the century, Billy Sunday (1862-1935) left professional baseball to successfully preach the gospel, becoming America's foremost revivalist during the 1910s and 1920s, his terse, colloquial speech making waves that reach us to this day.

On Christianity:

"They tell me a revival is only temporary; so is a bath, but it does you good."

"Let's quit fiddling with religion and do something to bring the world to Christ."

"Lord save us from off-handed, flabby-cheeked, brittle-boned, weak-kneed, thin-skinned, pliable, plastic, spineless, effeminate, ossified, three-karat Christianity."

"Going to church doesn't make you a Christian any more than going to a garage makes you an automobile."

On sin:

"One reason sin flourishes is that it is treated like a cream puff instead of a rattlesnake."

"The reason you don't like the Bible, you old sinner, is because it

knows all about you."

"I believe that a long step toward public morality will have been taken when sins are called by their right names."

"Listen, I'm against sin. I'll kick it as long as I've got a foot, I'll fight it as long as I've got a fist, I'll butt it as long as I've got a head, and I'll bite it as long as I've got a tooth. And when I'm old, fistless, footless, and toothless, I'll gum it till I go home to glory and it goes home to perdition."

On character-building:

"It is not necessary to be in a big place to do big things."

"Your reputation is what people say about you. Your character is what God and your wife know about you."

"Wealth is not the standard of worth. Some people put cash before character."

"Hypocrites in the Church? Yes, and in the lodge and at the home. Don't hunt through the Church for a hypocrite. Go home and look in the mirror. Hypocrites? Yes. See that you make the number one less."

On joy:

"If you lack joy, your Christianity must be leaking somewhere."

"God likes a little humor, as is evidenced by the fact that he made the monkeys, the parrot—and some of you people."

"…whenever a day comes when I can see men and women coming down the aisles without joy in my heart, I'll quit preaching."

"Yank some of the groans out of your prayers and shove in some shouts."

On Jesus:

"There are two hundred and fifty-six names given in the Bible for the Lord Jesus Christ, and I suppose this was because He was infinitely beyond all that any one name could express."

"Jesus gave his life on the cross for any who will believe. We're not redeemed by silver or gold. Jesus paid for it with his blood."

"Conversion is a complete surrender to Jesus. It's a willingness to do what he wants you to do."

"Jesus Christ was God's revenue officer."

BONUS FACTS!

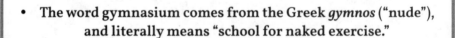

- The word gymnasium comes from the Greek *gymnos* ("nude"), and literally means "school for naked exercise."

- The Tsar Bomba was a 58 megaton Soviet hydrogen bomb tested on October 30, 1961, which remains the most powerful nuclear bomb ever detonated on this planet.

ODDBALL

Invented at Yale back in 1887, on Thanksgiving day, as an improvised indoor version of baseball, softball would quickly mature into its own outdoor, and internationally widespread sport; but what are the main differences between baseball and its fast-pitched offspring?

SOFTBALL:

Game length: 7 innings

Base distance: 60 feet

Outfield fence: 220 feet away from home plate

Pitcher's Circle: Flat

Ball: 12 inch circumference | Yellow

Bat: 34 inch length | 2 1/4 inch barrel diameter

Base stealing: After ball leaves pitcher's hand

Delivery: Underhand

BASEBALL:

Game length: 9 innings

Base distance: 90 feet

Outfield fence: 400+ feet away from home plate

Pitcher's Mound: 10 inches above ground

Ball: 9 inch circumference | White

Bat: 42 inch length | 2 5/8 inch barrel diameter

Base stealing: When "time" is not called

Delivery: Any (usually overhand)

BONUS FACT!

- Famous for his role as vampire Edward Cullen in the *Twilight* films, British actor Robert Pattinson (b.1986) is actually a distant relative of Vlad the Impaler (c.1428-1477), the real life inspiration of Bram Stoker's (1847-1912) Dracula!

A PLACE YOU CAN GO

Founded on the principles of muscular Christianity, the development of modern sports owes an awful lot to the YMCA!

1. Currently based in Geneva, Switzerland, the Young Men's Christian Association (YMCA) was founded in 1844 London by English philanthropist Sir George Williams (1821-1905), to address the terrible living conditions of working class young Englishmen during the Industrial Revolution. By 1851 it has expanded to the United Kingdom, Australia, Belgium, Canada, France, Germany, the Netherlands, Switzerland, and the United States.

2. Meant to improve the spiritual condition of young men, it was initially an evangelical social ministry, and many within the organization felt it had no business providing physical education.

3. The idea of turning the Y into a single global international movement was successfully proposed by Red Cross co-founder and Geneva YMCA Secretary Henry Dunant (1828-1910) in 1855, and by 1865 the Fourth World Conference of YMCAs finally agreed on the importance of developing complete spirit, mind, and body development.

4. In 1869, Boston YMCA staffer Robert J. Roberts (1850-?) began the association's first physical education plan, later coining the term "body building" for his pioneering fitness training program.

5. American YMCAs began offering low-income, temporary housing facilities in the 1880s, providing room and board for rural migrants, and homeless youth.

6. During the 1891 winter, Springfield (Massachusetts) YMCA physical education teacher and chaplain James Naismith (1861-1939) would invent a non-aggressive yet fast-paced brand new game to keep his students fit during a rainy day: basketball!

7. A few years later, with basketball catching on at YMCAs everywhere, Holyoke (Massachusetts) YMCA physical education director William G. Morgan (1870-1942) came up with a racquet-less version of badminton he called *mintonette*, the original volleyball!

8. Upon hearing a sermon about the newly recognized Mother's Day, Sonora Smart Dodd (1882-1978) pitched a Father's Day idea at a Washington regional YMCA meeting, which agreed to celebrate it for the first time on June 19, 1910.

9. A San Francisco YMCA catering mainly to the Chinese community was founded in 1875, its missionaries later would be credited for the introduction of basketball to China. These days, basketball is arguably China's most popular sport, played by 300 million of its citizens!

10. Softball was alternatively called "ladies baseball," pumpkin ball, country ball, kitten ball, diamond ball, and mush ball, before YMCA's Walter Hakanson (1898-1963) gave it its definitive name.

11. Modern-day YMCA promotes competition around the world through the Far Eastern Games, Pan American Games and the Inter-Allied Games.

12. The YMCA actually threatened to take legal action against the Village People over their 1978 hit single "Y.M.C.A." but ultimately made peace with band producer, and song composer, Jacques Morali (1947-1991), coming to embrace the song later on.

I SAID, YOUNG MAN!

Originally created at, and spread worldwide by the YMCA, basketball is undoubtedly the world's second favorite ball sport, behind soccer.

1. The original James Naismith (1861-1939) basketball game was played over 30 minutes on a much smaller court, by teams of nine players each, using actual peach baskets, and a soccer ball!

2. At first, dribbling was not allowed. Players could catch the ball, take a few steps, stop, and then pass or throw the ball from wherever they stood. Slam dunks wouldn't be allowed until 1976!

3. Peach baskets were originally nailed to the court mezzanine; since balcony spectators took to blocking some shots, the backboard was invented.

4. At the turn of the century, baskets came to be replaced with string nets hung around hoops, the game got rougher, and courts had to be fenced with chicken wire to keep players from falling over the crowd.

5. Formed in 1898, the first professional basketball league, the National Basketball League (NBL), was established to protect players, and promote an overall less rough game.

6. In the early decades of the twentieth century, the biggest professional teams were the Buffalo Germans, the New York Celtics, and the Harlem Renaissance Big Fives!

7. In 1946 the NBL would merge with the Basketball Association of America (BAA) to form the National Basketball Association (NBA), its oldest founding franchises being the Sacramento Kings (1923), and the Detroit Pistons (1941).

8. As strange as it sounds, we owe the inclusion of basketball in the Olympics to the Nazis, who gave it a place in the 1936 Berlin Olympic Games. The US team won the final over Canada, and would go on to win all but three Olympic basketball titles since, losing to the Soviet Union team in 1972, and again in 1988, and in the 2004 semifinals to Argentina (which would beat Italy in the final).

9. The *Fédération Internationale de Basket-ball Amateur* (FIBA) was originally formed in 1936 by Argentina, Czechoslovakia, Greece, Italy, Latvia, Portugal, Romania and Switzerland. The first FIBA Basketball World Cup was first held in Argentina in 1950, with FIBA Women's Basketball World Cup held in Chile in 1953.

10. A rival league to the NBA was formed in 1967, the American Basketball Association (ABA), which would be eventually absorbed by NBA ten years later. Four of its original ten teams (Indiana, Denver, New York, and San Antonio) are now part of the NBA (which also borrow the three-pointer from the defunct league).

11. The Boston Celtics have won the most NBA Championships (17), with the Los Angeles Lakers a close second (16), Golden State Warriors and Chicago Bulls winning six tournaments each for a third spot.

12. Michael Jordan (b.1963) has scored more points (5,987) during playoffs than any other player in history, while Kareem Abdul-Jabbar (1947) holds the record for most points scored in a career (38,387).

Wilt Chamberlain (1936-1999), on the other hand, scored the most points (100) ever, in a single game back in 1962!

13. Ron Artest (b. 1979) holds the longest suspension record at 73 games (and 13 playoffs), for punching fans on the stands, during the infamous 2004 "Malice in the Palace" brawl. Latrell Sprewell (b.1970) comes second, for choking coach P. J. Carlesimo (b.1949) for a whole 15 seconds in a 1997 incident which cost him a 68-game suspension. Also in 1997, Dennis Rodman (b.1961) got an 11-game suspension for knocking out a cameraman.

14. Attesting to China's long history with the game, that country's multibillion-dollar deal with the NBA involving media rights, streaming, and merchandise sales, has seen NBA championships viewed by 500 million Chinese, with the NBA itself opening offices in Beijing and Shanghai. Six Chinese players have also broken into the NBA, notably Wang Zhizhi (b.1977) who was the first, playing for the Dallas Mavericks in the early 2000s, and the Houston Rockets former star Yao Ming (b.1980), who remains one of the NBA's most popular players ever.

BONUS FACTS!

- American playwright Tennessee Williams (1911-1983) fatally choked on his sleeping pills' plastic cap.

- Bicycle pedal reflectors were invented by Anton Loibl (1900-1979), who happened to work as Hitler's driver!

SWEET GEORGIA BROWN

While not part of the NBA, nor originally from Harlem, the Harlem Globetrotters have been entertaining fans since 1926, playing well over 26,000 games in 124 countries since!

1. Ironically, the Harlem Globetrotters is an exhibition basketball team originating in Chicago, Illinois, with current corporate offices in Atlanta, Georgia, and Beijing, China, which couldn't be farther away from New York City!

2. The team was originally called the Savoy Big Five, all its original players from the Chicago South Side, but after a dispute, the members departing the team formed the "Globe Trotters," bringing in Abe Saperstein (1902-1966) as manager, promoter, and eventual coach. Saperstein would rebrand the team as the "New York Harlem Globe Trotters" in 1929.

3. Winning several tournaments during the 1940s, under Saperstein the Globetrotters would make history beating an all-white Lakers (from Minneapolis back then) lineup. The NBA took notice, and by 1950 had signed up trotters Chuck Cooper (1926-1984), and Nathaniel "Sweetwater" Clifton (1922-1990) as its first African-American players. In fact, one of the greatest centers in NBA history, Wilt Chamberlain (1936-1999), also began his professional career at the Globetrotters.

4. Baseball hall-of-famers Bob Gibson (b.1935), Lou Brock (b.1939), and Ferguson Jenkins (b.1942) also cut their basketball chops at the Globetrotters!

5. Joining in 1941, Goose Tatum (1921-1967) began incorporating comic antics into play, gradually turned the team from sports to entertainment over the following decade, before forming his own Harlem Magicians.

6. The 1951 sports drama *The Harlem Globetrotters*, was the team's first foray into film, followed up by the 1952 sequel *Go, Man, Go!*, starring Academy-Award-Winner Sidney Poitier (b.1927).

7. In 1952, Red Klotz (1920-2014) was commissioned by the Globetrotters to form an opposing team for their act, forever defeating the Washington Generals since … although that isn't entirely true: once, back in a mythical January 5, 1971, game, Klotz had to fill in for a player and managed to score a winning double in Tennessee!

8. By the end of the 1950s, the Globetrotters were already touring internationally, including a visit to the Soviet Union, being awarded the Athletic Order of Lenin medal by none other than Nikita Khrushchev (1894-1971)!

9. Derided by civil rights activists as "buffoonish," the team was defended by none other than Jesse Jackson (b.1941)."They don't show blacks as stupid. On the contrary, they show them as superior," the good reverend said. Of course, he was made an Honorary Globetrotter, an honor he shares with Bob Hope (1903-2003), Pope John Paul II (1920- 2005), Henry Kissinger (b.1923), Pope Francis (b.1936), and Whoopi Goldberg (b.1955).

10. The team would play its first-ever Harlem game in 1968!

11. Traditionally all-able-bodied, all-black, and all-male, the team recruited left-arm amputee Boid Buie (1922-1996) in 1946, while the first female Globetrotter was Lynette Woodard (b.1959) in 1985, and the team's first Hispanic player, Orlando Antigua (b.1973), was recruited in 1995.

12. The 1970s would see the Globetrotters break into television, with their own eponymous Saturday morning cartoon from Hanna-Barbera, followed by a 1974 live action show, *The Harlem Globetrotters Popcorn Machine*, another animated show from Hanna-Barbera, *The Super Globetrotters*, in 1979, and the well-remembered 1981 live-action TV movie, *The Harlem Globetrotters on Gilligan's Island*. Understandably, they received a star on the Hollywood Walk of Fame the following year!

BONUS FACTS!

- According to the Quran, an infant Jesus Christ made clay birds which would come alive!

- Latvia-born Sara Braun's (1862-1955) sheep farming company in Chile, the *Sociedad Explotadora de Tierra del Fuego* (Society for the Exploitation of Tierra del Fuego) controlled an area of Patagonia that was roughly the size of Belgium!

- Dissident Bulgarian writer Georgi Markov (1929-1978) was elaborately assassinated in London by the Bulgarian Secret Service, who shot him a ricin-filled pellet from an umbrella!

EL CONDOR PASA

Adapted in Scotland from the medieval Dutch game of kolf, golf would suffer ignominy and persecution in Britain until embraced by noblemen during the sixteenth century, and later taken by the Empire, like many other sports, across the world during the nineteenth century.

1. The first written mention of modern *gowlf* can be found in a 1457 James II (1430-1460) edict banning it. Two centuries later his descendants would avidly play it!

2. Golf would spread through the British isles in the 1860s, as everything Scottish became fashionable, and a new hardened latex ball came to substitute the old leather-and-feathers one (solid wood balls were also popular).

3. The word caddy comes from the French word *cadet* ("student").

4. Known to be costly, golf popularity tends to increase during financially booming times, such as the Jazz Age, the late 1950s, and the 1980s, while in times of scarcity it still endures despite many voices rising to question the practicality of maintaining its gigantic grass fields, or the labor practices of its clubs.

5. $600,000,000 are spent by Americans on golf balls every year! Balls may have anywhere between 330 to 500 dimples, the ideal number considered to be between 380 and 432.

6. Japanese golfers often carry "hole-in-one" insurance, in order to pay for the mandatory party they must hold to celebrate if they hit a hole-in-one!

7. The average golfer has a 12,500 to one chance of making a hole-in-one on a par-three, and 67,000,000 chances to one of making two holes-in-one on a par-three, but a hole-in-one on a par-five shot, known as a "condor," has happened only four times in recorded history!

8. Starting at 14,335 feet above sea level, the highest golf course is the Tactu Golf Club in Morococha, Peru.

9. So far, golf is the only human sport ever played outside Earth, back in 1971, when NASA's Alan Shepard (1923-1998), smuggled his club and two balls aboard the Apollo 14, to play on the Moon.

10. America's twenty-eighth president, Woodrow Wilson (1856-1924), was so devoted to the sport, he would golf in the snow, using a black ball! Other notable golf-loving presidents include: William H. Taft (1857-1930), Warren G. Harding (1865-1923), Dwight D. Eisenhower (1890-1969), John F. Kennedy (1917-1963), Lyndon B. Johnson (1908-1973), Richard M. Nixon (1913-1994), Gerald Ford (1913-2006), hall-of-famer George H. W. Bush (1924-2018), Bill Clinton (b.1946), Barack Obama (b.1961), and multiple course owner Donald J. Trump (b.1946).

BONUS FACT!

- Japanese tempura is actually a sixteenth-century Portuguese import, as the sailors and merchants arriving from that country would fry fish in an Ember days tradition known as *quatuor anni tempora* ("four seasons of the year") in Latin.

WITHOUT HOPE

A lifelong golfer, British-American comedian Bob Hope (1903-2003), hosted his own PGA Tour tournament and played for countless charities, eventually incorporating the golf club into his TV and USO standup shows, the game itself becoming the source of some of his best-ever punchlines:

"If you watch a game, it's fun. If you play it, it's recreation. If you work at it, it's golf."

"If you think golf is relaxing, you're not playing it right."

"Golf is a game that needlessly prolongs the lives of some of our most useless citizens."

"Golf is a funny game. It's done much for health, and at the same time has ruined people by robbing them of their peace of mind."

"Golf is a hard game to figure. One day you will go out and slice it and shank it, hit into all the traps and miss every green. The next day you go out and, for no reason at all, you really stink."

"It's wonderful how you can start out with strangers in the morning, play 18 holes, and by the time the day is over you have three solid enemies."

"Golf's really fun in Japan because of the women caddies. I saw one guy start out playing alone with his caddie. By the ninth hole they were engaged and when they finished on 18 they had a foursome."

"I've been playing the game so long that my handicap is in Roman numerals."

"I'll shoot my age if I have to live to be 105."

"I'd give up golf if I didn't have so many sweaters."

"I get upset over a bad shot just like anyone else. But it's silly to let the game get to you. When I miss a shot I just think what a beautiful day it is. And what pure fresh air I'm breathing. Then I take a deep breath. I have to do that. That's what gives me the strength to break the club."

"Bing (Crosby) always said my swing looked like Grandma Moses trying to keep warm."

"I once showed Pat Bradley my swing and said, 'What do I do next?' Pat replied, 'Wait till the pain dies down.'"

"Golf is my real profession. Entertainment is just a sideline. I tell jokes to pay my greens fees."

"Titleist has offered me a big contract not to play its balls."

"I've done as much for golf as Truman Capote has done for sumo wrestling."

"On one hole, I hit an alligator so hard, he's now my golf bag."

"A photographer kept shooting me every time I swung. I was very

flattered until I found out he was from *Field and Stream*."

"I never kick my ball in the rough or improve my lie in a sand trap. For that I have a caddie."

"It was a great honor to be inducted into the Hall of Fame. I didn't know they had a caddie division."

"President Eisenhower has given up golf for painting. It takes fewer strokes."

"Whenever I play with him (President Ford), I usually try to make it a foursome—the President, myself, a paramedic, and a faith healer."

"He (Sammy Davis Jr.) hits the ball 130 yards and his jewelry goes 150."

"Some of these Legends of Golf have been around golf for a long time. When they talk about having a good grip, they're talking about their dentures."

"If I'm on the course and lightning starts, I get inside fast. If God wants to play through, let him."

BONUS FACT!

- In 2004, a Disney employee dressed as "Tigger" was arrested for molesting a teenage girl and her mother!

BLOOD ON ICE

Its true origin lost in the icy mists of time, ice hockey is said to have evolved from stick and ball games played on ice in the northern hemisphere, until ...

1. On March 3, 1875, Canadian James Creighton (1850-1930) is said to be the first to organize an indoor ice hockey game at the Victoria Skating Rink in Montreal, using a wooden puck, but basically following English field hockey rules.

2. The Victoria Skating Rink would also become the location of the first Stanley Cup tournament held in 1893, named after Canadian Governor General Frederick Arthur Stanley, Sixteenth Earl of Derby (1841-1908), who donated the trophy, which has been awarded every single year except for two times (Spanish Flu pandemic in 1919, and the 2004-2005 NHL labor strike).

3. The Montreal Canadiens, since 1909 the longest running professional ice hockey team in history, have won 24 Stanley Cups, but 11 NHL teams have never won a single one: Buffalo Sabres, Columbus Blue Jackets, Minnesota Wild, Nashville Predators, Florida Panthers, Ottawa Senators, Arizona Coyotes, San Jose Sharks, St. Louis Blues, Washington Capitals, Vancouver Canucks and Winnipeg Jets.

4. A college tennis player of some repute, future American industrialist Malcolm Greene Chace (1875-1955) is credited for ditching his racquet for an ice hockey stick, bringing the new sport to the US, assembling his own team, and even touring Canada with it as a young man. Lord Stanley's sons, on the other hand, would export ice hockey "back" to England, and the rest of Europe.

5. The National Hockey Association (NHA) was formed in 1910 Montreal, establishing the game's modern rules. Changing its name to National Hockey League (NHL) in 1917, it expanded into the United States when the Boston Bruins joined up in 1924. The Chicago Blackhawks, New York Rangers, Montreal Canadians, Toronto Maple Leafs, and Detroit Red Wings would soon follow.

6. One of the first players to wear a helmet full-time (after a puck tore a piece off one of his ears), the Chicago Blackhawks' Stan Mikita (1940-2018) is credited for introducing the curved stick blade to the sport in the 1960s (all blades were previously straight).

7. Of a standard three inches diameter, and six ounces in weight, pucks are frozen before each game to keep them from bouncing on equally standard ice rinks measuring 200 feet long by 85 feet wide.

8. Historically, Russia and Canada are ice hockey's biggest international rivals. While Canada won almost every Olympic gold since ice hockey became a Winter Olympics sport in 1924, the state-supported USSR team won almost every match since that country first entered the Winter Olympics in 1956 until 1988, losing only twice to the US national team in 1960 and 1980.

BONUS FACT!

- A winner of several Paralympic gold medals, South African sprinter and double amputee Oscar Pistorius (b.1986), finally managed to be allowed into the 2012 London Summer Olympics. Regrettably, only a year later he was sentenced to prison for accidentally killing his girlfriend!

PUCK-MAN

While not as memorable as baseball pictures, ice hockey movies have managed to carve their own little industry niche.

Slap Shot (1977): Possibly the best ice hockey film ever made, it is an honest, working-class cult comedy which highlights the importance of community. It stars Academy Award Winner Paul Newman (1925-2008) in one of his best roles ever!

Miracle on Ice (1981): A quickly made-for-TV movie about the American semi-finals victory over the Soviet team in the 1980 Lake Placid Winter Olympics, it's risen over its live footage-recycling tropes by actors Karl Malden Karl Malden (1912-2009) and Steve Guttenberg (b.1964) from the *Police Academy* films.

Youngblood (1986): Clichéd and more 1980's than an A-Ha video clip, this drama starring heart-throbs of the day, Rob Lowe (b.1964) and Patrick Swayze (1952-2009), is perhaps best remembered by its final joust-like match.

The Mighty Ducks (1992): A feel-good Disney movie for kids, starring Emilio Estevez (b.1962) as the coach of, what else?, a youth league hockey team, it did so well it inspired two sequels, an animated series, and even a Disney-sponsored, real-life NHL team, Mighty Ducks of Anaheim (now called simply Anaheim Ducks)!

Sudden Death (1995): It would be like any other Jean-Claude van Damme (b.1960) action vehicle, but set during a fictional 1995 Stanley Cup final between the Pittsburgh Penguins and the Chicago Blackhawks, as van Damme's character, Canadian firefighter

Darren McCord, tries to save the US vice president from the equally fictional terrorist group that has rigged the Pittsburgh Civic Arena with explosives.

Mystery, Alaska (1999): This Jay Roach (b.1957) directed underdog comedy didn't do very well back in the day of its original release, but has since gained a cult following among ice hockey aficionados.

Miracle (2004): Starring Disney's favorite Kurt Russell (b.1951) as coach Herb Brooks (1937-2003), the film is a fictionalized account of the American victory over the Soviet team in the 1980 Lake Placid Winter Olympics semi-finals.

The Rocket (2005): This is a solid French-Canadian biopic about the Montreal Canadiens legend Maurice "The Rocket" Richard (1921-2000) played by Roy Dupuis (b.1963), which received many well-deserved awards in Canada and abroad.

Tooth Fairy (2010): A Dwayne "The Rock" Johnson (b.1972) all-ages high-concept film, about a minor league hockey player nicknamed the "Tooth Fairy," who sees himself turned into a real tooth fairy, and learns a few lessons along the way. It was panned by critics, but loved by families everywhere.

Goon (2011): The perfect bookend to *Slap Shot* (1977), this raunchy Canadian comedy starring Seann William Scott (b.1976) as kind-hearted-but-dim-witted enforcer Doug Glatt was a box-office flop, but a great success on streaming service Netflix, guaranteeing a 2017 sequel called *Goon: Last of the Enforcers*.

KINGPIN

The fun and relaxing sport we now call bowling has been around since Homo sapiens found the joy of knocking things down from a distance, and may be traced back through recorded history to the birth of civilization itself!

1. Five thousand years before Christ, ancient Egyptian children already bowled using porphyry (red marble) balls and alabaster pins!

2. An outdoor variation of the game without the use of pins can be found in classical Rome, from where it spread all over Europe, eventually becoming modern *bocce* in Italy, *pétanque* in France, and lawn bowls in Britain.

3. Medieval England saw the earliest outdoor bowling lane built in 1299 Southampton, but the game would be banned by Edward III (1312-1377) in 1366.

4. As is usually the case, sports banning never takes, and by 1455 lawn bowling lanes in London were roofed-over, for year-round fun!

5. While bowling aficionado Henry VIII loved the sport, the monarch took special care in banning it for poor and working-class Britons. In the continent, however, Martin Luther (1483-1546) loved bowling with his children!

6. The Dutch would bring lawn bowling to New Amsterdam (modern day New York) in the seventeenth century, as the Bowling Green park in lower Manhattan still attests.

7. In the nineteenth century, German immigrants brought their *kegelspiel*, or nine-pin bowling, to America, but working-class Germans not being immune to drinking, on the verge of that sport being banned, somebody added a tenth pin to the game to bypass the law, and modern bowling was born!

8. The very first ten-pin bowling alley, Knickerbockers, was built in 1840 New York, and by the end of that century over 200 such establishments could be found in that city alone. Back in those days, a "pinboy" had to manually reset bowling pins to their correct position, clear the fallen pins, and return the wooden bowling balls (with no holes!) to players.

9. Established in 1875, The National Bowling Association (NBA), was soon followed by the United Bowling Clubs (UBC), and the American Bowling Congress (ABC), all struggling to cleanse the seedy reputation that still clung to the game. Women had begun bowling early on despite being an considered an unseemly pursuit for them, and by 1910 had established their own association, the Women's International Bowling Congress (WIBC).

10. In 1902, hardwood balls were replaced by heavy vulcanized rubber ones, which became obsolete with the arrival of Polyester ones (with standard grip holes), in 1959. These in turn gave way to polyurethane ("urethane") ones with fingertip grips in the 1980s, and "reactive resin" ones in the 1990s, which currently still dominate the sport.

11. Prohibition would become an unexpected boon to bowling in America, as Deco-styled family-friendly alleys soon did what no association could, growing to 2,000 establishments by the end of the 1920s.

12. American Machine and Foundry (AMF) would finally commercialize its first fully automatic pinsetter in 1952.

13. Naturally, the US has the most bowling players anywhere in the world, where the bowling market generates a revenue of approximately $6 billion a year. The United States Bowling Congress (USBC) currently has over 2 million members.

14. The largest bowling alley in the world, however, is not found in America, but Japan, where the Inazawa Grand Bowl currently holds 116 lanes!

15. Notable bowling presidents include Harry S. Truman (1884-1972), who got a bowling lane installed in the White House for his sixty-third birthday (one of the seven pins he first knocked down is on display at the Smithsonian!), and Richard M. Nixon (1913-1994), who added an extra lane to play with his wife, first lady Pat Nixon (née Ryan, 1912-1993).

BONUS FACTS!

- The 1918 Spanish Flu pandemic lowered American life expectancy to 39 years of age, same as it has been during the Civil War!

- American novelist Sherwood Anderson (1876-1941) accidentally swallowed a toothpick which caused his untimely death.

- The 1962 book *Silent Spring* was instrumental in getting carcinogenic insecticide DDT banned worldwide.

OBVIOUSLY, YOU'RE NOT
A GOLFER

If you're not familiar with the title above, you're probably not aware it relates to the most beloved bowling movie in history, The Big Lebowski *(1998), and you should go and see it. If you are, it is also likely you haven't been exposed to all of the White Russian-soaked facts below.*

1. The film echoes Raymond Chandler's (1888-1959) *The Big Sleep* (1939) novel, but starring a good-for-nothing slacker, rather than a Phillip Marlowe type, the labyrinthine plot disguising the emptiness of the pursuit itself.

2. The film story begins on September 11, 1991, exactly 10 years before the 9/11 terror attacks, while George H.W. Bush (1924-2018) can be heard on the background delivering his "This aggression will not stand" speech.

3. The entire movie soundtrack is always played on the radio (the Dude's Walkman, the Supermarket, the bowling alley, and a cab).

4. Jeffrey "The Dude" Lebowski, played by Jeff Bridges (b.1949), is based on two real-life friends of the Coen brothers: Independent producer and Sundance Festival founder Jeff Dowd (b.1949) is said to have inspired the Dude's attitude and philosophy (not to mention his first name, and nickname), while screenplay supervisor Peter Exline (b.1946) coined the "really tied the room together" line, and also happened to find a schoolboy's homework in his car after it had been stolen, at some point in his life.

5. The Dude abiding stuff is a reference to the Bible's Ecclesiastes 1:4, "One generation passeth away, and another generation cometh: but

the earth abideth for ever. (KJV)" His rug being peed on is mentioned 17 times throughout the film, while the fact that it "really tied the room together," is repeated five times.

6. Keeping with film noir tradition The Dude is seen in every scene of the movie (even driving past while the Nihilists order pancakes!), but he is never seen bowling in it (it is Maude that throws the ball in the famous dream sequence)!

7. The Dude's garments came from actor Jeff Bridges's own, including the Kaoru Betto (1920-1999) t-shirt he wore seven years earlier in *The Fisher King*.

8. Inspired by real-life screenwriter and director John Milius (b.1944), of the Dirty Harry films, the Dude's friend Walter Sobchak, played by John Goodman (b.1952), converted to Judaism but the initials for his security business, Sobchak Security, are an ironic "SS." However, while the character always exhibits a rather fascist bent, he stays true to his friends, and single-handedly defeats Nazi stand-ins "the Nihilists," a billboard for Ben Hur Auto Repair prominently behind him—an obvious reference to the epic Jewish hero.

9. The Dude's friend Donny, played by Steve Buscemi (b.1957), always gets a strike when bowling in the film, except his last, but never wears his own bowling shirts. His cremation is also an inside joke, as Buscemi's characters in films *Miller's Crossing* (dead body), *Fargo* (severed leg), and *The Big Lebowski* (ashes) got smaller and smaller in death.

10. A White Russian, a.k.a. a "Caucasian," is a cocktail made of vodka, coffee liqueur, and cream The Dude drinks nine times during the movie (including a spiked one).

EVERYBODY LOVES KUNG FU FIGHTING

Who doesn't love martial arts? Popularized mainly by Bruce Lee (1940-1973) among many other film stars, Asian unarmed self-defense has been taking the West by a flurry of kicks and chops since the 1960s, and continue to grow in popularity all over the world.

1. The root of the word "martial" lies in Mars, the Roman god of war, different "martial arts" not only being developed in Asia, but throughout the world.

2. Wrestling is the oldest form of unarmed combat on record.

3. Unarmed martial arts are divided between those based on striking an opponent (Boxing, Wing Chun, Karate, Taekwondo, Capoeira, Savate, Lethwei, Muay Thai, Kung Fu, Pencak Silat, Kalaripayattu), and those based on grappling an opponent (Hapkido, Judo, Sumo, Wrestling, Aikido, Jujutsu, Brazilian Jiu-jitsu, Sambo, Kung Fu).

4. Probably originating in India, eastern martial arts are often indistinguishable from health and spiritual practices. Shaolinquan (shaolin king fu) in particular is inextricably linked to the spread of Buddhism.

5. *Wushu* (Chinese for "martial art") first came to international prominence with an 1899 anti-foreign and anti-Christian uprising in China the British popularly called the "War of the Boxers," because kung fu seemed like a form of boxing to them. Chinese boxers believing to be immune to bullets were quickly disabused of that notion by the allied American, Austro-Hungarian, British, French, German, Italian, Japanese, and Russian troops that quelled the rebellion.

6. When American military personnel became stationed in China, Japan, and South Korea, during and after World War II and the Korean War, some men began to learn and practice Asian martial arts. Notably, future karate and film legend Chuck Norris (b.1940) learned *Tang Soo Do*, a Korean karate variant, while an Air Policeman (AP) at the Osan Air Base.

7. Credited as one of the first instructors to openly teach Chinese martial arts to Westerners, TV and film legend Bruce Lee. Initially a Wing Chun student under the equally legendary Ip Man (1893-1972), he got into so much fighting trouble his parents shipped him to the US, where he got his first acting roles, and eventually invented his very own martial art: *Jeet Kune Do.*

8. Prominent martial artists and film stars Jackie Chan (b.1954) and Jet Li (b.1963) both began their careers in Bruce Lee's wake, and remain incredibly popular both in the East and the West.

9. Western wrestling and boxing have been part of the Olympics since their very creation in Ancient Greece. Judo was the first Eastern martial art to be included in the Olympics back in 1964, while Taekwondo became part of the competition only in 2000. Karate and Brazilian Jiu-jitsu are also expected to join at some point.

10. Genuine black-belt celebrities include Willie Nelson (b.1933), James Caan (b.1940), Ed O'Neill (b.1946), Dave Mustaine (b.1961), Forrest Whitaker (b.1961), Wesley Snipes (b.1962), Sean Patrick Flannery (b.1965), Michael Imperioli (b.1966), Joe Rogan (b.1967), Guy Ritchie (b.1968), Ryan Phillippe (b.1974), and Evan Rachel Wood (b.1987).

COWABUNGA!

Eastern martial arts not only took over movies and television, but printed media as well. The greatest fictional martial artists to ever grace comic books include:

Batman: The most popular superhero in the entire world, this Bob Kane (1915-1998) and Bill Finger (1914-1974) creation from 1939 needs no introduction. A polymath, Bruce Wayne is naturally an expert of not one but several martial arts, learning Asian ones while under writer/editor Denny O'Neil's (1939-2020) pen, himself a lifelong martial artist. In film, no Batman incarnation has been more proficient a martial artist (*Ninjutsu*) than in the Christopher Nolan (b.1970) trilogy, starring Christian Bale (b.1974), himself a Wing Chun practitioner!

Daredevil: Perhaps better known by his disability (blindness) than his martial arts prowess, martial arts were however, heavily introduced to the Daredevil mythos by young artist/writer Frank Miller (b.1957), who would also reboot Batman in the 1980s. In Miller's comic, the character's heightened senses are channeled via harsh martial arts training under *sensei* Stick, going on to face off against equally skilled martial artists (and a very complicated girlfriend assassin). Daredevil saw perhaps its most accurate portrayal on the eponymous TV show, starring Charlie Cox (b.1982).

Judomaster: Created by Joe Gill (1919-2006) and Frank McLaughlin (1935-2020) in 1965, for Connecticut's own Charlton Publications. Judomaster's origin story would set the basic template for martial arts fiction in the years to come: his alter-ego, Hadley "Rip" Jagger is a US Army sergeant during World War II. When he rescues the daughter of a Pacific island chief, the man repays the favor by teaching him Judo.

Karate Kid: Not to be confused with the film franchise from the 1980s, Karate Kid is a DC comics superhero created by Jim Shooter (b.1952) for the *Legion of Super-Heroes* comic book series. The son of a Japanese crime lord and an American mother (a story trope later emulated by Marvel's Shang Chi, and to a lesser degree *Star Wars*), Val Armorr is a master in every martial art ever developed by the 31st century that gave birth to him, which renders him a living weapon.

Shang Chi: "The Master of Kung Fu" was created by writer Steve Englehart (b.1947) and artist Jim Starlin (b.1949) back in 1973. An obvious Marvel attempt to capitalize on the 1972 "Kung Fu" TV show starring David Carradine (1936-2009), Shang Chi is the mixed-race son of Sax Rohmer's (1883-1959) evil mastermind Fu Manchu, and a white American woman, and therefore has to deal with his own father's wickedness (predating Luke Skywalker's daddy issues by several years). The formula worked very well, and the original title lasted until 1983.

Iron Fist: Another martial arts superhero from Marvel, Iron Fist was first created by Roy Thomas (b.1940) and Gil Kane (1926-2000). Inspired by the *Five Fingers of Death* (1972) classic film, Iron Fist features young millionaire Danny Rand, raised by shaolin monks in the mystical city of K'un-L'un after an accident during a trip to China. Danny would not only become a proficient wushu warrior, but also inherit his energy-charged fist after defeating dragon Shou-Lao in combat. The character would be portrayed by English actor Finn Jones (b.1988) on the Netflix live action show.

Kenshiro: First appearing in the "Fist of the North Star" Japanese *manga* ("comic book") series which debuted in 1983, Kenshiro, "the Survivor," is what could have happened if Bruce Lee had ever starred in the *Mad Max* film series. The practitioner of a deadly fictional martial art known as *Hokuto Shinken*, also inspired by the *Five Fingers of Death* film,

Kenshiro delivers swift, brutal justice to all sorts of aberrant mutant villains, while wandering a post-apocalyptic landscape. He is the creation of groundbreaking *manga* writer Buronson (b.1947), and artist Tetsuo Hara (b.1961).

Teenage Mutant Ninja Turtles: The brainchildren of Kevin Eastman (b.1962) and Peter Laird (b.1954), Leonardo, Raphael, Donatello, and Michaelangelo are four mutant turtles trained in the ancient art of *Ninjutsu* by mutated sewer rat Splinter. Self-published in a 1984 black and white comic, while originally intended as a Frank Miller's *Daredevil* spoof, the turtles would take the world by storm when their first cartoon and toy line premiered three years later. In 1990 a live action film produced by Hong Kong martial arts film powerhouse *Golden Harvest* became a box-office hit. It was followed by many more!

Son Goku: Created in 1984 by Akira Toriyama (b.1955), Goku is the enormously popular protagonist of Japanese *manga* series *Dragonball*. The character is a blend of the Monkey King from sixteenth-century folk tale *Journey to the West*, and Superman, with a little King Kong thrown in for good measure. The story, which borrows freely from martial arts classics like *Enter the Dragon* (1973), and *Drunken Master* (1978), follows the exploits of Goku and his merry band of friends, and the titular character trains and grows as a martial artist, fighting progressively more powerful foes.

Naruto: Heir apparent to Son Goku, Naruto Uzumaki's outwardly appearance as a young ninja-in-training hides within the power of the mythical Nine-Tails fox. Highly popular all over the planet, the best selling 1999-2014 *manga* series by Masashi Kishimoto (b.1979) has sold 250 million copies worldwide!

SPLIT

From the streets of Brussels rose the greatest martial artist and movie star the world has ever seen. The King of Split, the Muscles from Brussels, the one and only ... Jean-Claude Camille François van Varenberg ?

1. Born on October 18, 1960, the son of an accountant and a florist, Jean-Claude would enroll in a Shotokan Karate school at ten, and earn his black belt eight years later, while also finding the time to practice ballet, Muay Thai, and bodybuilding.

2. Earning a spot in the Belgian Karate Team, he won the 1979 European Karate Championship, and many a bout, while landing his first, yet uncredited role in the 1979 film *Femme entre chien et loup* ("Woman Between Wolf and Dog").

3. After moving to America, he got his first US film role as an extra on Cannon Films *Breakin'* (1984), and as a stunt man on Cannon's *Missing in Action* (1984), which led to a friendship with Cannon's main star, Chuck Norris (b.1940), who got him a day-job as a bouncer!

4. His first big role as the villain in New World Pictures' *No Retreat, No Surrender* (1986) film, would see his stage name credited for the first time, Jean-Claude van Damme! After quitting the 1987 *Predator* film, where he'd play the titular alien, Van Damme was running out of prospects, so he went to the only company that was always open for business: Cannon Films.

5. Catching Menahem Golan (1929-2014) at the Cannon building lobby, in a career-defining move, he proceeding to demonstrate his martial arts prowess by launching a kick to Golan's face, yet

stopping short from hitting him. This got him his big break at Cannon, *Bloodsport* (1988) and many more films followed uninterrupted through much of the 1990s.

6. But not everything was OK in Van Damme's life. Between a lifelong bipolar disorder, and the stress of uninterrupted filming, he became addicted to cocaine, a habit which would see him arrested in 1999. His career plummeted, as had his many (five) marriages, and he saw himself reduced to direct-to-video films for much of the following decade.

7. Quitting drugs cold-turkey along the way, 2008 would see him star in what many consider his best film ever, the semi-autobiographical French satire *JCVD*, directed by Mabrouk el Mechri (b.1976), which cemented Van Damme's cult stardom, and saw the man's Hollywood career rebound in a big way, leading to bigger roles in the 2010s, including starring in one of the most viewed commercials of all time,"Epic Split," which sees him musing while splitting between two racing Volvo trucks!

8. On October 21, 2012, a well-deserved Van Damme statue was inaugurated in front of the Westland Shopping Center in Brussels. Years later, another was unveiled at a park in the Azerbaijani town of, well, Vandam!

BONUS FACT!

- Engineer Thomas Hancock (1786-1865) named his rubber-hardening process "vulcanization," after Vulcan, Roman god of fire and forge.

BEES AND BUTTERFLIES

Boxing has had a long, distinguished history since 3000BC Sumeria, but we'll skip the details to focus on the sport's greatest pulp-beating, bone-crunching champs!

Onomastus of Smyrna (?): According to Philostratus (c.170-250AD) and Eusebius of Caesarea (c.260-340AD), the semi-legendary 688BC Olympic champion capitalized on his celebrity status by writing a best-selling boxing manual.

John L. Sullivan (1858-1918): Both the last bare-knuckle boxing champion, and the first gloved boxing champion. With a record of 40 wins (34 by K.O.), one loss and two draws, the Irish heavyweight pugilist was a superstar during his lifetime, and one of the world's highest paid athletes. It is said his burial ground was frozen so hard, they had to blast the coffin hole using dynamite—a fitting burial for a boxer!

Jack Johnson (1878-1946): In Jim Crow America, the Galveston Giant proved an African American could become world heavyweight boxing champion, and remained as such for seven years. Retiring with a record 70 wins (35 by K.O.), 11 losses, and 11 draws, Johnson made a good living endorsing various products, becoming a nightclub owner (founder of the original Cotton Club, no less!), and writing two memoirs, *My Combats* (1914) and *Jack Johnson in the Ring and Out* (1927).

Tommy Burns (1881-1955): The first and only Canadian world heavyweight champion, with 47 wins (35 by K.O.), five losses, and nine draws, what Burns lacked in height (he was 5'7", the shortest heavyweight champ in history), he more than compensated in

courage and sportsmanship, still being remembered for respecting every fighter, regardless of the color of their skin.

Luis A. Firpo (1894-1960): The Argentinian boxer, known as the Wild Bull of the Pampas, held a modest record of 31 Wins (26 by K.O.), and four losses, but is perhaps best remembered for stunningly knocking none other than Jack Dempsey out of the ring, in their legendary 1923 match, despite the later eventually winning the bout. He was the first Latin American to ever challenge for the world heavyweight title.

Jack Dempsey (1895-1983): The Manassa Mauler had arms like oxygen tanks and matching fists. With a solid record of 68 wins (53 by K.O.), six losses, and 11 draws, Dempsey retired, and would later join the Coast Guard during the World War II effort, participating in the invasion of Okinawa, later being honorably discharged having achieved Commander rank. Centuries after Onomastus ventured into the publishing ring, he would write his own *Championship Fighting: Explosive Punching and Aggressive Defense* (1950).

Joe Louis (1914-1981): Aptly nicknamed the Brown Bomber, his 66 wins (52 by K.O.), and only three losses record pales against his most memorable achievement: ramming "Aryan superiority" down Adolf Hitler's (1889-1945) throat by defeating Nazi favorite Max Schmeling (1905-2005) in two minutes and four seconds, in 1938! He would later serve in the US Army's Special Services Division, boosting troops' morale, being awarded the Legion of Merit in 1945.

Archie Moore (1916-1998): Famed for his stamina, the Mongoose had one of the longest careers in boxing, and remains the longest World Light Heavyweight Champion of all time, with a record of 186 wins (131 by K.O.—still unsurpassed!), 23 losses, and ten draws. The only man to have faced both Marciano and Ali—and lived to tell the

tale. After retiring from boxing Moore enjoyed a solid career in film and television, and is perhaps best-remembered as Jim, in the 1960 adaptation of *The Adventures of Huckleberry Finn*.

Sugar Ray Robinson (1921-1989: Considered the greatest boxer of all time, welterweight and middleweight Robinson's record includes 173 wins (109 by K.O.), 19 losses, and six draws. He's also remembered for denying an infant Cassius Clay (1942-2016), later known as Muhammad Ali, his autograph; an event which prompted the champ-to-be never to turn down an autograph request in his life.

Rocky Marciano (1923-1969: The undefeated 1952-1956 heavyweight champion of the world, Marciano holds one of the highest knock-out rates ever, 43 K.O.'s out of 49 wins and no losses, perhaps because he recognized the time had come for him to retire at age 32. Loving the sport still, he continued to work in and out of the ring as a referee and boxing commentator, dying in a plane crash a young man of 45.

Muhammad Ali (1942-2016): The legend that was Muhammad Ali could fill many books on its own—in fact, it has!—suffice it to say he won the Olympic gold at 18, took the world heavyweight championship from Sonny Liston (1930-1970 at 22, and following the stripping of his titles after refusing to be drafted into the Vietnam War, he took part in the heavily publicized matches "The Rumble in the Jungle" and the "Thrilla in Manila," retiring with a record of 56 wins (37 by K.O., and five losses; the greatest fight of his life, however, he took against Parkinson's until the end of his life.

EYE OF THE TIGER

Traditionally exempt from any obligations to a happy ending, the drama, excitement, and bloodshed of boxing has proven perfect material for the movies.

Champion (1949): Based on an original story by the great Ring Lardner (1885-1933), this great film-noir picture about the pitfalls of ambition follows a young Kirk Douglas (1916-2020) as Midge Kelly, a boxer willing to do whatever it takes to reach the top, even if that means betraying everyone that's ever been kind to him! Far from a redemption story , this film dares take all the familiar tropes and turn them on their head, which results in this little picture standing the test of time.

Requiem For A Heavyweight (1956): An original Peabody Award-winning teleplay by Rod Serling (1924-1975) which got remade several times (including in the UK, the Netherlands, and Yugoslavia, no less!), its gritty film treatment stars Anthony Quinn (1915-2001), who had been a boxer in his youth, as aging and down-on-his-luck champ Mountain Rivera. Best remembered for the Cassius Clay, later known as Muhammad Ali (1942-2016), cameo at the beginning of the picture, the film deserves a lot more credit for dealing with a man's broken dreams and ultimate humiliation, rather than narcissistic notions of "success."

The Great White Hope (1970): A romantic retelling of Jack Johnson's (1878-1946) life, it is based on the 1967 play, which earned the legendary James Earl Jones (b.1931) a Tony Award for the main role he reprised in the film, alongside the beautiful Jane Alexander (b.1939). Tackling an issue of the day (interracial marriage) via the distant past, it is also a film that ultimately deals not in victory, as later films would, but disaster for its protagonists, albeit outside of the ring.

Rocky (1976): Possibly the most iconic boxing film of all time, Rocky is also the straight-faced drama of a man standing on his own against not only a better, bigger opponent, but harsh, gritty reality itself pushing him down, which is exactly what screenwriter and actor Sylvester Stallone (b.1946) must have felt when he wrote the movie, and fought against all odds to be allowed to star in it. While the fictional Rocky doesn't win the match against Apollo, Stallone became the third man in history to receive Best Writer and Best Actor Oscar nominations for the same film, after Charlie Chaplin (b.1889-1977) and Orson Welles (b.1915-1985), the film deservedly winning the award for Best Picture, Director and Editing.

The Champ (1979): Remaking a classic is never easy, but this heartfelt, aesthetically polished drama directed by Franco Zeffirelli (1923-2019), effectively deals with a washed-up boxer, John Voight (b.1938), attempting to win back his son, and has a tear-jerker of an ending that never fails. While it didn't do so well in the US, it became one of MGM's greatest box-office hits ever thanks to its overseas ticket-selling power.

Raging Bull (1980): Based on middleweight slugger Jake LaMotta'a (1922-2017) 1970 autobiography, the film echoes *Champion* in more ways than one, and would later rise to prominence thanks to Robert De Niro's (b.1943) weight-gaining (60 pounds!) rather than its shoddy film making. Regardless, as painful and unforgiving a Martin Scorsese (b.1942) picture as can be, it is still better than most films out there, boxing or otherwise.

Rocky IV (1985): From the height of the Cold War, this pure 1980s blockbuster is hard to match in terms of sheer bone-crunching glee. It pits a Rocky, Sylvester Stallone, entrapped by a capitalist success which is breaking his family apart, against a humorless, steroid-pumped Ivan Drago, Dolph Lundgren (b.1957), who instead fights for

the State, and as such couldn't be further from his egotistical American opponents. Rocky, therefore is only able to beat Drago after going back to basics (being stripped of the advantages of home for a harsh USSR environment) and regaining the affection of his wife.

Gladiator (1992): Perhaps one of the most underrated boxing films in recent history, this movie needs to be rescued from oblivion, and put in its proper place among the greatest of its kind. James Marshall (b.1967) and Cuba Gooding Jr. (b.1968) star as two teens struggling to get out of poverty, who get exploited by ruthless underground boxing promoter Jimmy Horn, played by the great Brian Dennehy (1938-2020). Co-written by Robert Mark Kamen (b.1947), who also wrote the 1984 *Karate Kid* film, and directed by Rowdy Herrington (b.1951), this film is well worth seeing again!

The Boxer (1997): Set in Ireland during the violent final years of The Troubles, this rugged, violent Daniel Day-Lewis (b.1957) boxing drama with noir sensibilities escapes genre tropes by presenting boxing as an escape from violence (via community building), rather than the other way around; the bottom line being that, for all its troubles and downfalls, boxing is still a sport, its bloodshed never a match for the destruction engendered by political radicalism.

Million Dollar Baby (2004): Heart-wrenching as it is memorable, this Clint Eastwood (b.1930) drama is a boxing film in disguise which never lets you go, in or out of the movie theater. It stars Hilary Swank (b.1974) in a gritty role about—what else?—a down-on-her-luck struggling boxer, herself, as well as the film audience, not knowing that's only the beginning of her suffering. Swank, Eastwood, and the movie as a whole went on to win some well-deserved Academy Awards, despite it being panned by some critics who found it depressing, completely missing its underlying message.

A FRIEND IN ME

Walking into a toy store back in 1986, a professional football player realized the action figure shelves contained no real-life sports heroes, and the Starting Lineup toy line was born!

1. A *cum laude* Harvard Graduate, Pat McInally (b.1953) played for the Cincinnati Bengals as a punter and wide receiver from 1976 to 1985, and is the only NFL player to have reportedly got the only verified perfect score on the Wonderlic personnel assessment scale.

2. At the very end of his professional football career, McInally saw a gap in the toy market big companies had missed: realistic action figures based on well known athletes. He took his idea to a friend who worked as a manager at Cincinnati-based Kenner Products (known for their *Star Wars*, and Super Powers toy lines), and the rest, as they say, is history!

3. Starting Lineup debuted in 1988 with a 124 baseball players set. It did so well, it was soon followed with basketball and football sets. Of the 1988 sets, certain mint, unopened figures fetch prices as high as $375, with the Marc Wilson currently valued at $450.

4. 1989 saw Kenner release its first Baseball Greats dual-packs, featuring classic hall-of-famers as Mickey Mantle (1931-1995) with Joe DiMaggio (1914-1999), and Reggie Jackson (b.1946) with Don Drysdale (1936-1993). Other sports soon got their own Greats immortalized in such packs during the 1990s. Realizing they had tapped into a rich sports-collecting vein, the company also released its Slam Dunk line (no relation to the Japanese *manga*), featuring NBA stars dunking on a small hoop, with its backboard and hardwood floor included!

5. Over the 1990s, the line expanded to include players from all professional sports, including boxing, soccer, hockey, and many, many more. The Timeless Legends series at the end of that decade would also see figures of boxers like Joe Louis (1914-1981), Rocky Marciano (1923-1969) and Muhammad Ali (1942-2016), as well as other influential sporting heroes like Mary Lou Retton (b.1968) and Pelé (b.1940), for the first time in history!

6. While Kenner Products has been purchased by Hasbro in 1991, the Starting Lineup was continued throughout the decade, until the closure of the Cincinnati offices in 2000. Hasbro then discontinued the entire line in 2001, letting its trademark expire 16 years later, despite generating the company $400 million during its 14 year run.

7. Made a very rich man by the line, McInally was made director of marketing and testing of the Wonderlic Company in 2006. Still active after retirement, he supports a number of non-profits, and collects antique children's books.

BONUS FACTS!

- The root of the word "slave" is Slav, as it was originally white people from Slavic countries that were kept as slaves in Europe since Roman times, not Africans.

- Dating back to 1818, Brooks Brothers, one of America's oldest clothing companies went bankrupt in 2020, due to the Covid-19 pandemic.

LIVING ROOM INVADERS

During the last 20 years, as the entire planet switched over from the physical to the purely electronic, the rise of e-sports (competitive video gaming) came as no surprise. Quickly ingraining themselves within the sports marketing complex, with many real-life professional sports clubs currently branching out towards owning stakes and sponsoring teams in the e-sports circuit, the future of sports in general, it would seem, lies not on turf, but on the digital realm. So how on Earth did we get here?!

1. Inspired by radar displays he saw during World War II, Professor Thomas T. Goldsmith Jr. (1910-2009) patented the first ever arcade game in 1948. It used a cathode ray gun to "shoot down" vector screen dots which represented missiles!

2. In 1951, Christopher S. Strachey (1916-1975) would come up with a computerized version of draughts (known as checkers in the US), for the Pilot ACE computer. One of the earliest of its kind, it had memory capacity, which Strachey's draughts program completely drained!

3. 1952 would witness the arrival of OXO, a game of tic-tac-toe created by British computer scientist "Sandy" Douglas (1921-2010) in 1952 for the Electronic Delay Storage Automatic Calculator (EDSAC), one of the first computers with a memory that could be read from or written to.

4. Decades before Pong, tennis simulator Tennis for Two was designed by former Manhattan Project physicist William Higinbotham (1910-1994) back in 1958. Widely considered the first true, interactive video game, it played on an oscilloscope display with two custom aluminum controllers. First unveiled at the Brookhaven

National Laboratory's annual public exhibition, it naturally drew large crowds of—you guessed it—teenagers!

5. Eight years before America put two men on the Moon, MIT student Steve Russell (b.1937) created and designed the seminal (as in e-sports founding father) video game Spacewar on a DEC PDP-1 "mini" computer (the size of a cabinet), with fellow members of the Tech Model Railroad Club. Ten years later, on October 19, 1972, the earliest known video game competition took place at Stanford University. The game of choice? Spacewar. The prize? A one year subscription to *Rolling Stone* magazine!

6. Designed by Nolan Bushnell (b.1943) and Ted Dabney (1937-2018) as a coin-operated version of Spacewar, 1971 space combat arcade game Computer Space was the first commercially available arcade video game. In it, an ever-moving rocket fires at enemy flying saucers withing a black and white screen, all encased in a Bushnell-designed futuristic glittering indigo fiberglass cabinet, it still looks beautiful today. Though it sold a mere 1,500 units in its day, it was followed by anther Spacewar knock-off called Galaxy Game.

7. The first commercial home video-game system, the Magnavox Odyssey, would appear in 1972. Coupled with Computer Space, they would mark the end of the early era of experimental video games. The Odyssey was so ahead of its time, it even included the very first video game light gun accessory! By the time it was discontinued in 1975, it has sold an excess of 350,000 consoles in America alone!

8. The path becoming clear for Bushnell and Dabney, they founded Atari in 1972. The company, named after a Japanese word used in the Go board game meaning "to hit the target," produced an arcade knock-off an Odyssey ping-pong game they called Pong, which took the arcade market by storm that year. Magnavox later sued Atari for

patent infringement, but it didn't matter, Atari would become the dominant force in the nascent industry, moving beyond Pong into other games and eventually their own home console by 1977, now a full subsidiary of Warner Communications.

9. Meanwhile in Japan, a young programmer/designer at Taito Corporation named Tomohiro Nishikado (b.1944) was experimenting on his own on what became known as Space Invaders. Licensed for the Atari 2600 in 1980, the game sold an astonishing 2,000,000 cartridges that year alone. The first official Space Invaders Tournament, a large scale competition sponsored by Atari took place at the end of that year. It attracted an estimated 10,000 video game aficionados, and was reportedly won by Rebecca Heineman (b.1964), who would go on to become a game programmer herself.

10. The year 1980 would also see a young Walter Day (b.1949) found Twin Galaxies, an organization which kept track of video game high scores. This led to founding the US National Video Game Team, in association with the *Guinness Book of World Records* in 1983.

11. Business was booming for video-game companies. With frequent media coverage thanks to Day's efforts, video games even gained their own cable TV game show, TBS's *Starcade*, the first-ever televised e-sports events. *Starcade* ran four pilots, and 133 regular episodes from 1982 to 1983.

12. Just as industry revenues peaked at $3.2 billion in 1983 the home and arcade video game market reached its natural saturation point. The ensuing crash saw sales drop 97% by 1985. Atari folded almost immediately, paving the way for Japanese companies (which weren't as badly hit by the recession) like Nintendo to take the lead in the decades that followed. More affordable personal computers with far more memory and processing power than consoles, like the

Commodore 64, would also take the video-game torch relay, among other things by fostering a whole new generation of game designers.

13. PC's had also began connecting via phone lines, and by 1988, the first online sports game for a whopping 16 players, a multiplayer online battle arena (MOBA) game called Netrek was first posted on Usenet. In 1991, the first college Netrek game between UC Berkeley and Carnegie Mellon University took place, with the International Netrek League (INL) forming a year later. The game remained very popular until the mid 1990s.

14. In 1990, Nintendo of America would run the Nintendo World Championship (NWC) across 30 American cities, based on a special NES cartridge, which is now a valuable collector's item.

15. Previously relying on high scores, it would be 1991 fighting game Street Fighter 2 that made direct two-player competition fun, its popularity leading to the founding of the Evolution Championship Series (EVO) esports tournament in 1996.

16. In the 1990s Blockbuster Video would also implement its own *GamePro*-sponsored World Game Championships, which made TV take notice of video games again, and so did some politicians, which by the end of that decade were blaming video games for the evils of the day, like the Columbine High School massacre of 1999.

17. Meanwhile in Asia, the expansion of internet broadband networks meant that by 1997, the financial crisis in that continent suddenly created a mass of unemployed salarymen with time to kill. Internet cafés and LAN gaming centers mushroomed around this era, particularly in South Korea, where Ministry of Culture, Sports and Tourism approved the foundation of the Korean e-Sports Association

in 2000. It is currently an official member of the Korean Olympic Committee!

18. Between 2000 and 2002, Sony (in 2000), Nintendo (in 2001) and Microsoft (in 2002) would all give their consoles (PS2, GameCube, and XBox) online multiplayer capabilities, which are now an industry norm.

19. Since 2010, the never-ending proliferation of tournaments (such as The International, and the Intel Extreme Masters), leagues (Overwatch League, League of Legends Championship Series, etc.), and professionally sponsored teams (the top hundred of them earning between one and $35 million in prizes alone), has taken over physical space as well. With live, sold-out tournaments held in venues all around the world, even the International Olympic Committee (IOC) is currently considering incorporating e-sports into future Olympic Games!

BONUS FACTS!

- From its humble Mexican origin, the resilient and adaptable Colorado potato beetle (*Leptinotarsa decemlineata*), has become a widespread pest in all of North America, Europe, and Russia.

- George Plantagenet, Duke of Clarence (1449-1478) chose to be executed in style, by drowning in a wine barrel.

- Table sugar's name comes from the Middle East, where it was known as *al-zucar*.

VI
FLUSHING
PHENOMENA

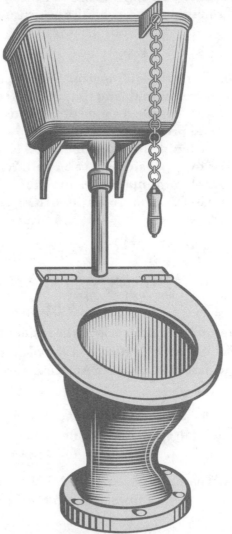

PLATO'S FOLLY

Plato (c.427-347BC) never would have guessed that out of all his philosophical and political treatises, it would be the fictional, cautionary tall tale of Atlantis that proved to be his most enduring.

1. Literally meaning "island of Atlas," in Plato's *Dialogues* (c.360BC) Atlantis was and island larger than Asia Minor and Libya combined, located just beyond the Strait of Gibraltar ("the Pillars of Hercules"). It was created by Poseidon, who left his son Atlas in charge of ruling its denizens.

2. Overtime, Plato's Atlantis would grow into a sophisticated and technologically advanced society, its arrogance leading it to try and conquer Europe, being ultimately defeated by ancient Athens (Plato's embodiment of the ideal government), and sunk into the ocean by the gods.

3. While adopted into politically allegorical works of literature by Thomas More (1478-1535), and Francis Bacon (1561-1626), it wouldn't be taken at face value until Olaus Rudbeck's (1630-1702) nationalistic *Atland eller Manheim* (1679). In it, Rudbeck set to prove without a shadow of doubt that Sweden was Atlantis, hence making Sweden the cradle of civilization!

4. Running into a dead end, Abbot Charles-Étienne Brasseur de Bourbourg (1814-1874), among other nineteenth century researchers, stated Atlantis may have been the source from which Mesoamerican civilizations stemmed, but it would be American Congressman and fringe historian Ignatius L. Donnelly's (1831-1901) *Atlantis: The Antediluvian World* (1882) that would bring Atlantis to the forefront of popular culture.

5. The founder of the esoteric Theosophical Society, Helena Blavatsky (1831-1891) would come to embrace Donnelly's work, incorporating his Atlantis theory into a thinly veiled racist cosmogony of her own invention, which purported Atlanteans to be a race of super-powered giants who built Stonehenge and the Moai of Easter Island, degrading into chaos when mating with apes to produce the Egyptians and indigenous Americans.

6. It was only a matter of time before serious crackpots took Blavatsky's preposterous theories, and gave them an even more racist spin. That's what happened in Austria when Guido von List (1848-1919) and Jörg Lanz (1874-1954) established their set of esoteric beliefs they called Ariosophy or Armanism. Blavatsky's olive-skinned, coastal Mediterranean Atlanteans suddenly became a "master race"of super-powered Norsemen. The stage was set for Ariosophy to be adopted by the Völkisch movement, ultimately giving birth to Nazism.

7. While plate tectonics and the continental drift have come to be regarded as undisputable fact, many people still look for historicity in Plato's allegory of government and power, alternatively "finding" Atlantis in the Bahamas, the Bosporus, Antarctica, or the currently in-vogue Santorini island.

BONUS FACTS!

- Only natural rubber can remain flexible after being subjected to extreme heat or freezing cold.

- None of Brazil's main agricultural exports (soybeans, beef, sugar, coffee) is native to the Americas.

LAND OF THE LOST

Atlantis isn't the only bygone continent produced by esoteric thought ... enter, Lemuria!

1. India's Tamil lore refers to the mythical land of *Kumari Kandam*, in the Indian Ocean, where their culture and society supposedly originated before a great catastrophe sunk it into the ocean.

2. Having found lemur fossils in Madagascar and India, but not Africa, nor the Middle East, zoologist Philip Sclater (1829-1913) proposed the existence of a long lost continent he named Lemuria, where these primates supposedly had originated from.

3. Helena Blavatsky (1831-1891)—who else?—would see fit to incorporate Sclater's trendy work, just as she did with Donnelly's, into the ever-growing Theosophical mishmash, as a precursor of Atlantis, revealed to her by the ancient Mahatmas ("saints") of Indian legend, going as far as identifying Australia's Aboriginal peoples as the offspring of Lemurians and animals (sigh). Fellow Theosophical Society member Charles Webster Leadbeater (1854-1934) somehow even managed to include a map of the place in his *The Lost Lemuria* (1904) book!

4. In 1926, author James Churchward (1851-1936) would take Augustus Le Plongeon's (1826-1908) "Land of Mu" (a stand-in for Atlantis), and merge it with Lemuria midway over the Pacific Ocean in his popular pseudo-archeology book *Lost Continent of Mu, the Motherland of Man*. In it, reaching from Hawaii to Easter Island, Mu's great civilization was, naturally, the cradle of Egyptian, Indian, and Mayan cultures.

5. Churchward's theories found fertile ground in "occultist" circles at both sides of the Atlantic, to the extent of even influencing the otherwise-rational *Atatürk*, Mustafa Kemal (1881-1938), who saw Mu as the legendary homeland not of the Tamil Indians, nor the Aboriginal Astralians, but the Turkish people!

6. In modern times, even reputed professors like Masaaki Kimura (b.1940) have fallen into the Lemuria/Mu trap, suggesting the Yonaguni Island rock formations are man-made in his 1998 book *A Continent Lost in the Pacific Ocean—Riddle of the Submarine Ruins in the Ryukyu Islands*.

7. Like Atlantis, Lemuria has found a home in pulp fiction, notably in the works of H.P. Lovecraft (1890-1937), and Robert E. Howard (1906-1936). Artist-writer Richard Sharpe Shaver (1907-1975) particularly claimed to have had true recollections of an ancient alien Lemurian civilization in his 1945 "I Remember Lemuria" tale for the *Amazing Stories* magazine!

BONUS FACTS!

- Muhammad Ali (1942-2016) saved a suicidal man's life in 1981, by talking him off of the ledge.

- Disneyland has only closed four times at JFK's 1963 assassination, the 1994 LA earthquake, the 9-11 attacks, and the Covid-19 pandemic.

- 80% of all golfers never achieve a handicap of less than 18.

MEN FROM ATLANTIS

Never failing from eliciting impressionable imaginations, mermen with ties to Atlantis, Mu, and Lemuria have sprung from comics, television, and the movies onto the cultural pool of mankind.

Namor: Introduced by Bill Everett (1917-1973) in the pages of *Marvel Comics* #1 (1939), the Sub-Mariner, whose name means "Roman" spelled backwards, is an ill-tempered Atlantean prince with Greco-Roman god attributes (including ankle wings which enable him to fly), and a dislike for humans which make him comics' first anti-hero. Over the years, the standard derivative supporting sea-dwelling cast has been added to the comic, including Namora, Namorita, and many more.

Aquaman: Created by writer Mort Weisinger (1915-1978) and artist Paul Norris (1914-2007) at rival publisher DC Comics, the blonde, personable king of Atlantis was originally meant as Namor's antithesis (yet with a similarly derivative cast of Aqualad, Aquagirl, and so on), until writer Peter David (b.1956) got him to lose a hand, while growing a beard and a temper equal to his Marvel counterpart, which ironically made the character more popular. Give or take, this is the version which was used in modern cartoons and the summer blockbuster movie of 2018 starring bearded Jason Momoa (b.1979) as the mean, bearded title character.

Mark Harris: A living, underwater-breathing Atlantean with webbed hands and feet, plunged into TV screens everywhere in *Man from Atlantis* (1977-1978). Created by Mayo Simon (b.1928) and Herbert F. Solow (b.1930), the amnesiac "Mark Harris," played by Patrick Duffy (b.1949), thought to be the last surviving denizen of Atlantis, is recruited by the fictional Foundation for Oceanic Research

to do the usual crime-fighting and world-saving, which until then had never been seen on the small screen. In this instance, the hero made the leap "backwards" from TV to the pages of US and British comics alike, though the show itself only lasted for 13 episodes.

TigerSharks: Developed by Rankin/Bass Productions in 1987, following the familiar template they had set with *ThunderCats* (1985), and *SilverHawks* (1986), as one of the animated shows in TV anthology series *The Comic Strip*, the show centers on a team of human explorers orbiting aquatic planet Water-O (sigh), using technology to transform into different sea-hybrid versions of themselves (shark, dolphin, walrus, etc.). Highly derivative, and cheaply made by Rankin/Bass standards, the show only lasted for 26, 20-minute episodes before cancellation.

Street Sharks: Made by Canadian animation company DIC Productions under commission by Mattel to promote its line of eponymous action-figures, this thinly-veiled *Ninja Turtles* knock-off managed to munch its chunk of that lucrative market for three seasons (1994-1997), inspiring a spin-off show, *Extreme Dinosaurs*, in the process. The story dealt with the cool, surfing sons of a scientists who accidentally see their genome spliced with different shark species DNA, transforming into mutated monster super heroes.

The Mariner: The protagonist of Kevin Costner's (b.1955) biggest career flop, *Waterworld* (1995), is only as original as the heroes it desperately imitates (Namor and Mark Harris), only thrust into a sea-park version of *Mad Max* (1979). In its time considered the most expensive movie ever made, *Waterworld* ultimately tanked (pun definitely intended) both at the box office, and among its many, many critics.

Abe Sapien: The brainchild of *Hellboy* comic creator Mike Mignola

(b. 1960) as his own homage to *The Creature from the Black Lagoon* (1954), the amphibious *Ichthyo sapien* creature christened Abraham Sapien was found in suspended animation by scientists, becoming an agent of the fictional Bureau for Paranormal Research and Defense (BPRD). The breakout character of the *Hellboy* comic series, Abe has seen his own comic miniseries published, as well as being prominently featured in the first two live-action *Hellboy* films, as played by Doug Jones (b.1960).

Aspen: Created and self-published by Michael Turner (1971-2008), Aspen Matthews is, as is usual with most aquatic super heroes, a child of both the human world and the sea, discovering she's part of a race of underwater super people who can control water and liquids to the point of creating tsunamis, much like Aquaman's Mera character.

The Deep: Kevin, a.k.a. The Deep, is the token merman in the Amazon satirical live-action series *The Boys*, played by Chace Crawford (b.1985). Holding all of the usual "Aquaman" powers (including telepathic communication with sea life), while its comic book counterpart is simply pathetic, Crawford plays a far more nuanced, vulnerable character with paraphilic inclinations, which soon mean his demotion to Midwestern sea park mascot, in a comedy of errors well-worth its own spinoff show.

Jacques-Yves Cousteau (1910-1997): While not fictional, the life of the pioneering inventor of modern scuba-diving and the Aqua-Lung is the stuff of legend. An Academy Award and Cannes *Palme d'or* winner, commander Cousteau set himself as the star of his own big and small screen documentaries. However, what earned him this spot is his 1962 speech at the World Congress of Underwater Activities in London, where he indulged into a long pseudo-scientific prediction concerning the evolution of surgically adapted "Homo aquaticus" which would supposedly populate the seas by the year 2000!

THE MYSTERIOUS CITIES OF GOLD

When sixteenth-century Spanish conquistadores *began to stumble onto affluent, culturally sophisticated, and very, very rich civilizations to plunder in the newly discovered Indies, the real and the mythical began to overlap. Soon a constant flow of fortune-seeking European soldiers and adventurers began to arrive into the Americas, seeking ever more treasure to loot!*

Tenochtitlan: Its name coming from the Nahuatl language's *tetl* ("rock") and *nōchtli* ("prickly pear"), the famed city-state of the Aztecs was founded in 1325 on an island in brackish (salty) Lake Texcoco (modern-day Mexico City). Soon the town would outgrow the island itself, with the Mexica building a lake-long dike to keep the lake's salty waters at bay, and a network of artificial smaller islands interconnected by bridges. When Hernán Cortés (1485-1547) and his ragtag band of soldiers reached it in 1519, it had 45 massive buildings (including palaces, temples, two zoos, a botanical garden, and an aquarium), a small army of "municipal" workers keeping its streets and channels clean, and was inhabited by at least as many people as Venice.

Qosqo: Its name meaning "Rock of the owl" in the native Andean languages Quechua and Aymara, this city started out as a mountain fortress, and by the thirteenth century had been taken over and expanded into a sprawling metropolis by the Inca. Surrounded by two artificial rivers, it was divided into four distinct areas, with palaces and temples built from gold-plated, perfectly cut blocks of stone, which naturally dazzled the Spanish who first set foot on it, and subsequently raided its treasures.

Machu-Picchu: Located 50 miles northwest and up of Qosqo, this abandoned palatial estate for the Inca emperor Pachacuti

(1438–1472), and his entourage of 750 *yanconas* ("servants"). Unearthed with great publicity by American explorer Hiram Bingham III (1875-1956), it was mistakenly thought to be the "last refuge" of the Inca for many years, until revealed otherwise by historians and the National Geographic Society in the early 1990's. Remarkably preserved and restored, it has been a UNESCO World Heritage Site since 1983.

Seven Cities of Gold: When Spanish *conquistadores* in Mexico began hearing rumors of rich cities located far up north (possibly originated by natives wanting to get rid of them), they naturally linked those to a popular folk tale of eighth century Portuguese monks who had sailed away from invading Muslims, to found "Seven Cities of Gold" in a faraway land. Setting out to find these golden towns, instead they came upon the much less glamorous Zuni Pueblo agricultural settlements of Hawikuh, Halona, Matsaki, Kiakima, Cíbola, and Kwakina, in modern day New Mexico.

El Dorado: Originally referring to a fabled king of the sophisticated Muisca people (of modern day Colombia) who supposedly bathed while covered in gold dust, the Muisca were indeed skilled craftsmen and goldsmiths whose intricate work with the precious metal caught the imaginations of many in Europe, and generated the golden city of legend. However, early expeditions led by the likes of Gonzalo Jimenez de Quesada (c.1496-1579), Francisco de Orellana (1511-1546), Lope "Wrath of God" de Aguirre (1510-1561), and even Sir Walter Raleigh (c. 1552-1618) proved futile, as did the many that came in the following century, until none other than Prussian explorer Alexander von Humboldt (1769-1859) conclusively disproved the existence of the mythical city and its legendary Parime lake during his Latin American sojourn at the beginning of the nineteenth century.

THE DEVIL YOU KNOW

As Europeans began to spread through the lush wilderness of the New World, they stumbled upon eerie places of native lore that gave them the creeps. Those places bear the devil's name to this day as a warning to us all not to tread lightly around those parts.

Devil's Backbone: Hidden in the Pine Hills Nature Preserve lies this uncanny rock wall, which has been the site of many disturbing sightings in Indiana. Shades State Park keeps hiking trails that lead to the ridge out of official maps, and occasional visitors are discouraged from bringing children and pets to this haunted place.

Devil's Bake Oven: The cave at the base of Tower Rock (a.k.a. Grand Tower), a tall rock island on the Mississippi River, inspired terror in the natives, who warned Europeans about a *manitou* ("evil spirit") dwelling there. Whatever the case, a foundry installed at that spot centuries later became the scene of a family tragedy, when the superintendent's daughter committed suicide by throwing herself from the outcropping, her wailing spirit said to wander the surroundings ever since.

Devil's Den: This boulder-strewn hill said to be the home of a devious, gigantic snake became part of the Gettysburg battle theater in 1863. Sown with the corpses of dead soldiers, visiting tourists continue to report ghost sightings in the area, including a Texas Confederate in a ragged butternut uniform directing visitors towards the Plum Run creek before vanishing.

Devil's Hole: In the equally, charmingly named Death Valley, lies this geothermal pool cavern where many have reportedly disappeared, and the place where notorious psycho-killer Charles Manson

(1934-2017) famously meditated for three days before realizing it was an actual gateway to the underworld!

Devil's Pulpit: The free-standing pillar of stone at the southwest side of Massachusetts's Monument Mountain has a long history of "Lover's Leaps," as in young Mohican maidens using it as a suicide spot, but the curse seems to have been lifted since the fateful meeting there between Nathaniel Hawthorne (1804-1864) and Herman Melville (1819-1891) in 1850.

Devil's Swamp: Located in Thibodaux, Louisiana, the place of the infamous Thibodaux massacre of 1887, in which a still widely debated number of black sugarcane workers and their families where slaughtered, their bodies dumped into the swamp, which still exudes unnatural fumes, some say are the product of chemical waste.

Devil's Tramping Ground: A 20-foot patch of barren ground within a forest located in Chatham Country, said to spook local dogs who dare not trespass its limits, has long been describe as the place where Satan ventures from the underworld to walk in circles, while plotting the downfall of man. Objects placed within this round patch by adventurous campers also seem to disappear overnight, as do the signs leading to the hellish spot.

Devils Lake: Originally known as *mni wakán* ("water spirit") by the Dakota tribes, the second largest body of water in North Dakota is home to many perch, which apparently feed its very own amphibious serpent monster, when not disturbed by the phantom steamboat still traversing its gentle waves.

Devils Tower: While officially named Bear Lodge Butte this Wyoming landmark butte, the product of a primal volcanic lava outburst, was sacred to the Lakota and Cheyenne who thought giant ghost bears prowled around it, leaving claw marks on its walls when attempting to climb it. It certainly came to prominence among UFO aficionados after being centrally featured in the Steven Spielberg (b.1946) film, *Close Encounters of the Third Kind* (1977).

El camino del diablo: Stretching through the Sonoran desert, "The Devil's Highway," or as it is also called, *El camino del muerto* ("The Dead Man's Path") has been littered with the corpses of natives, *conquistadores*, gold prospectors, drug traffickers, and unsuspecting backpackers since ancient times. Still a dirt road after all these years, spectral sightings have been reported in the area by the few who manage to survive it.

Mount Diablo: Originally *Monte del diablo* ("the devil's thicket") made reference to the seeming disappearance of Miwok natives fleeing the Spanish into the brushwood coverting that mountain, which dominates the Diablo Valley in California. Pious men have tried to change its name to "Mount Yahweh" unsuccessfully!

Hill of the Little Devils: Currently referred to as the Spirit Mound of South Dakota, the original Sioux inhabitants of that area called it to the attention of the Lewis and Clark Expedition, claiming devious little creatures with large heads had made it their home and protected it fiercely. However, the expedition party found no trace of such creatures when they climbed it in 1804.

US 491: Running through Colorado, New Mexico, and Utah, this highway used to be designated US 666, "The Number of the Beast," which was changed after pressures from Christians who nicknamed the route "Devil's Highway," after its sheer death rate caused some to believe it cursed.

SOMETHIN' STRANGE IN YOUR NEIGHBORHOOD

Not every spot on the map comes with a "Devil" warning attached. America's most haunted places include:

MANSIONS:

LaLaurie Mansion: This three-story mansion owned by socialite psychopath Delphine LaLaurie (1787-1849) in New Orleans witnessed the many slaves she tortured and murdered over a long period of time, until found out and escaping with her family to France. While the original building was burned down by a mob in 1834, many people walking around the rebuilt manor's corner at night have heard wailing and screaming coming from inside.

Winchester Mystery House: Straight out of some Victorian deranged fantasy novel, the building of this 161-room mansion in San Jose, California, was supervised by Sarah Winchester (1839-1922) herself, heir and widow of the famed rifle manufacturer. Working without any master plan (hence, having stairs leading nowhere, doors revealing bare brick walls, etc.), at the behest of a medium back east, she sought to keep the spirits supposedly hounding her confused and at bay. So confused, in fact, they apparently are still trying to find their way out of this gigantic ghost-trap.

Pittock Mansion: A French-style *château* overlooking Portland, Oregon, it was built by newspaper publisher Henry Pittock (1835-1919) and his wife Georgiana (1845-1918) in 1914. Used as a movie set on various horror and thriller films throughout the 1980s and 1990s, the keepers of the now-public landmark have felt the smell of Georgiana's favorite rose blooms, and seen a portrait of her husband unexpectedly appearing in different rooms around the manor.

HOTELS:

Hotel Monte Vista: Built in 1927, in Flagstaff, Arizona, and not far from Route 66, and long a den of Hollywood stars, as well as a set for *Casablanca* (1942), its guests have reported the appearance of a ghostly bell boy offering room service in the middle of the night, and two murdered women who attempt to asphyxiate male travelers, but it isn't clear which of these three specters managed to scare the daylights out of John Wayne (1907-1977) himself!

Crescent Hotel: America's most haunted hotel was built in 1886 as a lavish spa for the rich and famous, but turned into a cancer clinic in 1937 by quack "doctor" Norman G. Baker (1882-1958), who swindled hundreds of desperate patients with fake cures and injections until exposed and imprisoned. After a lengthy restoration process which returned it to its former glory, the building reopened as a hotel in 2003, but its hallways and rooms continue to be visited by different ghosts, one of which some claimed to be Baker himself.

The Stanley Hotel: It was founded in Estes Park, Colorado, in 1909, by Freelan O. Stanley (1849-1940) and his wife Flora (1847-1939), who apparently never really left the place, as Flora may still be heard playing the piano, her husband showing up in pictures, and children playing in the hallways. And if you're thinking this is a familiar trope from *The Shining* (1980), you'd be absolutely right, as Stephen King (b.1947) did indeed base the Overlook Hotel on this, its real-life counterpart.

INNS:

17Hundred90 Inn & Restaurant: Located in Savannah, Georgia, this beautiful establishment is full of southern charm ... and ghosts. "Anna", who tends to bother guests of room 204 is the best known, while "Thaddeus," the mischievous spirit of a boy leaves red pennies on tables at the restaurant and tavern. A third, unnamed phantom,

sometimes bothers the kitchen staff by tossing pots, pans, and jars around.

The Bourbon Inn: Once the red-brick family home of the L&N Railroad President, and currently an Inn where the ghost of an old woman in turn-of-the-century attire, regularly climbs the stairs of the building. Said apparition is linked to the former nanny of the house, rumored to dabble in the dark arts, who according to legend saw the summoning of an evil spirit backfire and take her life instead.

Lizzie Borden Bed and Breakfast Museum: Equally famed for its top-level hospitality as for its haunted dwellings, New England is also the home of one of history's most notorious axe murderers, Lizzie Borden (1860-1927). Accused, but later acquitted of hacking her father and stepmother to pieces in 1892, Lizzie continued to live at the family home until her death. Converted into a museum, and a bed-and-breakfast, allowing guests to sleep in rooms where all sorts of spectral shenanigans take place every night.

LIGHTHOUSES:

St. Augustine Lighthouse: A popular tourist destination to this day, this Florida beacon witnessed the death of its keeper, who fell while painting its walls, and has been seen at dusk roaming the surroundings. The laughter of three little girls who fell to the ocean and drowned is also heard from time to time by startled visitors.

Point Lookout Light: First lit in 1830, and abandoned in 1966, this lighthouse sitting at the entrance of the Potomac has been subject to serious paranormal investigations since the 1977 sighting of its first ghost, followed by several others, including a spectral old lady looking for the Confederate prison camp graveyard that used to lay nearby, and a Union soldier guarding the steps to a light that is no longer there.

Seguin Light: Lying two miles off the coast of Maine, Seguin Island houses the state's second-oldest lighthouse, and a dark, gruesome past. In the 1850s one of its keepers murdered his wife and killed himself, the repetitive piano tune the depressed woman used to play still haunting the place. Over the years, many keepers also reported the ghost of a girl running up and down the staircase, the disappearance of furniture, and utensils being tossed across the kitchen. Automated in 1985, a warrant officer charged with packing up the furniture claimed to have been visited by a man dressed in oil skins while staying the night. Still a magnet for paranormal investigators everywhere, the lighthouse was finally decommissioned in 2019.

PRISONS:

Eastern State Penitentiary: This 1828-built Philadelphia solitary confinement regime prison had prisoners stuck in stone cells. Though it abandoned the practice in 1913 due to overcrowding, and made allowances for criminal celebrities like Al Capone (1899-1947), after its 1971 shut down, visitors have often described seeing shadows and hearing footsteps and hushed words within the abandoned structure.

Pottawatomie County Jail: The "Squirrel Cage Jail" of Iowa became known for its then-state-of-the-art rotating three-tier cell blocks when it opened in 1885. Jailer reports of strange occurrences began almost immediately, with some of them refusing to sleep there at night. While only four prisoners died behind its bars, none under strange circumstances, apparitions of a former warden and a jailer have come to haunt it since its permanent closure in 1969.

Ohio State Reformatory: Best known as the infamous Mansfield Reformatory, this late-nineteenth-century prison built to resemble a German castle (deemed beneficial for inmates' morale)

over time became an overcrowded, violent, disease-ridden hell-hole. After being closed for good in 1986, its graveyard holding the bodies of the 215 inmates who never left its walls, it became and remains a museum, while also serving as the movie set for the award-winning 1994 prison drama *The Shawshank Redemption*. Unsurprisingly, it is still haunted all over by the spirits of prisoners and staff alike.

ASYLUMS:

Waverly Hills Sanatorium: Founded in 1909, this tuberculosis hospital is said to have witnessed the deaths of 63,000 patients, either from the disease itself, experiments gone wrong, and general mistreatment, it was finally closed in 1961 thanks to antibiotics rendering it useless. People visiting it on "ghost tours" have reported hearing screams and footsteps, seeing a boy named "Timmy" play with a rubber ball, and worst of all, the two spectral nurses of room 502 forever reenacting their suicides.

Trans-Allegheny Lunatic Asylum: Called the Weston State Hospital since opening its doors to patients in 1864, until its forced closure in 1994, this West Virginia facility was made to house 250 patients, but ended up holding ten times that, hundreds of which died there, either from neglect, or while enduring the most base, abusive treatment, which often included deadly electroshock and lobotomy therapies. Said to be the second largest hand-cut sandstone building in the world, the first one being the Kremlin, guided tours of the place now take place, with visitors and staff reporting strange occurrences, including screams coming from the former electroshock room, voices demanding people to leave, and the deranged ghost of a lunatic woman named "Ruth" attacking tourists.

Danvers State Lunatic Asylum: Originally known as the infamous Salem Village, where 19 women were hanged for witchcraft in 1692, the town of Danvers in Massachusetts opened its very own

psychiatric hospital in 1878. Initially housing 500 mentally challenged people, including children, its patients had risen to 2,000 by 1940, most of whom were left completely neglected and alone until forcefully dragged to the operating table for a procedure the place had become famous for: lobotomy! Despite being completely demolished in 2005, and the apartment complex erected in its place burning down two years later, paranormal activity and apparition reports abound in the area to this day; but the asylum is perhaps best remembered as the basis for H.P. Lovecraft's (1890-1937) own Arkham sanatorium (which in turn inspired the Arkham Asylum of the Batman comics).

BONUS FACTS!

- No other sport has more injuries than basketball, sprained ankle being the most common, while knee inflammation causes the most missed games to players.

- Industrial civilization relies mainly on three raw materials: steel, fossil fuel, and rubber.

- As a young man actor Liam Neeson (b.1952) was an amateur boxing champion while working a day job as a forklift driver at the Guinness Brewery.

- A Mexican import, *Phytophthora infestans*, a microorganism that behaves like a fungus, is the culprit behind the potato blight which caused widespread famine in Ireland from 1845 to 1849!

HOPE YOU GUESS MY NAME

As common as bedeviled places, "demon" sightings continue to scare Christian and heathen alike all across America.

Dover Demon: Popular since 1977, the small, humanoid creature with long fingers and a bulging head seen by three to four teenagers in Dover, a quiet, farm-dotted town at the heart of Massachusetts, presents striking similarities to the "little people" of Native American lore, but was dubbed the "Dover Demon" by American social worker and "cryptozoologist" Loren Coleman (b.1947), possibly influenced by the mythical "devil on horseback" spotted in the area a century earlier. According to an October 29, 2006, Boston Globe article, main witness William Bartlett (b.1960) still stands by what he saw.

Jersey Devil: From the Pine Barrens of New Jersey (famed among Native Americans as the abode of a dragon and later as a refuge for outcasts) rose this creature, akin to the Medieval England *wyvern* (a sort of bipedal dragon), said to be atop the Leeds family (of Leeds Point) crest. The family's esoteric almanac publishing business seems to have drawn criticism from local Quakers, leaving to them being labeled as "demons" by the populace. Said to be the cursed offspring of the family patriarch, it was still called the "Leeds Devil" at the turn of the century. Sporting a goat's head, bat wings, horns, tiny clawed hands, cloven hooves for feet, and a forked tail, its reported sightings came to a head in 1909, though it continues a popular folk legend to this day.

Pennsylvania Devil: At the height of the Jersey Devil's popularity, a similar monster was seen around the Springvale, Pennsylvania, woodlands. The wild, ferocious beast with powerful hind legs similar to those of a kangaroo, and quills like a porcupine, reportedly killed

a bloodhound and other farm animals in the area before vanishing off the face of the Earth on October, 1910.

Lone Pine Mountain Devil: Claimed by some to be a West Coast relative of the Jersey Devil, while others identify it with an extant species of prehistoric, flightless bird of prey, the purported "nineteenth century reports" of the creature marauding the California and Nevada mountains unfortunately lack credibility, and are likely part of an internet hoax from the early 2000s; which explains the subsequent rise in sightings, and supposed connections to people disappearing in the area.

Red-Whiskered Devil: Turn-of-the-century Brooklyn had its own demons. Described by witnesses as "a monster all covered in hair, with flaring red whiskers, and a Satanic howl" (*Alexandria Gazette*, No.82, April 6, 1891). A night train dispatcher by the name of William Bell, declared to have unsuccessfully chased down the creature armed with a monkey wrench, but it vanished from sight. While considered a hoax in its own day, the residents of Bath Beach and Gravesend Beach took to never leaving their homes unarmed in the event of further incursions by this particular devil.

Devil Monkeys: From Tennessee to Arizona, these four-foot-tall (on average), hairy, three toed, fanged baboon-like primates have been terrorizing Americans since first spotted in 1934. Unlike other "devils," they often run in packs, and have recently been spotted in places as far apart as Louisiana and Illinois, where reportedly one of these creatures viciously attacked a Chicago family dog.

Mothman: Five gravediggers working at the Clendenin (West Virginia) cemetery in 1966, claimed to have been accosted by a large flying man of gray skin and glowing red eyes, with similar "attacks" taking place in the days that followed. Author John Keel (1930-2009)

would later popularize the idea that these events were somehow connected to the 1967 collapse of the Silver Bridge in his book, *The Mothman Prophecies* (1975), which no doubt influenced the Russian ufologists who decades later would link similar sightings in Moscow to the apartment bombings of 1999.

Pope Lick Monster: According to the urban legend, a part-man, part-goat cryptid of unknown origin continues to lure people to their deaths at the Norfolk Southern Railway trestle bridge over Pope Lick Creek. Some of the reported deaths correspond to "monster-hunters" and "legend-trippers" who were either hit by incoming trains, or lost their grip of the side of the trestle (thanks to the passing train vibrations), plunging into the creek and drowning.

Pukwidgie: Not unlike the "Dover Demon," this mischievous, shape-shifting grey-skinned creature of short stature and bulging head, known as *Puck-wudj-ininee* ("little wild man that vanishes in the woods") by the Delaware and Wampanoag nations is indeed one of the many incarnations of Native American "little people" folklore. Encounters with the creatures still common, they've been immortalized by modern literature in the *The Song of Hiawatha* (1855) and the *Harry Potter* series.

Loveland Frogmen: As reported by several eye-witnesses in 1902 South Carolina, a humanoid frog was seen on the banks of the Colonial Lake pond in Charleston. After making some strange sounds, the amphibian went back into the water, never to be seen again, until sightings of similar frogmen in the town of Loveland began to surface again in the mid-1950s. Two decades later, the 1972 Loveland Police report of an encounter and shooting of a "frogman" turned out to be a hoax, the monster revealed to be an overgrown tail-less iguana by one of the now-retired officers in 2016.

Wendigo: An evil spirit among the Algonquian and other nations of North America, more than a simple parable or cautionary tale against greed and gluttony, the cannibalistic monster known as Wendigo also lends its name to a form of very real psychosis in which seemingly normal men are consumed by a craving for human flesh. Said bouts of cannibalism remained prevalent among the Algonquian until the early twentieth century, but its legend lives on in modern horror fiction and comic-books.

Chupacabra: Hailing from 1995 Puerto Rico, this creature which has alternatively been held to be an alien, a demon, or a science experiment gone wrong, the "goat-sucker" (named as such for preferring to devour the internal organs of its prey) took root in the imagination of people all over the world, with sightings reported throughout the late 1990s and early 2000s in the US, Russia, the Philippines, and South America. Its varying physical appearance depending where its attacks took place mark it as the astonishing case of an urban legend turned collective hysteria by the rise of the internet!

BONUS FACTS!

- The NBA logo silhouette is based on former Los Angeles Lakers all-star Jerry West (b.1938).

- The Buffalo Sabres are the only ice hockey team to have ever killed an animal (bat) during a hockey game in 1974!

- Muhammad Ali (1942-2016) once went without sex for two months in order to win a fight.

HARRY AND
THE HENDERSONS

Across cultures and continents, the presence of strong, hairy, and occasionally smelly hominids, popularly called "ape-men," have kept people everywhere on their toes since the dawn of time; yet, perhaps nowhere but in America have they taken such hold of human curiosity and imagination.

Yeti: While reports of a giant hairy creature in the Himalayas has been surfacing since the early nineteenth century, the mythical giant ape was first christened "The Wild Man of the Snows," in an attempt to translate Tibetan *metoh-kangmi* (*metoh* meaning "man-bear," while *kangmi* translates as "snowman") by British explorer Lieutenant-Colonel Charles Howard-Bury (1881-1963) in 1921, after finding unusually large footprints in the snow, while on a military reconnaissance expedition to Mount Everest; the "Abominable Snowman" was a later journalistic flourish or mistranslation, which quickly replicated in the news media of the day. Further Everest expeditions, including Edmund Hillary's (1919-2008) would uncover more footprints, and analyze feces in the snow, but no incontestable evidence. In particular a "Yeti scalp" kept in a local shrine proved to be neither a scalp, nor belonging to any sort of hominid creature. Twenty-first century Russian, Indian, and Chinese expeditions have yielded no conclusive results either.

Sasquatch: Colloquially referred to as "Bigfoot," the gigantic, hairy hominid of Washington and Oregon has proven as elusive as its Himalayan counterpart. Oral folk legends of the Lummi nation which describe a creature called *Ts'emekwes* have been recorded since the mid-nineteenth century, but it wasn't until 1940 that the term "Sasquatch" was coined from the native *sásq'ets* ("wild man"), while "Bigfoot" came to be used by newspapers by the end of the 1950s, when logger Ray Wallace (1918-2002) pranked the whole nation with a trail of fake footprints and other "evidence" (as revealed by his son

after his passing). Regardless, the creature became a pop-culture icon with the 1967 Patterson–Gimlin film lending it a degree of credibility, as no conclusive proof against the film's authenticity has ever been produced. It has also been widely reported that the FBI has had a file on the creature since 1976, but it only concerns a hair study, which concluded the analyzed samples belonged to a deer.

Wild Man: Possibly related to Silvanus, the Roman god of forests, "wildmen" covered in hair and living in the woods were a regular fixture of Medieval European folklore, much like their Asian and North American counterparts. It's no wonder then, that turn-of-the-century Bigfoot sightings in Idaho, Georgia, and Arkansas the creatures were described using that moniker, until their Pacific Northwest cousin took hold of the public's imagination.

Mogollon Monster: Seen as far back as 1903, the seven-foot-tall, alternatively white, gray, black, or red haired (depending on the account) hominid perfectly hiding within the Ponderosa forests of Arizona's Mogollon Rim, if it weren't for its strong smell, a common feature among local Bigfoot types. While commonly dismissed as a local folk legend, sightings of the creature striding across Fort Apache Indian Reservation land, and even peeking through home windows, have been reported as recently as 2006.

Fouke Monster: Though originally seen in the early 1950s, Arkansas's "Boggy Creek Monster" came to national prominence in 1971, after it reportedly attacked a local family. Said to be seven feet tall, dark haired, with big red eyes, and long arms, with a bounty on its head, its footprints and claw marks were said to be found around the mangled livestock it left in its wake. Forever immortalized by the 1973 "docudrama" *The Legend of Boggy Creek* and its sequels, sightings became more sporadic as public interest eventually waned.

Momo: The "Missouri Bigfoot" first came to prominence in the summer of 1972, with residents reporting sightings of a huge, shaggy black haired ape with a pungent smell, prowling around the outskirts of Louisiana. Two children told their parents it either attacked or defended itself form the family dog, which died after the incident. Two local women even accused the monster of stealing their picnic's peanut butter sandwiches, but sightings ended as winter came, and "Momo," as it came to be called, disappeared from the public eye for good.

Knobby: Named after Carpenter's Knob, North Carolina, where it was first seen, this ten feet tall giant hominid with a reportedly dark coat of hair and a grayish beard (though more recent accounts describe it as blonde) has been startling residents of Cleveland County since 1979, though according to the sheriff's office sightings are far less common these days. It is thought to be related to the *Tsul 'Kalu* of Cherokee lore.

Gugwe: Uncharacteristically aggressive and snout-faced, with an elongated head, this gorilla-styled cryptid, said to roam the northeastern US/Canada border woodlands, is closely related to the *Kukwe* man-eating ogre from Mi'kmaq folklore. Its only known modern sighting happened in 2005 when visitors took a panoramic photo at Quebec's beautiful *Parc régional des Sept-Chutes*, later discovering the blurry visage of the creature peeking from nearby thicket bush!

Honey Island Swamp Monster: First spotted in 1963 Louisiana, this smelly, seven-foot-tall, gray-haired hominid with big yellow eyes is said to have a distinctly webbed feet, possibly an adaptation to the swamp environment, though others have theorized it may be the divergent offspring of an escaped circus primate and alligator (sigh). To this day it is blamed for the deaths of livestock grazing near the swamp.

THE RETURN OF
⚬⚭⚬ SWAMPSQUATCH ⚬⚭⚬

Reports of an extant hominid dwelling in the Florida Everglades began to surface as early as 1957, but few have taken them as seriously as Dave Shealy (b.1963), founder of the Skunk Ape Research Headquarters, who has dedicated his life to researching the slippery and foul-smelling cryptid.

When and where were you born?

I was born on September 28, 1963 in Miami, FL.

What was your childhood like?

My childhood was wild and untamed, and I grew up in the heart of the Everglades.

When did you first see the creature known as the Skunk Ape?

When I was ten years old.

What were your first impressions of the creature back then?

It had just confirmed what the locals had been telling us about as children.

What prompted you to become the World's foremost Skunk Ape expert in the world?

An interest in my childhood findings evolved into what I do today.

Would you credit any other explorers, or zoologists as influential or inspiring you in this pursuit?

A gentleman by the name of Peter C. Byrne (b.1925) who is a Bigfoot

researcher, as well as J. Richard Greenwell (1942-2005) who studied the Bigfoot of China.

What research methodology did you use, and what did you uncover?

The research methods that I use to this day stem from my native Gladesmen traditions. I have plaster casts, photographs and videos of footprints as well as bedding areas found in the areas surrounding here. I was also able to estimate the population due to this, which would be seven or nine hominids residing within the southern Everglades.

Did you conduct any research on mythical or historical accounts of its existence? It is connected to the *Esti Capcaki* ("tall man") of Seminole lore?

I have spent years living and spending my time with the Seminole Indians and they have provided me with much useful mythical and historical information, as well as stories linking it to the *Esti Capcaki*.

How many more times have you come across the creature since your first sighting?

I have came across this creature a total of four times.

Have you ever managed to trap and capture one, physically or on camera?

I have not trapped or captured a Skunk Ape physically, but I have caught the creature on still film once as well as video another.

Could you make an accurate description, based on your latest findings?

A six to seven foot tall, hair-covered creature with four toes.

Is it intelligent or feral? To what degree?

Skunk Apes are relatively feral with primal tendencies towards family and food.

Is it a lone predator, or rather gregarious like modern primates and humans?

The majority of sightings encountered, they encounter the creature alone. It's very rare to come across more than one.

Is it in any way related to other extant hominids in America? What would you say makes it distinctive?

The distinctions made would be that the Skunk Ape has four toes, and can climb trees. Although, this creature looks identical to a Bigfoot.

How long has it be around?

Stories from the native Indians within the Everglades of a Skunk Ape or Bigfoot-like creature go back 300 years.

Why do you think it made Florida its home as opposed to colder locations, like the Pacific Northwest?

Bigfoot/Skunk Ape like creatures are found in various locations all over the globe, and in each location they seem to vary slightly. Typically they are always remote, meaning the Everglades would be a perfect location for a hominid as elusive as the Skunk Ape.

What would you say its eating habits and current geographical range are?

The creatures are omnivores, and Skunk Apes inhabit the southern states from Florida, onward up to Mississippi and Louisiana.

Is its smell as pungent as the name implies? If so, why you think that is the case? Could you describe it?

The name "Skunk Ape" describes the creature fittingly. They give off an odor that can be smelled for a very wide range, and we don't have skunks within the swamps this far south.

Is the Skunk Ape facing any immediate environmental or climate change threats to its existence?

Agriculture and development could potentially pose some sort of risk to the population.

Are you conducting any conservation efforts in addition to your research?

By being within the largest interconnected wild land environment east of the Mississippi, we are not so much worried about the conservation, but the awareness of such a creature.

When did you establish the Skunk Ape Headquarters?

Skunk Ape HQ started as a small building on property since I was about ten years old, as a small facility. I went public with the information that I'd collected in 1997.

What are the organization's current goals, and who do you currently collaborate with?

To bring awareness of the Everglades Skunk Ape and the surrounding ecosystems to the public, and we have collaborated with various film and media outlets for major news networks around the world.

Where can we currently find it? Are visitors allowed?

The number one hotspot to look for a Skunk Ape is the Big Cypress National Preserve. Visitors are allowed within designated park areas, so please refer to the NPS website for such information.

Note from the Author:

SKUNK APE RESEARCH HEADQUARTERS

40904 Tamiami Trail East, Ochopee, FL on the Trail Lakes Campground (Highway 41) property.

(239) 695-2275

everglardesadventuretours@gmail.com

BONUS FACTS!

- Tuchman's Law, as written by historian Barbara Tuchman (1912-1989), establishes that "The fact of being reported multiplies the apparent extent of any deplorable development by five to tenfold," which in layman's terms means nothing is as bad as it seems on the news.

- *Mary Poppins* creator P.L. Travers (1899-1996) hated the Disney musical film adaptation so much, that in her last will and testament she stipulated that only British writers, and no one from the Disney production, could ever be hired for future adaptations.

- Virgil Griffith (b.1983) created public database WikiScanner, which revealed FBI computers had been used to edit the FBI articles on Wikipedia.

SIGHTSQUATCH

Washington, California, Florida, Ohio, Illinois, Oregon, Texas, Michigan, Missouri, and Georgia are currently the states with the highest numbers of alleged Bigfoot sightings. In addition to being the state with the most sightings by a wide margin, Washington also passed legislation to protect the creature in 1969!

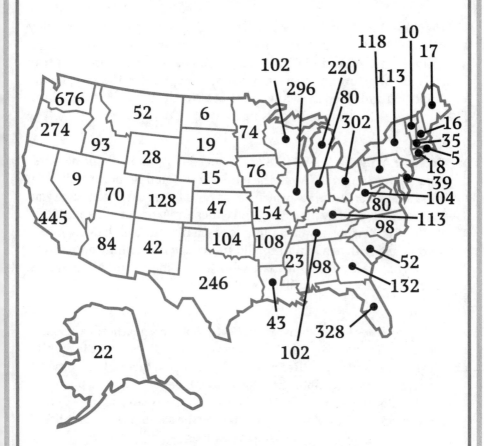

676
274
52
6
93
74
102
296
118
10
17
220
113
80
302
16
35
5
28
19
15
76
9
70
128
47
154
18
39
104
80
113
445
84
42
104
108
98
52
246
23
98
132
43
328
22
102

Hawaii is the only state of the US with no reported Bigfoot sightings—unless you count the Menehune, which aren't very big.

YOUTH IN REVOLT

A popular explanation for Bigfoot seems to be the most obvious too: homeless people making the forests and swamps of America their refuge. Whatever the case, accounts of "feral children" who were either abandoned or ran away from the trauma of abuse continue to be well documented.

Peter the Wild Boy (c.1713-1785): Found by a party of hunters led by George I of Great Britain (1660-1727) in the woods near Hamelin (Hanover, Germany) in 1725, this mentally handicapped boy allegedly survived in the forest for a year. Brought to England by the king, he was supported and cared for while living at a Northchurch, Hertfordshire farm until passing away at an old age.

Victor of Aveyron (c.1788-1828): Neglected by his alcoholic parents, young Victor ran off to live in the wilderness, fending for himself until found at age 12. Running away from several foster care homes, he was eventually adopted by physician and educator Jean Marc Gaspard Itard (1774-1838) who, despite failing to teach him the sign language he pioneered with deaf children, did succeeded in instilling empathy towards others in the young man, who died from pneumonia at age 40, still under Itard's care.

Marcos Rodríguez Pantoja (b.1946): Sold to a goatherder at age seven, he lived alone with the Sierra Morena wolves after the man's death for many years. "Rescued" at 19, he was returned to a human society he found disappointing, and though being subject to plenty of media attention—including the 2010 *Entrelobos* feature film—in his native Spain, the old man still longs for the solitary mountain life among the wolves.

Marina Chapman (b.1950): Living among capuchin monkeys in

the Colombian jungle from a young age, she was kidnapped by hunters as a teenager, and sold into prostitution until rescued by a family. Traveling to the UK as a nanny, in 2013 she published her autobiography *The Girl With No Name*, which was subject to much speculation, and a National Geographic documentary that year.

Saturday Mthiyane (1982- 2005): In 1987, a five-year-old boy was found on a Sunday by Sundumbili (South Africa) residents while roaming with monkeys and scavenging fruit. Put in the care of the Ethel Mthiyane Special School for the disabled, by the time he died in a fire in 2005, he still behaved in an ape-like way and refused to socialize.

John Ssebunya: (b.1985): Roughly four to five years old when found by villagers in 1991, this Ugandan boy had fled to the jungle when his father murdered his mother and lived with the vervet monkeys which protected him. Hairy all over, with long, curled nails, and a tapeworm-ridden tummy, little John was taken to the Kamuzinda Christian Orphanage, which did a remarkable job helping him readjust to life among humans.

Miguel Ángel Huiliqueo (1989-2011): Known as the niño de los perros ("dogs' boy") in Chile, he was abandoned at the age of five by his parents, and fled a child care home to live with a pack of stray dogs in a cave overlooking the ocean, where he was found in 2001. Five years later, however, he had returned to live on the streets of Temuco, always accompanied by his dogs, where he passed due to complications related to drug abuse and HIV at age 22.

Ivan Mishukov (b.1992): A young runaway from a fractured home, this Russian boy is said to have lived among stray dogs for two years, eventually becoming their pack leader! Managing to evade capture by the police three times, he was eventually caught at age six, and remains a local celebrity.

LOCH'D AND LOADED

Never thoroughly disproved, cryptozoology's poster-boy—or rather, poster-monster—Nessie, the Loch Ness Monster of Scotland, has reared its head in historical record since the sixth century. Still being seen wallowing through its lake deep, dark waters, its very existence still a matter of debate, many theories abound as to what it is, or may have been.

1. The earliest mention of Nessie can be found in a sixth-century hagiography of Saint Columba (521-597), the Irish evangelist who brought the Gospel to Scotland. The account in the pages of *Vita Columbae* states that the monster had already killed a Pict swimming in Loch Ness, so the saint sent one of his 12 disciples into the lake as bait, to lure the monster out. Just as the creature was about to kill this follower, Columba ordered Nessie back into the waters of the lake, from which it never returned until much, much later ...

2. Two unconfirmed accounts from the late nineteenth century have surfaced, revealing the famous cryptid did show itself before the explosion of its popularity in the 1930s. The first, attributed to a "D. McKenzie" describes a "log" wriggling about the lake before vanishing from sight in 1871. The second, an 1888 story about a mason known as Alexander MacDonald, who clearly saw a creature he compared to a salamander.

3. In 1933, a George Spicer and his wife pulled over their car when they saw a 25-foot-long and four-foot-high monster crossing the road near Loch Ness, as reported by the *Inverness Courier*, on August 4. The article became a local sensation, with people pouring over to the lake in hopes of finding the mythical animal, among which was a photographer by the name of Hugh Gray, who made a quick buck selling a blurry photo of an otter rolling backwards to several newspapers desperate for a scoop.

4. Not unlike the Spicers, a veterinary student named by the papers as "Arthur Grant" almost hit the monster with his motorcycle in 1934, as it again tried to cross the road unseen. Mr. Grant drew a sketch of a creature which looks like a cross between a seal and a plesiosaur (skeptics would, of course, link otter and seal together, dismissing the man's story entirely), but no Nessie depiction caused a greater sensation than the photograph taken by London gynecologist Dr. Robert Kenneth Wilson (1899-1969) that year. Latter dubbed "the surgeon's photograph," as to lend it credibility, it showed the unmistakable black silhouette of the head and long neck of a plesiosaur, a species thought extinct for 65 million years.

5. Reproduced and analyzed thousands of times in the following decades, by 1993 it had been revealed an elaborate hoax by film maker Marmaduke Wetherell (1883-1939), who took the photo (actually, it was two of them), Christian Spurling (1904-1993), who made the small scale motorized floating dinosaur, and Wilson who acted as front man for the whole affair.

6. A real 1938 letter which surfaced in 2010 at the National Archives of Scotland reveals the Inverness County Police Chief Constable believed the existence of the monster to be beyond doubt and sought to protect it from recently arrived monster-hunters, and gonzo film makers.

7. Not counting obvious publicity stunts by self-styles magician Anthony "Doc" Shiels (b.1938), from the late 1950s to the late 1970s, with the surging popularity of underwater exploration bringing the work of men like Jacques Cousteau (1910-1997) to the forefront, many university funded research parties from the UK and abroad took to scanning the lake using sonar technology, all of which yielded inconclusive results.

8. Outstanding yet still unexplained sightings include the Timothy Dinsdale (1924-1987) 1960 filming of a moving hump, the Gordon Holmes (b.1952) 2007 videotape of a "jet black thing, about 14 meters long, moving fairly fast in the water," and the 2020 Eoin O'Faodhagain (b.1965) webcam footage of something moving and splashing about in the lake.

9. In 1962, the Loch Ness Investigation Bureau (LNIB) was founded in the UK by BBC writer Norman Collins (1907-1982), naturalist R. S. R. Fitter (1913-2005) , MP David James (1919-1986), and conservationist Peter Scott (1909-1989). Aiming to study the Loch and test the veracity of the monster sightings, the volunteer organization reported over 1,000 members (half of them international) at the height of its fame, but ended up being disbanded a decade after its creation.

10. On September 5, 2019, the University of Otago (New Zealand) Gemmell Lab, which specializes in genetics, revealed the results of the research it had conducted in the Loch. Finding no genetic trace of large, modern animals like catfish, sturgeons, or Greenland sharks, nor any prehistoric animals like the famed plesiosaur, but plenty of human, dog, sheep, cattle, deer, badger, rabbit, bird, and European eel DNA, Nessie was concluded to be nothing but an oversized member of the latter species, which certainly made none of its fans happy!

BONUS FACT!

- Published by Selma Engler (1899-1972), "Die BIF" was the world's first lesbian magazine, exclusively made by women between 1925 and 1927.

LAKE PLACID

Nessie lovers do not despair! Your beloved Loch Ness Monster may be a gigantic eel but the world is still full of unexplained and legendary lake monsters just waiting to be captured on camera, the most notorious of which are listed below.

NORTH AMERICA

Cressie | Species: Eel | Lake: Crescent | Country: Canada

Gaasyendietha | Species: Dragon | Lake: Ontario | Country: Canada

Igopogo | Species: Mammal | Lake: Simcoe | Country: Canada

Manipogo | Species: Serpent | Lake: Manitoba | Country: Canada

Memphrémagog | Species: Plesiosaur | Lake: Memphré | Country: Canada

Mishipeshu | Species: Chimera | Lake: Superior | Country: Canada

Mugwump | Species: Serpent | Lake: Temiskaming | Country: Canada

Mussie | Species: Plesiosaur | Lake: Muskrat | Country: Canada

Ogopogo | Species: Serpent | Lake: Okanagan | Country: Canada

Winnipogo | Species: Serpent | Lake: Winnipegosis | Country: Canada

Alkali Lake Monster | Species: Alligator | Lake: Alkali | Country: US

Bear Lake Monster | Species: Serpent/Alligator | Lake: Bear | Country: US

Beast of Busco | Species: Turtle | Lake: Fulks | Country: US

Bessie | Species: Plesiosaur | Lake: Erie | Country: US

Bozho | Species: Serpent | Lake: Mendota | Country: US

Blue Dilly | Species: Plesiosaur | Lake: Dillon | Country: US

Champ | Species: Plesiosaur | Lake: Champlain | Country: US

Flessie | Species: Eel | Lake: Flathead | Country: US

Hamlet | Species: Plesiosaur | Lake: Elsinore | Country: US

Herry | Species: Chimera | Lake: Herrington | Country: US

Illie | Species: Fish | Lake: Iliamna | Country: US

Lake Chelan Monster | Species: Dragon | Lake: Chelan | Country: US

Man-i-too | Species: Serpent | Lake: Manitou | Country: US

Muck Monster | Species: Unknown | Lake: Worth | Country: US

Normie | Species: Plesiosaur | Lake: Norman | Country: US

North Shore Monster | Species: Chimera | Lake: Great Salt Lake | Country: US

Obokoji | Species: Plesiosaur | Lake: Obokoji | Country: US

Oklahoma Octopus | Species: Cephalopod | Lake: Thunderbird | Country: US

Pepie | Species: Serpent | Lake: Pepin | Country: US

Poco | Species: Plesiosaur | Lake: Pocomoonshine | Country: US

Rocky | Species: | Lake: Rock Lake | Country: US

Sharlie | Species: Serpent | Lake: Payette | Country: US

Smetty | Species: Plesiosaur | Lake: De Smet | Country: US

Skin Fin | Species: Plesiosaur | Lake: Powell | Country: US

Tarpie | Species: Plesiosaur | Lake: Tarpon | Country: US

Tessie | Species: Plesiosaur | Lake: Tahoe | Country: US

Teedy | Species: Unknown | Lake: Teedyuskung | Country: US

SOUTH AMERICA

El Cuero | Species: Stingray | Lake: Lácar | Country: Argentina

Nahuelito | Species: Serpent | Lake: Nahuel Huapi | Country: Argentina

Guallipén | Species: Chimera | Lake: Calafquén | Country: Argentina

Diablo Ballena | Species: Fish | Lake: Tota | Country: Colombia

Laguna Arenal Monster | Species: Plesiosaur | Lake: Arenal | Country: Costa Rica

EUROPE

Lagarfljótsormur | Species: Slug | Lake: Lagarfljót | Country: Iceland

Muckie | Species: Plesiosaur | Lake: Muckross | Country: Ireland

Lariosauro | Species: Reptile | Lake: Como | Country: Italy

Seljordsormen | Species: Serpent | Lake: Seljordsvatnet | Country: Norway

Brosnya | Species: Dragon | Lake: Brosno | Country: Russia

Gryttie | Species: Serpent | Lake: Gryttjen | Country: Sweden

Storsjöodjuret | Species: Serpent | Lake: Storsjön | Country: Sweden

Eachy | Species: Humanoid serpent | Lake: Bassenthwaite | Country: UK

Morag | Species: Plesiosaur | Lake: Morar | Country: UK

Muc-sheilche | Species: Eel | Lake: Maree | Country: UK

AFRICA

Irizima | Species: Chimera | Lake: Edward | Country: Democratic Republic of Congo

Lukwata | Species: Eel | Lake: Victoria | Country: Uganda

Makele-mbembe | Species: Brontosaurus | Lake: Makele | Country: Republic of Congo

Nyami Nyami | Species: Serpent | Lake: Kariba | Country: Zimbabwe

ASIA

Lake Tianchi Monster | Species: Plesiosaur | Lake: Tianchi | Country: China

Issie | Species: Plesiosaur | Lake: Ikeda | Country: Japan

Kussie | Species: Plesiosaur | Lake: Kussharo | Country: Japan

Seri Gumum | Species: Serpent | Lake: Tasik Chini | Country: Malaysia

Phaya Naga | Species: Serpent | Lake: Bueng Khong Long | Country: Thailand

AUSTRALIA

Bunyip | Species: Unknown | Lake: Modewarre | Country: Australia

BONUS FACT!

- One of the largest fossil fuel producers in the world, the United Arab Emirates (UAE) launched its first space probe mission to Mars on July 19, 2020.

CHARIOTS OF THE GODS?

Not every "monster" comes from Earth. Historical evidence of encounters with strange visitors from other planets is overwhelming and well worth a look.

Prehistory: Before the advent of the written word, cave paintings reveal astonishing alien-human contact. Paleolithic depictions of space-age helmet-hearing humanoids found at Valcamonica (Italy) seem to support this hypothesis, alongside Aboriginal art featuring strange, doe-eyed, bald-headed humanoids found in Kimberley (Australia), while according to a Russian independent researcher by the name of Vladimir Tyurin-Avinsky, the famous 5,000 year old Ural pictograms reveal complex organic chemistry structures beyond the grasp of the area's Finno-Ugric peoples. More recently, Robert K. G. Temple (b.1945), author of *The Sirius Mystery* (1976) found that the Dogon people living in Mali's central plateau, seem to have preserved 7,000 year old knowledge of the faint white dwarf companion of Sirius A, Sirius B, invisible to the naked eye. A knowledge, he insists shared with ancient Egyptians and Sumerians.

India: In classic Hindu, Sanskrit, Ayyavazhi, and Jain epics, mythological flying palaces called *vimāna* are used by the gods and their avatars to travel from place to place, which has been speculated to refer to spacecraft, particularly by Pandit Subbaraya Shastry (1866–1940) in his book *Vaimānika Śāstra*, as revealed to the author by the semi-legendary Maharishi Bhadadwaja, and published posthumously in 1959.

Israel: The ancient Hebrew *Tanakh*, the Old Testament of the Christian Bible, describes a race of giants, called Nephilim, said to be the offspring of angels and human women before the Deluge, according to the *Bereshit* (Genesis).

Considered apocryphal by most Jews and Christian denominations (including the Catholic and Orthodox churches), and canonical by Ethiopian Jews and Orthodox Christians, *The Book of Enoch*, offers supplemental information to the Genesis account of the Nephilim, including the fall of the Watchers, the angels who fathered this race of giants. Patriarch Enoch himself is said to have been taken to the heavens by archangel Uriel, his journey including precise descriptions of the movement of the sun, the moon, and the stars, and their application to a calendar.

The Bible's second book of Kings tells the story of prophet Elijah being taken to the heavens while walking alongside his disciple Elisha: "... they still went on, and talked, that, behold, there appeared a chariot of fire, and horses of fire, and parted them both asunder; and Elijah went up by a whirlwind into heaven." (2 Kings 2:11 KJV)

Also part of biblical canon, the *Book of Ezekiel*, with its description of a huge cloud of fire surrounded by light, piloted by four winged humanoid creatures followed by mechanical "wheels within wheels" deserves special mention, if only because former skeptic, NASA chief engineer Josef F. Blumrich (1913-2002) used it to hypothesize a real, working spacecraft, powered by the "Omnidirectional Wheel" he patented in 1974, the year he published the seminal book *The Spaceships of Ezekiel*.

Peru: While it was traditionally thought civilizations could only rise from fertile, richly irrigated plains, one region of the world, the steep Andean highlands of modern day Peru, defied all odds giving birth to many long-lasting cultures. One of these cultures, the Parcas are known for both artificially deforming the skulls of children, seeking to emulate their "gods," and for possibly drawing gigantic geoglyphs, now called the Nazca Lines, which depict animals, plants, and abstract patterns only visible from the sky above (in fact, first seen by modern man in the twentieth century!), which have been theorized to be a cosmic map for visitors from above!

Rome: Several reputed Roman statesmen, historians, lawyers, and political philosophers, wrote accounts of visitors from other worlds, including Marcus Tullius Cicero (106-43BC), who stated that "… deities have appeared in forms so visible that they have compelled everyone who is not senseless or hardened to impiety to confess the presence of the gods"; Titus Livius' (c.64BC –17AD) story of two Roman consuls visited upon by "a man of greater than human stature"; and Pliny the Elder's (23-79AD), Ariminium (modern day Rimini) sighting of a blaze in the sky and "three moons" becoming visible one day at night time, which was confirmed by Lucius Cassius Dio (c.155-235AD).

Renaissance: The German city of Nuremberg, and the Swiss city of Basel both experienced unexplained celestial phenomena in 1561 and 1566 respectively. Nuremberg residents were treated to what they described as a battle between a black triangular UFO, and many smaller spherical and cylindrical ones. The even above Basel involved many spherical UFOs seemingly coming out of the Sun!

80 years later, Massachusetts Bay Colony founder John Winthrop (c.1587-1649) reported two people rowing a boat on the Muddy River saw a darting ball of light, a sight echoed by other residents of the area.

Turn of the century: Between 1860 and 1913, a surge of close encounters with what was then deemed as "mystery airships" was reported across American newspapers. These include sightings of UFOs, as well as their occupants, described as humans of odd appearance and mannerisms, wearing equally strange garments. Notably, a large (200 ft.) object emanating a bluish light with three to four red glowing balls in tow, was seen in the night sky above Wilmington, Delaware, in 1860; an 1868 report—by none other than Charles Fort (1874-1932)—of an airship resembling a giant, shining bird landing in Copiapó, Chile; the 1897 burial of a crashed and burnt UFO pilot found

by local herdsmen in Aurora, Texas; Future US Navy Admiral, Lieutenant Frank Herman Schofield (1869-1942) seeing what he described as three soaring bright red "meteors" (one egg shaped and the other two round) from aboard the USS Supply in 1904; and the 1909 Otago (New Zealand) incident of strange lights witnessed in the sky, an sight echoed months later above Providence, Rhode Island.

BONUS FACTS!

- Originally intended as a Jean-Claude Van Damme (b.1960) video game, the original *Mortal Kombat* (1992) had to be changed to a fantasy fighting game when the deal fell through.

- NBA players run up to four miles during a game, burning 760 calories during a 48-minute game on average.

- In American comic books, Archie is a red-headed teenager, while in UK comics the name refers to a red-colored automaton!

- Tungsten carbide is the compound used to make the ball at the tip of ballpoint pens. It is ten times harder than steel.

- The International Academy of Sciences San Marino uses Esperanto as its official language.

- The co-founder of Atari Inc., Nolan Bushnell (b.1943), also founded the Chuck E. Cheese chain.

THE SPACESHIPS OF EZEKIEL

Founded in 1956 by inventor Thomas T. Brown (1905-1985), the National Investigations Committee On Aerial Phenomena (NICAP) catalogued every type of normally seen UFO until the organization's demise in 1980:

Flat: Includes circular, coin-shaped, ellipse-shaped, and lenticular objects.

Domed: The "flying saucer" of standard science fiction

Saturn disk: With a ring protruding from its center, this one looks like two domed disks glued together, and may be circular or oval-shaped.

Hemispherical: Comes in three "flavors," "Parachute" (domed top), "Mushroom" (domed top, extended bottom), and "Winged" (oval with deeper bottom than top).

Spherical: Perfectly round flying globes, though some may have a flattened section, and some may even have an additional "cockpit" at the top.

Elliptical: These are shaped like footballs or eggs, with the occasional non-protruding waist-band or "belt" slicing it in half.

Geometrical: Includes triangular, pyramidal, tetrahedral, cubical, pear and tear drop shaped.

Cylindrical: Tip-less rocket tubes, sometimes with reported portholes.

Light: Resembling shining stars or planets, as seen by the ancients.

Currently active civilian UFO organizations in the US include the Active Center for the Study of Extraterrestrial Intelligence (CSETI), the Center for UFO Studies (CUFOS or JAHCUFOS), the International UFO Congress (IUFOC), the Mutual UFO Network (MUFON), and the National UFO Reporting Center (NUFORC).

BONUS FACTS!

- On July 25, 2020, Norwegian Elvis impersonator Kjell Henning Bjornestad (b.1968) broke the world Elvis Presley (1935-1977) songs singing record at 50 hours, 50 minutes, and 50 seconds of continued performance.

- COINTELPRO (Counter Intelligence Program) was an illegal operation conducted by the FBI to discredit "subversives," which included both the Civil Rights Movement and the Ku Klux Klan … at the same time.

- Both Adolf Hitler (1889-1945) and Benito Mussolini (1883-1945) were voted into *Time* Magazine's "Time 100: The Most Important People of the Century," while Jesus of Nazareth (c.0AD-∞), and professional wrestler Ric Flair (b.1949), who got hundreds of thousands of votes, were disqualified by the editors for breaking the "spirit" of the list.

- Warm basketballs bounce more than a cold ones, because the hot molecules hit inside ball surface at a higher speed.

THE BLUE SCREEN OF DEATH

The mass UFO hysteria triggered by the 1947 Kenneth Arnold (1915-1984) sighting while flying near Mt. Rainier prompted a series of US Air Force (USAF) investigations, led by the preliminary code-named "Project Sign," the ill-fated "Project Grudge," and the now-legendary "Project Blue Book," the latter's scope and findings summarized below.

1. Launched in 1952 and terminated by USAF in 1969, it had two goals, a. to determine if UFOs were a threat to national security, and b. to scientifically analyze available UFO reports—12,618 of them!

2. In 1952, a panel of experts led my mathematician Bob Robertson (1903-1961) suggested controlling public opinion through propaganda and spying, as a means to "separate the wheat from the chaff," to insure accurate analysis. This was carried well beyond the project's termination. A year later armed forces "Regulation 146" would also criminalize the discussion with unauthorized civilians of classified UFO reports, while the investigation of the most important cases was diverted from Blue Book to the 4602nd Air Intelligence Squadron (AISS) of the Air Defense Command.

3. By 1954 said statistical analysis (contained in Special Report No. 14) yielded some interesting results, namely that 69% of the reports were known, 22% were considered unknown, and nine percent lacked enough information to be classified as either known or unknown. Known cases were split among the perfectly obviously explained (balloons, weather, etc.) 89%, the hoaxes (eight percent), and the psychologically delusional (three percent).

4. In 1955 USAF decided Blue Book would rather be used to minimize the unknown reports. The project was extremely efficient in this task,

and by 1956 it had clarified most reports and reduced the unidentified cases from 22% to just one percent. That year, the The 4602nd was disbanded, its still-ongoing investigations charged to the 1066th Air Intelligence Service Squadron.

5. When former Tuskegee airman Lt. Col. Robert J. Friend (1920-2019) was charged with leading Blue Book in 1958, he took steps to reverse its progressive defunding. His efforts were largely ignored or met by a wall of institutional indifference at USAF, but not by Congress, nor by civilian organization National Investigations Committee On Aerial Phenomena (NICAP), which put Blue Book under the public spotlight, forcing the Air Technical Intelligence Center (ATIC) to increase the project's budget and personnel in 1960.

6. Unfortunately, Blue Book was put under Major Hector Quintanilla (1923-1998) in 1963. Major Quintanilla had a physics degree, but the post was a not-so-subtle chastisement for refusing USAF jobs which would have seen him sent to Vietnam, so over the next three years he gradually drove the Blue Book to the ground by focusing mainly on the debunking of reports, until the project's termination and his retirement as a Lieutenant Colonel from USAF in 1969. A Quintanilla memoir, *UFOs: An Air-Force Dilemma* was published posthumously.

7. In 1966 an independent, USAF-funded, committee was established at the University of Colorado. Led by reputed Manhattan Project physicist Edward Condon (1902-1974), it determined there was no reason to give UFO investigations high priority, the results of its investigation, known as the "Condon Report" were published in book form as *Scientific Study of Unidentified Flying Objects* (1968), and meant the final blow to Project Blue Book.

8. The final conclusions of Project Blue Book were that a. no UFO reported, investigated, and evaluated by the Air Force has ever given

any indication of threat to national security, b. there has been no evidence submitted to or discovered by the Air Force that sightings categorized as "unidentified" represent technological developments or principles beyond the range of present day scientific knowledge, and c. there has been no evidence indicating the sightings categorized as "unidentified" are extraterrestrial vehicles.

9. In spite of the statement above, perhaps the most striking Blue Book "one percent" case, credited for turning previously skeptic Josef Allen Hynek (1910-1986) into a believer, happened on March 21, 1966, when a student at Hillsdale College (Michigan) reported a glowing object in the sky, which was followed by the police while hovering above a nearby swamp, under the astonished gaze of the school dean and over 100 other students. While Hynek originally attributed the event to a massive blurting of swamp gas, soil analysis later would reveal the ground to be contaminated with Boron (B) a chemical element produced at the heart of exploding supernovae, but very rare in our Solar System!

BONUS FACTS!

- Nobel Prize laureate Ivar Giaever (b.1929) is a global warming skeptic, comparing its believers to a religious cult.

- Many historians support the notion that globalization as we know it today began in earnest not with the advent of the internet, but when Spanish navigator Miguel López de Legazpi (c.1502-1572) made first contact with Chinese traders in the Philippines, back in 1565!

THE UFO EXPERIENCE

The scale devised by American astronomer and UFOlogist Josef Allen Hynek (1910-1986), who went from skeptical to apologist while taking part in Project Sign (1947–1949), Project Grudge (1949–1952), and Project Blue Book (1952–1969), and its subsequent extensions provide the right framework for rigorous observation of the skies.

Nocturnal Lights: Lights in the night sky at a distance of over 500 feet from the observer.

Daylight Discs: Daytime UFOs at more than 500 feet from the observer.

Radar-Visual: UFOs confirmed by radar.

Close Encounters of the First Kind: UFOs seen less than 500 feet away in considerable detail.

Close Encounters of the Second Kind: UFO event with perceived physical consequences (such as electronic device interference, the barking of dogs, scorched ground, etc.).

Close Encounters of the Third Kind: UFO encounters which include the object's occupants or pilots, whatever they may be. It includes the subtypes proposed by Ted Bloecher (b.1929):

A (Aboard): Entity observed only inside the UFO.

B (Both): Entity observed inside and outside the UFO.

C (Close): Entity observed near a UFO, but not going in or out.

D (Direct): Entity observed, with no UFO in the vicinity of the encounter. UFO activity, however, has been reported in the area.

E (Excluded): Entity observed, but no UFOs have been seen nor reported in the area.

F (Frequence): No entity or UFOs are observed, but the observer experiences attempts at intelligent communication.

Close Encounters of the Fourth Kind: Abduction of a human by a UFO or its occupants.

Close Encounters of the Fifth Kind: Direct and deliberate communication established between UFO occupants and humans.

Close Encounters of the Sixth Kind: UFO sighting which results in the death of the observer.

Close Encounters of the Seventh Kind: Human/alien hybrid creation by means of sexual intercourse or artificial insemination.

Celebrities that claimed to have seen UFOs include Jackie Gleason (1916-1987), William Shatner (b. 1931), John Lennon (1940-1980), Muhammad Ali (1942-2016), David Bowie (1947-2016) and Kurt Russell (b. 1951).

BONUS FACT!

- Born in Chihuahua, Mexico, legendary actor Anthony Quinn's (1915-2001) real name was Manuel Antonio Rodolfo Quinn Oaxaca!

NOT IN KANSAS ANYMORE

Famed British UFOlogist and author Jenny Randles (b.1951), coined the term "Oz Factor," to describe the altered state of consciousness which may occur during close encounters, including:

Blue lights: Cherenkov radiation, the kind emitted by particles traversing at faster than light speed, is seen by most UFO percipients.

Lost time: UFO witnesses report episodes of timelessness during a close encounter, in which they may lose the track or the recalling of time during the episode.

New dimension: People encountering UFOs often feel transported to another time and place, even if the surrounding sight remain the same.

Cone of silence: An eerie stillness and lack of all auditive stimuli is also common among UFO witnesses, but some have reported intermittent humming as well.

Paralysis: Some people report being unable to move during an encounter.

Drowsiness: Weakness and lightheadedness are often experienced by victims of the fourth close encounter type: abduction!

Carl Sagan (1934-1996) was also a famous debunker of UFOs, based on the realities of interstellar travel distance as stated by Thomas Huxley (1825-1895), and the famous statistical equation devised by astrophysicist

Frank Drake (b.1930) to determine the likelihood of advanced civilizations in our galaxy:

$$N = R^* \cdot fp \cdot ne \cdot fl \cdot fi \cdot fc \cdot L$$

N = Number of civilizations in our galaxy with which communication might be possible.

R = Average rate of star formation in our galaxy.

fp = Fraction of those stars that have planets.

ne = Average number of planets that can potentially support life per star that has planets.

fl = Fraction of planets that could support life that actually develop life at some point.

fi = Fraction of planets with life that actually go on to develop intelligent life.

fc = Fraction of civilizations that develop advanced communications technology.

L = Length of time for which such civilizations release detectable signals into space

None of the values of the equation factors, however, is known with any degree of absolute certainty.

BONUS FACT!

- MLB pitcher Joel Zumaya (b.1984) had to sit out of three games after injuring himself playing *Guitar Hero* in 2006!

ANAL ENCOUNTERS OF THE FOURTH KIND

Seeing a UFO is one thing, but being kidnapped by one is a whole new level of terrifying!

1. The Betty (1919-2004) and Barney Hill (1922-1969) abduction of 1961 is considered the case that sparked the nationwide UFO abduction craze that continues, if abated, to this day. The Hills were an interracial couple in a time when such a thing was frowned upon, even in New Hampshire. One day they were followed by strange lights on the road. When they arrived home, obviously shaken, they found they were dirty, Betty's dress was torn, and Barney's watch had stopped working, but neither could remember a thing about the last two hours. They put themselves in the hands of a psychiatrist who subjected them to now-controversial regression hypnosis (known, among other things, to trigger false memories of abuse), emerging from therapy with the startling revelation they had been kidnapped by beings from another planet.

2. Author Jason Colavito (b.1981) has pointed out that "nearly all of the imagery Barney Hill used to describe his alien encounter closely paralleled imagery from three episodes of the classic *The Outer Limits* television series that aired in the three weeks immediately preceding his hypnosis session." Regardless, the Hills published a book, *The Interrupted Journey* (1966) written by John G. Fuller (1913-1990), retelling their abduction, which caused a media frenzy around their case, similar reports skyrocketing as a result, including dubious "unearthed" accounts from the past, like the now-famous 1957 case of Antônio Villas Boas (1934–c.1991), a Brazilian farmer who claimed to have been kidnapped (by a sexy female alien who had intercourse with the man before releasing him) … the day after he read a science-fiction abduction story in a local magazine!

3. It is also worth pointing out that in 1965, during an investigation lead by NICAP's Walter N. Webb (1929-1971), Barney Hill (1922-1969) recalled being anally probed by the gray aliens that abducted him and his wife, despite this detail not being mentioned anywhere in *The Interrupted Journey*. Needless to say, this tidbit of information caught the morbid fascination of the public for years to come.

4. From then on most abduction claims, including those of celebrated abductees R. Leo Sprinkle (b.1930) and Budd Hopkins (1931-2011), would follow the Hills and Villas Boas pattern of overworked human subject, textbook "Oz Factor" memory loss, PTSD, and recovery of "memories" (including unpleasant anal probing) via dubious regression hypnosis. Hence, while statistically this does not rule out 100% of these cases, it does cast doubt over the truthfulness of most (after all, believing oneself a victim doesn't make it so).

5. Studying and interviewing 800 alien abduction "victims" at Harvard, Pulitzer Prize-winner psychiatrist John E. Mack (1929-2004), in particular, concluded that while we should remain open to the possibility of fourth kind encounters, abduction reports should not be considered to involve real alien entities, but rather the subjective accounts of imaginary grievances.

6. *The Interrupted Journey* (1966) was eventually adapted into the 1975 TV movie *The UFO Incident,* followed by Steven Spielberg's (b.1946) *Close Encounters of the Third Kind* (1977) and *E.T. the Extra-Terrestrial* (1982) which lead to a new surge of abduction claims well into the 1980s.

7. Currently, while abduction reports are at an all-time low (according to a Boston Globe survey from 2016), 20% of Americans still believe in them, while 40,000 of those are currently insured against alien abductions and/or alien impregnation!

RACE MATTERS

According to UFO aficionados, several archetypical alien races have come to this world. A few well-meaning ones try to protect us, while others remain intent on controlling the human race for their own cosmic domination goals.

Anunnaki: Author Zecharia Sitchin (1920-2010) alleged these deities from ancient Mesopotamia were in fact aliens from this Solar System. Their planet, Nibiru, located beyond Neptune, they came to mine Earth, crossbreeding with Homo erectus to create a new race, Homo sapiens, to serve as cheap labor for them.

Archons: Also known as Reptilians or Draconians, this shape-shifting race of inter-dimensional beings sprung from the troubled mind of English conspiracy theorist David Icke (b.1952), who claims they have interbred with humans, their descendants currently busy manipulating our world, seeking to turn it into a fascist, police state.

Arcturians: According to Edgar "The Sleeping Prophet" Cayce (1877-1945) these aliens come from a civilization so advanced, they have conquered and exist in five dimensions. Short, telepathic, loving, and God-fearing, some claim they are the reason Earth hasn't been conquered by less kind extra-terrestrial beings.

Grays: Popular across all media since the Hills' "abduction" in 1961, they are around four feet tall, hairless, with big largely featureless heads and faces, but for their huge eyes, and supposedly hail from binary star system Zeta Reticuli, 40 million light years away from earth. Some believe the reason they dislike humans is they were snubbed by Plejaren, who favored *Homo sapiens* above them.

Greens: Supposedly smaller than Grays and more goblin-like (as in large pointed ears, clawlike hands, yellow eyes), these aliens operate in groups of several individuals, and reportedly attacked a farm near Hopkinsville, Kentucky, in 1955. They are considered by UFO buffs to be the original inspiration behind elves in fantasy lore, as well as pop culture's "little green men." Like the Plejaren, Greens have almost completely been replaced by Grays in the media.

Plejaren: Formerly known as Pleiadians, Venusians, and Nordics, they represent a benevolent alien archetype which, as their name suggests has Nordic features (tall, blonde hair, blue eyes), though UFOlogists can't seem to agree on their origin—some have proposed they indeed come from the Pleiades star cluster, while others claim that they are, in fact, time-traveling humans from the future! In his 1976 best-seller **Gods of Aquarius**, they were dubbed "Star people," by New Age author Brad Steiger (1936-2018).

Sassani: This alien race, a genetic hybrid of Grays and Homo sapiens, is said to dwell on the planet Essassani, 500 light years from Earth near the Orion constellation … in a future timeline too! This privileged information was passed on to us by singer Paul Anka's (b.1941) cousin, Darryl Anka (b.1951), a medium who channels a Sassani alien known as "Bashar."

Yahyel: Another race of good natured aliens, UFO lore signals them as the most likely to reveal themselves to us in the near future, having already gauged mankind's readiness to make contact in the 1997 Phoenix Lights incident over Arizona, Nevada, and Sonora in Mexico.

J.C.
THE EXTRA-TERRESTRIAL

Was Jesus Christ an alien? Many UFO-based bespoke religions and pseudo-Christian basket cases believe so ...

1. After receiving a message ("Prepare yourself! You are to become the voice of Interplanetary Parliament") from an alien being known as Master Aetherius, London cab driver George King (1919-1997) funded the Aetherius Society in 1955 (later expanding it to California and New Zealand). This movement seeks to cooperate with its "Cosmic Masters" and heal Mother Earth through prayer. Who are these Cosmic Masters? Well, obviously Buddha, Krishna, Confucius and Jesus Christ.

2. Not counting Scientology (which deems Jesus an implanted memory), possibly the largest UFO religion in existence would be the International Raëlian Movement founded by French car-racing journalist Claude M. M. Vorilhon (b.1946), a.k.a. "Raël, the Messenger of Elohim," after elaborating on his alleged close encounter of 1973. This atheistic, hedonistic, and materialistic philosophy teaches mankind was created by technologically advanced aliens, the "Elohim." While humans often confused these aliens with gods, the Elohim sent forty alien/human hybrids to teach humanity their truth, including Buddha, Jesus, Muhammad, and Raël of course.

3. Defining Jesus as a "fine-vibrations being," the *Vesmírní lidé sil světla* ("Cosmic People of Light Powers"), also known as the Universe People, founded by Czech engineer Ivo Aštar Benda (b.1961) in the mid-1990's, is a modern cult largely based on American UFOlogist George Van Tassel's (1910-1978) claims of a Venusian "Ashtar Galactic Command" spaceship fleet currently guarding our planet; as well as elements from Swiss prophet Billy Meier's (b.1937)

Freie Interessengemeinschaft für Grenz- und Geisteswissenschaften und Ufologiestudien (Free Community of Interests for the Border and Spiritual Sciences and Ufological Studies) ideology, which Benda adopted as his own.

4. The fringe Theosophical "Ascended Master Teachings" beliefs espoused by Joshua David Stone (1953-2005), also embraced George Van Tassel's (1910-1978) "Ashtar Galactic Command" fringe philosophy, revealing Master Jesus true galactic name, Sananda, who was Commander Ashtar's second in command.

5. Not all claims regarding to Jesus being an alien come from strange cults. Presbyterian minister Dr. Barry Downing's (b.1938) *The Bible and Flying Saucers* (1968) cites biblical lines about the "other-worldiness" of Christ, as proof our Lord and Savior was indeed an alien-human hybrid, implanted into Mary's womb by aliens seeking to rid the world of sin. These aliens would have been responsible for resurrecting him with superior extra-terrestrial technology, later shipping Him back to their home world in another dimension.

6. Reverend Downing's findings were expanded by author R.L. Dione (1922-1996) in his 1969 classic *God Drives a Flying Saucer*, where the Father is posed to be an advanced UFOnaut, a.k.a. "Saucerian God," made immortal by the super technology of His home world, "Heaven," piloting His own flying saucer, "Star of Bethlehem," and making random people ill using hypnotism, so his Son would "cure" them afterwards. Dione then goes a step further by adopting popular Nazi esoterica claims of Hitler as an instrument of this Saucerian God, sent to punish the Soviets for their atheism!

I WANT TO BELIEVE

Beyond the crackpots, let's take a look at what rational, trustworthy people of good repute has had to say about UFOs.

"A purely psychological explanation is ruled out ... the discs show signs of intelligent guidance, by quasi-human pilots."
–Carl Jung (1875-1961)

"The nations of the world will have to unite for the next war will be an interplanetary war. The nations of Earth must some day make a common front against attack by people from other planets."
–General Douglas MacArthur (1880-1964)

"I can assure you that flying saucers, given that they exist, are not constructed by any power on Earth."
–Harry S. Truman (1884-1972)

"Flying saucers are real. Too many good men have seen them, that don't have hallucinations."
–Captain Eddie Rickenbacker (1890-1973)

"We cannot take credit for our record avancement in certain scientific fields alone. We have been helped, and we have been helped by the people of other worlds."
–Hermann Oberth (1894-1989)

"This 'flying saucer' situation is not at all imaginary or seeing too much in some natural phenomena. Something is really flying around.

The phenomenon is something real and not visionary or fictitious."
–General Nathan F. Twining (1897-1982)

"We have lost many men and planes trying to intercept them."
–General Benjamin W. Chidlaw (1900-1977)

"I think some highly secret government UFO investigations are going on that we don't know about—and probably never will unless the Air Force discloses them."
–Barry Goldwater (1909-1998)

"I have been privileged to be briefed and to know that we have been visited (by aliens). I do not have first hand experience in this regard, but I have been on investigating teams and I have been briefed by insiders who do know."
–Captain Edgar Mitchell (1930-2016)

"Of course it is possible that UFOs really do contain aliens as many people believe, and the government is hushing it up."
–Stephen Hawking (1942-2018)

"I think it's time to open the books on questions that have remained in the dark on the question of government investigations of UFOs. It's time to find out what the truth really is that's out there. We ought to do it because it's right. We ought to do it because the American people, quite frankly, can handle the truth. And we ought to do it because it's the law."
–John Podesta (b.1949)

LIKE A VIRGIN

UFOlogy and Catholicism meet at Marian apparitions, the supernatural events in which "seers," also known as visionaries, claim to have encountered Mary, the mother of Jesus, in physical form (hearing her, or seeing her silhouette on a slice of toast doesn't count). These account of close encounters of the divine kind have grabbed the world's attention over and over, despite an otherwise stern Catholic Church keeping its distance from them, at least until they become so popular, it becomes profitable to join in with the crowds.

Our Lady of the Pillar: According to tradition, around the year 40AD, the Apostle James was evangelizing Roman domain Hispania (modern day Spain), and one day while praying by the Ebro river, Mary, who was alive and well at Jerusalem at the time, appeared before him to offer encouragement. Whether the Blessed Mother teleported or bilocated is still a matter of much debate.

Our Lady of Mount Carmel: Said to have appeared to Carmelite Prior Saint Simon Stock (c.1165-1265) in the thirteenth century, bearing the gift of the Brown Scapular, or the habit of the Carmelite order, which has a smaller version for laymen consisting in two pieces of brown cloth joined by two straps or strings which overlap each shoulder (the word scapular means "shoulder blade"), which needs to be invested on the bearer by a priest, who from then on may count on the Virgin's special protection.

Our Lady of Guadalupe: On December 9, 1531, Mary appeared to recently converted Mexica Juan Diego Cuauhtlatoatzin (1474-1548) and his sick uncle Juan Diego Bernardino (c.1456-1544) five times. Newly appointed bishop of Mexico City, Fray Juan de Zumárraga y Arrazola (1468-1548) initially refused to believe the account, but caved in when, according to the stories (there's more than one)

Juan Diego brought roses gathered gathered atop the normally barren Tepeyac Hill, and dropped them on the floor from his *tilma* ("mantle"), which revealed the iconic Mary image everyone is familiar with.

Our Lady of Grace: On July 19, 1830, French nun Saint Catherine Labouré (1806-1876) claimed Mary's voice forewarned her of a mission from God, and then on November 27, 1830, appeared in full form inside an oval shape, standing on a globe while shooting rays from her hands, an image while Mary herself commanded to be engraved in a medallion, which was later called the Miraculous Medal, proving the mother of our Savior loves her bling-bling.

Our Lady of La Salette: On September 19, 1849, teenagers Maximin Giraud (1835-1875) and Mélanie Calvat, (1831-1904) reported seeing an apparition of a weeping Virgin Mary in the mountains of La Salette (southeastern France), visibly upset by people failure to keep the Sabbath, and respecting God's name, and threatening a famine the potato blight was already causing. It was also said she told each one of the seers a personal secret, they only shared epistolary with Pope Pius IX.

Our Lady of Lourdes: From February 11 to July 16, 1858, a lady identifying herself as the "Immaculate Conception" reportedly appeared to Saint Bernadette Soubirous (1844-1879) 18 times at the Massabielle grotto (in the outskirts of the town of Lourdes, France), requesting a chapel be built in that place. Needless to say, she got her wish tenfold, as that temple and many replicas got built all around the world.

Our Lady of Knock: On August 21, 1879, 15 villagers of the town of Knock, Ireland, witnessed the silent apparition not only of Mary, but also Saint Joseph, Saint John the Evangelist, angels, and even Jesus Christ as the Lamb of God, at the town church's gable.

The people gathered around it are said to have prayed the Rosary under the pouring rain until the vision vanished, while a farmer standing half a mile away claimed to have seen a huge ball light above the church.

Our Lady of Fátima: Between 1915 and 1916 three Portuguese cousins Lúcia dos Santos (1907-2005), Francisco Marto (1908-1919) and Jacinta Marto (1910-1920) saw what appeared to be the Guardian Angel of Portugal, who introduced himself as "The Angel of Peace," three times. The angel invited the children to prayer (taught them two prayer formulas) and penitence. Then on May 13, 1917, Our Lady appeared to them in luminous form as well, asking them to pray the Rosary and come back every thirteenth during the following six months, which they did, followed by larger and larger crowds every time. On the following appearances, Mary would predict Francisco and Jacinta's early demise, show the children hell, and on October 13 throw a show, "The Miracle of the Sun," before 100,000 people, which saw the sun spin and zig-zag in the sky before their very eyes. While Francisco and Jacinta did die on account of the Spanish Flu, Lúcia dos Santos became a nun, and claimed to have seen yet another Virgin Mary apparition on December 10, 1925, in Pontevedra, Spain, followed by a February 15, 1926, apparition of Jesus himself, though in child form.

Less known Marian sightings include Our Lady of Walsingham (England, 1061), Our Lady of the Watch (1490, Italy), Our Lady of Good Health (India, 1570-1587), Our Lady of Šiluva (Luthuania, 1608), Our Lady of the Good Event (Ecuador, 1594-1634), Our Lady of Laus (France, 1664-1718), Our Lady of La Vang (Vietnam, 1798), Our Lady of Good Help (U.S.A., 1859), Our Lady of Pontmain (France, 1871), Our Lady of Pellevoisin (France, 1876), Our Lady of Gietrzwałd (Poland, 1877), Our Lady of Beauraing (Belgium, 1932-1933), Our Lady of Banneux (Belgium, 1933), Our Lady of All Nations (Netherlands, 1945-1959),

Our Lady of Akita (Japan, 1973), Our Lady of Cuapa (Nicaragua, 1980), Our Lady of Kibeho (Rwanda, 1981-1983), Our Lady of the Rosary of San Nicolás (Argentina, 1983-1990), and the still ongoing appearances of Our Lady of Medjugorje (Bosnia and Herzegovina).

BONUS FACTS!

- Pulitzer prize-winning nonfiction book *The Guns of August* (1962) by Barbara Tuchman (1912-1989) influenced President John F. Kennedy (1917-1963) to avoid escalation with the USSR during the Cuban Missile Crisis.

- In 1969, an expedition led by Jacques Cousteau (1910-1997) reportedly found Lake Titicaca water frogs measuring two feet long, and weighing 2.2 pounds, with excessive amounts of skin, which help them breathe in freezing temperatures at 12,000 feet!

- Blonde, mischievous American cartoon character Dennis the Menace debuted in US newspapers on March 12, 1951. Coincidentally, five days later, a black-haired mischievous British cartoon character also named Dennis the Menace debuted in DC Thomson's *The Beano* comic book!

- While named in honor of the self-taught chemist who developed vulcanized rubber, the Goodyear Tire and Rubber Company has no connection to Charles Goodyear (1800-1860), who died poor and in debt.

THE CRYING GAME

A well-known hoax in Ancient Rome, if written accounts by Plutarch (c.46-119AD) concerning effigies of the goddess Fortuna are to be trusted, weeping and bleeding statues—paintings too—of the Virgin Mary and other saints have become a fixture of folksy Christianity since.

1. The Madonna of Syracuse, is a plaque of the Immaculate Heart of Mary at a Sicilian home which, between August 29 and September 1, 1953, wept what according to scientists of the day were real human tears. Sadly, DNA testing wasn't available back then, so this figure remains the only weeping effigy officially approved by the Catholic Church.

2. A great many icons have reportedly wept at St. Paul's Greek Orthodox Church in Hempstead, New York since 1960.

3. In 1973, the wood statue of Our Lady of Akita in Japan began to bleed from the center of its left hand after a reported apparition to Sister Agnes Katsuko Sasagawa (b.1931). Other nuns, however, reported the carved hand seem to have been cut with a tool and stained with ink …

4. A crying Virgin Mary bas-relief owner was caught in flagrante delicto (red-handed) while spraying "tears" on her face with a water pistol, back in 1980, in Pavia, Italy.

5. Apparently, Virgin Mary statues seem to burst into tears at the sight of Father James Bruce (b.1955), but the one at the priest's parish, St. Elizabeth Ann Seton Catholic Church in Lake Ridge, Virginia, made headlines back in 1992.

The flamboyant priest himself, nowadays keeping a much lower profile, was said to be baffled by these events, including his bleeding from the wrists (stigmata) during mass, but not by his three consecutive marathon roller-coaster riding Guinness Records!

6. The 16-inch "Weeping Madonna of Civitavecchia" hasn't wept blood since a 1995 DNA analysis ordered by the conscientious town bishop proved her tears to be the blood of a male, likely its owner, by the name of Pablo Grigori.

7. A Christ of the Hills Monastery (Texas) myrrh-weeping painting of the Virgin Mary drew many visitors in the 1980s, until allegations of sexual abuse saw its founder, Samuel A. Greene Jr. (1944-2007), a.k.a. Father Benedict, reveal it a hoax in the year 2000. Seven years later, Greene committed suicide while still on probation.

8. A bronze statue of Saint Pio of Pietrelcina (1887-1968), himself a suspect in his lifetime to be causing his own "stigmata," was revealed to weep blood in 2002, only for another useful DNA test to prove the blood belonged to a pious female believer.

9. Shedding "Sacred Chrism" (scented oil) tears between July and September, 2018, the statue at Our Lady of Guadalupe Catholic Church, in Hobbs, New Mexico, remains under investigation. Oil tears, however, are a hoax stalwart seen from Bangladesh to Lebanon, as it conveniently doesn't evaporate. Not so conveniently, in this particular effigy's case, is the alleged tears appear to have been dripped from above its eyelids!

SEND ME AN ANGEL

Soaring above a variety of religions and belief systems, both ancient and new, the supernatural creatures we refer to as angels have come to be embraced by all, but what are they really, and are they the wholesome, winged, and toga-wearing asexuals depicted in art and literature, or rather fearsome beings of light, fire, and brimstone?

1. As conceived by Greek philosopher Aristotle (384-322 BC) in his influential work Metaphysics, which was later picked by Thomas Aquinas (1225-1274), if God is the prime cause or "first mover" of the universe, it stands to reason other "secondary movers" must exist, but Greco-Roman polytheism lacked "angels" as described in Abrahamic religions.

2. The word "angel" derives from Late Latin angelus ("messenger"), most often used to translate the Hebrew term *mal'ākh*, also meaning messenger, divine or human depending on the context. However, only two messengers of the divine kind are mentioned by name in the Bible, their appearances significant but very brief: Michael ("Who is like God?"), traditionally protecting mankind, and Gabriel ("God is my strength"), usually sent to deliver justice, or messages of importance.

3. Christianity established angels and intermediaries between man and God, describing several human-angel interactions in the New Testament (not to mention Gabriel's pivotal role in the birth of Jesus Christ), and while Church Fathers struggled with proper classification, it was Saint Augustine of Hippo (354-430AD) who famously defined "angel" as the name of an office, rather than the creatures inherent nature.

4. Other that Michael and Gabriel, angels present in various traditions are considered non-biblical in reformed Christian canon, including Jophiel ("Beauty of God"), Raphael ("It is God who heals"), Uriel ("God is my light"), and Samael ("Venom of God"), the famed "angel of death."

5. According to the Catholic Church's Congregation for Divine Worship and Discipline of the Sacraments, assigning names to angels should be discouraged, other than those already present in Scripture, which in Catholic and Orthodox traditions includes Raphael, present in the Book of Tobit, which is absent from Reformed tradition.

6. Influenced by the writings of Lutheran theologian Emanuel Swedenborg (1688–1772), the New Church believes that, rather than strictly spiritual entities created by God before man, angels originate from humans, and there is not one angel in heaven who first did not live in a material body. If films like *Heaven Can Wait* (1978) and TV shows like *Highway to Heaven* (1984-1989) are any indication, this idea is particularly appealing to both folk and pop culture alike.

7. Swedenborg's theology, or rather "angeleology" also exerted a tremendous influence on Mormonism. According to the Church of Latter Day Saints, angels may be either the spirits of deceased, unborn, or resurrected humans in real physical form. Dispensing with the "el" ending traditional angel names, this religion's founder, Joseph Smith (1805-1844) was visited by the Angel Moroni, who had previously been a Mesoamerican prophet-warrior during the fifth century.

8. In Asia, there's a rich angelic tradition in Islamic literature, which mainly classifies them according to a specific function, though all seem to be beings of light, cold for those of mercy, hot for those imparting justice in Allah's name (Michael and Gabriel are

specifically mentioned in the Quran). For Zoroastrianism, on the other hand, angels were originally abstract emanations of Ahura Mazda, which later gained a conscience and personality of their own, including Guardian Angel Fravashi. Another Persian faith, the Bahá'í concept of angels is not very different from the one found in New Church and Mormonism.

9. A western esoteric movement, the Theosophical Society has also adopted angels as its own, incorporating them into a cosmogony of "etheric" creatures, which include gnomes and fairies, angels are called "devas," and dwell both in the atmosphere of planets or inside the Sun. This was superficially adopted by the New Age movement, which encompasses such a multitude of beliefs and conceptions, it is impossible to pinpoint a single exclusive angel notion pertaining to this philosophy.

10. For approximately four centuries, Christian art represented angels without wings, incorporating them around 395AD, based on the four- and six-winged fearsome creatures described by prophet Ezekiel and John the Evangelist in Revelation. According to Church Father Saint John Chrysostom (347-407), angels have no wings, but wings are meant to represent their sublime nature. The number of wings posed a compositional nightmare to Christian artists, however, who simplified them to just two, protruding between the shoulder blades, early on.

BONUS FACT!

- Introduced into boxing to increase hits to the head and knockouts., boxing gloves actually result in more deaths than old time bare-knuckle boxing!

GOD ONLY KNOWS

While hardly Biblical, angel and demon classifications which abounded between the fifth and nineteenth centuries, can be counted as early efforts to grasp the depth of human morality and behavior, even if they were not seen as such in their day.

ANGELS

Written by someone claiming to be Apostle Paul's disciple Dionysius the Areopagite, *De coelesti hierarchia* ("On the Celestial Hierarchy") is a fifth-century book describing the ranks and organization of angels in hierarchies, each containing three choirs of angels.

FIRST HIERARCHY

Seraphim: In charge of love.

Cherubim: In charge of intercession.

Thrones: In charge of justice.

SECOND HIERARCHY

Dominions: In charge of other angels.

Virtues: In charge of miracles.

Powers: In charge of the souls of the dead.

THIRD HIERARCHY

Principalities: In charge of protecting religion.

Archangels: In charge of human history.

Angels: In charge of protecting individuals and nations.

DEMONS

French inquisitor and exorcist Sébastien Michaelis (1543-1618), based the following classification of demons contained in *Histoire admirable de la possession et conversion d'une penitente* (1612) in *De coelesti hierarchia.*

FIRST HIERARCHY (Former Seraphim, Cherubim and Thrones)
Seraphim: Including Beelzebub, Leviathan, and Asmodeus.
Cherubim: Including Berith.
Thrones: Including Astaroth, Verrine, Gressil, and Soneillon.

SECOND HIERARCHY (Former Dominions, Virtues, and Powers)
Dominions: Including Carreau and Carnivale.
Virtues: Including Oeillet and Rosier.
Powers: Including Belias.

THIRD HIERARCHY (Former Principalities, Archangels, and Angels)
Principalities: Including Verrier.
Archangels: Including Olivier.
Angels: Including Luvart.

BONUS FACT!

- In 2005, Chilean film maker Alejandro Jodorowsky (b.1929) officiated the wedding of American rock star Marilyn Manson (b.1969) and vedette Dita Von Teese (b.1972).

TOUCHED BY AN ANGEL

Over the centuries, not all Christians have fallen under the angelic spell.

"The Devil often transforms himself into an angel to tempt men, some for their instruction, some for their ruin."

–Saint Augustine (354-430AD)

"Pride and nothing else caused an angel to fall from heaven. And so one my reasonably ask whether one may reach heaven by humility alone without the help of any other virtue."

–Saint John Climacus (c.579-649AD)

"An angel can only be called incorporeal and non-material in comparison with us. For in comparison with God, Who alone is beyond compare, everything seems coarse and material, only the divinity is totally non-material and incorporeal."

–Saint John of Damascus (c.675-749AD)

"A person is disposed to an act of choice by an angel ... in two ways. Sometimes, a man's understanding is enlightened by an angel to know what is good, but it is not instructed as to the reason why ... But sometimes he is instructed by angelic illumination, both that this act is good and as to the reason why it is good."

–Thomas Aquinas (1225-1274)

"The soul at its highest is found like God, but an angel gives a closer idea of Him. That is all an angel is: an idea of God."

–Meister Eckhart (1260-1328)

"Although the angels are superior to us in many ways, yet in some respects … they fall short of us with regard to being in the image of the Creator; for we, rather than they, have been created in God's image."

–St. Gregory Palamas (1296-1357)

"From the beginning of my Reformation I have asked God to send me neither dreams, nor visions, nor angels, but to give me the right understanding of His Word, the Holy Scriptures; for as long as I have God's Word, I know that I am walking in His way and that I shall not fall into any error or delusion."

–Martin Luther (1483-1546)

"Angels, being the ministers appointed to execute the commands of God, must, of course, be admitted to be His creatures, but to stir up questions concerning the time or order in which they were created bespeaks more perverseness than industry."

–John Calvin (1509-1564)

"In Scripture the visitation of an angel is always alarming; it has to begin by saying 'Fear not.' The Victorian angel looks as if it were going to say, 'There, there.'"
–C. S. Lewis (1898-1963)

BONUS FACT!

- On July 10, 2020, a mint quality copy of a packed and sealed 1985 *Super Mario Bros'* game cartridge was sold at Heritage Auctions for $114,000.

ANGELS IN AMERICA

Right alongside Power Rangers, Beanie Babies, pogs, and fanny packs, angels capitalized both their Christian and New Age following in unprecedented ways during the 1990s.

1. A 1993 Time magazine survey revealed 69% of Americans believed in angels back then. 46% of those believed they had a personal Guardian Angel. By 1994 that number had gone up to 72% according to a *USA Today*/CNN poll.

2. As belief increased, so did claims of real angel encounters (as proven by Bigfoot, Nessie, UFOs, etc.), which were tracked by the Angel Watch Network in New Jersey.

3. Beginning with *A Book of Angels: Reflections on Angels Past and Present, and True Stories of How They Touch Our Lives* (1990) by Sophy Burnham (b.1936), a whole new publishing niche sprung from the angel craze. Popular examples include *Chicken Soup for the Soul* and *Women's World Magazine* real-life encounter anthologies, author Doreen Virtue's (b.1958) never ending line of "angelology" titles and merchandise, and the *Your Angels Speak* daily syndicated comic-strip, by prolific cartoonist and country musician Guy Gilchrist's (b.1957) who more recently has launched a "Bearly-Angels" line of winged "Teddy" bear figurines!

4. As keenly observed by journalist Nancy Gibbs (b.1960) "... angels are the handy compromise, all fluff and meringue, kind, nonjudgmental. And they avail themselves to everyone, like aspirin." So, by the late 1990s many angel-exclusive merchandise stores had opened in the US—some reconverted from New Age paraphernalia shops, while others were Christian book stores or churches!

5. Dedicated to collecting and preserving angel merchandise, the Angel Collectors Club of America was founded in Colorado in 1976, and saw a considerable rise in memberships from 200 when it incorporated in 1989, to 1,600 by 1993. Even Hillary Clinton (b.1947) once claimed to wear an angel wings pin on her jacket whenever she faced a difficult day!

6. The trend even reflected on 1990s nonprofits adding "angel" to their names, such as the Angel Food Ministries (1994), the Angel Foundation (1995), and the Masonic Angel Fund (1998). While the Guardian Angels organization has been protecting children from violence since 1979, it became more prominent in the 1990s, branching out to patrol the internet with its "CyberAngels" program in 1995, which received a Presidential Service Award in 1998.

7. As is usually the case, Hollywood soon caught wind of the trend, angel movies becoming dominant in the 1990s, just as westerns had been in the 1960s, and super heroes would in the 2010s. Popular angel films included: *Almost an Angel* **(1990),** *The Dark Side of the Heart* **(1992),** *Faraway, So Close!* **(1993),** *Heart and Souls* **(1993),** *Angels in the Outfield* **(1994),** *The Hudsucker Proxy* **(1994)** *All Dogs Go to Heaven 2* **(1996),** *The Preacher's Wife* **(1996),** *Unlikely Angel* **(1996),** *Michael* **(1996),** *Angels in the Endzone* **(1997),** *A Life Less Ordinary* **(1997),** *City of Angels* **(1998),** *What Dreams May Come* **(1998),** *An All Dogs Christmas Carol* **(1998), and** *Dogma* **(1999), while TV audiences flocked to shows like** *Heaven Help Us!* **(1994),** *Touched by an Angel* **(1994-2003),** *All Dogs Go to Heaven: The Series* **(1996-1998),** *Teen Angel* **(1997-1998), and even the ironically titled vampire show** *Angel* **(1999-2004).**

THE LEGENDARY SUPER POWERS SHOW

Some people believe we are all born with psychic abilities, which may be harnessed through discipline and practice, once we become aware of their existence. Who knows? One of the following super powers could be your own!

Apportation: The materialization, appearance, disappearance or teleportation of an item from an unknown source. Many a guru and medium has claimed to have such power only to be proven a hoax, including Maria Silbert (1866-1936), Charles Bailey (1870–1947), Lajos Pap (1883-1941), Eva Carrière (1886-1943), and Sathya Sai Baba (1926-2011).

Astral projection: Popularized in the West by the Theosophical Society (along all sorts of other phenomena), the ability to eject one's consciousness, soul, or as the Theosophists say, "astral body," out of our physical bodies, has caught the imaginations of many, and become standard practice of fictional super heroes like Marvel's Doctor Strange. It's important to note that is said out-of-the-body experience carries any time distortion it is referred to as "astral," while if it doesn't—say, if your projection traverses only through your current space-time continuum—the correct term would be "etherical."

Automatic writing: Not to be confused with the academic literary practice of free writing, this is the ability to draw or write while guided by another supernatural being or source. Many, from Elizabethan astrologers like John Dee (1527-c.1609), to modern poetry geniuses like Fernando Pessoa (1888-1935) and W. B. Yeats (1865-1939) have claimed to write under what we hope was a strictly spiritual influence. Many modern false "mystics" has also claimed to have this ability, so be warned!

Channeling: Communicating with spirits of the dead, also known as mediumship, used to be standard practice among esoteric circles across cultures for centuries, but the nineteenth century adoption of stage magic tricks into the practice eventually caused it to fall into disrepute. Regardless, in this day and age channeling continues to be practiced in the English-speaking world. Mediums may be generally classified as "mental mediums," who connect to the spirit world through trance states, and "physical mediums" who connect with the spirits via objects either presented to them by séance attendees, or produced by them via apportation.

Clairvoyance: Literally meaning "clear seeing," it is the power to see invisible things via the "mind's eye" or "third eye." Similarly, there's a clairaudience ("clear hearing"), clairalience ("clear smelling"), and so on, each related to a supernaturally acute sense of the spirit world, beyond regular human perception.

Divination: This highly ritualistic process of gaining insight into a situation shouldn't be confused with the casual parlor practice of fortune-telling for personal purposes (I-Ching, Tarot, etc.). Oracles ("seers") and prophets ("interpreters") have been a fixture of organized religious history since the dawn of time, and continue to be so.

Dowsing: A form of *rhabdomancy* (divination via sticks) dismissed as quackery centuries ago, the capacity to find water via a Y-shaped twig or rod, would prove very useful nonetheless, if it ever worked which, according to most scientific studies, it doesn't. However, water dowsing has seen its comebacks into the cultural limelight, notably via the 1940s through 1950s Kenneth Roberts books (1885-1957) about the uncanny dowsing abilities of Henry Gross (1895-1979), who purportedly could locate deposits of water, petroleum, uranium, and diamonds using a twig.

Energy healing: Wouldn't you love to heal yourself or others through the power of your own etheric, astral, mental, or spiritual energy? Not to be confused with Faith Healing (channeling God's or Jesus' power to heal others), energy healing may be practiced with or without touching a patient, and even remotely, and may rely on the healers own power (think *Reiki* and *Qigong*), or contraptions (magnet therapy is a good example). If you indulge in this practice, however, be aware no clinical evidence supports its efficacy.

Enhanced Vision: The famed "sight beyond sight" of *ThunderCats* lore, this ability shouldn't be mistaken with clairvoyance or anything paranormal, but is in fact a physical gift subject to the constriction of time and space. This includes telesthesia, remote, or long range vision (seeing people, situation, or information across a distance), microscopic vision, infrared vision (seeing emanating heat), or if you believe Natasha Demkina's (b.1987) claims, X-ray vision … like Supergirl!

Levitation: Floating or flying by mystical means has been part of floklore since times immemorial, but levitation also includes widely accepted examples of walking on water by Gautama Buddha (c.563-483BC) and Jesus Christ (c.0-∞AD). Beyond mediums and stage magicians, Christian saints said to have levitated in their lifetime include Saint Francis of Assisi (c.1181-1226), Saint Teresa of Jesus (1515-1582), and Saint Seraphim of Sarov (1754-1833).

Psychic surgery: Sooner of later, everybody seeks a miracle, and this particular form of energy healing—or fraudulent sleight of hand depending who you ask—is based on digging out diseased tissue from the body via an "energetic" incision that heals right away. If it seems too good to be true, that's because it is, but while the deception has been exposed over and over, "spiritual healing" continues to be popular practice in countries like Brazil and the Philippines.

Psychokinesis: Commonly referred to as telekinesis, the term "psychokinesis," as coined by publisher Henry Holt (1840-1926), extends well beyond simply moving objects with the power of our mind, but physically alter matter in unpredictable ways. Regardless its seeming violation of the laws of physics, plenty of people have claimed to posses this power only to be discredited, like the spoon-bending Israeli illusionist Uri Geller (b.1946), while others like British healer Matthew Manning (b.1955) are yet to be disproved.

Psychometry: The concept of objects emanating an energy, or soul, which could be harnessed by sensitive people was developed by Joseph Rodes Buchanan (1814-1899) in his 1893 book, *Manual of Psychometry: the Dawn of a New Civilization*, which was quickly adopted by spiritualist and New Age movements in the decades that followed. Imagine touching an object and gaining immediate knowledge of its origin, history, and the people it had been in contact with. Not only it makes the perfect plot device for a great thriller, like the movie *Solace* (2015), but that would be one useful power to have!

Precognition and Postcognition: The extra sensory perception of future and past events respectively, has been desired by people for generations. Precognition or premonition in particular is the stuff prophets of different cultures and religions are either made of or unmade by, while postcognition, also known as retrocognition, is a lot harder to assess. Precognition may rely of messages from a deity, an external but unintelligible oracle, the seer's own power, or its focus through a given object ("crystal ball"). Postcognition, on the other hand, may be produced by previous knowledge, which would rule out any paranormal powers, but some cases, like the Charlotte Moberly (1846-1937) and Eleanor Jourdain (1863-1924) purported 1901 encounter with Marie Antoinette's (1755-1793) memories, still baffle most.

Telepathy: Comprised by Greek words *tele* ("distant") and *pathos* ("feeling"), "telepathy" seems to evoke a much less defined ability than its modern conception of being able to transmit or receive thoughts, as well as meddling around in the minds of others. Continuing to capture the imagination of audiences everywhere, from close-up magicians to comic-book super heroes like Professor X, all of its real life instances have been experimentally proven to be either psychopathic delusions, or downright hoaxes.

Not to be confused with the 1994 film, nor its following television spin-offs, the Stargate Project was the CIA's 1978 inquiry into the gaining insight on remote information, people, or situations though paranormal means. The project was terminated in 1995 after it demonstrated unequivocally that a paranormal phenomena have limited applicability and utility for intelligence gathering operations, according to the American Institutes for Research.

BONUS FACTS!

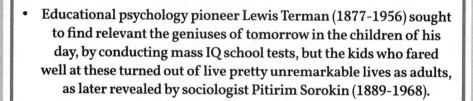

- Educational psychology pioneer Lewis Terman (1877-1956) sought to find relevant the geniuses of tomorrow in the children of his day, by conducting mass IQ school tests, but the kids who fared well at these turned out of live pretty unremarkable lives as adults, as later revealed by sociologist Pitirim Sorokin (1889-1968).

- Britain's most distinctive bird of prey, the red kite, was almost driven to extinction in the 1960s by egg collectors, but successfully reintroduced into the UK from Spain in the 1980s.

BE THE BATMAN

Picture yourself as the only plain human in the Hall of Justice, surrounded by charming people claiming to have superhuman abilities and powers beyond belief. Upon closer examination though, you realize Superman, Wonder Woman, and Aquaman are all frauds, just people in shiny, skin tight suits, while your own "super" power is real, and can't be proven otherwise. And no, money isn't it—though it's darn close—but your uncanny gift of acute observation, persuasion, and inductive reasoning. If that is the case, congratulations, you're Batman, and your power is a technique known as "cold reading," a skill well worth learning about if only to spot the con artists who use it to fake various supernatural gifts!

1. Cold reading begins with careful observation, and study of a subject's particular constitution, age, clothing, hairstyle, gender, ethnicity, and the various mannerisms given away by the person in question.

2. Observation is followed by persuasion. It is essential to elicit the subject's willingness to cooperate, first by admitting supposedly muddy signals, which will surely become clear reading with the person's aid.

3. Probing questions are then used to determine the degree of cooperation on the subject's part, as well as to gradually build up its confirmation biases. This is done via combing through various tidbits of information, and subtly focusing on the hits rather than the misses as revealed either verbally or subtly by the subject's facial expression and body language.

4. Trained cold readers are equally skilled at probing individuals

as well as large crowds, from which they usually pick an individual subject that's eager to participate, and therefore easier to manipulate.

5. Probing techniques include:

- **Shotgunning:** Bombarding an individual or group with a series of vague statements which will be narrowed down in a "father figure" to "your uncle Bill" fashion.

- **Barnum effect:** Faint statements such as "you have a need to be loved" that will be interpreted as personal attributes by an eager subject, as is usually the case with Horoscopes.

- **Warm reading:** Using the Barnum effect to give the impression the reader is a gifted psychic via inferred educated guesses.

- **Rainbow ruse:** Covering all bases by assigning an eager subject a specific trait and its opposite, both of which will be found true by the person in question, either by association ("if 'a' is true, then 'b' must be also), or self-criticism ("maybe I have overlooked this").

6. Cold reading is consciously used for profit by stage magicians who always admit it to be a trick done for entertainment purposes, as well as by swindlers and smooth talkers who try to pass as psychics, mediums, and healers, but there have also been instances in which a given esoteric practitioner thought cold reading a genuine supernatural ability, using it intuitively and without malice, completely unaware of the literature around its process and techniques. Either way, as those other American heroes—G.I. Joe—say "knowing is half the battle!"

THE MENTALIST

When evidence is lacking, leads grow cold, technology fails, and investigations reach a dead end, law enforcement agencies may occasionally secure the services of "psychic detectives," though its been found that, more often than not, it's exposure-hungry psychics who reach out to law enforcement offering their assistance.

Dorothy Allison (1924-1999): A widely publicized, but highly ineffective psychic detective, Ms. Allison reportedly provided Atlanta Police Department with 42 names of suspects supposedly connected to the Atlanta Child Murders of 1979-1981, none of which turned out to be the culprit, Wayne Williams (b.1958). **Success rate: 0%**

Greta Alexander (1932-1998): Claiming that being struck by lightning in 1961 turned her clairvoyant, clairaudient, and clairsensory, Ms. Alexander was said to help the police with cold cases and murder investigations, as well as psychically detecting diseases and underlying conditions in regular folk. A media personality, she wasn't shy at self-promotion, and appears to have genuinely believed to be helping people, despite her claims seemingly lacking any accuracy. **Success rate: 0%**

Sylvia Celeste Browne (1936-2013): A regular guest at TV and radio shows, Ms. Browne had a large fan base, despite a spectacular list of failed police case predictions including the murder of six-year-old Opal Jo Jennings, who Browne claimed had been sold to slavery in Japan, and Amanda Berry (b.1986), kept prisoner alongside two other victims by Ariel Castro (1960-2013), whose mother was brazenly told by Browne her daughter was deceased, and died thinking that was indeed the case. **Success rate: 0%**

Noreen Renier (b.1937): This celebrated "spirit medium" and psychic detective from Orlando, Florida, said to have been involved in hundreds of cases for various law enforcement agencies in the US and other countries, is without her detractors who claim most of her cases to be fabrications. She has published several books, including the how-to manual of psychic detective work, *The Practical Psychic: A No-Nonsense Guide to Developing Your Natural Intuitive Abilities* (2011), and the best-selling *A Mind for Murder: The Real-Life Files of a Psychic Investigator* (2005). **Success rate: Unconfirmed.**

Annette Martin (1937-2011): Featured in countless newspapers, TV, and Radio shows, she was the first psychic to ever testify as a witness in a murder case, and is said to have helped the police find several missing children, and notably the corpse of 71-year-old Dennis Prado, a retired paratrooper who died from natural causes during an evening stroll. **Success rate: 100%**

Nancy Myer (b.1945): A life changing religious experience in The Garden of Gethsemane in Jerusalem leaving her with her gift, Ms. Myer's first successful case was helping the police identify a Wilmington, Delaware, serial rapist in 1977, followed by many others. **Success rate: 80%**

Carol Pate (b.1945): Arkansas's best known psychic, Ms. Pate claims to have been born with her psychometric abilities, helping law enforcement find missing persons since she was 12. In 1991 she successfully helped the police locate kidnapping victim, 18-year-old Tyson Efrid, a case which led her to be called to help authorities locate physician Xu "Sue" Wang (b.1960) in 2000, but while she told the Chicago Tribune that she had provided the police with "details" they could use (and her belief that Wang's car was placed on the parking strip as a diversion), the truth of the matter is that, 20 years later, Ms. Wang still hasn't been found. **Success rate: 50%**

Etta Louise Smith (b.1948): While never claiming to be a psychic, Ms. Smith claimed a feeling or vision lead her to the body of nurse Melanie Uribe (1948-1980), but instead of being rewarded she was imprisoned and questioned for four days (she failed at the polygraph despite having no connection to the victim whatsoever), until another suspect confessed to the crime. Ms. Smith would sue the LAPD for the distress inflicted upon her, and was awarded $26,184 in 1987. **Success rate: 100%**

Troy Griffin (b.1965): The self-styled "Psychic Medium, Clairvoyant, Empath and Psychic Investigator," Griffin has managed to stay a media celebrity, by taking part in high-profile investigations like the disappearance of Kelsie Schelling in 2013, who was 21 years old and pregnant at the time. Ms. Schelling remains missing, while Mr. Griffin reportedly still charges $250-300 an hour for his "work," which hasn't been confirmed, nor denied by the authorities. **Success rate: 0%**

Charles Lindbergh (1902-1974): Not a psychic by a long shot, but when Lindbergh's 20-month-old son, Charles Augustus Lindbergh Jr. (1930-1932) was kidnapped in 1932, the Harvard Psychological Clinic conducted a study inviting the general public to contribute any precognitive visions they may have about the child's fate. Of the 1,300 total reported precognitions and dreams, 65 saw the child dead, and a mere four saw him buried in the woods. Statistically speaking, even blind luck would have been more accurate!

BONUS FACT!

- In 2020, a rock kept for 30 years in a man's garden in Blaubeuren, Germany, was found to be a 66-pound iron-ore space meteor!

THE HUMAN TORCH

Not all "superpowers" are gifts. If the phenomenon known as Spontaneous Human Combustion (SHC) is any indication, some may downright be considered a deadly curse!

1. The earliest SHC occurrence on record, dates back to 1673 when an alcoholic prostitute spontaneously caught fire in the streets of Paris.

2. In a 1725 morning, an innkeeper found his heavy-drinking wife burned to a crisp, but for her lower legs, part of her skull and a few vertebrae lying around in the kitchen. The man was jailed on suspicion of foul play, but cleared of all charges after a thorough medical investigation revealed the event as a "visitation from God."

3. Another early documented case of SHC happened to 66-year-old Italian Countess Cornelia Zangheri Bandi (1664-1731). Reportedly a brandy drinker who used to douse herself with the liquor to relieve herself from joint pain, Countess Zangheri went to bed one night, and by morning was found by her maid reduced to a pile of ashes atop her intact bed, but for her lower limbs, three fingers, and a fragment of her skull.

4. Further accounts from Italy (1776) and England (1788) reveal a Catholic priest bursting in flames during his devotions, and a chambermaid set ablaze while scrubbing the floor respectively.

5. According to *A Treatise on Medical Jurisprudence* (1823) by Dr. John Ayrton Paris (1785-1856) and John Samuel Martin Fonblanque (1787-1865), a series of common traits are shared by most in SHC cases:

a. The victims are chronic alcoholics.

b. They are usually elderly females.

c. The body has not burned spontaneously, but some lighted substance has come into contact with it.

d. The hands and feet usually fall off.

e. The fire has caused very little damage to combustible things in contact with the body.

f. The combustion of the body has left a residue of greasy and fetid ashes.

6. Russian author Nikolai Gogol (1809-1852) introduced his readers to SHC in his 1842 *Dead Souls* book, while Herman Melville (1819-1891) would use it in his 1849 *Redburn* novel, but it would be Charles Dickens's (1812-1870) 1852 serialized novel *Bleak House*, featuring SHC as the cause of death for one of the characters, Krook, that would catch morbid Victorian curiosity, the famed author being accused of "giving currency to a vulgar error," against which he cited as many as 30 real instances of SHC which had served as his inspiration.

7. Three shocking SHC cases from the last 50 years include:

- **Margaret Hogan** (1881-1970), an old Irish widow found as a heap of smoldering ashes in front of her TV set with the glass screen melted off, back in 1970 Dublin.

- **Henry Thomas** (1907-1980), an Australian gentleman incinerated in his New South Wales home, but—you guessed it—for his lower limbs and a portion of his skull.

- **Michael Faherty** (1934-2010), a 76-year-old Irishman suffering from diabetes and hypertension, who was found burnt to a crisp while lying in his living room. His death was the first officially attributed to SHC in more than a century!

8. Originally blamed on intemperance and divine justice, with more SHC events taking place during the past two centuries, new hypotheses regarding its cause have been proposed, including intestinal gas, static electricity, depression, sunspots, cosmic storms, ball lightning, ketosis, poltergeist activity, and *pyrokinesis* (flame manipulation), but American skeptic investigator of the paranormal Joe Nickell (b.1944) has suggested the cause may be as pedestrian as SHC victims being either toddlers or elderly, alone, and close to flames, and in the seniors' case often smokers and/or drinkers to boot!

BONUS FACTS!

- Formerly a medical student, George Francis "Doc" Medich (b.1948), saved the life of a fan suffering from a heart stroke during a 1978 Texas Rangers v. Baltimore Orioles game!

- DC Comics, the publishing company responsible for characters such as Superman, Batman, and Wonder Woman, was founded by notorious bootlegger Harry Donenfeld (1893-1965) as a respectable front for his racy magazines business.

- Unlike most literary works which become public domain 70 years after the deaths of their authors, the copyright of *The Diary of Anne Frank* (1947), controlled by the Anne Frank Fonds (AFF) organization will stay protected until 2050.

- Muhammad Ali (1942-2016) fought against Japanese wrestler Antonio Inoki (b.1946) in one of the first mixed martial arts (MMA) fights ever, the 1976 "War of the Worlds" match!

FLAME ON!

Through the lens of the imagination, of course, Spontaneous Human Combustion turns into the coolest superpower ever. The best ten super heroes blazing their way through highly-flammable comic book pages include:

The Human Torch: Originally created by artist Carl Burgos (1916-1984) for the pages of *Marvel Comics* #1 (1939), while also gracing the cover of the publication, in a beautifully rendered illustration by influential pulp magazines artist Frank R. Paul (1884-1963). One of Marvel's most popular characters of the 1940s alongside the Sub-Mariner, and Captain America, this version of the Torch is as original as they come. For starters, not even a human being, but a rogue android anti-hero. First chased down by the authorities, it would eventually assume the human identity of Jim Hammond, an NYPD officer, later joined by his very own sidekick, Toro, the mutant son of two nuclear scientists!

Firestorm: This Disco-era fire hero from DC Comics created in 1978 by Gerry Conway (b.1952) and Al Milgrom (b.1950) has some unique traits. First off, rather than being completely covered by fire, his head works like a smokestack releasing the atomic fire burning within. A nuclear freak, Firestorm isn't the alter ego of one person, but the atomic fusion of two, very opposite people: highschool jock Ronnie Raymond and physics professor Martin Stein! As with many a DC Comics character, it has been see on television, originally in animated form on the Super Friends and various Justice League cartoons, and also in the live-action CW shows *The Flash* (2014) and *Legends of Tomorrow* (2016), portrayed by Robbie Amell (b.1988), and the legendary Victor Garber (b.1949).

Johnny Storm: Created by Stan Lee (1922-2018) and Jack Kirby

(1917-1994) as a 1960s reinvention of Carl Burgos's original Human Torch, for the *Fantastic Four* #1 (1961) comic book, the brother of the Invisible Woman, Johnny Storm got his powers when bombarded with cosmic rays aboard a spaceship, and much like the original, he can engulf his entire body in flames, fly, shoot and control fire at will. The character has been seen in most *Fantastic Four* cartoon shows, but the 1978 serial replaced him with the robot H.E.R.B.I.E.! Legend has it the networks didn't want kids to "try this at home," setting themselves on fire, but in reality the character rights were tied in another licensing deal at Universal. Johnny Storm has also been seen the *Fantastic Four* live action films of 2005 and 2007, played by Chris Evans (b.1981), and the failed 2015 reboot, played by Michael B. Jordan (b.1987).

Sunfire: Sunfire was created writer Roy Thomas (b.1940) and artist Don Heck (1929-1995), in the pages of *X-Men* #64 (1970). The son of a Hiroshima A-bomb victim who died of radiation poisoning, instead of dying too Shiro Yoshida gained the ability to absorb solar radiation and convert it to plasma state which bursts into flame when shot through his hands. He may also fly surrounded with an aura of heat as strong as the sun, and see infrared light. His first appearance out of the printed page was as a villain-turned-hero in the *Spider-Man and His Amazing Friends* (1981-1983) cartoon show.

Ghost Rider: Or rather a plural "Riders," as the name was adopted from a previous series of cowboy/western comic-book heroes and applied to motorcycle stuntman Johnny Blaze, who made a deal with Satan to save his ailing father, becoming bound to the demon Zarathos, the "Spirit of Vengeance," which melts his flesh at night, transforming him into a burning skull motorcycle apparition from hell. Originally created by editor Roy Thomas (b.1940), writer Gary Friedrich (1943-2018), and artist Mike Ploog (b.1940) for *Marvel Spotlight* #5 (1972), Blaze's curse has since been transferred to other bearers, all sharing more-or-less the same traits and abilities.

Son of Satan: Motivated by the success of *Ghost Rider*, editor Roy Thomas commissioned writer Gary Friedrich with the creation of another satanic anti-hero, Daimon Hellstorm, the son of the devil himself and a mortal woman (he has a sister, appropriately named Satana too!), who gets raised in a Jesuit orphanage, and therefore steered towards using his demonic powers, including trident-projected "hellfire" blasts, for good. The character will soon be portrayed—sans the trident—by English actor Tom Austen (b.1988) in a gritty live action TV show named *Helstrom*, set to premiere on streaming service Hulu in late 2020.

Pyro: An evil Australian mutant with pyrokinetic abilities, Pyro was introduced as a villain in *Uncanny X-Men* #141 (1981) by creators Chris Claremont (b.1950) and John Byrne (b.1950). St. John Allerdyce (Pyro's secret identity) is a subversive with a talent for arson who finds he can control fire at will, but not generate it, therefore donning an adapted flame-thrower as his weapon of choice. Other than appearing on various X-Men cartoons, the character was brought to life by actor Aaron Stanford (b.1976) in the live action films *X2* (2003), and *X-Men: The Last Stand* (2006), as a turncoat "X-man" who joins Magneto's Brotherhood of Mutants.

Fire: Originally created as the Green Fury, Fire first appeared in the pages of the *Super Friends* #25 (1979) comic book as Beatriz da Costa, a Brazilian super hero fueled by a mystical green fire she controls at will. She may also exhale her green fire to fly and create illusions. The character's name was later changed to Green Flame, and finally Fire, when introduced to DC Comics regular lineup of heroes, but its original version was created by Edward Nelson Bridwell (1931-1987), and Ramona Fradon (b.1926). A live-action version of the character, played by Michelle Hurd (b.1966), appeared in an unsuccessful 1997 pilot for a *Justice League of America* comedic television show.

Firestar: First appearing alongside Spider-Man and Iceman in the *Spider-Man and His Amazing Friends* (1981-1983) cartoon show, rather than fire-based Angelica Jones is mutant whose body stores ambient electromagnetic energy, which she can project as microwaves, generating enormous amounts of heat, not unlike a microwave oven. She flew into the comic book pages of *Uncanny X-Men* #193, later getting her own mini-series back in the early 1980s.

Ash: Created and self-published by Joe Quesada (b.1962) and Jimmy Palmiotti (b.1961) in the pages of the hero's eponymous comic series back in the 1990s, firefighter Ashley Quinn got trapped inside a burning building, where a hidden "regeneration chamber" from the future gave his body the ability of generating heat up to 1260°F. Using special gauntlets to control the ensuing flames, and make fire-based weapons from it, Ash fought crime as best he could until his creators took different career paths at Marvel and DC Comics respectively.

BONUS FACTS!

- Shot and killed by Ku Klux Klansmen, white Civil Rights activist Viola Liuzzo (1925-1965) was framed as a promiscuous Communist, and a junkie by J. Edgar Hoover (1895-1972), in order to protect one of the Bureau's secret Klan informants who took part in the crime.

- Initially a home-school English project while on lockdown during the Covid-19 pandemic, British boy Arlo Lipiatt's (b.2010) punk music fanzine, *Pint-Sized Punk*, became a hit, selling out at home, and getting orders from the US and Australia!

AMAZING STORIES

Characters and stories are not the exclusive realm of professional writers, artists, and publishers, but sometimes spontaneously burst into existence. Triggered by our innermost primal fears, modern urban legends continue to thrive via word of mouth (not unlike the stories cavemen used to circulate before the advent of writing), and boosted by the rise of the internet, email, "memes," and social media, which propagate these tales ad infinitum!

Forty Licks

Going all the way back to a nineteenth-century folktale of a clergy man, his wife, and a jewel thief posing as their Labrador underneath the bed, comes a modern spin, featuring a young woman going to bed at night, and caressing her dog lying beside her. Woken by a dripping sound, the next morning she finds her dog slain in the bathtub, and a "Humans can lick too" lipstick graffiti on the mirror!

Michigan J. Frog

Long a staple of Forteana, reports of animals (usually reptiles or amphibians) entombed in building cornerstones and other places (quarries, mines, tree trunks) either alone or in groups, have appeared in the news media since the nineteenth century, and continue to do so. One of the most famous, Ol' Rip the Horned Toad, a horned lizard said to have been awaken from a 31-year slumber inside a time capsule, which had been placed into the cornerstone of the Eastland County Courthouse (Eastland, Texas) in 1897, made headlines. Ol' Rip, however, could only survive for another 11 months until the intensive touring killed it for good.

Wally Gator

Despite continued assurances by City Hall officials regarding the

nonexistence of alligators in the New York City sewer system, rumors persist after a string of gator sightings during the 1930s, which were reported across various media outlets, inspired part of Thomas Pynchon's (b.1937) fiction novel *V* (1963). In it, Pynchon speculated how baby alligators purchased in Florida by the well-to-do of the city, might have been discarded into the toilet like many a goldfish, and currently may be roaming the city pipelines, possibly blind and colorless. Likewise, a version of this story told in reverse, that of sewer rats swimming up the pipeline all the way into people's toilets is also going around.

The Baby-Sitters Club

Sitters make the best horror stories, and this cautionary tale one is no exception. It takes place in the 1960s, when a teenage baby-sitter indulging in unrestricted TV watching starts getting calls from a stranger, reminding her to check on the children upstairs several times, until she decides to alert the police, which comes to her rescue after finding the calls came from inside the house from a man who had killed the sleeping children, though an alternative version of the myth has the sitter checking on the children and being killed herself. All are largely based on the unsolved murder of babysitter Janett Christman (b.1936-1950).

Band on the Run

According to the "Paul is dead" legend making the rounds since 1967, Paul McCartney (b.1942) died in a traffic accident on November 9, 1966, and was secretly replaced by a look-alike named William Campbell or Billy Shears. Paul walking barefoot while holding a cigarette with his right hand (he's a lefty) in the cover photo of *Abbey Road* (1969) has been alleged as a clue to his demise. McCartney, still very much alive and well, used his 1993 album *Paul is Live* as a way to make fun of this theory.

Road Rage

The "High Beams" urban legend, also known as "Killer in the Backseat," began in the late 1960s, and involves a woman driving home one night, when a strange car begins to pursue her, flashing its high beams, and even ramming her vehicle. Ditching the chasing car, she finally arrives home only to realize whoever was driving that car was actually trying to warn her of the murderer, rapist, or deranged lunatic hiding in the back seat of her car.

1969, A Kubrick Odyssey

Everybody loves a good conspiracy, and the one supposedly surrounding the 1969 Apollo 11 moon landing is no exception, and have been in circulation since the 1990s. A fake viral video from 2015 in particular, shows a man it claims to be Stanley Kubrick (1928-1999) confess to have faked the moon landings … except the man only has a passing resemblance to Kubrick, and the whole thing is obviously a failed publicity stunt to draw attention to a low-budget film that never got made.

Procter & Beelzebub

This legend dating back to the 1970s states that President of Procter & Gamble appeared on a number of popular late-night shows to announce that due to the openness of our society, he was revealing his association with the church of Satan, making derogatory remarks about Christians in America, etc. It also mentions the supposed satanic symbolism of its 1930s company logo, supposedly depicting Satan, the number 666, and 13 stars when reflected. Caught in the 1980s "Satanic Panic," P&G had no option but to completely overhaul its corporate identity, and yet the rumor continues to be spread.

Winds of Change

The December 2, 1979, attempted suicide of Elvita Adams (b.1950),

a young African American woman who jumped from the Empire State Building's eighty-sixth floor, only to be blown back onto a ledge by a gust of wind naturally made headlines in its day, and though Ms. Adams's fate afterwards isn't known, during the following decades her story was distorted beyond recognition into the tale of a white male executive attempting suicide from the Twin Towers, only to be lifted by miraculous winds and deposited … at the floor of a TV network newsroom!

Risky Business

Popular all over the world, and for good reason, the story of a woman "caught in the act" as she smears her private parts with peanut butter (alternatively also margarine, whipped cream, marmalade, pate, macaroni, sugar, and dog food) to be licked by her dog (sometimes a horse), only to be surprised by her friends (including but not limited to the fiancee, boyfriend, husband, *Candid Camera* show crew, and even Ricky Martin himself!), and fleeing the country (sometimes quitting her job, calling off her wedding, etc.) as a result, has been an urban legend staple since the early 1980s at the very least.

Blow

Coca-Cola's New Coke beverage from 1985 has been subject to many a myth, including the replacing of cane sugar with inexpensive high-fructose corn syrup (HFCS) in the new formula; being forced to remove cocaine from the formula by the Drug Enforcement Administration (DEA); removing thousands of air-brushed retail posters in Australia and the South Pacific, supposedly for containing lewd images hidden in the reflections of the ice; and creating it on purpose to boost classic Coca-Cola sales. But, alas, HFCS began to be allowed in the early 1980s; the DEA knew the minute traces of coca leaves (produced for the company by Peruvian government-owned fields) were not in any way harmful; that poster never existed (the image circulating online has been clumsily doctored); and the company isn't so smart.

Three Men and a Dead Baby

When *Three Men and a Baby*, the 1987 American blockbuster remake of French comedy *Trois hommes et un couffin* (1985) made its way to VHS, some people couldn't help but notice a mysterious figure, staring menacingly behind the trio's shared apartment window curtains, said to be the ghost of a murdered boy who used to live at the New York flat where the film was shot ... except filming never took place in any apartment, but a Toronto soundstage, and the "dead boy" was nothing but a cardboard cutout of Ted Danson's (b.1947) Jack Holden character, a stage performer in the movie.

Kentucky Fried Cloning

Part of the activist populace will always be determined to bring down the fast food industrial complex. That's how persistent rumors of worms in McDonald's hamburgers, cockroaches in Taco Bell tacos, and toxic gasses in Coca-Cola soft drinks have come into existence, and that's how the story (which originally featured six-legged chicken) of Kentucky Fried Chicken shortening its brand name to KFC in 1991 not to incur in false advertising charges. After all, they don't fry real chicken but nondescript, force-fed, genetically manipulated organisms with no beak, no feathers, nor any feet!

Bloody Mary

Catoptromancy, from the Greek *katoptron* ("mirror"), and *manteia* ("divination"), is as old as people's fascination with reflecting surfaces. Picked from a Victorian "husband-catching" ritual for young pageant girls, "Bloody Mary" started as a 1960s slumber party game in which teenage girls were supposed to chant her name into a mirror (conveniently placed in a dimly-lit or candle-lit room) thirteen times, until this character (unrelated to the British Queen, the cocktail drink, and the "Mary Worth" comic strip), shows up to scare the hell out of anyone invoking her ... or killing them. With the advent of the internet, baby boomers apparently saw it fit to propagate this tale

via chain messages in the early 1990s.

A Nightmare on Elm Street

A popular "creepypasta" (online horror "meme" pictures) character created by a forum user in 2009, the "Slender Man" is a very tall, very thin man wearing a suit, with no discernible face, and freakishly long fingers, that supposedly goes about murdering unsuspecting millennials, which is exactly what two disturbed 12-year-old girls decided to do on May 31, 2014, in Wisconsin, stabbing another girl 19 times to prove the character was real!

Free Willy

Hailing from Russian social networks in 2016, as originally reported by dubious Russian tabloid news outlets, the "Blue Whale Challenge" is supposedly a social media game, giving a series of challenges to kids, which grow progressively more harmful, and end with the player's suicide, over a 50-day period. Nothing but a rehash of the 1980s Dungeons & Dragons controversy fabrication, "Blue Whale" caught the attention of the media and alarmed parents all over the world, with child self-harm and suicide cases linked to the non-existent game, being reported from Brazil to Bangladesh!

BONUS FACTS!

- Wanting to take part in World War I, Walt Disney (1901-1966) dropped out of highschool to join the Red Cross Ambulance Corps, same as another high-school dropout, Ray Kroc (1902-1984), future founder of McDonald's!

ACKNOWLEDGMENTS

The initial idea for this book came from the wondrous mind of Roberto Barreiro, writer, pulp-fiction collector, and dear *amigo*. It wouldn't have been possible without his enthusiasm, support, and quota of research assistance.

Editor Jason Schneider (1975-2019) is also to blame, as he took to my original proposal, and championed it forward at Skyhorse until approved. His torch was relayed to the great Jesse McHugh, who entrusted editor Caroline Russomanno, and proofreader Matt Lehman to help me polish this volume to fact-filled perfection.

A special thanks to cryptozoologist Dave Shealy, the World's foremost Skunk Ape expert, for graciously answering the many questions this Bigfoot aficionado had to ask him.

Last but not least, a print "kiss" to my loving soul-mate Maritza "Icha" Mardones, who made sure I could write unhindered, well fed, and sheltered from a world gone bonkers.

ABOUT THE AUTHOR

Diego Jourdan Pereira is a world-trotting puzzle designer, and nonfiction writer. Growing up in cannibalism-prone Uruguay, his travels saw him dodge bullets in crime-ridden Buenos Aires (2005), survive the swine flu pandemic (2009), endure an 8.8 magnitude earthquake in Chile (2010), sojourn through Easter Island (2011), and travel back in time from Japan (2015). He currently finds himself braving both the 2019 Chilean Uprising, and the 2020 worldwide coronavirus pandemic!

ABR
590

OTHER TITLES BY DIEGO JOURDAN PEREIRA

Giant Book of Games and Puzzles for Smart Kids

More Than 1000 Fun and Educational Activities

448 Pages

ISBN: 9781631583292

The Big Book of Brain-Boosting Puzzles

Word Games Designed to Keep the Mind Young!

600 Pages

ISBN: 9781631585111

Bible Power Puzzles

Learn the Word of God Through the Power of Puzzles

586 Pages

ISBN: 9781680996104